Whitechapel Noise

Whitechapel Noise

Jewish Immigrant Life in Yiddish Song and Verse, London 1884–1914

Vivi Lachs

Wayne State University Press | Detroit

© 2018 Vivi Lachs. All rights reserved.
No part of this book may be reproduced without formal permission.
Manufactured in the United States of America.

ISBN 978-0-8143-4488-0 (hardcover) | ISBN 978-0-8143-4355-5 (paper)
ISBN 978-0-8143-4356-2 (e-book)

Library of Congress Control Number: 2017960708

Publication of this book was made possible through the generosity of the Bertha M. and Hyman Herman Endowed Memorial Fund.

Wayne State University Press
Leonard N. Simons Building
4809 Woodward Avenue
Detroit, Michigan 48201-1309

Visit us online at wsupress.wayne.edu

This book is dedicated to the memory of my father, Henry Lachs, and my grandmother Manya Lachs, who brought Polish Yiddish into my life and whose constant presence within me infuses these pages.

It is also dedicated to David Cesarani, who supervised my PhD on which this book is based and who sadly passed away just before my viva.

Cover of the *Londoner kupletist*, ca. 1903. Advertising one hundred new concert and theatre songs sung in London and published by the London Actors Society. From the collections of the National Library of Israel.

Contents

List of Illustrations   ix

Acknowledgments   xi

Transliteration of the Yiddish and Pronunciation Guide   xv

List of Abbreviations   xvii

Introduction   1

Part I. The London of the Lyrics

1. Immigrant Labor, Political Activism, and Socialist Poetry   23

2. London Yiddish Music-Hall Culture   40

Part II. The Lyrics of London

3. The Transnational Scope   67

   Politics: The Poetry of Morris Winchevsky's London Years

4. Debates and Ballads   91

5. Making Socialist Activists   109

   Sex: Innuendo in the Immigrant Halls

6. Transforming Courtship   135

CONTENTS

7. Marriage, Lodgers, and Transgressive Sex   154
   Religion: Subverting Religious Motifs
8. Religion as a Socialist Tool   175
9. Religion Updated and Improved   192

   Conclusion   219

   Notes   227

   Bibliography   287

   Glossary   309

   Appendix 1: Location of the London Yiddish Lyrics   311

   Appendix 2: London Immigrant Personalities   319

   Index   323

Illustrations

Cover of the *Londoner kupletist*, ca. 1903   vi

Advertisement for Yiddish gramophone records, 1905   4

East End Russian restaurant, 1901   21

Concert at Jewish working girls' club, Soho, 1901   21

Front page of the *Poylisher yidl*, 1884   29

Arn Nager, "Maydn, vos shvaygt ir maydn," ca. 1903   48

Princess' Hall, 1901   49

York Minster music-hall program, ca. 1902   54

Satirical drawing: "Avreml Swims to the Bloffer Concert," 1911   61

Front page of the *Arbayter fraynd*, 1887   65

Beki Goldstein, "A het oder a get," ca. 1903   66

Goulston Street market, 1901   73

Victoria Park sandpit, 1901   82

Morris Winchevsky, 1880s   89

Winchevsky's SDF membership card, 1893   95

Front page of the *Fraye velt*, 1891   116

Satirical drawing: "How Jews Sit in a Yiddish Theater," 1912   133

ILLUSTRATIONS

Beki Goldstein and Joseph Markovitsh, ca. 1910   136

Poster for the song "A boytshik ap to deyt," ca. 1902   150

Advertisement searching for missing husband, 1904   161

Advertisement searching for missing sister, 1904   167

Satirical drawing: "The Giving of the Torah in Whitechapel," 1912   173

Cover of the *Kinnous oder arbayter klogelider* (Workers' laments), 1888   186

Avrom Margolin (Avreml)   202

Acknowledgments

This book is the product of a number of years of research. My interest in Yiddish songs about London started me on a journey that led to performing, composing, and scholarship. Many people helped me along the way, and I am truly grateful for their encouragement, support, criticism, and love.

This book developed from my doctoral thesis, and I am grateful to my wonderful supervisors. To the late David Cesarani, who was enthusiastic about this project and hugely supportive with his tough criticism, warm encouragement, and valuable insights. I miss him greatly and feel very fortunate to have worked with him. This book is dedicated to his memory. To Rachel Beckles Willson for her guidance into the world of ethnomusicology, for taking on this project with such interest, and for her incisive comments that enlarged the scope of my thinking. I also want to thank David Feldman and Shirli Gilbert, who so meticulously examined my thesis, have been encouraging and supportive in my writing this book, and continue to advise. I am very grateful to the Royal Holloway history and music departments, which provided the academic environment for this research; for the financial support of a Royal Holloway history scholarship award, for funding Yiddish language courses, conferences, and for generous Friendly Hand grants for archival trips abroad. Thanks to the late Louise Forsyth and Hannah Davis for hospitality and conversation while I was researching in New York.

I am grateful to the patient and knowledgeable archivists who helped me find material and made useful suggestions: Fruma Mohrer, the late Chana Gordon Mlotek, Gunnar Berg, Ettie Goldwasser, Leo Greenbaum, Lorin Sklamberg from the YIVO archive, the informative librarians in the YIVO Library, Zmira Reuveni at the National Library of Israel, Chris Rawlings at the British Library, Chana Pollack from the Forward/

ACKNOWLEDGMENTS

Forverts Archives, the Klau Library, record archivist Michael Aylward, and song collector Derek Reid.

Chapters 4 and 5 of this book are a development on two articles, and I am grateful to Shane Nagle and the Association for the Study of Ethnicity and Nationalism (ASEN) and Daniel Renshaw of *Socialist History* for suggesting that I talk at their conferences, which led to my publishing the articles in their journals. I would also like to warmly thank Sarah Glazer for inviting me to give a Ruth Gay lecture at YIVO.

I am particularly grateful to my informal academic community of friends who gave their time and expertise to read chapters and give me detailed comments, broad challenges, and lots of ideas, in particular Sarha Moore, Nadia Valman, and Davina Cooper, and the late Sheila Shulman, Didi Herman, Adam Sutcliffe, Zoe Weiman-Kelman, Denis Paz, Ben Gidley, Abbi Wood, Rachel Pistol, and Penny Florence.

A *hartsikn dank* to my community of Yiddishists, both academic and not, who talked over ideas, corrected Yiddish, gave detailed feedback on chapters, advised, suggested, and encouraged: David Mazower, who shared his private collection of London-Yiddish songsheets, books, and manuscripts—his wide knowledge of London Yiddish popular culture, his criticism, and his friendship have been hugely appreciated; Khayke Beruriah Wiegand, for her meticulous expertise in language and transliteration; and my wonderful fellow Yiddishists Ester Whine, Ellen Cassedy, Miryem-Khaye Seigel, Sima Beeri, Barry Davis, Itzik Gottersman, Haya Vardi, Michael Wex, Eve Sicular, and Chaim Neslen. The Ot Azoy Yiddish course in London has been a part of my Yiddish language development, and I am grateful to Helen Beer, Heather Valencia, and Sonia Pinkusowitz.

Many friends and family talked through ideas, read sections, gave me new perspectives through their questions, and advised on religious contexts. My sister Jude Lachs was a meticulous reader. Edith Lachs and Nicky Lachs listened to hours of my translations of gems from the archives in Jerusalem. I also thank Dave Rosenberg, Marion Brady, the late Rhona Schein, Gabriel Ellenberg, Julia Doyle, Ruti Lachs, Nic Pollinger, Shimmy Lopian, and Stuart Lachs. Also my Facebook friends—Tomas Wdski, Shane Baker, Michael Alpert, Daniel Zylbersztajn, Judy Waldman, Esther Grinfeld, Michael Pertz, and Ross Bradshaw—who have been a great source of advice on idiomatic Yiddish expressions.

ACKNOWLEDGMENTS

My musical community has inspired me by encouraging me to find new material and compose music, and has worked with me on new ways to perform Yiddish songs of London. I would like to lovingly acknowledge the late Adrienne Cooper, and to thank Karsten Troyke, Klezmer Klub, Tantsunlid, Katsha'nes, and all those in the Great Yiddish Parade. I have been supported and encouraged to focus on this work over the years by the Jewish Music Institute, and would particularly like to thank Geraldine Auerbach, Jennifer Jankel, Gil Karpas, and Noa Lachman.

Finally, I am delighted to be publishing with Wayne State University Press, and would like to thank my editor, Kathy Wildfong, for the enthusiastic support and advice she has given me. Also Lisa Stallings, Rachel Ross, Emily Nowak, Erin Davis, Ellen Lohman, the people at Westchester Publishing Services, and the two anonymous reviewers of my book for their insightful and helpful comments.

Transliteration of the Yiddish and Pronunciation Guide

Yiddish is written right to left using the Hebrew alphabet. This alphabet is not reproduced in this book, and the Yiddish mostly appears according to the standard YIVO transliteration system. The words sound as below.

Looks like	Sounds like	Looks like	Sounds like
a	as in *art*	o	as in *lost*
ay	as in *spy*	u	as in *spoon*
e	as in *empty*	kh	as in *chutzpah*
ey	as in *brain*	dzh	as in *jelly*
i	as in *pin*	zh	as in the French *je*

Unlike in English, the *e* is pronounced on the end of a word. So you hear the final vowel in *drite* (third).

There are some exceptions to the YIVO system. The poetry and song texts have a variety of nonstandard spellings. When these do not affect the sound, they have been standardized in the transliteration. However, they are written as they sound when they reflect different styles of speech and dialect, "theatre" pronunciation, and anglicized words. I have tried to be faithful to the Yiddish; thus the transliteration comes with a number of caveats:

- I have not invalidated any rhymes. So the Standard Yiddish *yung* (young) becomes *ying* in Polish dialect to rhyme with *gring* (easy), and *geyt* (goes) becomes *gayt* to rhyme with the anglicized word *fayt* (fight).

TRANSLITERATION AND PRONUNCIATION

- I have not changed nonstandard Yiddish titles of journals or texts—for example, *Idisher ekspres* instead of *Yidisher ekspres* and "A khoydesh on arbayt" rather than the standard spelling *arbet*. In the case of the *Poylisher yidl*, I have not followed my own rules, and used *yidl* rather than *idl* due to common usage.
- When journals include a nonstandard Yiddish transliteration of their title, I have kept the original transliteration, such as the magazine *Der bloffer* or the pamphlet *Kinnous*.
- If there are known transcriptions for Hebrew-based Yiddish words, these forms are used in the narrative, such as *shechita* or *Torah*. However, if these words come up in the Yiddish lyrics, I have used the YIVO transliteration, *shkhite* and *toyre*.
- For people's names I have used the most common spelling from YIVO or the entry in Leonard Prager's *Yiddish Culture in Britain*, for example, Morris Winchevsky or Kalman Marmor. However, if the names come up in a Yiddish source, they are transliterated, such as *Moris vintshevski*.

Yiddish does not use capital letters. In transliteration I have capitalized the beginning of sentences, people's names, and the first names of journals, articles, and poem and song titles. Any other capitalization is from emphasis in the Yiddish text. In translating this emphasis I have used italics.

When referring to newspapers, apart from the first times they are mentioned, I have generally removed the Yiddish definite article, as in *Der poylisher yidl* (itself nonstandard), replacing it with English, "the *Poylisher yidl*," in order to maintain the narrative flow. There are a few grammatical instances that are not standard Yiddish, but I have quoted from the grammar in the published texts.

YIDDISH TRANSLATION

The poems and songs are translated to be literal rather than to create lyrical verse. If this strategy is at the expense of sense, I have changed the English word order to make it readable. All translations from Yiddish to English are my own unless stated.

Abbreviations

AF	*Arbayter fraynd*
ELO	*East London Observer*
FV	*Fraye velt*
IE	*Idisher ekspres*
IS	*Idishe shtime*
JC	*Jewish Chronicle*
JW	*Jewish World*
LG	*Lider un gedikhte*
LK	*Londoner kupletist*
LLM	*Londoner lider magazin*
MF	*Morgen freiheit*
MPC	Mazower Private Collection
NLI	National Library of Israel
PY	*Poylisher yidl*
SG	Songsheet Goldberg
SM	Songsheet Mazin
SR	Songsheet Ruderman
SY	Songsheet Yozef
YK	*Yidishe kultur*

Introduction

Hostu gezen a "grinem" yid	Have you seen a new immigrant
hir blondzhendik aleyn?	Wandering about here alone?
Keyn koyrev nit, keyn goyel nit	Without relatives, without a savior
un elnt vi a shteyn?	And acutely lonely?
Di raykhe "kenen gornit ton,"	The rich "can't do anything,"
zey hobn tekhter, zin . . .	They have daughters, sons . . .
Di londoner "komite-layt"	For the London "committee members"
far zey iz er tsu GRIN.	He's too *new* an immigrant.[1]

This is a book of tales of Jewish East End immigrant lives before World War I. The tales are about work and politics, leisure, religion, and community. They are full of talk, debate, laughter, and bickering. Yiddish filled the air as people struggled with their changing identities, challenged authorities, fought for fairer conditions, and rethought their religious practice and family roles. The hubbub of noise from immigrants' lives was reflected in the poetry of socialists demanding a different future where poverty and inequality were eliminated, in the lyrics of popular song making fun of relationships between the sexes, and in the verses of the satirists denouncing hypocrisy and double standards.[2] It was a noisy place. It was the sound of the Jewish immigrant population meeting Whitechapel. This book explores the complex character of acculturation. It was not linear, straightforward, or easy and resulted in immigrants' rethinking core concepts of self and community. Finding these new aspects of Anglo-Jewish history through popular culture is uncharted territory, and the rewards are a fascinating exposé of Whitechapel immigrant lives.

INTRODUCTION

As the immigrant population increased, Yiddish language cultural institutions developed in London's East End with the left-wing Yiddish newspaper *Der poylisher yidl* (The Polish Jew) in 1884, leading to a small but active Yiddish press, Yiddish publishing houses, Yiddish theatres, and a handful of Yiddish music halls.[3] This cultural life partly re-created aspects of the Eastern European community the immigrants had left, but more significantly it responded to the new life in England, new ways of practical living and new social mores.

Over four hundred Yiddish poems, songs, and verses, which I call "London's Yiddish lyrics," were written between 1884 and 1914 and published in local Yiddish newspapers, pamphlets, magazines, penny songsheets, and songbooks.[4] All in *kupletn* (rhyming couplets), they conjure up and fictionalize incidents in known localities. There are pickpockets outside Broad Street Station, couples courting in Crystal Palace, families struggling to pay rent in Berner Street, child prostitution in Victoria Park, and children selling matches on the streets by the Stock Exchange in Cornhill. Characters include people who were well known, such as Nathan Mayer, the first Lord Rothschild; Prime Minister William Gladstone; and anarchist leader Rudolf Rocker, and lesser-known personalities such as local Yiddish theatre stars Beki Goldstein and Joseph Sherman. The lyrics create entertaining scenarios with strong conviction, clever wordplay, powerful narratives, and schoolboy jibes.

Sometimes, to make the locality clear, the Yiddish is scattered with anglicizations, such as *ridzhent strit* (Regent Street), *bavelkomt* (welcomed), and *votsh un tsheyn* (watch and chain).[5] The immigrant community was in a state of flux, and the anglicized Yiddish reflected the spoken language of the Jewish East End. Immigrants lived with growing bilingualism, and the writers' ability to switch between languages in a creative way celebrates their resourcefulness.[6] Adding "foreign" expressions to Yiddish songs and poems brings a surprise element and portrays a changing identity and growing compatibility with the new language.[7]

The lyrics do not give a simplistic portrayal because they criticize and comment, addressing community wrangles and internal anxiety and discord. They indicate the importance of an issue, because the issue would not crop up in the lyrics unless it had already assumed considerable prominence. Literary texts of this era not only reflect political conflict but are significant agents in shaping debate, rehearsing arguments, and preparing the ground for political action.⁸ In this sense, the London Yiddish lyrics act as sites of debate, pushing forward agendas in a variety of political and social spheres.

Some lyrics articulate opinions on current politics and events such as the 1892 general election, the 1905 Aliens Act, and controversies surrounding the building of the Feinman Yiddish People's Theatre in 1911. Others depict the pressures immigration has brought to religious practice and the changing roles of men and women. There are lyrics that concern the broad problems of poverty, working conditions in the sweated trades, child labor, and the age of consent. And there are those that focus on internal controversy over the decline of religious observance, religion teachers' pay, problems of gambling in the community, exploitative sexual behavior, and the clash between exponents of highbrow and lowbrow Yiddish theatre.

Yiddish verse and song lyrics offer an alternative approach to Anglo-Jewish historiography because creative texts do different work to prose and alter the nature of intervention in debates. The lyrics are the bearers of messages and insights that heighten our understanding of the immigrant community and, as such, describe aspects of immigrant life previously unrecorded. Poetry imagines things in different ways offering new perspectives, and can thus move and transform, becoming a force in consciousness raising.⁹ Rhyming couplets are an unconventional historical source. They are not official documentation such as minutes of meetings or parliamentary reports. Lyrics of pop songs, satirical verse, and polemical poetry offer hints and clues rather than concrete information, and a sense of the past is gleaned from the crevices of the rhyme. This makes the view of the past one from within the culture, from below, and addresses details of the everyday which make up a vital aspect of understanding the immigrant community. This view transforms parts of what we already know and points to areas that have been occluded or overlooked. In addition to the content, the London lyrics also display the vibrant cultural life from which they emanated.

Many London lyrics were published to be read, and were perused in workplaces, cafés, or the home, local satire merely surviving until the next week's newspaper.¹⁰ Other lyrics were not accessed on the page, but were heard sung, direct and unmediated. There was socialist poetry that was read aloud at political events or declaimed from the Yiddish stage,

INTRODUCTION

Advertisement for Yiddish gramophone records. © British Library Board, *Idisher ekspres*, 1905.

and their full layered meanings may not have been grasped on first hearing. Socialist anthems became rousing choruses during demonstrations, were performed by choirs at socialist events, and were sung to accompany the rhythm of sewing machines in factories and workshops. The rhyme could become a hook to pick up and memorize the lyrics. The music-hall songs were heard in performance in the Yiddish halls and clubs or between acts in the Yiddish theatre. Local celebrities became associated with their songs, and once they became popular, they were sung on the streets by sellers touting penny songsheets to be bought and sung at home. Only after 1905 did some well-known Yiddish songs appear on gramophone records.[11]

The performative aspect of the songs is vital in interpreting them because they demand audiences interact and respond with emotions, heckling, and applause. In deciphering the way performance and music affect meaning, we can add to how we understand and appreciate the lyrics.

Rhyming *kupletn* were only one aspect of Jewish East End popular culture in Yiddish. Yiddish newspapers, journals, and pamphlets published creative prose, fiction, political cartoons, features, reviews, and serialized translations into Yiddish of well-known English and European

INTRODUCTION

literature. Yiddish plays on local English themes and famous Yiddish classics were performed on the London Yiddish stage, and toward the end of the period discussed, Yiddish cinema was becoming popular. Wider East End Jewish culture, which may or may not have been conducted in Yiddish, included boxing, gambling, street bands, cafés, and workingmen's clubs.[12] The growth of this immigrant culture brought a new vibrancy to Jewish life in England, yet it was a culture that was deeply strange to the established Anglo-Jewish community.

THE ANGLO-JEWISH COMMUNITY AND THE NEW IMMIGRANTS

London iz nisht vi es iz amol geveyn...	London is not as it once was...
di yidn redn english az men ken zey nit farshteyn.	The Jews speak English so you can't understand them.
Oy london hot zikh ibergekert.	Oh London has turned upside down.[13]

The East End's Yiddish-speaking ghetto developed after 1881 when the immigration of Jews from Eastern Europe rapidly accelerated. The established, settled Anglo-Jewish community was thrown into chaos trying to support those arriving in England. Differences in class, language, style of religion, outlook, culture, and political activism, however, gave the Anglo-Jewish establishment little in common with the immigrants. The dissimilarities seemed too great a gap to cross, and there were huge conflicts of interest and misunderstandings between them. Opinions and satire about the relationship between the immigrants and the Anglo-Jewish establishment are scattered throughout the lyrics, and in order to understand the content, we need to consider the change in England's Jewish demography.

Before 1881 the established Anglo-Jewish community was upwardly mobile, increasingly prosperous, and middle class, with an exceedingly wealthy elite. The elite consisted of established dynasties of families, both Sephardi and Ashkenazi, who financed and ran all the major Anglo-Jewish institutions. The largest section was middle class, with a small number of professionals and many active in commerce, and a small

INTRODUCTION

section were working-class immigrants from Poland and Russia. The East End of London contained all classes of Jews, but most of the elite had moved to West London and the West End, and the middle classes were moving to North London. The poorer immigrants remained in the East End.

The Anglo-Jewish elite was composed of English people with English values and mores who were practicing Judaism. The Anglo-Jewish authorities tried to produce unity within the community, assisting all Jews to become middle class with English values. To achieve this, they modernized existing institutions. The Jewish Board of Deputies, with delegates from the major synagogues, represented the Jewish community to government agencies. They were allied to the Chief Rabbinate, who held religious authority across the British Empire. London Ashkenazi synagogues were brought together in the United Synagogue, which tried to bring in a common orthodox style which engaged with modernity by modeling itself on the Anglican Church. The United Synagogue did not change the ancient liturgy, but abandoned certain sacrificial prayers and created a more accessible English translation in an attempt at making synagogue services acceptable to English Jews and the more orthodox.[14]

Although the United Synagogue wanted to unite orthodox practice in Britain, most immigrants were not members of the large synagogues within the United Synagogue's remit. Immigrants were unable to afford the high synagogue fees, and many did not recognize the authority of the chief rabbi. The Anglo-Jewish Rabbinate practiced what they considered a diluted form of Judaism that was too anglicized. Immigrants preferred to pray in *khevres*, which were small, informal, and gregarious prayer rooms in the Russian/Polish style of prayer. They charged low fees, and although many khevres could not afford rabbis, others employed immigrant rabbis from Eastern Europe.[15] However, because the khevres were not included in the United Synagogue structure, they had no representation in Anglo-Jewish orthodoxy.[16]

The major Anglo-Jewish synagogues had charitable arms offering support to members, so this excluded most of the immigrant community. The Jewish Board of Guardians had been set up decades earlier with a remit to provide relief to the Jewish poor who were not members of Anglo-Jewish synagogues. The board was particularly anxious to keep poor Jews out of the workhouse, where families were split up and it was impossible to keep kosher and the Sabbath. Their principal aim was to provide assistance that would stop people living on relief and move them out of poverty. They gave advice on sanitation and inspected homes to put pressure on landlords to fulfill their obligations for building maintenance. They offered loans and medical aid and ran apprenticeship schemes.[17]

From 1881 the Anglo-Jewish institutions were put under tremendous pressure as the demography of London's Jewish community radically changed. The 60,000 members of the established Anglo-Jewish community expanded with the accelerated influx of thousands of immigrants from Russia and Poland. Between 1881 and 1914, 100,000 to 120,000 Yiddish-speaking Jews settled in London, mostly in the East End. These population numbers did not account for transmigrants en route to America, so at any one time, numbers were up to three times higher than official figures.[18]

Yiddish-speaking immigrants entered an overcrowded labor and housing market where they struggled to get a foothold, find work, and earn a living, and immigrant institutions, such as khevres, multiplied. The struggle to create a new life was chaotic and pressured, yet it was not only new immigrants who were disorientated and confused. Established Anglo-Jewry was unprepared for the changes that immigration wrought. The Board of Guardians found itself overwhelmed by the demand for poor relief, and a separate Mansion House Fund was established to help refugees fleeing persecution. Immigrants were looked after on arrival; protected from dockside impostors; given furniture, tools, clothing, and other household necessities; and provided with opportunities to learn trades. However, by 1891 the Mansion House Fund money was used up, and the Russo-Jewish Committee was formed to take over dealing with the influx of refugees.[19]

In an attempt to bring the expanding number of khevres together, modernize them, and give them a voice in Anglo-Jewry, Samuel Montagu, Liberal Member of Parliament (MP) for Whitechapel, established the Federation of Synagogues in 1888, with Lord Rothschild as its president. Their aim was to unite East End khevres and immigrant synagogues, amalgamate *khadorim* (religion classes), and improve sanitation and the condition of the buildings by giving loans.[20] This aim was not entirely successful, and the expanding immigrant community was immersed in debate and conflict, not only with the established Anglo-Jews but also between immigrant orthodox and the vocal and activist socialists and anarchists.

The thirty-year span covered in this book coincides with political events that changed the nature of the Yiddish-speaking audience in England and had an effect on the material being published and performed. In the 1880s most immigrants were poor and uneducated workers trying to improve their economic status. The end of the century coincided with the establishment of the Jewish Labor Bund in Russia, with its concentration on the status of the Yiddish language and creating cultural activities in Yiddish, and many immigrants from this period would have been familiar with the growing Yiddish literature. The period after 1905 also brought immigrants who were political refugees from the abortive Russian revolution.[21] These new audiences raised the bar and brought greater debate on the quality of performance in Yiddish.

THE CONTENT OF THE YIDDISH LYRICS

The lyrics are varied, coming from three distinct and somewhat disconnected genres: socialist poetry, music-hall songs, and satirical verse. The socialist poetry was published in the London Yiddish socialist press, mostly between 1884 and 1894: *Der poylisher yidl*, *Di tsukunft* (The future), *Der arbayter fraynd* (The Worker's Friend), *Di fraye velt* (The free world), and *Der veker* (The awakener). These papers were largely established and edited by the popular writer and poet Morris Winchevsky, who wrote the large majority of the poems, ballads, and anthems.

Music-hall songs were performed in East End immigrant music halls and published as penny songsheets and songbooks, such as *Der londoner kupletist* (The London rhymester) and *Der londoner lider magazin* (The London song magazine).[22] Leonard Prager, in his invaluable *Yiddish Culture in Britain*, lists 244 songsheets published in London.[23] They are not individually dated, but were likely to have been published between 1900 and 1905, and sung from a little earlier.[24] Immigrant music-hall performers and songwriters, such as Arn (Aaron) Nager, Beki (Rebecca) Goldstein, and Yoysef (Joseph) Markovitsh, became well-known figures, and traveled across the Yiddish world with their repertoire.

The satirical verse was mostly published in the five years prior to World War I, with the majority between 1911 and 1913. They appeared in *Der idisher ekspres* (The Jewish express), *Di tsayt* (The times), and *Der bloffer* (The bluffer).[25] The most prolific satirist, and editor of the *Bloffer*, was Dr. Avrom Margolin, who wrote under the pseudonym Avreml.[26]

The three genres, with writers from different perspectives, agendas, and goals, are sometimes in tension with each other, and sometimes overlap, yet each genre adds richness to the developing picture of the Jewish East End. Taken together, they portray some of the conflict and debate that existed within the community. The *kupletn* analyzed here are chosen for the stories they uncover about the themes of politics, sex, and religion in the immigrant sphere. They are creative and contain imaginative ideas, and give us a sense not only of the lived life but how it was variously interpreted. The writers, situated within an immigrant world, a Yiddish world, and an English world, engage with all three. As commentary on the worlds that they inhabit, the texts offer challenges and an alternative approach to Anglo-Jewish historiography.

Parts of these stories have been told before; however, this research illuminates totally new aspects of the history of Jewish immigration to England by speaking with a different register to histories taken from more established sources. Jewish labor relations and the impact of the Russian revolutionary socialists in the East End are well-trodden ground.[27] The socialist poetry, however, shows an attempt at direct and accessible communication with working people, with a desire to inform, influence, and convert the reader to socialism. Morris Winchevsky was the subject of many articles in Yiddish. Some writers were contemporary critics, and many were uncritical fans praising his work.[28] In English there has been little written about him, and he is often just mentioned in passing in larger works.[29] This book is the most in-depth exploration of Winchevsky's London poetry.

There is almost no Anglo-Jewish scholarly research on the history of intimate sexual relations.[30] When it appears in Anglo-Jewish history, it is generally within the context of crime and prostitution.[31] Yet the themes of courtship, relationships, marriage, sex, and sexual exploitation appear regularly in the Yiddish music-hall songs. They allude to the changing nature of sexual roles and relationships in the immigrant

London community, and offer perspectives, albeit exaggerated and laden with music-hall humor and double entendres, on how sexual relations are changed both by engagement with modernity and by the process of immigration.

The institutional side of the practice of Judaism is well researched by scholars, including conflicts between religious and radicals.[32] However, popular song and poetry nuance what we know. They offer glimpses into how religious practice and growing secularization were changing immigrants' daily lives in the encounter with modernity. The lyrics highlight how some religious immigrants were trying to change orthodox practice without losing the quality of their religious lives, and others were abandoning any religious practice for new philosophies or ideologies. In addition, many texts use concepts, language, and imagery from liturgy, the Bible, and the Talmud. Whether engaging with religious, secular, or atheist ideas, these poems and songs display how religion structured the way the community thought and communicated.

There has been little scholarly work on Yiddish popular culture in Britain, and this book seeks to address that by offering a chapter on the history of the Yiddish music halls in the London sphere.[33] Aspects of the experience of being a singer, an actor, an audience, a reader, or a writer are gleaned from a variety of Yiddish primary sources other than the poems and songs themselves, such as theatre reviews, newspaper articles, and memoirs. These sources build a picture of a Yiddish-speaking East End where writers, performers, and audiences are in close communication, producing and consuming Yiddish language culture. Whether perusing Yiddish newspapers for news and opinions, crying at a moving scenario at the Yiddish theatre, or giggling and flirting in the music halls, the London lyrics made up a significant proportion of East End immigrant popular entertainment.

This book raises questions and offers perspectives that resonate across many areas of historiography. The history of Jewish immigrants to London and the way they acculturated to English life are an important part of the history of London, working-class immigrant histories, and London cultural and social histories.[34] This analysis will also add to histories of Yiddish popular culture and Jewish diaspora histories, in particular that of New York's Yiddish-speaking Lower East Side. There were many connections in ideas and in transfer of people, and similar issues

INTRODUCTION

were encountered in both locations.[35] An equivalent analysis of American Yiddish popular songs is yet to be done.[36] Finally, this study draws on ethnomusicology, sociology, and cultural history.

The analysis of the poems and songs in this book focuses on three themes that were aspects of immigrant life that were most challenged by the experience of immigration: politics, sex, and religion. Yet the overall understanding is framed by two, sometimes overlapping, lenses. The first explores how the texts engage with acculturation to England, and the extent to which they encourage the process of anglicization. The second focuses on how the London lyrics illustrate the transnational nature of the London immigrant community. These two perspectives offer alternate ways of understanding the nature and function of the London Yiddish lyrics.

ANGLICIZATION

Tsu kemfen far englands frayhayt mit shverd in hant
di volentirn zet nor vi freylekh geyen zey...
oykh a yid var tzvishn zey.

To fight for England's freedom with sword in hand
The volunteers seemed happy as they went...
Also a Jew was among them.[37]

The debate that dominated the agenda of the Anglo-Jewish community of this period was the anglicization of the Eastern European Jewish immigrants.[38] Yet understanding what constituted anglicization was fiercely contested, and the limits of anglicization were questioned by different parts of the Jewish and English communities. For the gentile English community, anglicization was on a continuum from the acculturation to English norms, to assimilation, or even conversion to Christianity. The Liberal Party was ambivalent. It had brought in Jewish emancipation over twenty years earlier, releasing Jews from legal restrictions, yet was wary about emancipated Jews maintaining their collective and international ties with other Jewish communities.[39] In contrast, the Far Right rhetoric of anti-Semites such as Arnold White and William Evans-Gordon demanded Englishness should be a "re-Christianisation of democracy."[40]

Israel Zangwill's short story "Anglicization," written in 1902, examines some of these tensions.[41] The story portrays how the limits of anglicization are tested when an anglicized Jewish veteran of the Boer War hopes to marry an English Christian girl. Here, even anglicized Jewishness has become a stumbling block to national belonging. The story suggests that the definition of anglicization by Jews and English gentiles did not coincide. A Jew could be English enough to fight in the Boer War, risking death and saving another soldier's life. He could be part of established English society and wish to marry a Christian. Yet a marriage of these opposites could not happen because ultimately Englishness did not include the Jew. The story drew out the contested nature of the term "anglicization" between Jew and gentile. The patriotic Yiddish music-hall song quoted at the start of this section tells of a Jewish soldier in the Boer War, dying a hero and saving his fellow soldier. The song, like its English music-hall equivalents, written to encourage Jews to fight for England, does not make the social comment Zangwill makes. Instead, it suggests that the death of one Jewish soldier raised the profile of Jewish involvement in English life.[42]

The meaning of anglicization within the Jewish community varied greatly. The Anglo-Jewish establishment saw the impoverished immigrants as coming from a backward culture and desired their urgent transformation, improvement, and integration into English society. Charitable institutions funded and encouraged social mobility to move immigrant workers out of poverty. They wanted to eliminate the Yiddish language but preserve a strong Jewish identity and orthodox practice. To this end Anglo-Jewry set up and funded educational programs to "iron out the ghetto bend."[43] The Jews' Free School (JFS) was established long before emancipation to educate the Jewish poor, who were largely immigrants or children of immigrants. The school's mission was to turn immigrant children into English boys and girls.[44] Rich in its praise for the JFS, the *Jewish Chronicle* explained that the school provided immigrant children with a "bridge by which mentally and morally, they may pass from Russia to England."[45] The school's head teacher, Moses Angel, banned the speaking of Yiddish, and the school taught mainly secular subjects. The lack of a full Jewish education left East End parents sending their children to *khadorim* and *talmetoyres* (religion classes for younger and older boys), which ran before and after school and on Sundays. Angel led a crusade against the standard of teaching and the sanitation of the premises of these establishments.

INTRODUCTION

The desire for anglicization also came from within the immigrant community. Socialists and anarchists saw immigrant workers as clinging to outmoded ideas that they needed to reject in order to embrace modernity and fight for a socialist future. They saw engagement with local radical politics and an understanding of international socialism to be part of a self-improvement program. They offered political lectures, English classes, and cultural entertainment. The socialists were left-wing assimilationists and internationalists, so their engagement with acculturation to England needs to be seen as a step toward their wider aim of political revolution.[46]

Anglicization looked very different in the orthodox *Machzike Hadath* synagogue. The *Machzike Hadath* was established in 1898 as an amalgamation between a North London German synagogue and a large khevre, to agitate for stricter communal orthodoxy. The congregants were anxious that being part of anglicized Anglo-Jewish structures would bring a dilution of strictly orthodox practice. They therefore remained outside the Federation of Synagogues, whose anglicization drive tried to expunge Yiddish from their proceedings. They argued separately for tighter strictures in *kashres* (kosher food) and *shechita* (ritual slaughter of animals). Yet the synagogue embraced a form of patriotism to Britain. It was not opposed to anglicization as long as orthodoxy remained stringent. It adopted liturgy that acknowledged a debt to Britain yet continued teaching its children in Yiddish in the *khadorim* and *talmetoyres*.[47]

Many "ordinary," nominally religious Jews simply wanted their children to learn English so that they could move up the social ladder. They did not imagine that their children would become estranged from Jewish tradition. They welcomed the London "Board" schools yet also sent their children to *khadorim* to supplement the Jewish education they got at home.

Anglicization had many faces, depending on context. It could be revolutionary, patriotic, or conversionist. It could be paternalistic, didactic, or pragmatic. And it could be inconsistent, stressing the need to acculturate yet desiring communal unity.[48] Although previous historiography on Jewish immigrant acculturation has focused on institutions and prominent individuals, this work investigates what attitudes and perspectives are revealed in popular culture and concerns lesser-known people in the community. Conflicting ideologies and approaches offered rich material for poems and songs, polemics, narrative, and satire.[49] The London Yiddish lyrics refer to local and national politics: internal workings of the East End Yiddish-speaking community, tensions between Anglo-Jewry and the immigrants, and topical events of the wider English world. The texts embrace English culture and poke fun at those left behind in the old world. They grapple with the cultural clash with a mixture of nostalgia and defiance. Taken as a whole, the poetry and song can be viewed as a way for immigrant writers to encourage their own community to participate in and adapt to life in England.

It may appear paradoxical to suggest that the Yiddish popular lyrics were a force for anglicization. The Anglo-Jewish authorities were unhappy about the prevalence of the Yiddish language, seeing it as a stumbling block to engagement with England. Yet the poems and songs expressed progressive ideas specific to English diaspora life, such as debating aspects of voting in the coming election or filling in census data, or the need to consider how to change religious and family life to move with the times. Sometimes known Yiddish texts were changed to update them and make them relevant. In Salli and Philip Weisenfreund's East End music hall, a sketch by the famous playwright Avrom Goldfaden was updated to include local references to the London fog and Disraeli.[50] In addition, the Yiddish of the lyrics often reflected local East End speech with the incorporation of anglicized words. As such, Yiddish acts as a bridge between identities, becoming part of the medium of cultural transmission. The Yiddish texts are conglomerates. They are not translations of English texts, even though writers may ape the style of English music-hall song or be influenced by a tradition of English poetry and satire. They are also not identical to similar texts from Eastern Europe, even though they may share themes and cultural knowledge. The lyrics mix "local London color" with elements of a common background in an Eastern European past, and as such, mirror the complexity of the immigrants' state of flux within a transnational Yiddish-speaking world.[51]

TRANSNATIONALISM

Andersh nit vi got in kas   It can't be anything else than God being angry

oyf der velt iz (ir farshteyt?)   With the world (you understand?)

INTRODUCTION

dos ir hant di "strayk khalas"
oyf der velt hot itst tseshpreyt.

Lang in london straykn beker.

That its hand has spread
The "strike disease"across the world.
Bakers have been on strike in London for ages.[52]

The London East End Yiddish-speaking immigrant milieu was not a cultural bubble. It was a vibrant mixture of influences from multiple locations and communities. Locally there were the wider English gentile society and the Anglo-Jewish established community. Further afield, there were connections from immigrants' past lives in Eastern European Yiddish-speaking towns and *shtetlekh* (small towns). There was contact with other immigrant diaspora locations, such as New York, and an awareness of wider international politics and radical internationalist ideas. The way these locations and ideas combined within the Yiddish lyrics of London produces a transnational creative force. This can be seen in the satirical poem "Strayk epidemye" (Strike epidemic), written in London in 1913. This poem is packed with topical references to London strikes of bakers, housepainters, and the local Yiddish press. Yet it is characterized as an epidemic, so there are also American women "striking" against men and Russia being a "sea of mass-strikes." The poem includes reference to the Eleventh Zionist Congress in Vienna, Polish workers, anarchists, the Russian government, and the trial of Mendel Beilis. The local and transnational references are scattered throughout the poem, jumping from one location to another and back. The song portrays not only how conflict and activism exist across the Jewish world but also that there are links between these worlds.

In 2009 historian Moshe Rosman threw down a challenge to fellow Jewish historians concerning their approach to the geography of Jewish history. In *Rethinking European Jewish History*, he identified two routes taken by historians. If historians see Jewish history as having a unified wholeness and view Jews in a global aspect, the particularity of Jewish experience in one individual place gets subsumed. Yet by focusing solely on Jews in one country, the transnational perspective is lost: "The local context was only one context of the Jewish historical experience. Jewish experience was also contextualized within the frameworks of Jewish

INTRODUCTION

history, Jewish tradition, and the mutual influences of Jewish communities in various parts of the world."[53] Rosman suggests that we consider regionalism in our analyses of Jewish culture and argues for the concept of Ashkenaz as a transnational "Jewish country." Ashkenaz signifies a culture that crosses locations. So when exploring a Yiddish-based diasporic culture such as London, it should be considered within the context of the whole Yiddish-speaking world.

This approach is useful when analyzing the acculturation of Jewish immigrant communities in London. The acculturation process is a careful balance between entering into a new diasporic culture with unfamiliar mores in the new country of settlement and maintaining old cultural forms of the homelands of Eastern Europe. Immigrants may leave one society and join another, yet they often maintain contacts, business links, and political interests through letters, journeys, and sending money. The change in geography can even increase communication, support, and trade. Advances in transportation in the late nineteenth century allowed considerable to-ing and fro-ing and circular movement creating transatlantic networks. The multilayered aspects of identity and lifestyle were fluid and indeterminate.[54] Interactions between the old and new cultures were complex and entangled and not unidirectional. A transnational perspective offers a way of analyzing how immigrants participate in both societies at the same time, and how they develop a new identity transcending both new and home communities.[55] The culture that is created is an integral part of Ashkenaz because, as a "Jewish country," Ashkenaz contains the cultures of the Eastern European homeland and all of its diasporic locations.

Within this milieu, popular culture gains particular significance because the purveyors of that culture—the actors, singers, musicians, directors, even writers—move among the locations in the course of their work, taking plays, songs, and music across the Yiddish-speaking world. They maintain ties, circulate ideas, and transcend the existent cultural forms to create new mixes.[56] The variety of artistic influences on the songwriters and poets creates a transnational aesthetics that reflects multiple locations, cultures, and changes simultaneously.[57]

Transnational Ashkenaz may cross geographic borders, but it is still centered around Jewish communities. Yet in England, the East End Yiddish-speaking enclave was small, and the outside English gentile

INTRODUCTION

world had considerable influence. Ethnomusicological research has often explored how migration from one country to another has affected cultural output and identity, analyzing how migrants adjust the songs they bring with them to the cultural context of the new country. Cultural baggage can have symbolic power as the new cultural artifact is created from the tension between the rupture, displacement, and dispossession of the old life, and the acculturation into the new country.[58] This process is not smooth and does not happen without resistance, as cultural symbols are reinterpreted in new structures. However, when transnational elements are grafted onto local music, it can both bring a sense of emancipation and give the music a complex and ambivalent meaning.[59]

If migration is not simply viewed as movement from one territory to another, facing indigenous people in an "us and them" situation, this allows for the complexity of migrants inhabiting multiple locations. Artists are often supported by transnational networks of hubs, such as people, spaces, or institutions. Performers can move between them, keeping meaningful contacts in all places. These hubs help migrant artists to use influences from those multiple locations, producing "transcultural capital" in their creative work.[60]

These transnational locations become incorporated into the creative work to make simultaneous multiple constructions of identity, history, and culture.[61] The resulting cultural artifact cannot be easily pulled into constituent parts. Rather, the influences on it produce its originality. The challenge then shifts into questions of how to define the various styles of cultural mix. It is difficult, if not impossible, to define a cultural boundary, particularly in immigrant and diaspora communities, because no one expression of culture can define any individual group. Instead, immigrant societies can be seen to live at the intersection of three cultures: their new land of settlement, their old homeland, and a diaspora culture that they share with those in other countries.[62]

The idea of diaspora is an important identity marker in Jewish migration.[63] This is exemplified in Rebecca Kobrin's research on the immigrant experiences of émigrés from the town of Białystok. She argues that some émigrés see themselves as torn from their lost homeland, while others identify as part of a transnational diaspora. Because Jewish migration happened with such speed, new solidarities were created through newspapers and organizations that kept links to the homeland but were full of

INTRODUCTION

local concerns for the diaspora locations. The Jews in the different diasporas of Białystok did not consider their Białystok identity as being erased. Instead, their identity seemed to be reinforced. In this example, regionalism is not limited by borders, and the Białystok model shows the collision of global, national, and local concerns.[64]

The transnational elements of the London Yiddish lyrics give them a layered impact. Yet it would be simplistic only to name the layers as home country, new country, and diasporas, because there are multiple perspectives and a variety of cultural experiences within each place. London's cultural mix is entwined in the lyrics, yet this did not make the texts so specific that they could not travel. London may have been a small Yiddish-speaking diaspora, but there was overlap in immigrant experience between London and New York. Similarly, there was much in common with the Eastern European experience because cultural and generational change and modernization were happening everywhere, and Eastern European Jewish mores were also in flux.[65] Thus the London lyrics held meaning throughout a geographical space, and it is through popular culture that the transnational nature of Jewish culture is particularly visible.

This book is split into two parts. Part I, "The London of the Lyrics," gives an overview of two histories of Jewish London, portraying the daily context in which the lyrics are situated. The first historical chapter, chapter 1, describes the politics of work and unions and the Jewish socialists' position as union activists. It addresses the importance of poetry to both the English and Jewish socialists, and includes political developments that led to the Aliens Act and the conflicts that this wrought within the community. The second historical chapter, chapter 2, offers a history of London's Yiddish theatre and music halls that provided a home for the London songs. It places the Yiddish halls within the context of the English halls, and focuses on the battles concerning the quality of art in English campaigns and the Yiddish press.

Part II, "The Lyrics of London," is the main part of the book. It analyzes the poems and songs, using them to reveal hidden social histories of Jewish London. Chapter 3 gives a detailed analysis of how the lyrics demonstrate the way the immigrants were entwined within a transnational Yiddish-speaking world. This is followed by pairs of chapters (chapter 4 to chapter 9) which focus on politics, sex, and religion. The

INTRODUCTION

"Politics" chapters 4 and 5 analyze the socialist poetry of the most renowned and prolific London socialist writer of the time, Morris Winchevsky. The large amount of poetry from his London years promoted political engagement and activism. Chapters 6 and 7 explore the sexual content of Yiddish music-hall songs and how the immigrant process affected intimate relations in courtship, marriage, and transgressive sex. Chapters 8 and 9 analyze how religious language and ideas are incorporated into a variety of texts to make comment on both religious and nonreligious aspects of life.

Whitechapel Noise gives a hitherto unseen view of London's social and cultural history. It shows a lively, vibrant, and noisy community facing immigration problems head on, sometimes with anxiety, sometimes with anger, and sometimes with humor.

PART I

The London of the Lyrics

East End Russian restaurant, and concert at Jewish working girls' club, Soho. Both from George Sims, *Living London*, 1901. From the Mazower Private Collection.

I

Immigrant Labor, Political Activism, and Socialist Poetry

Meyle, s'iz bizi, be-me
ober in slek, oy vey
aleyn vi a shteyn bin ikh do
   na-ve-nad
Dem gantsn tog shteyn dort in blek
   leyen yard

Well, in the busy season, so-so,
But in the slack, oh no
Alone as a stone I'm here wander-
   ing homeless
Standing there all day in Black
   Lion Yard.[1]

The first priority of a newly arrived immigrant, after securing housing, was finding work in the overcrowded job market. In London after 1901, almost two-thirds of the male immigrant workers worked in the sweated trades of tailoring, footwear, and furniture.[2] Their hard lives became material for dozens of songs and verses, and in particular the socialist poetry. Socialist poets wrote about immigrant workers' conditions, acute poverty, and child labor. They offered a class analysis, stressed the importance of activism in fighting for better conditions, and provided anthems to be used in demonstrations and marches.

The background for the London lyrics' representation of immigrant labor consists of the ideological and political clashes between Anglo-Jews and immigrants about work and unions, between English and Jewish socialists about ideology and aesthetics, and between English anti-alienists and immigrants about immigration and Englishness. Jewish immigrant socialists, despite being revolutionary internationalists, were trade union leaders who at times worked together with their English comrades. Both English and Jewish socialists used song and poetry as an integral part of the struggle for a fairer future. Immigrant labor was used as an excuse for anti-alien sentiment and immigration restriction. It was in the atmosphere of anti-alienism that the London Yiddish lyrics were produced.

SWEATING AND UNION ACTIVISM

Lomir in yunyons zikh ale farbunden	Let's all be bound to the unions
s'vet dokh undz gebn i koyekh, i mut . . .	It will surely give us strength and courage . . .
es tsitert in vorkshop der maysterl dort.	The small master quakes there in the workshop.[3]

In London's sweated workshops, immigrant workers endured long hours, received low wages, and worked in overcrowded and unsanitary conditions.[4] The word "sweater" was commonly used to refer to the workshop master and subcontractor of the tailoring, footwear, and furniture workshops. Subcontracting was the process of repeatedly contracting out jobs of work from wholesalers to workshops in order to make garments at the cheapest possible rate. A West End wholesale tailoring firm would get an order from a retailer, buy the cloth, cut it, and give it to subcontractors for a deposit. The subcontractor would receive a fixed price per piece returned by a certain time. He would contract the work out to his own workshop or masters in other workshops, who may, in turn, subcontract to smaller workshops and to home workers.[5] As the workshops taking the work became smaller and smaller, based in cellars, kitchens, back rooms, or outhouses, it became easier for the master or sweater to disregard restrictions, demanding longer hours and a fast pace of work and allowing very poor working conditions.[6]

Demand for unskilled labor was increased by the system of subdivision of tasks. Rather than one well-paid, skilled craftsman completing a whole item, the process of making a garment was split into smaller jobs: sleeves, cuffs, pockets, fixing, basting, and pressing. These were divided between workers of different skills and experience, with the simpler tasks being done by unskilled, poorly paid workers.[7] A small workshop would be a hierarchy. At the top were contracted workers who had permanent jobs, such as a machinist, a presser, and a baster. Under them would be subcontracted workers such as subpressers and plain machinists, and beneath them would be a range of unskilled workers, such as buttonhole makers and finishers. Often women and boys only had to become proficient at one task.[8]

The difficulties of earning a living wage were exacerbated by the seasonal nature of the sweated trades, connected to when consumers were buying clothing and shoes. Busy times in the Jewish trades when work was pressured by deadlines, and when workers might work through the night, were October to December and March to April in the run up to Passover. During slack times, many workers were laid off, with only some skilled workers kept on in the workshop.[9] This left much of the workforce in "casualized limbo," having to find bits of work such as street trading, or reliant on the money they had saved during the busy season.[10] Some years had additional pressures, such as trade depressions or severe winters when the Thames froze. This affected the jobs of dock workers, whose wives would take on homework to assist the family income, which in turn would increase competition for immigrants working in the sweated trades.[11]

Jewish women were conspicuous in the workplace in clothing workshops, shops, and market stalls, with others less visible working from their homes and taking in lodgers to supplement the family income. It was common for a woman to work before marriage, in widowhood, and to supplement her husband's income during the slack season.[12] However, women were paid significantly less than men and were rarely in skilled jobs. The lowest-paid women's work was homework, which consisted of finishing garments that required little training and no machinery and which provided barely sufficient pay to support one person.[13]

English national unions dominated the three main industries in which Jews worked: tailors, cabinet makers, and boot and shoe makers. Jews could join, although few did. The English trade union movement was small, with no tradition of multiethnicity in English life and no precedents for political organization based on a foreign language. English trade unionists claimed that Jewish immigrants were difficult if not impossible to unionize and were not good unionists when they did. They believed that immigrant workers undercut native workers by being prepared to work for so little and that Jews were unused to British institutions, ignored union officers' instructions, went on strike without authority, were riven by political disputes between socialists and anarchists, and did not want to join unions because they wanted to become masters.[14] It was apparent that Jewish workshop masters and workers aligned with religious, kinship, and community ties of loyalty, and this made unionization unpopular among Jewish workers. Seasonal work meant that workers were out of work during the slack, and women working from home were often isolated.[15]

One reason for the reluctance of Jews to join unions was their aspiration for upward mobility, which prevented their organizing for improvement in basic wages and working conditions. Becoming an entrepreneur was one way to minimize the effect of seasonal fluctuations. The constant supply of unskilled immigrants not only pushed established workers out of their jobs; it sometimes pushed them upward into more skilled positions. Historians disagree about the meaning of the immigrants' drive toward upward mobility: whether it demonstrates the Jewish working-class entrepreneurial spirit and drive for independence, or whether it is not connected to ethnicity but was a result of Jewish immigrants' access to capital loans.[16] An immigrant could take a loan from the Jewish Board of Guardians in order to hire essential tools, such as a sewing machine or a pressing iron, and set up a workshop. Contemporary social reformer and labor researcher Beatrice Potter claimed that "with £1 in his pocket any man may rise to the dignity of a sweater." He would begin by living on immigrant labor, then employ a machinist and presser. The new master might earn little more than those he employed, but even if he earned less, he was more likely to be in work during the slack season.[17] The ease of movement from worker to master increased competition and often pitched masters back into the ranks of workers.

The upwardly mobile immigrant became an "alrightnik." The alrightnik was a bridge between the established Anglo-Jewish middle class and the immigrants. He rose to a management position within immigrant society and began to sponsor immigrant organizations, such as *landsmanshaftn*, and friendly societies, *khevres*, or perhaps paid for the salary of rabbis to be brought over from Eastern Europe.[18] Alrightniks were often not in good favor with the Anglo-Jewish establishment, who saw their leadership position and power in the immigrant community as a direct threat. Such was the case with the alrightnik Simcha Becker. Becker, a Polish refugee and a baker, set up a shelter for immigrants in 1885 with housing, kosher food, and a prayer room. The Board of Guardians opposed it as a private initiative and closed it down, claiming that providing a harbor for refugees would invite "helpless foreigners" to England.[19] A *Jewish Chronicle* editorial decried the shelter as encouraging "loafing and idleness."[20] Becker, however, was a folk hero among the immigrants, and the action against him caused an outcry. In a bid to reestablish community power, Samuel Montagu and other leading members of the Anglo-Jewish elite set up the Poor Jews Temporary Shelter.[21]

Despite aspirations toward upward mobility and the reluctance of many Jewish workers to join trade unions, between 1872 and 1915 thirty-six independent Jewish tailoring trade unions were formed, and if the Jewish branches of English unions are counted, then the figure rises to over fifty. In 1889 and 1890 there was partially successful mass strike action by Jewish workers. In 1889, inspired by a spate of strikes by English unions, notably the dockers' strike which had ended in success, trade union activist Lewis Lyons and socialist strike leader William Wess called a general strike in the Jewish tailoring trade.[22] The strike dragged on and eventually succeeded. However, with the constant influx of new immigrants, it proved impossible to sustain and ended with the collapse of the union.[23] In the 1890 shoe and boot strike, David Schloss, civil servant and member of the Jewish Board of Guardians, described how Jewish subcontractors appealed to Jewish manufacturers, arguing that the maintenance of the sweating system was a *khilel hashem*—a desecration of God's name—and passed the responsibility to them to change it. There was an unsatisfactory victory that again was impossible to maintain.[24] In 1912, however, there was a successful mass strike of tailors and tailoresses in the East and West End. The men's strike was over in three weeks and did not achieve much. The women's strike, however, though lengthy, ended with secured trade union workshops, a twelve-hour day, a 10 percent increase in wages, and the abolition of having both piece and time rates in the same workplace.[25] Many of the Jewish trade unions involved in these strikes were short-lived, some lasting months, some years, and only two survived a decade.[26]

CHAPTER 1

SOCIALIST ACTIVISM

Likht farshpreytn—rekht farbreytn	To spread Light—extend Justice
kum ikh un tsebrekh di keytn	I come and break the chains
fun der tiranay.	Of tyranny.[27]

Socialist activists, escaping Bismarck's anti-socialist laws, had been arriving in London since the 1870s. One of these was Aaron Lieberman, a socialist militant from Grodno who had been involved in revolutionary activities in Eastern Europe and had written a socialist manifesto titled "Call to Jewish Youth." In 1876 Lieberman established the *Agudah Hasozialistim Chaverim* (Hebrew Socialist Union), aiming to start a movement that included Jewish and non-Jewish socialists and aspired to improve the lot of Jewish workers in London. He was outspokenly anti-religious, which backfired with orthodox and traditional workers. He was accused of being a conversionist, which spread alarm in the orthodox community, which already saw the numbers of orthodox Jews depleting and had to endure Christian missionary activity across the East End offering help and support to impoverished workers.[28] Although Lieberman was unsuccessful in inspiring the mass of workers, he influenced many young socialist leaders, one of whom was Morris Winchevsky.[29]

Winchevsky, a radical revolutionary, was inspired by Lieberman's ideas but was less dogmatic in his approach, wanting to interpret socialist ideas and practice in a language that spoke directly to the workers.[30] In 1884 he and a friend, Elye Rabbinowitch, set up the *Poylisher yidl*, aimed at educating and supporting newly arrived Yiddish-speaking immigrants.[31] In addition to news and features, the *Poylisher yidl* published Yiddish fiction, translations of classics into Yiddish, and new socialist poetry, written almost entirely by Winchevsky.[32]

The *Poylisher yidl*, later named the *Tsukunft*, folded after less than a year on account of an ideological difference when Rabbinowitch accepted an advertisement from Samuel Montagu, who was both orthodox and a member of the Anglo-Jewish elite.[33] Winchevsky left the paper to found the overtly socialist *Arbayter fraynd* (Worker's friend), which published articles on sweated trade and capitalist exploitation, regularly criticizing Montagu and Chief Rabbi Hermann Adler in its pages.[34] Its aim was to raise consciousness and create a socialist movement.[35] In 1885

Front page of the *Poylisher yidl*, 15 August 1884. From the Mazower Private Collection.

the socialists established the Berner Street Club as a hub for the movement; for union and political meetings and activities, language classes, lectures, and entertainment; and as a base for the *Arbayter fraynd* press.[36]

As union activists, the Russian Jewish socialists were unlike their counterparts in the British trade union movement, because the Russian Jewish socialists' main aim was revolution across the Yiddish-speaking world. The *Arbayter fraynd* editor, Philip Krantz, was influenced by Ferdinand Lasalle's "iron law of wages." Lasalle considered it impossible for the workers' standard of living to improve because any rise in wages would bring a rise in prices, so that winning a small increase would not last and workers would revert to being on the same level as before.[37] Isaac Stone, a regular contributor to the *Arbayter fraynd*, wrote: "Trade unions alone cannot end the wretched life of the worker. . . . They lead workers off the right road with their belief in self help. . . . We socialists say the role of the union should not be only to make strikes but to completely rebuild society."[38] The fight for better working conditions was seen as important by the socialists, but it was only a starting point for revolutionary talk.[39]

These ideological perspectives did not attract workers en masse, whose priority was immediate amelioration of their condition. Workers may have felt that the socialist activists were more interested in dogma than in helping them feed their families, a stance that led Jewish socialists to temper their revolutionary ideas to a level that the workers could relate to. Indeed, by 1889 the revolutionary socialists began to regard trade unions as institutions that could propel workers toward a greater understanding of exploitation in a capitalist society.[40]

LONDON SOCIALIST POETRY AND SONG

Nemt aykh tsuzamen ir mutike brider	Come together courageous comrades
bildet in eynem a mekhtiken khor!	Form together a mighty choir!
Zoln dershaln di arbeter lider	Workers' songs should ring out
tsu undzer fertsntn yubiley-yor!	For our fourteenth anniversary![41]

The immigrant socialists, as well as being active among the Yiddish-speaking workers, joined the English socialist movements, such as the

Social Democratic Federation (SDF) and William Morris's Socialist League (SL).[42] These movements were, in the mid-1880s, developing a body of socialist poetry. The English socialists wrote within a long tradition of political songs. There were eighteenth-century industrial songs written by working people about their experience of work and sung by workers at workplaces, pubs, and clubs.[43] Broadside ballads, known as the "journalism of the poor," were topical and political songs, with often irreverent reports of daily events, published as songsheets and sold on the streets. They had a reputation for being scurrilous and sensationalist, but went into decline when the music halls started producing similar songs.[44] The loss of the broadside ballads left a void, to be filled in the 1880s by political poetry which was published in the English radical press and songbooks. The English socialists were concerned with the power of verse as education, propaganda, and activism, rather than entertainment. Poetry and song could teach about socialism, and be sung on the streets to raise funds for striking families and display socialist ideas.[45]

The Jewish socialists in London had similar needs to their English counterparts and attempted to develop a body of poetic material in Yiddish that included socialist polemic, anthems, and ballads about working conditions. However, they did not have the same well of poetry to draw on. In the 1880s Yiddish poetry had barely begun as a genre.[46] The *haskole* (Jewish enlightenment) writers had considered Yiddish a jargon: a domestic language that was spoken rather than a literary language, and therefore unsuitable for writing poetry. Most *haskole* poets wrote in Hebrew, German, or Russian, and although some dabbled in Yiddish, they were generally held in very poor regard.[47] This meant that the early socialist poets, such as Winchevsky, had few models of Yiddish poetry, and for a poetic aesthetic they were more likely to have looked for their inspiration toward Hebrew and biblical poetry or European works in German, Russian, or English.[48]

The Yiddish verse known to immigrant poets came from the generations-old Yiddish folk songs, which had made up their childhood landscapes of tune and rhyme imbibed from lullabies, childhood games, and community singing. As adults, the major Yiddish language influences were three popular writers. Berl Broder wrote song-dialogues in rhyming verse and performed them in taverns in Bessarabia in the mid-nineteenth century with a troupe of "Broder singers." Elyakum Zunzer was a prolific Lithuanian *badkhn* (wedding jester) and the first to publish his *kupletn* (rhyming couplets), which were widely read.[49] Avrom Goldfaden established the first Yiddish theatre in 1876 in Romania and wrote dozens of poems and songs to be performed in his plays on the new Yiddish stage. However, socialist poets who drew inspiration from these examples of popular song were disdained by critics who rejected the *kupletn* that Winchevsky and the sweatshop poets penned.[50] Decades later, when Yiddish poetry had developed substantially, very little of the poetry of the socialist writers was included in the canon of Yiddish poetry, being seen as overly concerned with the political message it was portraying and too unconcerned with aesthetics.[51] Yet the popularity of socialist poetry attested to its place in Yiddish culture.[52]

One reason for the popularity of socialist poetry was that it was not only read but sung, and music was seen by socialists as being particularly important to the struggle. For English socialists, the edifying possibilities of music were partly inspired by the conservative-led mid-Victorian idea of "rational recreation." Rational recreation promoted the use of leisure time in a way that would lead to desirable social change. Conservative reformers strove to limit drinking and brawling by providing mentally stimulating alternatives, and arranged free concerts on the streets and organized festivals and competitions for working-class choirs singing classical repertoire. However, their desire to offer leisure activities to workers was tempered by their anxiety that too much intellectual stimulation might open workers to radical politics.[53]

Such an engagement with radical politics was exactly what socialist activists hoped for. They believed that if they got it right, as well as holding the socialist message, the arts could open people's minds and release their potential, enabling them to respond to progressive political ideas.[54] They used similar strategies to the reformers, organizing choirs and arranging concerts in workers' clubs, using specially composed music and selected songs and poems to open and close meetings.[55] The socialist weekly *Clarion* described choral singing as "a lesson in discipline and socialism of the most convincing sort."[56] The Clarion Vocal Union considered the formality of a choir as having edifying qualities with its use of Victorian part-harmony and the Tonic Sol-fa method of sight reading.[57] Their choirs provided entertainment at socialist gatherings and festivals across the country. As well as singing classical repertoire, choirs sung new socialist song material, and songbooks were published with new labor hymns, "chants for socialists," and poems taken from the *Workman's Times* and *Clarion*.[58]

Some of the Jewish socialists' Yiddish lyrics mirrored English work songs, such as Winchevsky's free-translation of "The Song of the Shirt."[59] The immigrant socialist community also encouraged choirs, which were advertised in the *Arbayter fraynd*, and workers' songbooks were published by London Yiddish presses.[60] Generally, Yiddish material was written for particular immigrant strikes and events in London's East End, where songs were sung by crowds on marches and at meetings.

The nature of socialist poetry was a subject of debate. William Morris and other English socialist poets, artists, and writers were trying to create a new and distinct socialist aesthetic that would contribute to the long tradition of English poetry. They tried to combine a concern for aesthetics with socialism, believing that revolution would come from beauty as well as from a proletarian uprising.[61] Winchevsky's activist and anti-aesthetic stance stood in opposition to this approach. Winchevsky's sole aim was to be a *veker*, an awakener, and for him content was all-important. He criticized as ineffective the way Morris wrote poetry in a "spotless authentic Anglo-Saxon" which told "immortal tales in an immortal way," because those lyrical forms were unfamiliar to the uneducated worker, and were therefore less immediately accessible.[62] Winchevsky claimed that the workers needed a translation of Morris's poetry into nineteenth-century speech.[63]

This argument is not without its contradictions. In his love of the poetic form, Winchevsky also claimed that when Morris gave speeches in more vernacular and comprehensible English, he lost the heroic muse which made his poetry so valuable.[64] And Winchevsky himself was not always successful in practicing what he preached. Abraham Cahan, editor of the New York *Forverts*, used a similar criticism of Winchevsky's language, calling it "a bit too highbrow ... for the simple Jewish worker." Cahan claimed that "Winchevsky wrote magnificent Yiddish and had a beautiful Yiddish humor, but most of this humor also demanded a certain grade of development on the part of the reader."[65]

Yet accessibility was certainly the aim of the Jewish socialists. Russian Jewish intellectuals of this period came from a society where poetry, novels, and plays were the only accessible forums for making political comment in the public sphere. The role of literature was not only to inspire revolutionary acts but was itself a revolutionary act.[66] This blurred distinctions between different types of political activity. For these early socialists, the importance of content, a poem's social relevance and usefulness, completely overrode questions of style.[67]

For poems to become the lyrics of political agitation, they needed to have a rousing effect on workers and demonstrate solidarity.[68] Anthems had to be designed to be sung by large groups at demonstrations, rallies, open air meetings, and marches, to accompany the rhythm of marching and to create a rousing finale to a speech. They also had to have a universal quality and convey a sense that victory was possible. It was vital not only that words were easily understood but that they were entirely fit for purpose. A careful balance had to be struck. If lyrics were too fiercely revolutionary, they might alienate the public; however, if they described the daily hard conditions and greed of the sweaters and showed why strikers were taking a particular action, they were more likely to win the sympathy of the working-class public.[69] Anthems were often commissioned by trade unions and political parties, and written by professionals and circulated in the press. Some anthems traveled between contexts and countries, becoming international emblems of the Left and translated into other languages.

Probably the best-known anthem sung internationally was "The Marseillaise." Originally written for the French Revolution a century earlier, the song still resonated with the working class, and socialist and anarchist groups used "The Marseillaise" to protest in the present while claiming a historical connection to the past.[70] "The Marseillaise" was a stock anthem of the Yiddish-speaking Left. Anarchist Thomas Eyges describes hearing it in Whitechapel at the end of a political meeting.[71] A Yiddish version, "Di marseyese," written by Winchevsky in 1889, was reprinted many times.[72] Although his version has the same structure and meter of the original, and can be sung to the same tune, it is a different song. The title became used in a more symbolic way. Indeed, the rousing song "Es rirt zikh" (It's moving), written for what was later called the Bloody Sunday demonstration in Trafalgar Square in 1887, became known as "Winchevsky's Marseillaise."[73]

Most of the Jewish socialist meetings took place in pubs such as the Sugar Loaf and Berner Street Club in London's East End.[74] Eyges describes the scene:

The club was a spacious room, with a capacity of over 200 people, and contained a stage. Here were performed by amateurs mostly in Russian language plays by well known Russian revolutionists— Tchaikovsky (not the famous composer), Volchovsky, Stepniak, Winchevsky, Gallop; later came Simon Kahn, Krantz, Feigenbaum, Yanovsky, and others . . . intellectuals that came frequently in Berner Street Club, taking an active part in spreading the gospel of revolutionary socialism.[75]

William Morris regularly visited the Berner Street Club, where he was treated as a respected and honored guest. He gave speeches at meetings and read his poetry, and the choir sang his songs.[76] In turn Morris supported the fledgling Yiddish-speaking socialist groups with the sort of encouragement not always meted out by the English socialists to their Jewish counterparts. Anarchist leader Saul Yanovsky remembers a "tea-party" where he moaned to Morris about his single-handed work for the *Arbayter fraynd*, giving weekly lectures and free English classes. He recalls that Morris "shook my hand with great warmth, telling me, that people like me make him certain that the time of freedom is not far away. This compliment made me feel in seventh heaven and his handshake was the greatest reward for me."[77] In 1890 Morris chaired and gave the opening speech at the fifth anniversary celebration of the *Arbayter fraynd* at the Berner Street Club. He warmly introduced Winchevsky as "our beloved friend." After the poetry reading, the choir sang Morris's "Down among the Dead Men."[78]

During the second half of the 1890s, amid lots of infighting, the anarchists began to take over the Jewish leadership of the Left. Many of the socialist leadership moved to New York, and Rudolf Rocker, a non-Jewish German anarchist, became the charismatic leader as the anarchists took over the *Arbayter fraynd*. They moved from the Berner Street Club to new headquarters in Jubilee Street, took over Jewish trade union positions, and actively campaigned against the sweating system. Rocker argued that the struggle for working people to join the movement had to be not only about economic conditions but backed by an ethical desire for justice.[79] When Winchevsky left London in 1894, socialist poetry almost completely disappeared from the pages of the socialist press.

CHAPTER 1

ANTI-ALIEN SENTIMENT AND IMMIGRATION RESTRICTION

Ver hot geharget dem bil?   Who killed the bill?
Ikh, zogt tshertshil.   I, said Churchill.
Ikh hob geshosn in tsil,   I shot the target,
un geharget dem bil.   And killed the bill.[80]

Since the mid-1880s there had been popular and political demands for legislation to restrict immigration. It was a response to the view that massive unemployment was due to immigrants bringing unskilled labor into the country. The Liberal Party opposed such legislation on the grounds of free trade in goods and people, but East End Conservative candidates demanded restriction.[81] In 1888 a House of Lords committee examined sweating, concluding that wage problems were also in trades not affected by the immigrants. In 1889 a House of Commons committee on immigration found immigrants dirty but good citizens. However, this had no effect on the spiraling momentum of public opinion. In 1891 Arnold White set up the Association for Preventing the Immigration of Destitute Aliens. Between 1892 and 1895, the Trade Union Congress passed resolutions against free immigration, arguing that alien Jews undercut British labor.[82] Local anti-alien groups argued that Jews sent women to work, were averse to heavy labor, did not join trade unions, worked on the Christian Sabbath noisily from their homes, stored rags in their yards, and were an affront to respectability.[83] Historian David Feldman argues that demands for immigration restriction can be seen as an attempt to define or redefine the state in terms of who belongs. This suggests that the immigrant community fails the conservative and anti-Semites' test of Englishness. Despite ongoing acculturation programs from within the Jewish community, the immigrants remained foreign and poor, and their internal anglicization attempts insufficient.[84]

In 1901 William Evans-Gordon, Member of Parliament (MP) for Stepney, set up the British Brothers' League, an anti-alien pressure group demanding restrictive legislation. Evans-Gordon published his political argument in 1903 with the book *The Alien Immigrant*. The book developed ideas about London's Jewish immigrants from Evans-Gordon's travels researching conditions in Jewish communities in Eastern Europe. He argued that in London Jews were forcing out English inhabitants in two ways. Firstly, he argued that Jews were buying up properties, bypassing paying legal fees, and becoming landlords who demanded rents and key money that no English worker could afford. Secondly, he argued that aliens were able to compete successfully with native workers because, from their Eastern European background, they were prepared to accept a "disastrously low standard of living."[85] Not only Tories joined the league; there was cross-party support including Jewish MPs. Membership rose to 12,000 people but could raise 45,000 signatures on petitions.[86] There were, however, few violent clashes, and it may have been that the British Brothers' League acted as a "safety valve" for frustrated emotions, and had they not taken that role, there could have been more violence against Jews, such as that in South Wales in 1911.[87]

A small but influential group of the Anglo-Jewish elite supported the proposed legislation as long as it did not violate the right of asylum. Most communal leaders, however, did not support the legislation. They wanted to reduce immigration through actions within the community, such as publicizing anti-Semitism in Russia, arguing that if the government put pressure on Russia to relieve the situation for the Jews, it would slow down emigration.[88] The aliens bill failed to be passed in 1904, and the poem heading this section alludes to Churchill's part in arguing against it. The poem is a Yiddish parody of the children's song "Who Killed Cock Robin?" Indeed, this phrase was used in July 1904 when the bill's failure was being discussed in Parliament.[89] By the time the Aliens Act was passed in 1905, it had undergone a number of revisions making it less exclusionary. In 1906 the Liberal Party came back to power, yet it did not repeal the act.[90] This time coincides with the heyday of the Yiddish music halls, and Yiddish culture was becoming more visible on the streets of the East End, yet so too was what was seen as immigrant crime.

After the abortive 1905 revolution in Russia, a stream of Russian anarchists and revolutionaries arrived in London. They had been involved in violent underground activity in Russia, and they saw the state police as their enemy. Wanting to raise money for revolutionary causes back home, they staged armed bank raids, known as "expropriations," to steal money for the cause. Rocker tried to stop any violent anarchists and Russian spies who came to London attempting daredevil feats that would cost civilian life. But Rocker was not successful, and the Tottenham Outrage, a bungled robbery led by Latvian Social Revolutionaries in 1909, left two people dead and twenty-seven injured. The Houndsditch Murders and subsequent Siege of Sidney Street in 1910–11 left three revolutionaries and three policemen dead. The siege ended with a gunfight in the East End and was headline news long after. The remaining members of the gang were arrested and taken to court but were released on insufficient evidence. These actions spread alarm in the East End and across the country that England was being taken over by anarchist terrorists. Meanwhile, Rocker's socialist anarchists continued their union activism. In 1912 there was a successful mass strike of tailors and tailoresses in the East and West End.[91] Yet, not discriminating between violent revolutionaries and nonviolent anarchists, the general population, with the help of the press and politicians' statements, linked violence to anarchists and anarchists to Jews, leading to an upsurge in anti-alien feeling.[92]

In 1911 Churchill introduced a bill that attempted to tighten the Aliens Act, including registering aliens and demanding that alien offenders be expelled. The Board of Deputies' response to these amendments was cautious. The lack of condemnation by the Anglo-Jewish establishment led to East End activists setting up the Aliens Defence Committee (ADC) in 1911, which was supported by thirty-five immigrant organizations. The ADC attempted to take on the board's role by attacking Churchill's bill on specific points. The bill did not pass, and by the summer of 1911 the aliens issue and the ADC were fading. However, the ADC had developed new political structures outside of the Anglo-Jewish institutions.[93]

The 1914 Jewish landscape on the eve of war was a very different place from the relatively calm Anglo-Jewish world prior to 1881. The Anglo-Jewish elite was no longer the most visible aspect of Anglo-Jewry. There was anxiety that the image of a Jew had become that of a poor, badly educated immigrant identified with crime, violence, and anarchism. The East End was filled with tension, conflicts for daily survival, and fierce debates on ideology. Differences between and within Jewish groups were huge, allegiances were not simple, and strange and paradoxical alliances were forged. On the one hand, orthodox and socialist Jews united in trade union meetings, sometimes held on khevre premises, fighting for better pay and working conditions. On the other hand, socialist conversionism was decried from the pulpit in Yiddish by fiery preachers. Another instance saw trade union leaders creating an alliance of workers and small masters to fight together against contractors. Yet workers would abandon trade union gains in order to keep work during the slack season.[94] Anglo-Jewish leaders assisted workers in union disputes specifically to wrest control from the socialist union leaders. Socialists would speak Yiddish in order to work within the community, drawing workers into educational improvement and modernization while believing that Yiddish was a stopgap in lieu of using the language of the country.

For an example of the discord between Jewish groups, we can return to 1903, when the whole community—immigrants, orthodox, anarchists, Zionists, and Anglo-Jews—was united in its shocked response to the Kishinev pogrom.[95] However, the delayed response of the Anglo-Jewish establishment in condemning the pogrom caused friction with the immigrants, and the inclusion of the Zionists in the Hyde Park protest against the pogrom caused anger among the socialists. There were arguments between political groups as to where fundraising money should go, and the incident showed how the differences of ideology within the Jewish community were heartfelt, deep, and irreconcilable.[96]

The Yiddish-speaking East End, full of angry political and social debate, developed a cultural life that both reflected and engaged with the political ideas, while providing entertainment and spaces where new identities could be forged and tried out. Popular culture was an integral part of immigrant life, sometimes a part of the debate, sometimes a trigger, and sometimes a source of humor. But always engaging, questioning, and redefining.

2

London Yiddish Music-Hall Culture

Un fun fiber hits geplaplt	And in the heat of fever I babbled
folks—pavilion—pales	Folk—Pavilion—palace
sketsh, opere, drame,	Sketch, opera, drama
gevalt shund, dales, dales!	Help, *shund*, poverty, poverty![1]

In the decade around the turn of the twentieth century, the stages of the London Yiddish theatre and music hall played to packed auditoriums of hundreds of East End immigrants.[2] Posters were displayed on the streets, songsheets were sold by peddlers, and the melodies of popular Yiddish tunes could be heard in the clubs and bars. The vaudeville sketches and music-hall songs were a Yiddish theatre experience that for a short space of time became part of the fabric of London East End cultural life. The public may have flocked to the popular theatre, but conflict inevitably followed.

EARLY YIDDISH THEATRE

The commercial Yiddish theatre had begun in Russia instigated by the actor and prolific playwright Avrom Goldfaden. Goldfaden wrote popular plays and songs from the mid-1860s, which were constantly performed across the Yiddish-speaking world. His satirical comedies, biblical romantic operettas, and serious dramas on biblical themes were popular for the heightened emotion and spectacle.[3] The Yiddish theatre style, drawn from popular theatre more broadly, was melodramatic, declamatory, and unsubtle and included an outpouring of gestures and feelings.[4] Essential to the drama were its songs, which appeared whether or not the play was an operetta or a musical comedy and whether or not the songs had any relevance to the narrative action. In addition, music-hall songs and *kupletn* (rhyming couplets) were sung as entertainment between acts or at the end of the play.[5]

These commercial plays and songs were nicknamed *shund* (trash) by those who wanted to raise the standard of literary creativity. Yet they were loved by the working-class immigrant audiences who, despite coming from poverty and deprivation, could feel a sense of pride in their heroic Jewish history.[6] A division evolved between *kunst*, artistic, literary theatre that was pedagogic, enlightened, and nation building; and so-called shund, popular theatre and song that were seen as lowbrow, not educational, and unruly.[7] Trying to find an alternative to the popular comedies, musicals, and melodramas, playwright Jacob Gordin began writing more realistic theatre. His plays addressed difficult social issues, such as marriage difficulties, insanity, suicide, or murder, and both connected with traditional mores and challenged them.[8] In New York, Gordin and Abraham Cahan, editor of the *Forverts*, campaigned to transform shund theatre into new theatres for highbrow and cosmopolitan European culture. They considered realistic Yiddish theatre a vital force for education and enlightenment that could politicize the masses by helping them understand how power worked in society, and thus be a catalyst for change.[9]

However, it was the commercial theatre that got the audiences, and with repertoires changing every week, a large amount of new material was needed to keep up with demand. Playwrights often "baked" plays. They took plays in other languages, famous or not, changed them to have a Jewish flavor in names and locations, translated them into Yiddish, and put them out as their own compositions.[10] This was not always successful. A *Poylisher yidl* reviewer was unconvinced by a translation of Schiller: "Mr. Herman Fiddler's translation is not bad. However, he moved it to Russia and Schiller's characters were converted to Judaism. . . . The translation would have been much better had he left Schiller's play where it is in the world and not changed the Gentiles to Jews with troubles, particularly because in the last act they all die."[11]

It is important not to simplify this debate, as it is more contested than the polarized positions suggest. The word *shund* (trash) is a problematic term that conveyed the elitist views of the highbrow critics who derided popular culture as worthless. They may not have appreciated the value of popular culture, yet that does not mean that the commercial theatre had no value. The highbrow journalists and writers who were published in the Yiddish press may have been generally of one mind, yet the actors, singers, and writers knew that they could produce quality across both genres without distinguishing between kunst and shund.[12] Theatre historians Joel Berkowitz and Barbara Henry agree with this position in suggesting that performance of Yiddish theatre should be seen as a "network of intersecting paths," where some led to aesthetic plays, and some were entertainment, but many possessed qualities that appealed to both a popular audience and critics.[13]

Most performers and writers were versatile and relied on the entertainment value of the Yiddish theatre to earn their living. Writers had to produce material quickly and for mass appeal. They knew that some of it was trivial and irreverent, but it made them money, so they juggled the types of work they did. For example, Joseph Markovitsh had toured Eastern Europe as a classical chorister, but began life in London on the music-hall stage. He wrote both edgy music-hall songs, with sexual double entendres and comic themes, and serious songs about anti-Semitic violence and generational anxiety at growing secularization.[14] Even Jacob Gordin, under the pseudonym "Dr. Jacobi from London," wrote popular plays like the ones he claimed to detest because those were the plays that got audiences, and he had a large family to feed.[15] Similarly, the London Yiddish lyrics had fluid boundaries. Music-hall songs, layered with meanings and suggestions, offered levels of engagement that ranged from belly laughs to serious thought. Even poems by radical socialists were being put to music, published in songbooks, and declaimed from the stages of the London popular theatre.[16]

Early East End Yiddish theatre consisted of performances by amateurs and semiprofessionals, producing plays in clubs or halls.[17] In March 1880, a play by Goldfaden was performed in "Yosel's pub." Performances took place in unauthorized places on makeshift stages where people threw coins into a pot for payment. If there was not enough in the pot to pay the actors, an appeal would be made for more money before the play began.[18] During the 1880s theatrical productions in London were prohibited anywhere other than in an official theatre, so Yiddish theatre did what small English theatre troupes were doing: they set up nominal private clubs. Clubs were generally located in the back rooms of bars, club members would pay around a shilling a week, and nonmembers "made arrangements" on the door.[19] The club nature of the early London Yiddish theatre served the immigrant community well because the theatre had, as actor Bernard Mendelovitch remembered, "many functions apart from being a house of entertainment and culture. It was a meeting place for *landslayt* (kinsmen) to meet and discuss their problems, to seek help and advice, to provide a sense of belonging."[20] Jewish immigrant workers could go out with their whole family to play cards and chess, talk politics, and eat and drink in addition to watching the Yiddish show.[21]

In 1883 Yiddish theatre was banned in Russia, and its actors moved to find new homes and theatre bases. This changed the quality of the London Yiddish stage, as it now became professional with the arrival from Riga of the already famous actor Jacob Adler, later nicknamed "The Jewish Irving."[22] Adler (a distant relative of Chief Rabbi Nathan Adler) recalled in his memoirs that when he arrived, clubs were abundant: "A thousand clubs! Wherever you looked, clubs, splits, shouting, quarrels, and before you knew it—a new club! They were a training ground for our acting recruits, the chief source of our theatrical merchandise."[23] Adler and his small theatre troupe set up the Russian Jewish Operatic Company in January 1884 in Princes Street. Over the next two years they performed in clubs and halls with a range of work from operettas to vaudeville, performing three plays a week in repertory, and changing plays frequently.[24] One review in the *Poylisher yidl*, not without a dose of satire, relates the following: "For two years, edifying us here, there has been a small troupe of bad actors (with one or two good ones). On a small stage they have *sung* very poorly and have *spoken* very badly. I have been there a few times, have seen, heard, sweated, and caught a cold. The acting did not please me, I didn't understand the singing, the sweat annoyed me. . . . There was a quarrel. The quarrel became a fight, from the fight came a few black eyes. After an hour I began to curse the whole event."[25] Other reviews in the *Poylisher yidl* were more positive and complimented good acting, yet more often criticized overacting and actors' not knowing their lines.[26] Adler tried to develop local talent for the London Yiddish stage. He hired a music teacher to teach music notation and singing, advertising in the radical Yiddish press for people to sing in his chorus and to enroll in his new music school. These students became the chorus for larger operettas.[27]

Wanting to expand into more serious theatre, Adler found a sponsor in the "alrightnik" butcher and theatre lover Dovid Smith, and in March 1886 the new Hebrew Dramatic Club opened in Princes Street. In his memoirs, actor Boez (Bernard) Young describes how, as members of an official club, they had to conduct themselves as a club with a committee and a president: "In the middle of the theatre was a long table with bottles, and the committee sat around the table, with their backs to the stage. The president held a hammer in his hand. The waiters served food. When the president had finished eating, he gave a ring on a bell, and the curtain lifted up."[28]

Despite the prestigious opening of the Princes Street Club, and the success of full houses and actors finally being paid a good wage, tensions within the community were a constant strain on the new theatre and antagonism came from different quarters.[29] The Anglo-Jewish establishment saw support for Yiddish culture as a provocation to their desired process of anglicization, the orthodox saw the content and running of the theatre in opposition to Jewish religious law and custom, and the socialists wanted a more highbrow medium.

The Anglo-Jewish leadership saw the popularity of Yiddish theatre as maintaining the status of the Yiddish language and therefore it came to represent the immigrants' lack of desire for acculturation. The chief rabbi saw the use of Yiddish as divisive and an obstacle to his authority, and considered the Yiddish theatre as a forum for the socialists and anarchists to disseminate their ideas and give out provocative radical literature.[30] Both Anglo-Jewish and immigrant orthodox had a particular concern that the Yiddish theatre and music hall encouraged a move away from religious practice into immoral behavior. Orthodox Jews opposed the Yiddish theatre for its profanation of the Sabbath by opening on Friday nights and Saturday afternoons, which were, indeed, the most profitable times.[31] On the stage, the actors might smoke on the Sabbath. Off-stage, actors' behavior was seen as provocative. Adler, a married man, was known to have affairs, and one young actress, Jenya (Jenny) Kayzer, used to come to rehearsals with her three-year-old son, Charlie Adler, in tow.[32]

These considerations made both Anglo-Jewry and the orthodox immigrants consider the theatre as a dangerous place for their young people to congregate.[33] United in their opposition, the Chief Rabbinate and the religious leaders of the immigrant orthodox tried to find ways to close down the Yiddish theatre. They put pressure on Dovid Smith to stop financing the Princes Street Club by threatening to blacklist his butcher's shop, jeopardizing his kosher license. Smith retaliated and declared that he would not be terrorized, and if they would not permit him to sell meat under the kosher *shechita* he would sell non-kosher meat, leaving Jews unknowingly eating meat that was *treyf* (unclean).[34]

The chief rabbi Nathan Adler preached from the pulpit against the Yiddish theatre, calling it a "synagogue for sin and apostasy," seeing it as competition for the synagogues. He offered a bribe to Jacob Adler to go to New York, but in the flush of the success of the Princes Street Club, Jacob Adler saw no reason to leave.[35] The chief rabbi kept up the pressure, complaining so strongly that a production of *Hannah and Her Sons* was sacrilegious that the play was changed to another. He created an outcry when a *shofer* (ram's horn) was blown onstage in the play *Uriel Acosta*, calling it desecration of a holy object. It was replaced with a paper one.[36] Dovid Smith encouraged actors not to antagonize religious Jews when not on stage, not to smoke on the Sabbath, not to eat non-kosher food, and not to socialize with the Jewish underworld.[37] Jacob Adler was affected by the religious pressure, and in his memoirs he wrote that he lived "a life of fear [with] the stick held over our heads by the orthodox community. . . . We were always afraid they would report us, and had to give in to their every caprice. . . . We had to watch every move, every word, or in the middle of the play there would be a scandal."[38]

Tragically, the Princes Street Club came to a premature end on 18 January 1887, when mid-play, at the shout of "Fire," there was a rush for the doors of the theatre. There was no fire, but amid the stampede seventeen people died.[39] The Jewish East End, in mourning for months afterward, kept away from the theatre. The club closed, and Jacob Adler, finally taking the money offered by Nathan Adler, took his company to America. This left no resident professional company or permanent home for Yiddish theatre, although it continued in a hall in Vine Court in Whitechapel, and from the early 1890s, in greater earnest, in the Pavilion Theatre on Whitechapel Road.

CHAPTER 2

From 1900, the Anglo-Jewish press began begrudgingly to recognize Yiddish as a serious language and Yiddish theatre as a permanent feature. The *Jewish World* published articles on the critic Abraham Cahan, poet Morris Rosenfeld, and Goldfaden. In its introduction to "Max Rosenthal: The Forbes-Robertson of the Yiddish Stage," it acknowledged: "'Yiddish' is no longer so despised as was the custom in former years, and the men and women who in that language have charmed the ears and eyes of thousands of people, need no longer hide their light under a bushel. . . . There are some singers and great actors, who utilise nothing but the language spoken by the Jews of Russia, Galicia, and Rumania."[40] The *Jewish Chronicle*, which rarely focused on the Yiddish-speaking community, produced a long, rather surly, article in 1902 when it looked like a Yiddish theatre was going to be established in Hackney: "There are no doubt those who view such an enterprize with displeasure, but granting that it is to be, they would hope that the promoters would work on the very best lines." The article demanded restrictions in line with Sabbath observance, and reassured its readers that "no gags will be permitted of the slightest 'risky' business, [as] they believe the higher the tone, the greater will be their success."[41]

THE MUSIC HALLS

Punkt halb nokh akht	At precisely half past eight
di nayeste kupletn vet men zingen . . .	The newest couplets will be sung . . .
un shpiln a vodevil . . .	and acting a vaudeville . . .
Es vet oyf der pyano tantsn toyzent hint.	On the piano there will be A thousand dogs dancing.[42]

The anxiety expressed in the *Jewish Chronicle* was in response to the increase in both popular theatre and Yiddish music halls, in part due to new writers and performers arriving from Eastern Europe. Ayzik (Isaac) Lubritski had come to London from Poland possibly as early as the mid-1880s and worked as a *badkhn* (wedding jester). By the mid-1890s he was writing songs to be sung in the music hall. Arn Nager arrived around 1898 and Joseph Markovitsh at the turn of the twentieth century. Both Nager and Markovitsh worked as actors and singers and wrote plays and songs. By the early 1900s publisher, printer, bookseller, and binder R. Mazin was producing and selling Yiddish music-hall penny songsheets.[43] The publisher and bookseller M. Yozef wrote parodies to known melodies to be sung on the street advertising Yiddish songbooks.[44] Both Yozef and Mazin wrote songs themselves or added relevant local verses to known songs.

By 1900 Yiddish theatres were running in the Pavilion Theatre in Whitechapel, the Standard Theatre in Shoreditch (from 1896), and from 1902 the Manor Theatre in Hackney. The Yiddish music hall came into its own for around a decade and a half. The York Minster music hall in Philpot Street, Whitechapel, was managed by Salli and Philip Weisenfreund, whose son Muni later became the American actor Paul Muni.[45] There were also Yiddish music-hall nights at "Wonderland" on Whitechapel Road and the Princess' Hall on Commercial Road from 1907. Any space was commandeered for a Yiddish stage, including covering over the Goulston Street baths.[46]

By the turn of the century, when Yiddish songwriters were writing for the early Yiddish music halls in London, the English halls had been in full swing for half a century. The English music halls had developed from the informal pub culture of the "free-and-easy," an amateur singsong. In the back room of a pub, singers and performers from the audience would do a turn on a makeshift stage. Turns could be folk songs, political or comic ballads, sung to the drinking audience of men and women who would join in the raucous choruses.[47] Partly motivated by the police cracking down on the rowdiness of these evenings, but more generally motivated by the commercial possibilities of professionalizing popular entertainment, purpose-built music halls were set up by publicans and entrepreneurs, who became proprietors of these new establishments.[48] These ventures became huge commercial successes, and from their working-class beginnings, new halls developed with large middle- and upper-class variety theatres and music halls in the West End and suburbs. Smaller music halls still proliferated and continued in poorer districts.[49] It was in this environment that the Yiddish halls operated. The smaller halls had an informal atmosphere where the audience was often mobile, rather than seated, and people would come in for their favorite acts and leave afterward. It was affordable, and men and women could socialize, drink, and be entertained without being disciplined or improved by reformers or socialists.[50]

דאס ליעד
מיידט וואס שוויינט איהר מיידט
פערפאסט אונד געזונגע פין אן פ. נאגער

אין שיינע
זיא מעג זיין דאר אדער זייער פעט
א הויבע אדער גאהר א קלוינע
א מאליע וויא א ברעט
זיא מעג זיין א גוטע אדער א
קליפע
זיא מעג ריידען הויך אדער שווינגען
שטיל
דאן שטעל איך גלייך מיט איהר א
חופה
אין זיא קריגט שוין וואס זיא וויל.
רעפריין
מיירען וואס שווינגט איהר
מיידען א. ז. וו.

—3—

דאס מיידעל וואס וועט זיין מיר
בעשערם
וועט איהר זיין וואיל וויא דיא וועלט
פרעסען וועט זיא ביא מיר וויא א
פערד
נאר אן א פעגע געלט
זי וועט לעבען ביא מיר אין פראכט
וויא א פוינגל איגע אליון
נאר אין מ׳טען מאג אז איך זאן
סאיו נאכט
וועט זיא מוען .... עטסען גיין
רעפריין
מיירען וואס שווינגט איהר
מיידען א. ז. וו.

איך בין א בחור דאס ווייסטם איהר
אללע
מיט מעלות פיעל אין דאך בין איך
געפלעפטם
ווען איך קריעג אצינד א כלה מיט
א גרויס געשעפטם
פון דזוולערי פון אנדרע סחורות
דאס וואלט געווען פיר מיר א פיינער
פלאן
נאהיראט וואלט איך נאר אן מורת
געווען וואלם איך א געטרייער מאן
—רעפריין—
מיירען וואס שווינגט איהר מיידען
איהר זעהטם א בחור ער שטיים
פיר אייך
מיידען אוי לעבם אין פריידען
און נעמם דעם בחור און היירטם
גלייך
—2—

סיין מיידעל דארף נישט זיין דוקא

Song lyrics of "Maydn, vos shvaygt ir maydn" (Girls, why are you silent girls) with image of Arn Nager, *Londoner kupletist*, ca. 1903, 91. From the collections of the National Library of Israel.

Princess' Hall, Commercial Road. From George Sims, *Living London*, 1901. From the Mazower Private Collection.

There was significant overlap in the structure and content of the English and Yiddish halls. The evening's entertainment consisted of professional performers doing turns, of mainly comic songs. Music-hall stars would buy songs from songwriters and develop their own exclusive repertoire, often singing to piano accompaniment.[51] Performers generally sang in character and became associated with, and known for, their characters and songs. In the English halls, stock characters included the upper-class swell and the fake swell, the working-class coster and the working girl, husbands, wives and mothers, and the cheeky female comic.[52] In the Yiddish halls, stock characters were the harassed husband, the confused immigrant, the gentile seducer, the naive orthodox man, and the canny landlady.

Yet there was one more stock character worth noting in the English music hall, namely, "the Jew." The Anglo-Jewish community expressed anxiety about shund in the Yiddish music hall, yet Anglo-Jews frequented English music halls, where the stock character of "the Jew" was a common act. Although Jewish theatre historian Myer Landa claims that in general the stage Jew was "delineated as a pleasant fellow in the variety theatres," this view is at odds with contemporary commentator Y. Finkelshteyn.[53] A furious article published in the *Tsayt* in 1914 denounced the way Anglo-Jewish actors were prepared to propagate a stereotype of "the Jew" in the English music hall as a butt of comedy. Finkelshteyn complains that the "Hebrew comedian" was complicit in making anti-Semitic stereotypes that were the butt of tasteless humor: "The 'Hebrew comedian' is not properly a Jew hater. He is usually himself a Jew and he makes fun of Jews for a living. It is a fact that he cannot distinguish himself in his profession and can only be successful as a good 'Jewish' comic, yet his 'jokes' about Jews are full of venom and brand the Jew as a lower creature, a swindler, an arsonist and the like."[54] Hebrew comedians were popular fare of the English music hall, where the stereotypes played into the prejudices of the English audiences, although the "Jew" was one of a range of other cultural stereotypes.[55] The audiences of the immigrant halls sometimes frequented the English halls, and the character of the Jew appears in some Yiddish texts, one of which appears in chapter 9.

In both English and Yiddish music halls there were many roles for female performers. Women had a rare opportunity to gain some financial independence, with the additional potential to cross-dress and subvert the norms around gender roles.[56] However, these possibilities were often offset by the association of actresses with prostitution, putting pressure on women to conform, and mostly women's roles were highly traditional.[57] English songs concerned marriage, lodgers, and mothers-in-law, beer and holidays, patriotism and war, work, and London.[58] Yiddish song content included marriage, lodgers, and rabbis, immigration and pogroms, work, and London. The songs and characters did not attempt realistic portrayals of working-class life; rather, they exaggerated class differences, immigrant woes, and family relationships. The verbal repartee was full of puns, wordplay, street-language, and comic dialects, and drew in audiences with the "all-join-in" choruses. The different styles from vulgar to pretentious provided the edgy feel to the songs.[59] In order to gain attention in the melee of audience activity, the solo singer would shout and sing, wink and gesture, and jerk his or her body at the beginning of each line, in street style.[60] The music hall's evening entertainment was announced by a chairman in formal wear who introduced acts, covered for missing acts by singing, dodged missiles thrown by the audience, and was generally subjected to mockery.[61]

Between verses of singing in character, performers would ad-lib and patter out of character as themselves. They could skillfully manipulate the audience both to respond to the character they were performing and to communicate more directly and intimately with the artists themselves. Peter Bailey argues that the audience was thereby included, could see the "joins in the performance," and could get a sense of being an active participant in that performance. He calls this sense of moving the boundaries, removing the fourth wall, "knowingness." It is the basis of the humor, as the audience participates with heckling, cheering, booing, and joining in choruses.[62]

The concept of knowingness is particularly apposite in the Yiddish music hall. In addition to the shared immigrant experience using an insider language, there was a subtler sense of shared understanding of the stages of anglicization. Immigrants' insider knowledge of England was relevant. As waves of immigrants ceased being "greeners" (*new* immigrants) and became more acculturated, newer immigrants took their place. Using anglicisms in song texts was a way of identifying where one was in this process. Not getting a bilingual joke made you an outsider.[63] If you understood the anglicisms, you were more acculturated. If you understood the London references, you were more londonized.[64] Performers and audience in the Yiddish halls were a small immigrant community. People knew each other, shared the same streets and markets, cafés, and synagogues. The theatres and music halls were in the middle of residential areas and shopping thoroughfares where both performers and audience lived. The relationship was therefore already an intimate one.

An example of this intimacy can be seen in the experience of Joseph Markovitsh, who describes coming to London as a penniless young professional singer around 1900 and searching for the Yiddish theatre. He finds the York Minster music hall: "a three-cornered room, a few hard wooden benches, a piano, a stage a yard and a half wide and three quarters of a yard deep." Markovitsh impresses the management with his singing and his ability to write songs and is hired on the spot. However, he is unimpressed by the out-of-tune piano and the vulgarity of the pianist, who seems to treat life as an opportunity for crude music-hall humor. In response to being asked why he plays with only one hand, the pianist replies: "I keep my left hand in my pocket so nobody should steal my two pennies." Markovitsh, used to being treated with more dignity as he toured across Russia singing his classical and liturgical repertoire, was taken aback by such coarseness and the rough environment.⁶⁵ In his first performance on the York Minster music-hall stage, Markovitsh sang a Russian soldier's song. This was followed by a man whistling, a sketch, a dancer, and a range of double entendre and comic songs and ended with an actor singing a carol.⁶⁶ Markovitsh, inspired by this music-hall experience, wrote the song *A kholem* (A dream). The dream imagined coming to London and being warmly welcomed by Rothschild, driven in carriages, and given fish with *khreyn* (horseradish sauce). In the chorus he wakes up to the reality of poverty in London's East End:

Oy a kholem, a tayerer a giter	Ah a dream, a dear and lovely dream
ober in der fri iz oyfn hartsn zeyer biter,	But in the morning my heart is bitter,
azelkhe khaloymes nit far aykh gedakht,	Such dreams should not happen to you
kholemen zikh mir ale nakht!	That's what I dream every night!⁶⁷

Markovitsh performed this new song the next evening to a packed hall, where the audience "wouldn't let me leave the stage and people started throwing pennies and one or two sixpences as well. I had to sing the refrain until the whole audience sang along with me, 'A dream, a dear and lovely dream, but in the morning my heart was bitter.'"⁶⁸ The song was so popular that Markovitsh performed it night after night, developing a relationship with the audience. His popularity was in part due to the shared experience of the sentiment in the song, and of the audience watching a new immigrant, newer than themselves, struggling to acculturate to England.

Markovitsh was thrown into the unruly world of the Yiddish music hall, and his description of the ramshackle and informal nature of the hall is backed up by later reviews. A gentile English visitor to the York Minster hall in 1902 describes a noisy and demonstrative but well-dressed Jewish audience of over 400 people in a crowded shabby room. He lists the songs: a comedian singing a popular comic song, serious and semireligious songs, and a couple of English songs. In the second half, there is a sketch of Russian Jewish life, with a rabbi made to look like a buffoon, and "a little love-making and a little domestic trickery thrown in." The anonymous reviewer concludes his article with the assertion, "Nothing appeals so strongly to their feelings and sensibilities as those reminiscences of the continental Jewries where their earliest years were spent, and which they find so effectively reproduced in the Yiddish music-hall."[69]

The *Standard*'s reviewer was certainly intrigued by the ethnic quality of the Yiddish music hall and the stylish Jewish youths who were dressing in the latest "Oxford Street" clothes. He was also amused by the Yiddish-accented English words as the audience joined in the chorus of an English song. The reviewer notices how acculturation to British norms combines with maintaining a specifically Yiddish culture.

In contrast, journalist Leyb-Sholem Kreditor wrote that the Jewish East End was so Yiddish centered that the Anglo-Jewish establishment were terrified that the "whole English Jewish community would be yiddishized."[70] And yet the Yiddish writers were strongly influenced by their parallel English worlds around them, and they were keen to be a part of that world too. Theatre critic and author Chance Newton assessed the "extraordinary" mixture of cultures at the Wonderland Yiddish music hall on Whitechapel Road in 1902:

> They include little plays, songs and sketches, given first in Yiddish dialect and afterwards translated into more or less choice English by, as a rule, a Hebraic interpreter. This interpreter often improves the occasion by calling the attention of kind—and mostly alien—friends in front to certain side shows consisting of all sorts of armless, legless, skeleton, or spotted "freaks" scattered around the recesses of this galleryless hall. When once the "freaks" have been examined, or the "greeners" and other foreign and East-End "sweated" Jew toilers have utilised the interval to indulge in a little light refreshment according to their respective tastes, the Yiddish sketches and songs—comic and otherwise— are resumed until "closing time."[71]

Already in 1902 the songs and sketches were being translated for children of immigrants who were losing their Yiddish, for anglicized immigrants, and for English audience members. The Princess' Yiddish music hall also displayed a strong cultural mix. The *Jewish Chronicle* of 1907

Program for the York Minster music hall, Philpot Street. The cover shows Salli Weisenfreund cross-dressing, ca. 1902. © Jewish Museum, London.

described a "thoroughly free-and-easy, go-as-you-please unconventional affair." It lists a conventional program of music-hall turns you would see in any English music hall, yet intrinsically Jewish:

> To the superficial it was the ordinary music-hall program—songs, sketch, biograph [sic] and so forth, but in reality it was . . . a program steeped in the Ghetto, so to speak. It was not merely that the peculiar humor of the Jew dominated its comic songs. But the atmosphere of the Ghetto was there the tailor's shop, the immigrants, the shrewd exploiters of the immigrants, the "golus" [exile], and even the more pious side of Israell'ish aspirations. It was the life of a Jew set in a Gentile framework.[72]

The *Jewish Chronicle* reviewer addresses how the cultural tension between the old world and England influenced the content of the Yiddish music hall. This hybrid performance is further illustrated by the reviewer recounting a performance of the song "The Old Bull and Bush," "quaintly adapted to some sulfurous lines about the Russian tyranny."[73] Parodying English songs highlights the connections between cultures, and the fact that this was noticed and commented on by reviewers makes some claim to its importance.

OPPOSITION TO THE MUSIC HALLS

Oyb ir vet kumen morgen . . .	If you come tomorrow . . .
kupletistn vet men farkoyfn . . .	You will buy the *Kupletist* . . .
Bir un bronfn vet men	You will drink beer and brandy
trinken, men vet vern meshuge dul.	And become crazily mad.[74]

Music halls had to balance competing demands. On one hand, music hall proprietors were eager to maximize their income from the popularity of the halls. On the other hand, the authorities and reformers wanted to regulate working-class thought and behavior. Both demands had a significant effect on the content of songs.[75]

From 1889 the control of London's music halls was under the authority of the newly established London County Council (LCC). There was no censorship of music halls, and the LCC could inspect music halls only if it received complaints from the public. An LCC inspection was serious because it could result in demands for building repairs or changes to performance material, and the inspectors could ultimately revoke the music-hall license. The music-hall proprietors wanted to keep the edge that gave the music hall its attraction yet also ensure that the authorities were kept happy. Music-hall management did its utmost to forestall complaints that would elicit an inspection with a form of self-censorship. Some halls would invite audiences to report any improprieties to them directly, bypassing the LCC, and, in effect, doing their own policing.[76]

The fear that complaints about song content would result in an inspection led to English music-hall proprietors encouraging "safe" subjects that carried few risks, such as patriotic songs and heroic narratives.[77] Thus their music halls were popular for providing escapism and did not challenge the status quo. Rather, songs reflected a conservative acceptance of the working person's place in society, accepted the norm of class divisions, and did not offer any escape route or alternative futures.[78] Although subversive material could creep in, songs generally avoided or distorted working-class concerns to such an extent that they could be deemed propaganda against the working class. They depicted working-class people as vulgar and superficial, and the content of the songs did not touch their real struggles.[79]

The area of greatest concern for music-hall managers was performers' unscripted patter and off-the-cuff comments that they could not control. Some managements brought in contracts and had rules designed to limit talking to the audience, forbidding vulgar language or offensive allusions to official figures and institutions. They curtailed direct reference to local political and religious matters.[80] This sort of self-censorship may have produced better lyrics as writers were forced to find novel ways of saying things obliquely.[81] Some proprietors went as far as fining artists for bad behavior offstage, such as lack of punctuality or drunkenness.[82] Yet LCC policy on music halls was inconsistent. Some complaints about sexual allusions would result in the offending material being removed. Yet similar material might be ignored if the LCC felt there were aesthetic qualities to the songs. Some material slipped through the net because the written version did not show the suggestive nature that a nod or a wink could create in performance.[83]

It is hard to ascertain how much self-censorship applied to the material in the London Yiddish halls. Crude Yiddish songs were able to slip through into performance, and edgy material was published. Yiddish may have been unintelligible to the LCC but not to the immigrant community, and there was condemnation and pressure on one side from religious immigrants and on the other from the intellectuals and radicals. Despite the rather overt sexual double entendres, generally songs showed Jewish patriotism to England and did not contain overtly political messages or state ideological positions. In this way they also confirmed rather than tried to subvert the status quo.

The debate about quality in the Yiddish theatre and music hall was conducted in the pages of the London Jewish press. The critique of shund was directed at the popular Yiddish theatre, and the Yiddish music hall was singled out as the most vulgar example because coarse lyrics and sexual innuendo were commonplace and generally divorced from any narrative context. The same argument was happening in New York, where intellectuals and socialists attempted to change audience behavior and shut down the Lower East Side Yiddish halls. They berated vulgar material, prostitutes in the audience, and the sale of alcohol as morally dangerous to Jewish society.[84] Although significantly smaller in scale, the battles in London were fiercely fought in the pages of the *Idisher ekspres* with articles demanding changes to the East End Yiddish music halls and popular theatres. In December 1901 a furious indictment of the London Yiddish stage and the shund it performed was published under the alias "Eyner vos iz dort geven" (One who was there). The article began by berating the posters outside the Pavilion Theatre of a man dressed as a woman striking different poses. He used this image as an example of the loose morals of the London Yiddish stage with its "unnatural clumsy pantomime," where the genre is impossible to deduce and the melodramatic and unnaturalistic acting style is simply embarrassing: "This is speech with a tone that was developed in the Yiddish theatre, the tone and the sort of speech of the Purim clown and the Purim-shpilers. Yes this is our old, well-known Mondrish who has come back in another form. He doesn't come to us on Purim any more for a few minutes, to grab a tote of brandy and a few coins and go away. Here is Mondrish under another name who lets his picture be printed on huge posters and invites you to come to him instead of him to you."[85] The comparison of a sketch to a *purimshpil* and actors to Mondrish, the Purim clown, was derogatory. The *purimshpil* was a tradition of plays performed on the one-day festival of Purim. Purim commemorates surviving an anti-Semitic attack, but the celebration includes dressing up as characters in the story and getting drunk until one cannot tell the difference between the villain and the hero.[86] The custom began in Eastern Europe where Purim players would walk from house to house performing sketches and singing songs in a buffoonery style using language filled with curses and obscenities.[87]

A follow-on article by the same writer appeared in the *Idisher ekspres* five months later, this time focusing on the repertoire and audience. This article decried the corruption of the Yiddish theatre repertoire that offered "crude music-hall jokes, with vulgar songs that did not have anything to do with the contents." The article argued that the unquestionable *shund* of the music-hall comedy had now become the standard fare of the Yiddish stage: "In every theatre one is happy to play to the gallery and throw out a comic role but this is nothing but an add-on. In the Yiddish theatre this add-on has become the main thing, the comic role takes over the main role, and one sees that the management is more concerned with the taste of the gallery than the intelligent audience in the good seats. This is for business, but not for art."[88] Yet, as will be apparent in this book, the popularity of the genre shows that the "taste of the gallery" was important, and these highbrow critics could not see past the exterior of popular culture texts. Far from being merely the *shund* that these critics derided, songs and sketches engaged with a wide variety of ideas. It is true that some were silly, some vulgar, but many were deeply meaningful interventions into important parts of immigrant life. The battle against so-called *shund*, however, did not disappear; indeed, it intensified with further waves of immigration bringing more educated and political writers and audiences.

NEW AUDIENCES CHANGING THE YIDDISH THEATRE

Der "Bloffer"gloybt, az dos teater	The *"Bloffer"* believes that the theatre
dos "naye" vet efenen zikh bald,	The "new" one will open soon,
un gloybt oykh in nokh: bobemayses,	And also believes in: tall stories,
fun velkhe es lakht yung un alt.	That young and old laugh at.[89]

In 1906 there were two Yiddish theatre troupes in London. One was based at the Pavilion Theatre showing operettas and melodramas.[90] The other performed at the Standard Theatre showing more serious dramas and life-stories by Gordin and other playwrights concerned with realism. The two theatres catered to the desires of new audiences. The Russo-Japanese war of 1904 had prompted thousands of young men to escape conscription into the tsar's army by emigrating to Western Europe. A year later, during and after the abortive revolution, thousands of Jewish revolutionaries streamed into Western Europe. Many of those entering Britain were educated Russian immigrants who had been a part of the development of the Jewish Labor Bund.

The Jewish Labor Bund, founded in Vilna in 1897, organized strikes, distributed revolutionary literature, and tried to build a movement of workers to help improve living conditions. The Bund was illegal in Russia, and in 1898 there was an unexpected wave of arrests of Bundist leaders which decimated the core activists. As new leaders emerged, some of those arrested escaped bail or prison and fled to other countries in Europe, setting up Bundist cells there. Under Plehve, the Russian minister of the interior, thousands more members of the Bund were arrested in 1901–2, leading again to members escaping abroad.[91] These changes in the immigrant population entering Britain affected both who was writing material and the audiences they were writing for.

The Bund had set up cultural programs in Russia with lectures, poetry, and the arts, and gave Yiddish a new status as an appropriate language for high art. Both the intelligentsia and the workers who made up the Bund had had access to a significant amount of highbrow Yiddish culture. After 1905 there was therefore a willing audience in London for a more serious Yiddish culture. The subject of the changing status of Yiddish was even acknowledged in the *Jewish Chronicle*, which in 1909 advertised an event organized by the Young Hebrew Debating Society. The motion was that "Yiddish is a literary language and should be encouraged."[92]

London's print culture continued to expand, and with it, opportunities for printing London Yiddish lyrics. The daily *Idisher zhurnal* appeared in 1905. Poetry was still published regularly in the *Idisher ekspres* as well as in the satirical *Fonograf*, which appeared in 1908. The journalist Joseph Brenner worked in Naroditski's printing shop and wrote for the anarchist fortnightly paper *Di fraye arbayter velt*. Brenner's East End

CHAPTER 2

Hebrew novel, *Min Ha-Meitzar* (From the depths) published in 1909, vividly portrays a printing house in Whitechapel, with its tensions and conflicts over ideology. The news editor tirelessly puts the paper together while dreaming of "writing a searing tragedy drawn from the life of emigrants, revolutionaries and members of the self-defence units, and presenting it in the local Yiddish theatre."[93]

The satirical magazine *Der bloffer* was published between 1911 and 1913, sometimes fortnightly and sometimes monthly. The *Bloffer* was closely connected to the Yiddish theatre world. It endlessly lampooned antics at the theatre and music halls, targeting known personalities. The major focus of the satire was "hypocrisy," and no one was exempt: actors, singers, poets, playrights, editors, Anglo-Jews, orthodox immigrants, and radicals. The editor of the *Bloffer* was the Russian-born writer Dr. Avrom Margolin (Avreml). In 1911 he was brought over to London from Berlin amid fanfare, and was welcomed with excitement, a special concert, and a front cover of the *Bloffer*. In the front-page satirical cartoon, Avreml is seen floating over the English Channel on a copy of the *Bloffer* with a crowd of well-dressed anglicized Jews (probably immigrants, and well-known faces) wearing suits and hats and waiting on the shore to greet him. The sun is rising to reveal the name and address of the publisher, Moyshe (Morris) Sussman of 90 New Road, Whitechapel.[94] Avreml became a prolific poet of topical satire in London, writing extensively in each issue of the *Bloffer* between 1911 and 1913. He also wrote poetry regularly for the *Idisher ekspres* in 1912, and for journalist Morris Myer's new daily paper the *Tsayt* (Times) in 1913–14. He was a well-known figure in the Yiddish press and the intellectual café world. Margolin's coeditor was the theatre critic Leon Kussman, who wrote under the pen name of L. Izraeli in the *Idisher ekspres*. Kussman was dismayed by popular Yiddish culture and attacked it vigorously in print.

The debate about high and low art was intensifying. Intellectuals wanted more realistic theatre, and activists were still attempting to move audiences out of the music halls and commercial theatre into more serious art. Even the *Jewish Chronicle* participated in the debate on the occasion of a new Yiddish music hall opening in 1909. In an article suggesting that it would not be a bad thing to find a "Yiddish Robey" (George Robey was one of the most famous English music-hall stars at this time), it warns: "If his jokes are fresh and his 'patter' lightsome, then the Yiddish

"Avreml Swims to the Bloffer Concert," *Bloffer*, no. 6 (December 1911). From the collections of the National Library of Israel.

music-hall stage has cause for congratulation. Otherwise it were far better to keep his 'light' hidden from the gaze of men."[95]

This suggests a fondness for the music-hall genre, at least by this *Jewish Chronicle* writer, but there were demands for quality control between good and bad popular culture. This distinction was not held by most critics. Kussman condemned all popular theatre and decried the encouragement of audience participation. In an article slating the lack of artistic merit in Yiddish plays, writing as L. Izraeli, he described a performance of a song in a play by the popular dramatist Rakov: "When Motl Noz (Mr. Shilling) sang *shuldik iz di noz* [The nose is guilty] he was soon helped by the gallery, after that by the circle and the porter and then the whole theatre sang with him just like, *lehavdil*, if such a comparison can be made, Yom Kippur . . . in synagogue."[96] Kussman saw that atmosphere was an integral part of popular entertainment, which led to writers such as Rakov creating shund songs for the gallery rather than aspiring toward high art. He makes a comparison between the music-hall atmosphere and that created on the holiest day of the year in the synagogue. The word *lehavdl* denotes, with some humor, the unsuitability of the comparison; however, it does suggest that creating atmosphere was an intrinsic part of cultural life, in both religious observance and Yiddish popular culture. On Yom Kippur, even nonregular attendees of the synagogue would be found there, joining in with singing solemn prayers. The comparison is a heartfelt yet mischievous jibe implying that the Yom Kippur singing crowds of nominally religious people made the synagogue as unholy a place as the popular theatre.

Over the next few years an idea was proposed by East End theatregoers to build a new purpose-built Yiddish theatre in the East End for the staging of operas and serious drama. One immigrant journalist suggested that London's popular theatre had had its day: "Every theatre visitor now knows the difference between an artist and a *purim shpiler* . . . and there is no place any more for such uproar in London."[97] Yet even in 1911 there was a *Bloffer* front cover cartoon of two London theatres: the "Temple" showing *Hamlet* with one person buying a ticket and the popular theatre with a long queue at the box office.[98] In 1912 the *Faynmans idishe folks teater* (Feinman's Yiddish People's Theatre) or "Temple of Art" opened in Commercial Road with money raised from East End immigrants. Its announcement in *Der idisher zhurnal* underlined how this was quality theatre by demanding quiet, respectful, and appropriate behavior from the audience: "Please do not forget that the Yiddish People's Theatre is a temple and make sure that an atmosphere of holiness prevails."[99] The performance of *Rigoletto* in Yiddish even brought superlatives from the *Jewish Chronicle*.[100]

However, in the height of its early success, the Yiddish People's Theatre incurred conflict. The *Idisher ekspres* letters pages debated the appropriateness of opening on the Sabbath, the religious shareholders stating that it was against Jewish law and the secular shareholders claiming that it was unfair for the religious to set the limits. The wrath of the religious about performances on the Sabbath and the high cost of tickets (with no gallery of cheaper seats) meant that locals did not go.[101] With mismanaged and inadequate financial backing, after only four months the Yiddish People's Theatre closed. London was simply unable to contain two theatres.[102] So the Pavilion Theatre survived on its own, giving home to both the popular theatre that the East End fans flocked to and a smaller amount of more serious Yiddish theatre.[103]

The developments and subsequent failure of the Feinman's People's Theatre were closely followed by the satirists in the *Bloffer*. They mercilessly ribbed the actors, the managers, the writers, and maybe most of all, the ordinary *moyshe*, the frequenter of the popular theatre and music hall. All of them were blamed for the failure of the high-art Yiddish theatre. Kussman despaired of the Yiddish theatre repertoire that "sinks with every day to the abyss of trash, comic dance, song and cheap jokes." Yet he had to admit that that was what Yiddish theatre audiences preferred.[104]

The three decades between 1884 and the start of World War I saw Yiddish popular theatre and music halls develop and flourish in London's East End, although their progress was halting. The music-hall songwriters and satirical poets (sometimes the same people) came from diverse backgrounds, with influences from Jewish and Russian education. They came into a London that was full of new influences from English culture and old debates about Yiddish culture. Songs and satire, primarily for entertainment, engaged with issues of daily immigrant life and conflict. They raise questions about modernity, religious observance, and processes of acculturation. Yet they are funny and naughty and rarely raised the issues with great earnest. The attempt by the Anglo-Jewish community and even the Jewish socialists to edify the immigrant workers was not successful across the board. Rather than going to serious theatre or reading translation of the classics into Yiddish, the younger immigrants were more likely to parade down Whitechapel Road in all the finery they could muster, spending their hard-earned money taking their sweethearts to the Yiddish music hall.

PART II

The Lyrics of London

Front page of the *Arbayter fraynd*, 8 March 1887. From the Mazower Private Collection.

א הוט אדער א גט

שינגען מיט טעקסטעס פון מאדאם ב. גאלדשטיין

שפײ איך אויף דײן באטען אונד ניב
דיר באלד א גט
איך דארף קײן קלײד אונד קײן שיך
נור אהעם וויל איך
ווען ניט כאפט דיך דער רוח
זעסט יענע שכנה פון נעקסטן דאהר
יעדע פעדער פון איהר העט
נרײכם בײ דעם זעקסטען פלאה־ר
איך וויל אויף דיר ניט קיקען
איך דארף ניט דײנע גליקען
א העט אדער א געט   (בים)

2.

עס איז געווען א צײט
איך האב געהאט א פײם
מיט מײן מאן
אוי אוי אי
ווײל איך ברען א זועלם
אונד ספענד פיעל געלם
אויף א העם
וואם ווערט ניט גיט

פראזא

הערם מענשען פון אינזערע
העמס ווערם ניט גים ? דער פאר
האם עד זיך מים מיר נעקרינגם
אוי האב איך איהם געגעבין...
מים אײן האנם האב איך איהם
א נעם געטאן פאר דיא האהר
אונד מים דער צווײטער אין
דיא אויגען אונד האב געשמען
שרײען
(קאהר)
מוזיק: דיא גימער ברידער

זײנע פרײנד
ווא געפעל איך אײך הײנם
מים מײן נײען העם !
יזו ! אוי ! אוי !
װאס איך מהוע װעלען
צו מײן מאן געפעלין
יען ניט כאך איך א געװאלד
אונד שרײ אױם באלד

פראזא

װיא מײן ליבער כאן דיר געפעלם
אם מײן העם ! װײסם דו מײן ליבער
שװערעלע איך בין ניט װיא יענע
װײבער װאם לאזען זיך פון א מאן
פרעמין מים דיא פים בײא ביז אז
קארץ אונד שארף

(קאהר)

פרום װילכם דיא טימער שװנה,
נאך ניט קויפען קײן העם

3

The Transnational Scope

Ikh kum in england a griner
ver a preser, a mashiner . . .
O, rusland, fraynt, vi ze ikh dir haynt.

I come to England a new immigrant
Become a presser, a machinist . . .
Oh Russia, friend, how I see you today.[1]

London's Yiddish lyrics are not a simple or accurate portrayal of the lived life of the immigrants. Instead, they create a complex picture that comments on and analyzes the immigrant experience from different perspectives. Through selective emphasis, parody, and satire, they transform immigrant life into a crafted artifact for entertainment or in pursuit of an emotional or political response. Entwined in the lyrics are reflections of the changing landscape of experiences and locations, creating a patchwork of ideas and themes derived from multiple sources and set within an environment that is itself diverse and changing. Written into, sometimes hidden inside, the words, the phraseology, and the concepts, there are details and particularities that incorporate places and cultures that had become the world of the Jewish immigrant. Even the most apparently straightforward of lyrics about everyday topics often show a complex, multilayered, and "messy" composition.[2]

Whitechapel's background noise of discussion, argument, acculturation, and controversy did not only relate to London's Whitechapel, and among the hubbub it is possible to hear the wider influences on immigrant life. There were five major milieus that impacted on the Yiddish-speaking immigrant in England: the *heym* (homeland) of Eastern Europe; the Yiddish-speaking community in the East End of London; the Anglo-Jewish establishment; the English community; and other Yiddish-speaking immigrant diaspora communities, particularly that of New York. These locations are referenced implicitly or explicitly throughout the London lyrics, yet each milieu is itself heterogenous and in the process of change.[3]

There is no single Eastern European homeland of the immigrants. Coming from Lithuania, Galicia, or the Ukraine meant differences in the experience of politics, religious traditions, and access to modernity and education. These differences affected the landscape of the immigrant East End as people clustered in micro-communities in *landsmanshaftn* (organizations supporting people from the same home town), *khevres* of particular denominations and trades, or internationalist socialist groups. Migration brought a diminishing of the importance of religion, a fracturing of family structure, and greater secularization. Differences from Eastern Europe were exposed and often exaggerated in the Yiddish-speaking East End, at times resulting in hard-fought conflict within the immigrant community. The Anglo-Jewish establishment was also far from homogenous, and embraced a range of opinions. The *Jewish Chronicle* letter pages were full of internal controversy, struggling with the lack of unity within anglicized Anglo-Jewry.[4]

Although some aspects of Jewish culture were broad enough to include the whole Jewish community, there were no simple ways to divide and categorize a culture that had grown and developed from a range of sources, places, and languages. Thus the Yiddish texts sometimes use broad strokes in their cultural mix, but more often include subtle subtexts. This transnational cultural mix is ubiquitous in the poetry and songs, and is the engine behind the vibrant London Yiddish lyrics.

There may seem, at first glance, to be a paradox in the idea that this transnational hybridity produces a specifically *English* Yiddish-language popular culture. On the one hand, the Yiddish lyrics are full of local allusion, language, and concepts, debating ideas, and events happening in England. They enact the process of anglicization *despite* the fact that they were written in Yiddish. On the other hand, the lyrics include allusions to the politics of the wider Yiddish-speaking world and a geography of

Eastern Europe. This is partly *enabled* by the fact that they were written in Yiddish. It is these contrary forces, clearly exhibited in the poems and songs, that make the London lyrics so unique. This does not mean that there are not similarities in experience with life in Eastern European communities and other immigrant diasporas such as that of the Lower East Side in New York. Indeed, these similarities are important enough to be easily transferable between different locations. However, the extent of the use of "Englishness" in the lyrics is too important to ignore, in their writers' attempts to embed the Yiddish-speaking community into Britain.

Transnational elements of the lyrics may have been written intentionally, but may also be intuitive. Writers generally keep multiple audiences in mind, and layer hints, markers, and codes and switch between them.[5] When subcultures copy or borrow aspects of the dominant culture, they both reflect and invert it to create a very different and subversive product.[6] This type of code switching and inversion is identifiable in the London Yiddish lyrics as they engage with the complexity brought about by change.

Yiddish-speaking actors and singers had always inhabited a transnational world, visiting and performing wherever Jews migrated and lived. Troupes of *klezmorim* (musicians) traveled across Eastern Europe in search of work. As Yiddish-speaking diasporas grew and transport developed, actors traveled across the globe, including Western Europe, America, South Africa, Argentina, and even the Far East. They performed in real and makeshift Yiddish theatres and carried the songs with them, songs that had relevance for all Yiddish-speaking Jews, immigrants or not.[7] Every Eastern European Jew was affected in some way by immigration, and the impact and influences went in multiple directions. The location of Yiddish theatre in key cities such as Odessa, Warsaw, London, Paris, New York, Johannesburg, and Buenos Aires can be seen as a part of a transnational network of hubs.[8] Not only Yiddish theatres, but *landsmanshaftn* became central in cultural communication between different Jewish centers.[9] The use of a sense of place in song lyrics and performance style creates a bond with an audience, where memories are tapped.[10] The London Yiddish lyrics, with their evocation of a variety of places, exemplifies the transnational and transcultural Yiddish Ashkenaz.

HASHIVEYNU NAZAD: COMPLEX ENTANGLEMENTS

Many lyrics use already existant songs as their basic structure, drawing audiences in with a sense of familiarity. Writing new words to famous songs creates parodies, which add color and symbolic associations to the new song through connotation, or emotional manipulation.[11] This type of "creative indexing," which uses familiar melodies to index loyalties to the context of an original song, can be seen in the example of *hashiveynu nazad*.[12] There are three London songs and a poem that use a version of the words *hashiveynu nazad* (returning back) in their title: "Dem nayem hashiveynu nazad" (The new hashiveynu nazad), "A ferter hashiveynu nazad" (A fourth hashiveynu nazad), and "A finfter hashiveynu nazad" (A fifth hashiveynu nazad), all written in around 1900, and a satirical poem just called "Hashiveynu nazad" published in 1913. The lyrics are all specific to Jewish immigrant life in London, mentioning places and people, and using anglicized language. Yet they are all parodies of an original of the same title, and are mostly written in a meter to sing to the original melody.

The original "Hashiveynu nazad" was a famous song by Avrom Goldfaden from his opera *Der yidisher faust* (The Jewish Faust).[13] The title is unusual and not commonplace Yiddish, but a carefully crafted Yiddish hybrid. The word *hashiveynu* comes from a Hebrew word meaning "return us." It is a familiar term to synagogue-going Jews, as it is part of the Sabbath morning liturgy when the Torah scrolls are returned to the Ark. The word *hashiveynu* appears in the phrase *hashiveynu adonoy elekho venoshuvo, khadesh yomeynu kekedem* ("Return us to you God and we will return. Renew our days as of old"). This verse comes from the Book of Lamentations, and is part of a lament for the destruction of Jerusalem and of a yearning for a utopia or a messianic era.[14] In the Sabbath morning liturgy it is often sung, and the word *hashiveynu* is emphasized and lingered on. The familiarity of the liturgy gives the word *hashiveynu* intense and deep resonances. Goldfaden's choice to use such evocative language was in style with his operatic melodramas that used historical events with much emotive feeling to drive the action of his plays. The second word of the title, *nazad*, is also not standard Yiddish, and comes from Russian meaning "back there." The title in full means "return us back" or "take us back." The mixture of classical Hebrew and Russian both reflects and augments the content of the song.

Goldfaden's "Hashiveynu nazad" has a Zionist message. The song describes the archetypal wandering Jew, living in exile through hardship and poverty, being uprooted and driven out of Spain and Russia, and yearning for a home but not knowing which way to go. The answer offered by Goldfaden is *keyn tsien! hashiveynu nazad!* (To Zion! Take us back!).[15] The Zionist theme was strengthened by the use of biblical language giving depth and gravitas to the lyrics, and implying that going back to Zion included getting closer to God. Any later song that used the same title and melody as Goldfaden's hit song would carry resonances, and the audience of "Dem nayem hashiveynu nazad," a song about the hardship of immigration to London, would know both the Goldfaden song and the liturgy.

The London song "Dem nayem hashiveynu nazad," not attributed to an author, describes the real cost of living in a "free" country where the hopes of new immigrants are dashed by the reality of London's East End.[16] The narrator describes escaping tsarist violence and tyranny, only to be beaten up on the streets of London for being an immigrant. The escape from the hunger of Eastern Europe with the promise of a living wage in England is frustrated by starvation during the slack season. Workers skilled in the old country are left doing menial jobs in London. The punch line of each verse is the repeated hashiveynu nazad crying out to be taken back to Eastern Europe, suggesting that London is worse than Russia and it would be better to return.

The song uses a similar image as Goldfaden's archetypal lost, tired, and dispirited Jewish victim, but transfers the geography from Russia as the diaspora of Zion to England being a diaspora of Eastern Europe. This places a local song about London into a much broader context of the eternal Jewish condition. The song is imbued with local London color, which can be seen clearly in the final verse:

Git a blik in der leyn	Glance down the lane
vet ir dort zen	You'll see there
file mentshn shteyen	Many people
aropgelozt dem kop.	With slumped heads.
Tsvishn zey in dermit	Among them

in der korner gulsten strit	On the corner of Goulston Street
shteyt a griner yid	Stands a new immigrant Jew
un kukt oys a dzhob.	Looking for a job.

"The Lane" refers to the busy, sprawling Petticoat Lane market centered around Middlesex Street, and the unemployed new immigrant was probably standing on the corner of Wentworth Street and Goulston Street. The English feel is maintained through the use of many anglicized words. The use of *leyn* (lane) and *strit* (street), rather than the Yiddish *gesl* or *gas*, may be obvious for conserving place names. There are also anglicisms for words that have no equivalent in Yiddish, so in a later verse there is a reference to the *bizi tsayt* (busy season). *Bizi* evokes English working practices and the sweating system, which uses the terminology busy and slack (*slek*). Another type of anglicism is used simply as an aesthetic choice, such as the word *korner* in the verse quoted above or, as in the verse below, where we encounter an immigrant wandering around London alone and confused:

A yokl hot bald derkent	A yokel recognizes
az a griner dort gayt	That a new immigrant is walking by
un hot oysgetsoygn zayne hent	And stretched out his hands
un hot im bavelkomt mit a fayt.[17]	And welcomed him with a fight.

The words *yokl*, *bavelkomt*, and *fayt* have perfectly good Yiddish alternatives, but the choice to use them makes an aesthetic point about the londonized Yiddish used on the East End street, and the use of them in popular song builds a vibrant picture.[18] The code switching between languages is fun; it creates a richness of bicultural language games.[19] It is a nonpurist vernacular Yiddish used for its familiarity.

On a basic level, "Dem nayem hashiveynu nazad" expresses discontent for life in England and offers a better alternative, to return to Eastern Europe. The title, *Dem nayem* (The new) suggests that the song is saying something different and novel. We are left to speculate. The chorus line is powerful and can be read with nostalgia, satire, or irony. It could be a religious agenda with a nostalgic hankering back to the old

THE TRANSNATIONAL SCOPE

GOULSTON STREET ON SUNDAY MORNING.

Goulston Street market on Sunday morning. From George Sims, *Living London*, 1901. From the Mazower Private Collection.

country, the old faith, and the family. It could be a Bundist agenda satirizing the Goldfaden song, to say the answer is not Zion and is not England but staying and improving Eastern Europe.

There may be another reason. At the same time as providing charitable support to immigrants, both the Jewish Board of Guardians and the Russo-Jewish Committee were putting energy into trying to stem the tide of immigrants. The Board of Guardians put advertisements and warnings in the Eastern European Jewish press describing the torment of finding work in England and discouraging Jews from coming. It made arrangements with committees on the continent to encourage Russian emigrants not to come to London. The Russo-Jewish Committee tried to send refugees onward to America, where they felt immigrants would have better prospects of finding work and housing.[20] The song "Dem nayem hashiveynu nazad" could be a piece of designed Anglo-Jewish propaganda, discouraging migration to London.

CHAPTER 3

By using the form of the Goldfaden chorus of "Take Me Back," this song about London was placed within the context of a wider Jewish nation. The songwriter could count on allusions to other parts of popular culture or politics being known not only in name but as ingrained implicit knowledge of Yiddish Ashkenaz. This text is transnational in the sense that it lays out the Jewish world from Eastern Europe to the London diaspora, and even includes the hidden reference to Zion. It portrays Jews as a people settling in new places but connected as a transnational group. This is not an unusual strategy, and it is commonplace to describe the Jews of one country as part of a nation. The important aspect here is how it was a part of the London immigrant popular culture: sold as a songsheet, reprinted in the *Londoner kupletist*. Acculturation to England is entangled with a sense of being the "Jewish People."

One must be careful, however, not to overstate the significance of putting a known song to new lyrics. Well-known songs were often used simply because doing so was easier and quicker than writing a new one. Or there may be a light or tangential connection, as can be seen in the two songs titled "A ferter hashiveynu nazad" (fourth hashiveynu) and "A finfter hashiveynu nazad" (fifth hashiveynu), published at around the turn of the twentieth century.[21] These songs were both written and published by Yozef the bookseller and are double parodies, both of the Goldfaden original song and of "Dem nayem hashiveynu nazad." The fourth and fifth "Hashiveynu" songs are essentially the same song: a lively advertisement for songsheets, songbooks, and sheet music of Yiddish popular songs that can be bought in his shop. The two songs are almost identical, but the changes are significant. The first verse of each song gives the address of Yozef's shop. In the fourth hashiveynu, this was on the *korner of kanen strit* (Cannon Street [Road]), and in the fifth hashiveynu, the address was the corner *of litl terner strit* (Little Turner Street, now Rampart Street). The two addresses were one street away from each other on Commercial Road.[22] The use of the lyric *korner* parallels the verse quoted earlier from "Dem nayem hashiveynu nazad," which must have been popular enough to create the humor in these parodies. Prager's list of Yiddish songs published in Britain includes a first and a third hashiveynu nazad song. Although there are no known surviving copies of these songsheets, it can be assumed that Yozef recycled the song to advertise his shop each time it changed address.[23]

Both the fourth and the fifth hashiveynu songs advertise a new "invention," which is a songbook. Yet the songbooks are different. In the fourth hashiveynu the advertised songbook contains the latest songs of "the best singers in the world / Like Weisenfreund, Gutentag, Sherman and Akselrod." These singers were all well-known actors appearing on London's Yiddish stage and singing lyrics about London.[24] The songbook being advertised, however, was the *Idishe bine*, an 800-page American publication of theatre songs published in a double volume in 1897, which did not contain any songs with London lyrics.[25] In the fifth hashiveynu song the London actors' names have disappeared, but this time the songbook advertised was the *Londoner kupletist*, which was a local songbook that included lyrics of London songs. The London Yiddish music hall had become popular enough to have a songbook in its own right, not an American import.

In both of these advertising songs, the chorus line words *hashiveynu nazad* change their meaning with each verse. This is sometimes used to acknowledge Goldfaden's original in suggesting that the reader now has the lyrics to "sing along with [Goldfaden's] *hashiveynu nazad*." One verse has the shop advertised as a library where books can be borrowed for a deposit, so the returning, the hashiveynu nazad, is to return the book and reclaim the deposit. Another verse claims that with songbooks life will never be dull, and then, totally out of context, finishes "There would be time / And we should go / To Zion, *hashiveynu nazad*." Yozef was a known Zionist, and this is not the only occasion that he added a Zionist verse out of context to express his politics, and of course, this is Goldfaden's line and so is both political and amusing. The final verse of both songs uses the term *hashiveynu nazad* with emphasis. Come back to the shop, hashiveynu nazad.[26]

Yozef's bookshop did not only sell books. At the bottom of the songsheets there is small print with details of the shop and a list of what else it sells: "*sforim, tfilin, mezuzes, sidurim, makhzorim, bils shir hamaylesn, kortn, domines, matses, vayn oyf peysekh, vintshkartn oyf rosheshone.*" These are all religious items, study and prayer texts, cards, *matzah*, and wine for Passover. We can imagine that many songsheets were bought by music-hall lovers, and they would generally be less orthodox. So it is possible that the song contains a further nuance on the idea of "returning," implying that returning to the shop with all its religious accessories could also be a return to a more active religious observance of Judaism.

These advertising songs present a Jewish world of transnational carriers of popular culture. It is not only the singers who were moving to and fro between Eastern Europe and various diasporas to perform and sing; the songs were traveling with them, and some became popular enough to be published as songbooks to be sold locally. The traveling songs ended up in surprising places. Canadian Yiddishist Chaim Neslen recorded his grandmother, Esther Djzaldovsky, singing the song "Dem nayem hashiveynu nazad" when he was a twelve-year-old boy in 1950. Djzaldovsky, originally from Poland, learned the song when she was living in Denmark with her family and worked as a seamstress from her home. Denmark was on the route for traveling actors who would often stay with her family. Djzaldovsky remembered the song well enough to sing all four verses some forty years later. Yet this song is a local London song, and she had never visited and had no knowledge of London. Consequently, the street name Goulston Street was muttered unintelligibly on the recording because Djzaldovsky could not pick up the unfamiliar name she had heard the actors sing.[27] This example demonstrates how cultural texts were carriers of the local to the wider Yiddish-speaking world, and it exposes parallels in experience as well as making claims to specific local places and people.

A final ditty is a short, satirical verse simply titled "Hashiveynu nazad." It was published in the *Bloffer* of May 1913 and dedicated to the London actor Joseph Sherman. The meter precisely fits the tune of "Hashiveynu nazad," but there is little connection other than the title, and there is not even a final chorus line of the words *hashiveynu nazad*.[28] What it does reference is a forlorn, poor Jew uncertain about where to go. The Jew in question is an aging, badly paid actor who has lost his role in the theatre. It is light and satirical and involves local theatre politics because at this time Sherman was at the height of his career and a popular household name in London.[29] This version of "Hashiveynu nazad" makes the famous actor become an age-old wandering Jew, a character he might have played on the stage hundreds of times. Indeed, it could refer to his role in Goldfaden's *Faust*, the opera that the original "Hashiveynu nazad" came from.

This collection of hashiveynu nazad songs shows a local popular culture steeped in the wider Jewish world of Eastern Europe. The local is tightly connected to the Eastern European homeland through the subject matter and through the connection to Goldfaden's original song. These texts are layered with the geography of Ashkenaz, to include London, Zion, and New York. The collage of references allowed the songs to be enjoyed and accessed in multiple directions simultaneously.

LONDON BAY NAKHT: THE TRANSPLANTATION OF SONG

Using London as a location to make political points assures the possibility of a transnational scope, when the politics can be related to a wider sphere. Winchevsky's poem "London bay nakht" was published in the *Poylisher yidl* in 1884. It begins with a description of streetlamps that illuminate London's streets and walls, with the purpose of providing a clear view of what happens in London at night. Each subsequent verse explores what the lamps do not reveal. These are the poorest people who are hidden from view, hopeless, and desperate. It describes hunger and homelessness, unemployment, sickness, and death. It considers the loneliness of the new immigrant without a family, and still too new an immigrant to get help from the *londoner komite layt* (the London Committee members). In the final verse, the streetlamps become symbols and a political statement:

Zey zenen vi KOMITE LAYT	They are like *committee members*
tsum SHAYNEN *nor gezetst,*	Just placed there to *shine,*
un zeen nit, un visn nit—	Without seeing, without knowing—
der shukh bay vemen kvetsht.	Whose shoe pinches.[30]

The image of the cobbled streets and the local hospital conjure up the East End. The description does not specify that the characters are Jewish apart from the verse about the new immigrant, so the characters are generic. They could be Jew or gentile, although, writing in Yiddish, readers may have identified with the characters as if they were Jews. Winchevsky's inclusion of Jews in descriptions of poverty in the wider English society may have been an attempt to encourage Yiddish-speaking immigrants toward an internationalist socialist perspective, rather than maintaining an identity based on religion or ethnicity. The local referencing reaches more widely when it describes the *londoner komite layt* (London Committee members). The Metropolitan Board of Works (MBW) was responsible for the upkeep of the capital; however, they were seen as corrupt and are the likely London Committee of the poem mentioned in reference to their lack of support for new immigrants. The English establishment did not generally support Jewish immigrants upon arrival, making it necessary for Anglo-Jewish charities to take that role. However, even the Jewish Board of Guardians would not support immigrants until they had been living in the country for six months. In the context of the poem, being "too new" an immigrant meant falling through the support gap and being hidden, not illuminated by the streetlights.

Winchevsky footnoted the poem to explain that "the form is taken from an old Russian poem." The poem is "Fonariki" (Streetlights) by Ivan Miatlev.[31] The Miatlev poem is also a satire where streetlights represent the power of the government and the aristocracy. Miatlev's narrator asks the streetlights if they have seen a young woman waiting for her love, an orphan, a sad writer. Literary critic Nokhem Minkov, writing in 1956, argues: "Winchevsky uses the same form, but the social message is much deeper. It is through and through concrete and proletarian. Here we have a starving boy who cannot find a roof over his head. The girl in Winchevsky's poem is not waiting for her beloved. She's waiting by the hospital where her father is dying—and five children at home, and the mother three years dead. Winchevsky introduces an unhappy actor, a 'half-confused old man,' and the new immigrant Jew. . . . They are all real, living in London at the beginning of the 1880s."[32]

In his memoirs Winchevsky explained that even if Russians do not remember Miatlev's name, they would know the opening lines of this poem.[33] So "London bay nakht" took on a starker political hue when seen in intertextual relation to Miatlev's poem. A benefit of using Miatlev's structure was that Winchevsky could profit from the lyricism of an established poet. But by changing the words to become more radical than the original, he implied a sardonic critique of Miatlev's politics. "London bay nakht" highlights the restrictions of Miatlev's artistic freedom, and the greater freedom that Winchevsky had to write political satire in England.

Winchevsky's biographer, Kalman Marmor, noted that "London bay nakht" was popular on both sides of the Atlantic, put to music, and sung for decades.[34] The poem that was sung in America, however, was a slightly different version. References to London were removed and the title was changed to "Di lempelekh" (The streetlights), the same title as Miatlev's poem. The *londoner komite layt* was changed to *di nyuyoriker 8te strit layt* (The New York 8th Street people), reflecting its new location as a Jewish immigrant area of the Lower East Side. The body of the retained text conveys the transnational nature of the poem. The themes are concerns shared by Londoners and New Yorkers. "Di lempelekh," with its New York words, was popular enough to be republished back in London, not in the socialist Yiddish press as its first incantation was, but as a penny songsheet by the publisher Yozef.[35]

The impact of this poem is manifested in its critical acclaim and circulation. The layered codes offered London audiences a feeling that they were part of a larger community that encompassed both the English world and the wider Yiddish-speaking world. In the intersection of Ashkenaz locations, home country becomes displaced from its privileged position and becomes another diaspora location.[36] In effect, the multiple locations then cease to be prioritized, and all become elements of the poem. Winchevsky explicitly references London and New York and deliberately refers to Russia in the footnote. In pre-copyright publishing some authors chose to make similar statements about their sources, although many did not. This shows Winchevsky, a socialist, acknowledging his debt to Miatlev, but it also shows the importance to Winchevsky, an internationalist, of using a Russian source in a Yiddish poem about London.

The movement of songs across the Yiddish-speaking diaspora was commonplace when there was enough relevant content to transfer between contexts, and many songs with local content were adapted in a similar vein to "London bay nakht." "Der bal-toyvnik" (The do-gooder) was written by Isaac Reingold, a Polish immigrant to America, and adapted by the London-based Arn Nager to remove the American references and replace them with English ones.[37] Other songs had substantially new versions written, based on an original. "A het oder a get" (a hat or a divorce) was written by the prolific vaudeville writer Louis Gilrod, who emigrated from the Ukraine to America as a child. The song was published in the American *Lider magazin*, yet a new version with the same title was published in the

Londoner kupletist, showing Beki Goldstein as the performer.[38] The two versions are significantly different. Thus Goldstein created a new version of the song, inspired by Gilrod, to perform to a London audience.

Other songs that were written in one location remained the same but with verses added to locate them in the new country. The song "Gevalt es iz a shlekhte tsayt" (Help, it is a terrible time) has seven verses as published in a 1910 reprint of the American *Idishe bine*. No author is attributed; however, it uses the words "boarder" and "alright," which generally mark it as an American work. The song was also produced as a songsheet by Yozef, in which an additional verse composed by him was added at the end. Yozef's final verse suggests that one way to bring relief from the "terrible time" is to read books, and he gives the address of his bookshop.[39] He also replaces the Americanism "boarder" with the English word "lodger." With almost identical songs produced in both places, it is not always clear which came first. New York had a much larger music-hall scene and produced so much more than London that the American version is often assumed to be the original. Another song, "Azoy geyt dos gelt avek" (And so the money disappears), describes boys courting girls in Crystal Palace. The chorus title line coupled with the local allusions is very similar to the lyric, "That's the way the money goes" in the popular mid-Victorian English song "Pop Goes the Weasel," which refers to locations in East London. The Yiddish song was published twice in London: as a penny songsheet and in the *Londoner kupletist*. It was also published in the American song collection *Yidishe teater lider*, where the term Crystal Palace is replaced with *ekipazhen*, which means coaches or carriages.[40] Whichever version came first, it remains the case that songs were interchangeable across the Yiddish-speaking world, showing the similarity of experience in the Yiddish-speaking diaspora.

VIKTORYE PARK: THE "GLOCAL" IMAGINARY

Converting a local space to a transnational location offers an opportunity for critique, and this is what happens in Nager's song "Viktorye park" (Victoria Park). In 1909, the *Jewish Chronicle* reported that on a Friday afternoon in Victoria Park the grass was "black with thousands of children."[41] Immigrants from Whitechapel's model dwellings, the Rothschild Buildings, built to alleviate slum conditions, were not allowed to play sports in the courtyards of their East End buildings, so a bus trip two miles north to Victoria Park gave them the space to play cricket and football, go swimming and boating, and listen to a band.[42] The park was so popular with the Jewish immigrant community, it was nicknamed the "Polish Brighton," and the tram or bus heading there the "Polish Express."[43]

Local historian Charles Poulson describes the park at the time as a mainly left-wing public forum, "an East End version of the more famous Speakers' Corner in Hyde Park," yet serious rather than entertaining. Political meetings, rallies, and processions were held there regularly. Poulson quotes from a letter from William Morris to his daughter in 1886, where he described his visit to Victoria Park: "Had a good meeting, spoke for an hour in a place made noisy by other meetings near, also a brass band not far off."[44] Music can conjure up places, and those places can then be used to define a community in relation to the world around it.[45] Nager manages to achieve this in his music-hall song "Viktorye park." He chose this specific place in London to describe the multiple communities that Jewish immigrants inhabit.[46] The actual location becomes symbolic. The borders of its bounded world create a self-contained medium through which to make critical comment.

Nager's song is set in a Yiddish-speaking Victoria Park community. A fictional image of this familiar place is constructed, peopled with an assortment of comic, vulgar, and prosaic Jewish characters, including Moyshe Reytekh (Moses Radish) and Meymi Loksh (Mamie Noodle) with false teeth. The word *loksh* (noodle) is slang for a dollar, so Meymi may be rich or an American, or maybe a transmigrant. Many of the characters are described in a traditional Yiddish style with adjectives (often not complimentary) before the person's name. So there is fat Annie, red Benny, spotty Fanny. The eclectic mix includes a porter with a red neck, and Edi Bor, the biggest kike (an offensive word for Jew). Some of the language is vulgar, although with a word like "kike" it may be subverted in this context to be comic and could refer to his being a new immigrant.[47] The description of the park is boisterous and noisy, a comic rendition of a familiar place satirizing the East End immigrant community at leisure.[48]

However, the local flavor of the song is layered with references to the East European *heym*, the Anglo-Jewish community, and the wider English culture. The song parodies an image of the Eastern European shtetl with its similarly eclectic mix of Jewish characters. The shtetl is

CHAPTER 3

VICTORIA PARK: THE SAND-PIT.

Victoria Park sandpit. From George Sims, *Living London*, 1901. From the Mazower Private Collection.

evoked by two clear links to Eastern Europe. Firstly is the character of the prostitute Khaye-Ite, who is deliberately located as being from Lithuania. Secondly is the use of the line *landslayt zukhn dort a dzhob* / (*Landslayt* are looking for a job there). The word *landslayt* means people who come from the same town in Eastern Europe. So the evocation of the shtetl connects the London diaspora community to the Eastern European homeland. The picture drawn of the shtetl in "Viktorye park" is grotesque in many ways but it is a caricature, and no less realistic a portrayal than the idyllic homeland created from diasporic nostalgia. In this sense it is comparable to other portrayals that do not represent real situations. Thus the song elicits nostalgia for the *concept* of homeland, and shows the local London Yiddish-speaking community as a part of the wider international Jewish world, what I call parochial internationalism.[49] Parochial internationalism refers to the relationship between local and international, and invokes a narrow-mindedness in the local, and an insularity in the evocation of the shtetl.

Nager's portrayal of a shtetl can be augmented to some extent by Dan Miron's argument that the shtetl had to be portrayed as solely Jewish so that it could become the butt of satire and could be "exposed as benighted and reactionary, soporific, resistant to initiative and innovation, or, alternatively, portrayed nostalgically and romantically as the quintessence of spirituality and communal intimacy, the nucleus of a besieged civilization that nevertheless enjoyed internal harmony and perfect internal communication."[50] In this case, the Victoria Park shtetl comes across as a dysfunctional hodgepodge of people who are generally behaving in antisocial ways. It critiques both the Eastern European shtetl as dysfunctional and Jewish London as vulgar and conflicted. In the final verse, among sexually coarse descriptions, we have *Itsik*, whose nose is *shpitsik* (pointed), and because his nose is *shpitsik*, he is called *Itsik*. This line may, to stretch the point a little, be an allusion to the anti-Semitic stereotype of a Jew, often portrayed by Anglo-Jewish actors, known as "Hebrew comedians" in the English music hall. This allusion to the stage Jew makes fun of the use of the stereotype. However, by juxtaposing it in a verse that also uses vulgar sexual terminology, the stereotype is shown to be in bad taste, and as such makes a comment on the bad taste of its usage in the English music hall.

There is yet a further layer to this text concerning the melody line. Music plays an important part in defining space, and when a song's melody is connected to a specific place, it brings additional meanings and significance.[51] The melody of the verse of "Viktorye park" has a striking resemblance to the song "London Bridge Is Falling Down." This gives the piece local flavor and removes it somewhat from its Yiddish-language environment. Counterpointing the English feel with the image of homeland and the image of the East End, it invites the listener to combine these experiences of location. The chorus melody is almost identical to the traditional square dance "Little Redwing," an American song from 1907 which was almost immediately parodied with British words.[52]

This text can be seen as connected to the current discourse on glocalization that claims that commercial music always requires some local identification despite its transnational scope.[53] Here, the local identification in "Viktorye park" serves to expose the transnational elements of the Yiddish culture.

CHAPTER 3

DER BLOFFER LAKHT: TELLING THE TRUTH

Satire generally relates to particular local events and people, yet the satirical magazines in London and New York often shared (or stole) stories from each other, epitomizing the transnational nature of the diaspora experience.[54] "Der bloffer lakht" (The *Bloffer* laughs) is a series of five poems published in five issues of the *Bloffer* between 1911 and 1912.[55] They describe people's actions that show hypocrisy and expose them by the *Bloffer* laughing at their behavior. The name of the journal is vital in understanding the poem. It is similar but not identical to the English word "bluffer." The English word is lighter and has a sense of good-natured assurance in hoodwinking someone.[56] Prager translates the Yiddish *blofer* as "Fibber,"[57] and although *blofer* can include the lighter tone of the English "bluffer," in Yiddish bluffing is lying or cheating and the magazine's aim was to expose hypocrisy in a satirical way. The byline of the magazine rather paradoxically reads: *Ale mentshn zogn lign / kumt der bloffer zogt emes* (All people lie / The *Bloffer* comes to tell the truth). So, although it explains that it will expose the lying, it does also question whether a bluffer can tell the truth. This satirical edge may in fact be the license for the magazine to regularly name and shame or embarrass. Indeed, the final poem of the series satirized how the *Bloffer* magazine had come in for criticism and opponents had tried to close it down, but the *Bloffer* had survived the "hypocrites," the "capitalists," and the "flatterers," and was still laughing.[58] This verse was from the thirteenth edition of the *Bloffer*, and the magazine continued for another twenty-six issues.

The five "Der bloffer lakht" poems contain twenty-one verses in total, and each verse looks at another instance of hypocrisy. Some verses tell of generic events, such as a journalist writing from a position that he does not hold or a street beggar who has money in the bank.[59] However, it is likely that they were topical at the time, pointing at particular people in the small Yiddish-speaking enclave. Targeting individuals is clearer in a verse where a woman is being unfaithful with a lodger, and the cuckolded husband is named as Mr. Kimmel, presumably alluding to a real person, possibly a coded reference.[60] Other verses are directed at more obvious local targets. One tells of the new Yiddish theatre employing immigrant tradespeople as actors and the audience not noticing the lack of professionalism. Another tells of a fiery preacher using Talmudic references in his sermons, yet being a philanderer. A third describes how an unnamed "Lord" gives his gentile coachmen generous gifts, but will not support Jewish organizations such as the establishment of a Jewish hospital for the immigrants of the East End.[61] This news story was well known, strewn across the pages of the Jewish press in 1911, and hotly debated.[62] Immigrant East Enders were giving their hard-earned pennies to buy a plot of land that would become a Jewish hospital. Yet this was fiercely opposed by many in the Anglo-Jewish establishment, and in particular Lord Rothschild. His opposition was on the issue of Jewish separatism, and he argued that East End Jews should be using the London Hospital in Whitechapel.[63] The *Bloffer* exposé was not, therefore, the known news story; rather, the poem produced evidence that Rothschild gave generously to gentiles before East End Jews.

The cultural differences between the Anglo-Jewish community and the Yiddish-speaking immigrant community is raised again and again in "Der bloffer lakht," often pointing out the tension between sanitized philanthropy and real poverty on the ground in the East End. One verse praises a charitable institution that pays its workers well, yet when a pauper comes to its doorstep begging, the institution dismisses him unthinkingly. Another verse describes an Anglo-Jewish establishment figure, involved in community institutions, who gives charity to the East End soup kitchen yet also owns a sweatshop subjecting workers to low pay and long hours. Another engages in a more angry debate on the attempts to control the immigrant community by Anglo-Jewish authorities. The verse attacks the president of the Board of Deputies of British Jews for being familiar with the tenets of Judaism yet betting on races and behaving in a non-religious way, and still striving for total power and influence over *shechita* (ritual slaughter of animals for kosher food). These verses could be seen to draw a list of tensions and inequalities between the two sections of the Jewish community in England.[64]

A significant number of verses expose how opportunism is possible specifically because of the transnational nature of the immigrant community. Migration enabled a man to reject his past and re-create himself in a new place. He could use migration as an opportunity to improve his

CHAPTER 3

life, but moving countries could also be opportunistic and deceptive, as the verses of "Der bloffer lakht" attest:

Derlozn a vayb in der heym hot eyner,	He left a wife at home,
un keyn London iz er gekumen	And came to London
do hot er als bokher, fayner un shener	As a bachelor, more refined and beautiful
an ander vayb zikh gevolt nemen.	He wanted to take another wife.
Dervust hobn zikh di landslayt zayne	The people from his home town discovered it
un dos vayb im tsu der khupe gebrakht—	And brought his [original] wife to the wedding canopy—
gezen hot der bloffer di komishe sene	The *Bloffer* saw the comic scene
un zikh gut fun im oysgelakht.	And had a good laugh at him.[65]

The problem of deserted wives was well known. Some of the Yiddish press contained a classified section where people searched for missing husbands, attempting to reunite them with their responsibilities.[66] The same theme emerges some months later in another "Bloffer lakht" poem, suggesting their grounding in real life stories. The second poem tells of a man of letters who has two wives, maybe the same man as the previous poem. Clearly the *Bloffer* has already named him because the verse tells of how the twice-married man is so angry at being exposed in the *Bloffer* that he tries to close the journal. But the *Bloffer* further exposes these attempts and in the last line of the verse the *Bloffer* "sticks out his tongue and laughs."[67]

Not all problems of immigration were so high on the political agenda of the community. One verse concerned work and how lack of training of religious teachers could make deception easy. The verse runs:

Dort loyft a yidl, in a kurtsn rekl,	There runs a Jew in a short jacket
untern orem a sider, in der hant a shtekl.	Under his arm a prayer book, a stick in his hand.
A melamed iz er do, er lernt mit kinder,	He is a religious teacher here, teaches children.

86

THE TRANSNATIONAL SCOPE

un in der heym iz er gor—hert a vinder!	But back home—listen to this miracle! He was
A koval geven, ferdishe potkeves gemakht.	A blacksmith, made horseshoes.
Der bloffer veyst es, nor er shvaygt un lakht.	The *Bloffer* knows this, keeps quiet and laughs.[68]

This religion teacher has re-created himself through moving from Eastern Europe to London. It implies that he would not be deemed suitable to be a teacher if he was known to be a blacksmith because as a blacksmith in the old country he would not have been learned or religiously observant enough to be a religion teacher.

The *Bloffer* is critical of people who "change sides," and sees inconsistency in political thought or allegiance as hypocritical. One verse describes a fervent Zionist who tells other Jews to get away from anti-Semitism by going to live in the "motherland," but would never consider going there himself. Another scenario tells of a young man who was a Zionist in the old country and involved in community activities. Yet when he came to London he became first an anarchist and then a social democrat, and had an active role in a Jewish paper. The *Bloffer* laughs at his involvement in community politics and events in London with people who do not know his background.[69]

The London Yiddish lyrics contain an entangled cultural mix. They acknowledge the life that exists and is lived in London yet are part of a transnational framework that alludes to the Eastern European Jewish homeland, politics, and culture. The texts are messy, and despite being carefully constructed by Winchevsky, Nager, and other authors, references are often mixed up, merged, layered, and thrown one on top of the other. The texts seem to be crafted to reflect both the confusion of the cultural clash brought about by immigration and the richness of cultural depth as new ideas are encountered.

Lyrics that seem to be engaging with the acculturation process may not have aimed at making Jewish immigrants as English as those around them. Rather, they suggest the possibilities of a hybrid culture that can be inclusive of the multiple elements of the immigrants'

CHAPTER 3

changing identities. Long before multiculturalism, these texts hint at the reality of multiple identities. The texts described here are not isolated instances. The large quantity of Yiddish verse and song lyrics pushing similar messages creates a very animated and vibrant East End immigrant culture.

Politics: The Poetry of Morris Winchevsky's London Years

Morris Winchevsky, 1880s. From Abraham Cahan's memoir *Bleter fun mayn lebn*, vol. 3. New York: Forverts Association, 1926, 110a. From the Mazower Private Collection, with the permission of the Forverts Archive.

4

Debates and Ballads

Aroyf tshipsayd, nit vayt funem monument,	Up toward Cheapside, not far from the Monument,
shteyt oyf dem trotuar tog teglekh	Every day there stands on the pavement
a blinder man, vos halt in dare hent,	A blind man, holding in withered hands,
an opgenitstn instrument,	A worn out old instrument,
un shpilt a nign umgehoyer kleglekh.	And plays an immensely pitiful tune.[1]

From the early 1880s Jewish socialists were visible and audible on the streets of the East End. They were involved in labor struggles, and could be heard speaking at rallies and political meetings. Their main aim was getting workers involved in radical and revolutionary politics, and their views could also be found in print in the new Yiddish socialist press. One of the earliest socialist leaders was Morris Winchevsky, who spent fifteen years in London, writing and editing for the Yiddish press. He became a well-known poet who, from his mid-twenties in London, was nicknamed the *zeyde* (grandfather) of the sweatshop poets. His London poetry offers an insight into local politics of the time, and this chapter and chapter 5 consider a range of his poems and explore what they tell us about socialist perspectives on London immigrant life.

Morris Winchevsky was born Leopold Benzion Novokhovitch in 1856 in Yanove, a small town in Kovno, Lithuania, and brought up with

Yiddish as his mother tongue.² He had a traditional religious education in the Bible and Hebrew at home, and from the age of eleven studied in a Russian government school, where he learned Russian and later German. After finishing school he worked as a clerk interpreter in a bank while translating Russian poets into Hebrew and writing his own poetry.³ At age twenty he was influenced by the work of Aaron Lieberman and started writing for Lieberman's Hebrew socialist magazine *Ha-Emes* (The truth). A year later he moved to Königsberg, working for the German socialist movement and setting up a socialist journal in Hebrew, *Aseyfes khakhomim* (Meeting of the wise). During his time in Germany he read Bakunin and Lavrov and became involved in socialist activity. However, under Bismarck's first anti-socialist laws in 1878, Winchevsky was arrested for having letters from Lieberman in his possession. He was in prison for five months before being released on bail.⁴

Winchevsky arrived in London on 23 March 1879. In Whitechapel he was confronted with the desperate conditions for the mass of Jewish workers and he struggled to earn a living. A friend, shocked at seeing his squalid living situation, managed to get him work as a bookkeeper in a London branch of Zeligman's bank. Using the name Leopold Benedict in his job, Winchevsky continued to write socialist material under a number of pseudonyms. In order to communicate directly with Yiddish-speaking workers, Winchevsky chose to write in Yiddish, rather than Hebrew, Russian, German, or, indeed, English.⁵ He established, edited, and contributed to the London Yiddish socialist press, and set up the *Poylisher yidl*, writing most of the articles, editorials, feuilletons, and theatre reviews. In 1885 he was involved with creating the *Arbayter fraynd*, where he wrote the popular satirical column in the character of "Der meshugener filozof" (The crazy philosopher), and translated classics, such as Ibsen, into Yiddish to be serialized.⁶ He wrote *notitsn* (notes) on political events in the *Arbayter fraynd* and *Fraye velt* (Free world) and later edited and contributed to the social democratic *Veker* (Awakener). His poetry was published in all of these papers.

POSITIONING WINCHEVSKY

Winchevsky's overall aim was to be a *veker*, and so influence political debate. His desire was to help produce a cognitive rupture, where the political awakening was more important than the aesthetic means.[7] Although the power of poetry was the reason for his prolific output in verse, literary critics strongly criticized his poetic style, and his position in the canon of Yiddish poetry was hotly contested. The influential socialist writer A. Litvak saw Winchevsky as a successful *veker* but an unsuccessful poet, using childish couplets which were no more than "revolutionary *badkhones*" akin to Zunzer.[8] On the other side, biographers Abraham Bik and Kalman Marmor defended and analyzed the lyricism within his poetry.[9] Countering the criticism himself, Winchevsky argued that he was intentionally more an activist than a lyrical poet and would use any means in his power of writing to achieve his goal:

> If anyone who sings my praises finds more activism in my work than poetry, they should not forget that ... I did not publish anything that did not aim to awaken the Jewish worker: wake him, his brain, his heart and his class consciousness: force him to stand up, rub his eyes and ask himself: Who am I? What sort of world is this around me? How did I get fettered by religious cobwebs and political nonsense.... If you call this activism, very good. It makes no difference to me how I awaken. A stab in the ribs is as good as shining a large torch into closed eyes. If a laugh can awaken, I laugh. If a complaint does so, I complain. If a smile can draw a sympathetic look—I smile, if not I will try a sigh.[10]

Winchevsky lived in Whitechapel among the Jewish immigrant workers he wrote for, and he tried to engage them by writing poetry that was concerned with local issues and political and community debate. He drew pictures in his poetry of people and places that his readers could recognize and relate to, and gave opinions on current affairs and social and party politics. Some of these debates were happening in the wider English sphere, such as those on the nature of work and society, poverty and prostitution. Others were internal cultural controversies concerning religious inequalities and class corruption within the London Jewish world. The poems unequivocally state positions, do not hold punches, and are clear and direct. As such Winchevsky was a thorn in the side of the Anglo-Jewish establishment, who wanted to limit socialist activity and socialist publications.

CHAPTER 4

A dominant issue for socialist activists was not only class conflict and the attempt to integrate into existing labor organizations and trade unions but also engaging with modern secular thought.[11] Winchevsky's poetry encouraged acculturation by demanding that workers become involved with local union activity and English politics. As an internationalist, he was certainly not pushing an anglicization agenda, although that may have been a by-product, but rather suggesting engagement with current ideas as a first step toward revolution. The aim of the poetry was to move readers to a new way of thinking, a new way of understanding the world and a way of engaging with sophisticated ideas. Poetry, as a higher art form, could bring elegance and rhythm and encapsulate sharp, satirical punch lines in order to convey difficult ideas.

Winchevsky's first poem was published in the third issue of the *Poylisher yidl*. "Tsvey geslekh" (Two alleys) is a satire on gambling, written because "the plague of cards at that time . . . devastated many families' lives."[12] The poem tells the story of two rooms in two alleys on a Friday evening, the beginning of the Sabbath. In one a young woman is sitting with her hungry children waiting for her husband to come home with the week's pay. In the other room, the husband is gambling the pay away. The poem was so well received that the famous Yiddish actor Jacob Adler added it to his current theatre program and declaimed it from the stage of the Hebrew Dramatic Club in the same week it was published.[13] Winchevsky's friend and collaborator Philip Krantz, although positive about the subject matter, strongly criticized the "absurd" overusage of diminutives.[14] This contemporary criticism of his first poem stayed with Winchevsky for years as critics argued over his use of rhyme. Winchevsky was, in these early years, a pioneer, with few models for Yiddish poetic style, and although both Elyakum Zunzer and Abraham Goldfaden addressed social questions in their verse and song lyrics, they were not making the sort of political statements that Winchevsky had made in his Hebrew verse and wanted to continue to do in Yiddish.[15] Winchevsky began to write poetry regularly for the Yiddish press, contributing scores of poems. His complete works, edited by Marmor, comes to nine volumes, only one of which is poetry, yet it was his poetry that was popular, sung, and remembered.[16]

The Jewish socialism that Winchevsky propounded was not situated in any one socialist philosophy. The critic Shakhne Epstein claimed that

Winchevsky, Social Democratic Federation (SDF) membership card, 1893. From the Archives of the YIVO Institute for Jewish Research, New York.

Winchevsky "was from the beginning, not a socialist, not an anarchist, but simply a revolutionary."[17] It is true that Winchevsky did not ally himself with any one political party on the English left, supporting both the Social Democratic Federation (SDF) and the Socialist League (SL), and encouraging them to work together. Similarly, among the Jewish Left, he worked with both socialists and anarchists. He was situated in the camp of Marx and Engels, yet was "all party" and saw differences between socialists and anarchists as academic, calling the anarchists "stepbrothers" and "cousins." He considered it vital that they cooperate to establish unions, lead strikes, and maintain a community press and a club with a library and a reading room.[18] The *Arbayter fraynd* took on this principle of broad coalitions, as its first editorial stated: "The *Arbayter fraynd* will not chiefly be a one party paper. This means it will embrace all important opinions on different socialist questions, even when these opinions do not agree with ours. Our party is simply against today's society, against all injustice in the world, but we are friends of all socialists whatever opinions they have about socialist questions, which divide us now."[19]

CHAPTER 4

Winchevsky's transparent, nonpartisan stance allowed both socialists and anarchists to claim him as one of their own and to see him as fighting for their cause.[20] The anarchist sweatshop poet Dovid Edelshtadt had firsthand experience of New York's Lower East Side sweatshops. He admired Winchevsky's unique position and his ability to write about the effect of the sweating system on workers even though he himself had not worked in a sweatshop. In "Tsum meshugenem filozof" (To the mad philosopher), published in prime place on the front cover of the *Arbayter fraynd* in 1890, Edelshtadt penned the following:

Ikh bin farlibt in zayne tsayln . . .	I am in love with his lines . . .
Zayn shraybn derfilt mir mit hofenung un mut,	His writing makes me feel hope and courage,
dokh ken ikh zikh gut nit derklern:	Yet I cannot explain to myself well:
vi kumt in zayn tinter mayn harts blut?	How does my heart's blood come into his inkwell?
Vi kumen tsu im mayne trern?	How do my tears reach him?[21]

Yet, despite Edelshtadt's respect for Winchevsky, he felt hugely let down when, by 1890, the *Arbayter fraynd* was taken over by the anarchists, and Winchevsky and editor Konstantin Gallop left with other social democrats to set up the *Fraye velt*.[22] Edelshtadt regarded Winchevsky's departure from the *Arbayter fraynd* as an abandonment of both the anarchists and the principle of a broad Left and criticized him in the poem "Mayn muze":

Mit gleklekh kon mayn muze nit klingen . . .	My muse cannot ring with bells . . .
Zi vet ir kegner di hant nit derlangen,	She will not offer her hand to her opponent,
zi vet nit kushn zayn giftike lip,	She will not kiss his poisonous lips,
zi veyst, az ir kegners beste farlangen	She knows that her opponent's greatest desire
iz zen dem toyt fun ir printsip.	Is to see the death of her principle.[23]

Edelshtadt saw Winchevsky as defecting to the social democrat camp, and no longer prepared to fight under a banner inclusive of anarchism. His outrage, written with the passion of an abandoned lover, indicates the importance of Winchevsky's position as a nonpartisan figure of the Left and the strong feelings he evoked. Winchevsky's poetic response to Edelshtadt is full of injured feelings and righteous anger, evidently suspecting other agendas in play:

Du shtrofst mikh, shtrenger kritiker,	You reprove me, stern critic,
mit halb farshtelte reyd;	With half-disguised words;
ikh bin nit keyn politiker	I am not a politician
un zog: dos tut mir leyd.	And say: I am sorry.
. . .	. . .
Dayn ziser lider-klang,	Your sweet poetic sound,
volt klingen shener, herlekher	Would sound more beautiful, more magnificent
on kine in gezang.	Without envy in the verse.[24]

As the *Arbayter fraynd* was taken over by the anarchists in 1890, the leading lights of the Jewish socialist press migrated from London to New York.[25] It became impossible for the two groups, socialists and anarchists, to continue friendly contact. Winchevsky stayed in London, describing his new paper, *Fraye velt*, as the continuation of the *Arbayter fraynd*. The *Fraye velt* was run by socialist intellectuals who embraced the communist maxim as a front cover slogan: "From *each* according to *his ability*, to *each* according to *his need*." In its pages Winchevsky continued to argue his nonpartisan position. The 1892 poem "Parti politik" was an explicit statement of how he did not want to be pigeonholed into taking one position:

Ikh loz nit fartsamen	I won't let my way be barred
mayn veg durkh programen,	By political programs,
ikh ken keyn partey-man nit zayn;	I cannot be a party-man;
ikh ken mayn gevisn	I cannot bind and lock
nit binden un shlisn . . .	My conscience . . .
Ikh vil nit bashrenken	I do not want to limit

mayn moyekh tsu denken   My mind to think
azoy vi es denkt di partey.   Just as the party thinks.[26]

Marmor argued that Winchevsky was no longer seen as "all party" as much as "anti-party."[27] The poem earned him a rebuke from hardliners, and he was condemned as a party political activist who simply would not adhere to party discipline.[28]

In 1892, Winchevsky was involved in the establishment of a Jewish "general council." This council brought together almost all of the Jewish unions in London, including workers' associations and social democrats, into the Jewish Socialist Workers' Union. Their principal aim was to unite workers in strikes, boycotts, demonstrations, and political activism. From 1892 the Socialist Workers' Union published the weekly *Der veker*, with Winchevsky as the most significant and influential contributor of poetry and prose.[29]

AKHDES: PARTICIPATING IN LOCAL DEBATE

The short satirical poem "Akhdes" (Unity), published beside the *meshugener filozof* column in the *Arbayter fraynd*, can be seen to survey the Jewish landscape in London in 1890.[30] It lampoons a range of often religious positions including Anglo-Jewish and immigrant orthodox. However, a poem titled "Unity," written by the grandfather of Jewish socialism in 1890 when fierce debates were taking place across the community, cannot be taken at face value. One of the concepts that most angered socialists and, indeed, those who became Bundists a few years later, was the notion that Jews are a nation and united because they are Jews. The socialists did not consider any unity that cut across class, believing that Jewish workers had more in common with non-Jewish workers than with Jewish masters. Winchevsky, in this satire, attacks the phony unity of religion, and promotes the authentic unity of the proletariat, of workers of the world uniting.

"Akhdes" moves between broad statements about Jewish religious practice and the socialist position on workers' unity to the specificity of England and the peculiarities of debates happening within Anglo-Jewry. The poem is in three sections. The first starts with the assertion that everyone is united:

Yo mir zaynen ale eynik!	Yes we are all united!
tsi mir hobn fil tsi veynik,	Whether we have a lot or a little,
un mir zaynen ale brider,	And we are all brothers,
un mir davnen fun eyn sider.	And we pray from one prayer book.

These lines set the tone for what is to follow, oblique satire where the meaning is opposite to what is written. The claim that Jewish unity is based on religion, not class, indicates how this poem will turn ideas on their head. The idea of Jews praying from the same prayer book was not simply a version of the colloquial expression "singing from the same hymn sheet." "Akhdes" was published a mere four weeks after the publication of the Authorized Daily Prayer Book of the United Hebrew Congregations of the British Empire translated by Rabbi Simeon Singer. This was a long-awaited publication which attempted to be inclusive in two ways. Firstly, it included all important prayers, both daily and Sabbath prayers and a range of prayers for specific occasions usefully collected in one book. Secondly, there was a new English translation that aimed at using English that was comprehensible to all English speakers. The *Jewish Chronicle* reviewed it: "The translation is accurate without being pedantic, while the language, graceful and melodious though it be, is equally simple and prayerful. Mr Singer has gone to the age of Milton and of the Authorised Version of the Bible for inspiration: and the result is that the new edition of our prayer-book presents a pure and idiomatic rendering in place of the high-flown extravagances that disfigure so many of the earlier edition ... [of] more than a century ago."[31] This attempt to produce a unified prayer book across the Anglo-Jewish communities may have been scholarly, useful, and beautiful; however, it was not a prayer book for the whole Jewish community. It was for the Anglo-Jews, translated into *English*, and deliberately designed to look from the cover like the Christian Book of Common Prayer.[32] The attempt at unity in the prayer book was one of selective unity which did not include the culture of the Yiddish-speaking East End *khevres* where Jews did not speak or read English.[33] The statement about all praying from one prayer book therefore satirized the way that Anglo-Jewish culture was not representative of the community.

This is made clearer in the second section of the poem, which lists the differences among Jews living in England. Winchevsky makes fun of the smaller and smaller units of identity where people cannot unite:

CHAPTER 4

Kurtse peyes, lange peyes,	Short sidelocks, long sidelocks,
yidn mit un on matbeyes...	Jews with and without money...
frume kep un kep fun zinders,	Religious heads and heads of sinners,
kep in yarmelkes, tsilinders,	Heads in skullcaps, top hats,
ale zaynen nor eyn folk.	But everyone is one people.

The different length of sidelocks refers to different types of immigrant orthodox sects. Sidelocks were worn by both Hasidim and *misnagdim*, yet philosophies and styles of prayer were different between the two groups and also between subgroups. Khevres and *shtiblekh* (Hasidic prayer rooms) were often bitterly divided by different customs, outlook, and attendant fashion. One could see by the style of clothing and sidelocks which sect an orthodox man belonged to. Because the orthodox were generally immigrant workers, Winchevsky reiterates the inversion of the socialist dogma like a running gag, claiming that differences are irrelevant, that unity exists across class, and that there is unity between rich and poor because everyone is a Jew.

The poem continues by alluding to antagonism between Anglo-Jewry and immigrant orthodoxy. With short phrases and amusing rhymes, the poem suggests the absurdity of the idea that we are all equal. The word *zinder* (sinner) is rhymed with *tsilinder* (top hat). The obvious jibe here is that the skullcaps are on the religious heads of the poor Jews without money, and the top hats, which mimic the style of the Anglican churches, are worn by the moneyed and sinning Anglo-Jews. The humor is at the expense of any nuance, because the broad categories of good and bad, rich and poor, immigrant and Anglo-Jewish are easy jibes.

The final section of the poem returns to addressing the immigrant community, suggesting that all workers are united whatever their belief, with the line *frum un link, fareynikt ale* (Religious and left, all are united). The word *frum* denotes immigrant orthodox rather than Anglo-Jewish, and perhaps this phrase is the East End Jewish version of "workers of the world unite." Then follow nine lines of inseparable unions:

Vi der khosn mit der kale,	Like the bride and groom,
vi der bezem mitn shtekn,	Like the broom and stick,

vi di tsitses mit di ekn	Like the fringes with tassels
vi di tir mit der mezuze . . .	Like the door with the mezuzah . . .
vi der khumesh mit der rashe	Like the Torah with Rashi [commentary]
vi der kugl mit der kashe . . .	Like the potato cake and the buckwheat . . .
vi der klezmer mitn tants.	Like the musician and the dance.

Amid the religious items of *tsitses* (ritual fringes worn by men under their clothes) and *mezuze* (a scroll with prayers placed on the doorpost) and the Bible and the Sabbath foods, there is a dig at the conflict on the Left, alluded to by the broom representing anarchism. This poem was published during the time when divisions between socialists and anarchists were becoming intense with constant angry debate in meetings and in the socialist Yiddish press. It was only six months later that the socialists felt compelled to leave the *Arbayter fraynd* as it became an anarchist paper.

The unity of the poem's title may refer to the false unity of religion and the real unity of class. However, the subject of unity was also being debated in the Anglo-Jewish community. Chief Rabbi Nathan Adler had died six months earlier, leading to discussion about continuity. In February 1890 two letters were printed in the *Jewish Chronicle* under the title "Unity, Not Uniformity." Both letters argued that Adler's death was a turning point, creating an opportunity to overtly address disagreements within the Anglo-Jewish community concerning synagogue practice.[34] Responses argued variously: that the debate must include the Federation of Synagogues for the sake of "communal unity"; that the incoming chief rabbi should "steer a middle course between the extremes"; that Reform should be included; that there should be a united Jewish divorce procedure; and that the chief rabbi should live in the East End.[35] "Unity" was high on the topical agenda, with the word itself repeatedly used. Winchevsky's poem of the same title sat in the midst of this topical discussion.

The first line of "Akhdes" begins with the word *Yo* (yes), implying that there was a question to which this was an answer. However, whether there was a specific question or not, Winchevsky's poetic response was his contribution to the debate. The central idea asserted that rather than unity, there was antagonism between rich and poor Jews, Yiddish-speaking orthodox and Anglo-Jews, Yiddish-speaking orthodox and socialist Jews, socialist and Anglo-Jews, and factions within orthodox Yiddish-speaking Jews. It even hinted at fractures in the Left.

Although Winchevsky may have used the word *akhdes* to highlight the discussion on unity in Anglo-Jewry, the poem is mostly lampooning the debate by asserting that Anglo-Jewish forms of unity are fictive. The only objective unity is that of the working class and its relation to the means of production, as opposed to any fellow feeling based on religion. The poem was written for a socialist audience, who would no doubt have appreciated the creativity of its celebrity activist producing a satire with a lightness of touch and a fearless lack of deference. Despite the poem's local and political flavor, a reworked and depoliticized adaptation, *Ale brider* (All brothers) became a popular song across the Yiddish-speaking world.[36]

KINDER FUN'S FOLK: LONDON SILHOUETTES

Winchevsky's engagement with local issues did not always take the form of satire. In his memoirs, he recalls how he produced a series of poems "written under the influence of the terrible poverty around me,—from this poverty in all its nakedness, tattered, rancidity that one can see only in London."[37] They were published individually in the Yiddish press between 1884 and 1891, and later twenty-four poems were brought together under the title *Kinder fun's folk: londoner siluetn* (The nation's children: London silhouettes).[38] We have already encountered two of these poems, "London bay nakht" and "Tsvey geslekh." Both these poems connected with local ideas and social problems, and are indicative of the *siluetn* as a series of poems. Although Winchevsky had experienced poverty in his youth in Lithuania, he regarded the poverty in London as worse than that of Kovno, because he was seeing it with the eyes of a conscious socialist. It was therefore a deliberate strategy to write lyrical, sentimental, and despondent ballads that describe the bitterest parts of working-class life and the fight for survival.[39] Ballads are an accessible form of storytelling, and Winchevsky's ballads do so with pathos, and usually with a sharp social comment in a chorus line. The descriptions, directed at the worker, explored the inequality of a system that created poverty, and they appealed to the worker to respond with anger, as anger was the only emotion that would be productive of change.[40]

Winchevsky's determination as to the value of anger can be seen in the poem "Tsum nayem yor" (To the New Year), not in the *siluetn*. It tells the story of the emotions of a seventy-year-old man who never shows anger. The old man condemns the old year with sadness, prays for food with bitterness, buries his child with grief, and finally dies calmly. The New Year responds with the argument that the appropriate response to all these events should have been anger. Anger alone has the power to make change.[41]

Winchevsky's approach to stimulating the anger he regarded as necessary to combat poverty was to portray the worst of what he saw in a simple narrative, explaining that "the worst" meant the sight of a child languishing, hungry, starving, sick, and begging.[42] He therefore focused on tales of children in poverty in London working for their living and the effect hardship had on their lives. In "Oremer yosel" (Pauper Joe), a small boy sells wares from a couple of boxes on the street. The poem's narrator questions the boy about the importance of cleanliness, education, and honesty. Despite the narrator's increasing insistence that knowledge is the only way out of poverty, to each question the boy replies in a repeated chorus chant: *Ikh muz fardinen mayn broyt*, that his only priority is to earn enough to eat.[43]

"A meydele in der siti" (A little girl in the city) follows a homeless orphan selling matches in Cornhill, London's financial district. The tiny girl stands in the rain and thunder repeating *Koyft bay mir metshes mayn her!* "(Buy my matches, Sir!) / Two boxes a penny, one penny the pair!" as she is surrounded by brokers and office workers, rushing past her to their workplaces.[44] This poem, published in 1885, carefully constructs the place where the child is selling by pinpointing its exact location. *Lebn der berze, dem templ fun shvindl* (Near the stock exchange, the temple of swindle). And to refine it further, the poet asks in verse three, does she sleep, like Rowland Hill, in Cornhill? Rowland Hill was a Victorian postal and education reformer, who himself has no connection to the poem. However, in 1881 a statue of him was erected opposite the stock exchange. So sleeping like Rowland Hill meant outdoors and homeless. The mention of Rowland Hill may further refine the location, yet

CHAPTER 4

comparing a small sleeping child to a huge stone statue reinforces the difference between rich and poor, respected and ignored, stone and flesh. The visual picture is striking and demands that readers imagine the little girl on her own selling matches in an area of huge wealth. Although Cornhill is not far from the East End, it is unlikely to be an area that immigrants frequented, yet they would have known the name, heard about the new statue, or read a financial story in the papers.

One of the clearest examples of a sentimental poem demanding a response is "Dray shvester" (Three sisters), which also begins with a familiar landmark. It tells the story of three sisters working in Leicester Square in the West End of London:

In england iz do a shtot lester,	In England there is a town called Leicester,
in london iz do aza skver,	In London there is such a square,
in skver shteyen teglekh dray shvester,	Each day three sisters stand in the square,
di meydlekh,—zey ken ver-nit-ver.	The girls—everybody knows them.[45]
Di yingste farkoyft dortn blumen,	The youngest sells flowers there,
di mitelste—bendlekh fun shikh	The middle one—shoelaces
un shpet in der nakht zet men kumen	And late at night you can see approaching
di eltste vos handlt mit zikh.	The oldest, who sells herself.[46]

"Dray shvester" not only described and commented on poverty, but was written within the context of campaigns on the age of consent, prostitution, and the white slave trade. In 1885 William Stead, editor of the *Pall Mall Gazette*, had produced a sensational piece of journalism published as "The Maiden Tribute of Modern Babylon." Stead had gone undercover to expose child prostitution abuses in London, aiming to publicize and campaign against the low age of consent. The report gave detailed accounts of the trade in young women and girls, publishing anonymous interviews and testimonies with people involved in the trade including trafficked girls, and disclosing the process of procuring underage and virgin girls. The "Maiden Tribute" shocked the public and may have been a contributing factor to Parliament's raising the age of consent from thirteen to sixteen in the Criminal Law Amendment Act of 1885.[47] In Winchevsky's poem, age is a clear focus. The sister who sells her body is the oldest of the three, although that does not tell us whether or not she was over the age of consent. However, Winchevsky did not simply reference a topical issue; he added a socialist perspective through the words of his characters:

Di yingere beyde batrakhtn	The two younger ones both think of
di eltere shvester on has;	Their older sister without hatred;
den ale dray meydlekh farakhtn	Because all three girls despise
di velt un di shtot un di gas.	The world and the town and the street.

The last line of the verse makes the sisters the instrument for arguing that the capitalist system is the problem, not the individual. The sisters hate society, not each other. Yet their anger is mixed with helplessness. The final stanza shows the sisters at home with their tears drenching the shoelaces and flowers.[48] This poem captured the imagination of its audience, became immediately popular and set to music, and was still being sung decades later.[49]

"Dray shvester" is not the only poem in the *Siluetn* that raises the subject of prostitution and how it affects children. Only a few hundred yards from Leicester Square was the Strand, an area "crowded with prostitutes . . . openly soliciting in broad daylight."[50] The poem "Oyfn strend" (On the Strand) concerns the young child of parents who take her with them to the pub to drink their pay rather than buying food for the Sabbath.[51] The pub is seen as a place where the horrors of hunger can be forgotten. We see the neglect of childhood superimposed on the busy Strand. Theatreland is conjured with dandies and a murky world. The poem raises the question as to whether this approach to bringing up children will give the girl *a tam fun a laykhtern lebn, /a lebn fun meydlekh in strend* (a taste of the easier life, / the life of a girl in the Strand). The poem's last lines are *fardungene libe vert munter, / di shande mit tunkl farshtelt* (Rented love becomes cheerful, / shame is disguised in the darkness). The poem tells a story; it observes rather than condemns, questions rather than suggests. It pits the decadent theatre world against the world of immigrant poverty, where the dandy's behavior is counterpointed with the child's innocence.

The *Londoner siluetn* are full of memorable images of youngsters in London, showing them as victims in their parents' lives, and often ending tragically. "Rent" describes the fate of a family after the death of the father and wage-earner Barnet Mass of Berner Street in the East End, leaving his pregnant wife unable to pay the rent, and ending in the death of her baby.[52] Another shocking poem, "Di farfroyrene" (The frozen ones), tells of parents and three children wandering homeless in the English frost. The setting is not London, but a mythical English "forest" where they freeze to death.[53] Abraham Bik compared "Di farfroyrene" to a similar poem by Heine where two unfortunates freeze to death in an attic on a winter night. Heine's children die from cold and hunger and the message is a tragic one. Under Winchevsky's pen, the deaths are not tragedies but sacrifices to the system. Bik argues that the comparison between Heine and Winchevsky strengthens the socialist message by highlighting the differences between the poems.[54] Of course this assumes that the audience would know the Heine poem, but using the structure of a known poem is a useful strategy, as seen in the analysis of *London bay nakht*, which uses the same device, in chapter 3.

Most of the poems in the *Siluetn* are full of sentimental pathos, attempting to create representative images that make general points about poverty, child labor, education, and prostitution. The children in the ballads "Dray shvester" and "A meydele in der siti" may or may not have been Jewish. Winchevsky often makes no mention of ethnicity, so that when he does it changes the emphasis and is clearly a conscious choice. The aforementioned "Oremer Yosel" was first published in the *Tsukunft* in 1885 and uses the Jewish name Yosel in the title, even though the boy's name is not mentioned in the poem itself. When later published in the *Siluetn* in 1910, the poem was renamed "Der yoseml" (The young orphan), removing the reference to his Jewishness.

The choice of making the characters in the poems universal potentially gave them a wider audience. The song "Dray shvester" survived over a hundred years, and is currently in the repertoire of the singer Karsten Troyke. Troyke explained that he had learned the song from the Argentinian actress Cipe Lincovsky, who had been singing it as part of her own repertoire. Troyke explained: "Cipe told me, that Helene Weigel [widow of Bertolt Brecht and then chief of his theatre] handed the lyrics to her, saying that Brecht loved the song for being so strong with the social idea—because the sisters blame the circumstances and society for being a prostitute, not their sister herself."[55] Brecht's response to the song was not as a Jewish poem but as a socialist poem with an international message.

Winchevsky wanted to ensure his readers would relate to the poems, but making the sisters in "Dray shvester" clearly Jewish may have been too shocking. Writing in Yiddish for a Jewish audience, however, Winchevsky did not need to make the children Jewish to touch a raw nerve sparking people's fears for their own families. The poem "Di oreme maria" (The pauper Maria) tries to shock his reader into anger with a mixture of comedy, satire, and a sharp punch line. The poem describes how British justice binds the poor into an impossible cycle of poverty. Maria, probably a teenager, is left to look after her orphaned siblings. Unemployed during the slack season, she is destitute and desperate. First she begs, then steals, then solicits to make money for food. When given a shilling, she drinks it to drown her sorrows, and finally tries to drown herself. Each time she is caught and jailed by a pompous magistrate who declares begging, stealing, soliciting, being drunk in public, and attempting suicide to be "strictly forbidden in England." The seventeen-verse poem is split into six sections, with the first five sections repeating the same three lines, substituting the first word:

Betlen in england iz shtrengstens farbotn.	Begging in England is strictly forbidden.
Un dos derklert ir der her magistrat,	So the magistrate explained to her,
velkher zet oys zeyer kreftik un zat.	Who appeared healthy and well fed.[56]

The magistrate and Maria are caricatures. They could be characters in a music-hall song with a running gag: the poor and feisty Maria set against the pompous arrogant magistrate. The poem is on the edge of comedy, where the repetition, rhythm, and song-like rhyming structure create a wry humor. The story is tragic, yet makes fun of the legal system where even attempted suicide is forbidden in England. At the end of the poem, Maria dies of hunger on the streets. The shock of the final verse slams a lid on the humor, ramming home the message that a system that gave no legal assistance to the most poor is unjust. Maria lies dead in an unknown place, and the poet asks:

Ver veyst, tsi veyst zi—az shtarbn fun noyt,	Who knows if she knows—that starving from want,
mit a GEZETSLEKHN, RUIKN toyt,	With a *legal, peaceful* death,
IZ NIT in fraye medines farboten.	*Is not* forbidden in free countries.

"Di oreme maria," like other poems in the *siluetn*, takes the side of the debate that blamed the capitalist system that kept the poor in poverty, and are ultimately anti-capitalist. The silhouettes depicted are shadows or outlines of young people and, as such, serve to show the stories as examples or generalizations of a wider political message. These poems were written at a time when there was a particular focus on poverty. In 1885 the *Pall Mall Gazette* published the results of a survey by the Social Democratic Federation (SDF) that showed that 25 percent of Londoners lived in poverty. The social reformer Charles Booth, skeptical about these figures, did his own ethnographic research. His survey of the East End was published in 1889 and found that the degree of poverty was even higher than the SDF had claimed.[57] Winchevsky was a member of the SDF, and his poetry can be seen as writing from within the debate about the extent of poverty in London, encouraging workers to take part in the discussion.

Setting poems in a London context is a strategy to draw in readers through local knowledge, and this has additional poignancy when the readers are immigrants just getting to know the city. Jewish immigrants may never have been in London's business district or West End. Indeed, the words *strend*, *lester skver*, and *Roland hil* may never have been written in Yiddish before. Although the *siluetn* and *Akhdes* are set in a London context, they offer glimpses into wider debates. Through satire or sentiment, they challenge the reader to generate an opinion. Winchevsky wanted to go further, however, than just creating empathy through his poetry: he wanted to create activists.

5

Making Socialist Activists

Ven es vet der shtrayt baginen	When the fight begins
far di frayhayt, gegn gelt,	For freedom, against money,
vet ir efsher mikh gefinen	You may find me
in di reyen oyfn feld.	In the ranks in the battlefield.
Dortn vel ikh mayne brider	There I won't lead my brothers
firn nit als general,	Like a general,
ikh vel nor mit frayhayts-lider	Instead I will encourage them everywhere
zey ermuntern iberal.	With freedom poems.
Den tsum kamf vet men badarfn,	Since for the struggle we will need,
yenem tog fun hits un drang,	On that heated and driven day,
khuts dem biks, dem shverd dem sharfn,	Besides the rifle and sharp sword,
a bagaystertn gezang.	An inspired song.[1]

Winchevsky repeatedly stated that his sole purpose was to be a *veker*. He wanted to transform workers from being indifferent to politics and paralyzed by poverty and exhaustion to being informed and interested activists in the struggle. He demanded concrete engagement with intellectual and practical ideas. This chapter analyzes poetry that can be seen to use three different strategies to achieve this aim. Firstly, there are poems that use socialist polemic to explain theoretical concepts and provide a memorable mnemonic for understanding socialist philosophy. Secondly, there are rhyming *notitsn* (notes) that engage with current politics, proffering opinions and stimulating discussion of political events. Thirdly, there are sung poems, with anthems and marching songs for union activism, designed for crowds to sing at demonstrations and rallies. The final section of the chapter explores how contemporary critics assessed the body of Winchevsky's poetic work.

TSUM ARBAYTER FRAYND: DISPLAYING SOCIALIST IDEAS

The reality of many workers' daily lives was work in the sweating system, and Winchevsky wrote several poems that attempted to explain sweating and capitalism from a socialist perspective. Poems are not polemical essays, yet these socialist verses can be seen as political tracts. They use similar techniques to oratory: repetition of ideas in different forms, simplification of ideas, and a personal approach in speaking directly to workers. These are the types of poems sung or read out in political events.[2] They are forthright and do not shy away from criticizing the worker for inactivity.

One of Winchevsky's techniques drew on generalized "types," such as contrasting narratives that focused on the opposites of "rich" and "poor." The rich are shown as corrupt and heartless, squandering resources for their own pleasure. The poor are portrayed as downtrodden and, more often than not, ignorant. The poem "Tsum Arbayter fraynd" (To the *Arbayter fraynd* [the meaning is "worker's friend," but the poem is an ode to the newspaper of that name]) written in 1885 seeks to explain the inequality arising from the split between workers and masters, consumers and producers. It questions who owns the fruits of one's labor and who benefits from them, and answers that the workers "sacrifice their brain for their body." It is workers

Vos neyen un trogn aleyn nit di kleyder,	Who sew but do not wear the clothes themselves,
vos boyen far andere hayzer mit mi,	Who labor to build houses for others,
un voynen aleyn in a finstern kheyder,	And live alone in a dark room,

MAKING SOCIALIST ACTIVISTS

tsuzamengeshtupt, vi in shtaln di fi;	Stuffed together like cattle in stalls;
vos horeven nor, um tsu makhn di gvir'n	Who only work to make the rich
alts raykher durkh dem, vos dem oremen felt,	Even richer through that which the poor worker lacks,
un lozn zikh kireven, traybn un firn,	And submit to being steered, driven and led,
vi oksn in sokhe, vi oksn in feld.	Like oxen in the yoke, like oxen in the field.[3]

The theme is a standard socialist axiom repeated in much of the poetry. It offers a theoretical perspective on workers' alienation that is a step toward understanding a Marxist idea. The folklorist Ruth Rubin traced the theme of workers creating and producing what they cannot own in a number of Yiddish, German, and American poems, all taking their inspiration from Shelley's "Song to the Men of England," written in 1819.[4] By using the standard tropes of the movement, Winchevsky's verse was part of a wider poetic tradition of socialist verse.

As part of their self-elected role as paternalistic educators, the socialists were often didactic with the nonresponsive worker, and Winchevsky was not shy in admonishing workers for their passivity. The thirteen-stanza poem from 1891, "Tsu di arbayter: nokh a tsuruf" (To the worker: Another call), moves beyond the description of starving workers sowing seeds and naked workers sewing clothes, and urges them to be proactive in changing the situation:

Dokh ir kvart un dart	Here you shrivel up and wither
un derlangt zikh keyn rir;	And do not stir yourself;
farblendt, farnart,	Deluded, fooled,
ot zitst ir un vart,	You just sit and wait,
zogt, oyf vemen vart ir?	Speak, who are you waiting for?[5]

The reprimands are taken further in the poem of 1892, "More shkhoyre" (Depression), which offers an explanation of how workers make the tools of their oppression, and ends up blaming the worker:

CHAPTER 5

Di fabrikantn lozn aykh on kreftn . . .	The manufacturers leave you without strength . . .
Fun ayer dumheyt makhn zey gesheftn . . .	They make businesses from your stupidity . . .
Ir shmidt aleyn far ayer guf di keytn,	You forge the chains for your own body,
ir flekht aleyn far ayer haldz di shtrik;	You braid the rope for your own neck;
ir helft aleyn far zikh dem nets farshpreytn,	You help spread the net for yourself,
ir boyt aleyn dem fangers festn brik.	You yourself build the capturer's firm bridge.[6]

The workers' employers may be a variety of people: master tailors (sweaters), manufacturers, and businessmen, and all of them are *raykhe* (rich). Also written in 1892, the poem "Vi di raykhe layt lebn" (How the rich live) runs to forty-eight verses. The six-line descriptions of rich people's lives are vignettes of moments that build up to an understanding of the other side. The rich include an elegantly dressed flatterer, a traveler squandering his money on happiness, a journalist of sleaze, a banker's gambling son, a hypocritical preacher, and a corrupt lawyer. The descriptions highlight their hypocrisy, and show how their wealth makes them gamble, womanize, and patronize balls and concerts. The poem's first vignette describes a man who became rich through an upwardly mobile path from worker, to master/sweater, to usurer:

Eyner iz a sveterl	One is a sweater
biz er vert a feterl	Until he becomes a pawnbroker [literally "little uncle"]
un layt gelt oyf protsent;	And lends money for interest;
layt gelt ruik zitsndik,	Lends money calmly sitting,
roykhndik, nit shvitsndik,	Smoking, not perspiring,
vi frier arbeter-hent.	Like earlier worker's hands.[7]

For the socialists, the path of upward mobility was fraught with ideological problems. Workers had to remain workers and fight as workers. If they were upwardly mobile and became sweaters, they had abandoned the fight and become traitors, the enemy, the rich. Upward mobility is shown to be a dirty business with a momentum that leads from worker to master to lending money for profit. Winchevsky's solution to poverty is not to leave the working class through upward mobility.

The dignity of work is a theme that emerges in a number of poems. The poem "Akhdes" (Unity), analyzed in detail in chapter 4, sets up disunities:

Yo mir zaynen ale eynik! . . .	Yes we are all united! . . .
Say mir shnaydn pantalones,	Whether we are cutting trousers,
say mir shnaydn op kupones.	Or whether we are cutting out coupons.[8]

This couplet contrasts two ways of making money: working in the tailoring trade within the sweating system, and cutting coupons. The coupons refer to charity coupons given by organizations such as the Jewish Board of Guardians in preference to cash handouts.[9] The socialists abhorred the idea of financial assistance by a paternalistic organization because it went contrary to workers identifying as workers and earning their money from their labor. "Akhdes" argues that these different ways of acquiring money are not equal. The message of the dignity of work was so important to Winchevsky that he used it as the front motto of the *Poylisher yidl*, in a quote from Psalm 128: *Yegiye kapekho ki soykhel ashrekho vetoyv lokh* (When you enjoy the fruits of your own labor you will be happy and prosper). In the first edition of the *Poylisher yidl* in 1884, Winchevsky's editorial explained the motto as the raison d'être of the newspaper. It argued that when the *Poylisher yidl* became a paper that the workers were proud to call their own, "then we will hold the awl, the needle, the plane, and the hammer in more esteem than the scissors that cut the coupons."[10]

Later in the same year, the *Poylisher yidl* published "A khoydesh on arbayt" (A month without work), which begins as follows:

Ikh bet nit NEDOVES	I ask for no *charity*
fun vegn ZKHUS-OVES,	For the *merits of the fathers*,
farhoreven vil ikh mayn broyt.	I will work for my bread.
Nit betlen, nit shnoren,	Not beg, not plead,

CHAPTER 5

tsu ktsinim nit forn,   not go to a rich man,
nit vartn oyf raykhe layts toyt . . .   not wait for a rich man to die . . .
Mayn shtolts iz mayn HANDVERK   My pride is my *handiwork* alone.[11]
aleyn.

The emphasized phrase "merits of the fathers," in this context, means the luck of being born a Jew, because it was only Jewish workers who could partake of the charitable support provided by the Jewish Board of Guardians. In his memoirs, Winchevsky described how he came to write the poem. Coming out of a meeting in Whitechapel at one o'clock in the morning, he saw the effect of the slack time, which left workers unemployed and hungry. Outside the meeting there were beggars: "People who lick rich people's plates, who assume that their poverty is a natural phenomenon. . . . Their remedy for the 'slack' is going to the Board of Guardians. . . . With boys coming over having to work for London sweaters, never having been an artisan back home, it's easy for them to fall into being a beggar. One has to get them from the beginning, to feel the importance of work and the lowliness of begging."[12]

The word "handiwork" in the poem is written in anglicized Yiddish, and reflected the fact that the debates about productivity and taking pride in physical work were taking place in English socialist circles. At the time Winchevsky was writing, there was debate between William Morris and Oscar Wilde, Morris arguing for an aesthetics of labor and Wilde skeptical about the talk of the dignity of manual labor.[13] Winchevsky's contribution draws immigrants into the debate by putting his poetry in the workplace, as he wrote of "A khoydesh on arbayt": "Within two weeks there is a borrowed melody and the song is in every workshop."[14]

Winchevsky's poetry that explains socialist politics does so in sound bites with rhythmic momentum and memorable phrases. They demand an overthrowing of the class system, and an end to poverty and inequality in concepts that are broad and generic. Yet he also focuses on more specific local politics with greater detail.

NOTITSN: CURRENT AFFAIRS

As early as 1885 there had been complaints by readers to the *Arbayter fraynd* editor about the level of complexity in their articles. They were seen as too theoretical and complicated and did not relate to their worker-readers' lives. *Arbayter fraynd* editor Philip Krantz, in an attempt to increase readership, commissioned Winchevsky to write a column called *notitsn* (notes). The column concentrated on topical politics, but was written in short, concise paragraphs. Krantz hoped that shorter articles would be more accessible and draw the reader in more quickly than longer pieces.[15] When Winchevsky left the *Arbayter fraynd* and set up the *Fraye velt*, he took the notitsn column with him, but now added a rhyming verse to follow the prose.[16] These verse-notitsn created an additional perspective and, although connected to the prose, stood alone as poems. On the page they were eye-catching and accessible and tended to encapsulate the nugget of an idea. They added sentiment and humor to the argument and created a different type of contribution to the debate.

Between 1891 and 1892 there were dozens of notitsn. Around half the poetic notitsn concerned British politics and Irish Home Rule. The other half comprised news from abroad, often from the immigrants' countries of origin. One *notits* was in the form of a conversation between "Alexander the idiot" and "Wilhelm the insane" (Tsar Alexander III and German emperor Wilhelm). Others included an angry piece on the death of "the swine" Moltke the Elder, a piece on the sad love life of the son of the Romanian king, a death notice for the Chilean president, and a piece mocking Bismarck. The notitsn analyzed in this section, however, concern British politics made relevant to the immigrant Jews of Whitechapel.

A notits of May 1891 offers an opinion on the national census of the previous month. The prose section argues that the census collection only counted heads because it was convenient. Had it counted the sufferings of those heads, it would have produced an altogether different statistic. The verse follows a similar line of argument:

Zey tseyln di kep, ale tsen yor amol,	They count heads every ten years,
tsu visn oyf klor fun di mentshn dem tsol,	To know precisely the number of people,
vos voynen in dize gebentshte medine;	Who live in this blessed country;
zey tseylen di kep, on a shum nafke-mine,	They count heads without differentiating,

Front page of the *Fraye velt*, July 1891, showing the notitsn column. From the Mazower Private Collection.

tsi zaynen di aynvoyner zat, oder nit,	Whether the inhabitants are well fed, or not,
oykh hertser tsebrokhene tseylen zey nit.	And they do not count broken hearts.[17]

These highly rhythmic couplets, with rhymes both midline and end-of-line, allow for a punch line that gives it an emotional edge missing from the prose section. The verse implies that the census is useless because bald statistics do not tell you about lived life, and it does not see the people it counts. This notits must have connected with immigrants' suspicion or cynicism of filling in official forms, wondering how it would help or damage their situation and their abilities to feed their families and deal with loss and readjustment. Winchevsky's viewpoint touches on their particular experiences.

A notits of three months later responds to the Elementary Education Act of 1891, which offered grants to schools so that parents would not have to pay directly for schooling. Winchevsky was critical of this measure, seeing it as funded by raised taxes:

> The government throws down a bone; free schools. The workers' children finally get free schools and universities. The English worker will be in the same happy position as the Jew in Whitechapel.[18] He will lose the few pennies a week that could have been earned. The [government] money [to make free schools] comes from the 90 million pounds they tear out annually from the people. This [the workers'] money comes from the extra bits a family would have saved for their children's education. "What a swindle the whole story is."[19]

The verse that follows is written in the style of a playground skipping song:

Zey gibn a peni un nemen a fund,	They give a penny and take a pound,
ir zayt di bal-khoyves,	You are the debtor,
un zey di bal-toyves.	And they, the benefactor.
Zey gibn aykh makes un nemen gezund.	They give you plagues, and take your health.[20]

CHAPTER 5

Although the prose carries more detail, the verse extends the argument, pitting the government against parents in a similar way to pitting master against worker. Writing the piece in the form of a skipping song put the child at the center of the debate. This law affected all parents, and the prose notits compared English and immigrant families, showing the connection between them and demanding that immigrant parents respond to their English world.

Commenting on British politics may have been a first step toward engaging the worker in progressive politics. Winchevsky's practical yet profoundly radical attitude is exemplified in a short notits of July 1892 concerning the upcoming British general election:

Der liberale zogt, dzhek muz im helfn, vayl er iz zayn fraynd.	The Liberal says, Jack must help him Because he is his friend.
Der konservator zogt: mayn buzem efnt zikh far dzhekn haynt.	The Conservative says: My heart Opens to Jack today.
Baym sheynker kumt oys, dzhek iz zayner un er lozt im nit avek.	The publican contends that Jack is his And will not let him go.
Der vaser-mentsh shrayt: ikh bin dayner un du mayner, liber dzhek!	The teetotaler shouts: I am yours And you are mine, dear Jack!
Der git im tey, der git a shnepsl	One gives him tea, another gives him a drink
yener firt im in karetn;	Someone else leads him in carriages;
primroz-damen kushn, gletn;	The primrose-women kiss, caress;
un dzhek—er shtimt far zey, der shepsl.	And Jack—he votes for them, the sheep.[21]

The poem mocks the strategies used by different parties to court the worker to vote for them. Yet the critique is really directed at the worker for falling for their promises. Winchevsky does not suggest whom the worker should vote for, and merely goads the voting worker to think independently. The humor in the satirical final line assumes that they would not want to be taunted as a "sheep," and that this stinging accusation would act as a motivator. It was not a very subtle attempt at both questioning the party political process and demanding a thoughtful engagement with party politics.

Although many Yiddish-speaking workers were not naturalized citizens due to the high £7 fee, unnaturalized immigrants were put on the electoral register if they paid rates, even through a landlord. This situation brought heated debate between political parties, and objections were raised by Conservative anti-alienists.[22] Winchevsky's use of the name Jack is significant. Jack can mean any man (as in Jack-of-all-trades), and in this case any Englishman. Yet Jack is an anglicization of the biblical Jacob, and was a popular Jewish name, which in Yiddish is *Yankef.* The notits, however, does not use the Yiddish version of the name, but instead transliterates the English Jack into Yiddish *d-zh-e-k*. Winchevsky's choice to use Jack can be seen as a way of mainstreaming the immigrant Jews. Winchevsky wanted Jewish workers to be activists within English unions and socialist groups rather than segregated. Of course, he really wanted integration into revolutionary socialist politics, and all of the three notitsn described above are antiestablishment, critical, and deriding of parliamentary policies.

None of these three verse notitsn mention Jews, yet they had direct relevance for the Jews of Whitechapel who had just filled in the census, were sending their children to school, or were about to vote in the coming elections. The next example clearly shows how a news story without an overtly Jewish angle is made so under Winchevsky's pen. Written in 1891, it concerned the Baccarat affair of that year, a gambling scandal involving the Prince of Wales. Rather than condemning Prince Bertie's connection to the affair and criticizing his gambling habit, Winchevsky put forward a different view. Notice that the rhyming scheme is not simple couplets. There are rhymes on lines one and three, but alternate lines have midline rhymes, which slows down the rhythm when reading the verse aloud:[23]

Ven mentshn fun ale kolirn un sortn,	If people of all colors and sorts,
vos horeven shver, mitn nodl un sher,	Who work hard with needle and scissors,
farginen zikh gelt tsu farlirn in kortn,—	Let themselves lose money at cards,—

varum zol a prints, velkher hot mames mints,	Why should a prince, who has mother's money,
nit makhn a kertl un klingers farlirn?	Not have a game of cards and lose cash?
Varum nit kleyn-shas take lernen tsum shpas,	Why not play cards for fun,
un zikh nor mit vayber un sport amuzirn?	And amuse oneself with women and sport?
Dzhon bul, zay nit shtum, zog, entfer—varum.	John Bull, do not be silent. Speak, answer—why.[24]

On one level this poem contends that since people gamble away their money who cannot afford to, why should someone not gamble who can afford it? This is meant ironically, but Winchevsky did not lose an opportunity to harangue the Jewish workers on their gambling habits. In this notits the poem carefully draws in the Yiddish-speaker through the choice of the word for a deck of cards. Winchevsky uses two words, *kortn* and *kleyn-shas*. The word *kortn* (cards) is clearly understood, but *kleyn-shas* is a slang expression. It is a very Jewish term because it literally means "little Talmud." Gambling is forbidden in Jewish law, except on the festivals of Hanukkah and Purim, where one is obligated to refrain from studying Talmud and instead to play cards and dice. So cards become a little Talmud or *kleyn-shas*.[25] The poem directs criticism not only at Bertie playing *kortn* but at gambling East End Jews playing *kleyn-shas*. Indeed, the term *kleyn-shas* even gives the Jews' gambling the status of a commandment, where they do not play cards but *lern* (study) them, as they would Talmud. Using this humor, Winchevsky subtly connects an English story of gambling royalty with the Yiddish-speaking street, putting Jewish immigrants into the English mainstream. Jewish immigrant behavior may not be the same as English behavior, but it is similar.

But the connection between Jewish immigrants and English mainstream is not seen as simple. One of the most significant notitsn displays Winchevsky's anxiety about what he calls anti-Semitism. "Anti-Semitism" was a new and contested term in England in the 1880s, and Winchevsky knew Arnold White's rhetoric. White wanted to espouse anti-alien views without being called an anti-Semite, as he felt that would backfire on his effectiveness. He attempted to manipulate public opinion by suggesting that anti-Semitism was an old eternal word, and so diminish the negative power of the term and allow race to be brought into discussions of immigration and poverty.[26] Winchevsky was alarmed by White and his followers. In a prose leader from the *Poylisher yidl* of 1884, titled "A kleyner volkn oyfn himl" (A small cloud in the sky), Winchevsky declared that "a pogrom in Brick Lane, in the crossroad of Commercial Road could be terrible and bloody . . . like a pogrom in the Baltic."[27] In a poem written that year, "Rikblik oyf dos alte yor" (A glance at the old year), he conjures images of ancient anti-Semitism in the names Torquemada and Haman, and argues that the nineteenth century is doing just as badly with the Tiszaeszlár blood libel and pogroms.[28] He repeatedly called Jews "stepchildren" in the countries that already have emancipation as well as those that do not.[29] In July 1891, one notits deplored the "anti-Semitic" stance of two newspapers: "The two papers that have exploited the lie the most, that have shouted about it more than others; that this country will be attacked by Jews; who have thundered more than any others, that England NOW has already got more Jews than is healthy for it,—these newspapers both belong . . . to JEWS. These anti-Semitic Jewish papers are—the 'Telegraph' of Levy-Lawson and the *Evening News* of Harry Marks. If this is not a scandal what is it?"[30]

The naming and shaming of the prose is heartfelt and angry. Yet it is followed by a chilling interpretation in verse, of how aristocratic Anglo-Jews could be responsible for local anti-Semitic incidents:

Ven england zol di tir farshlisn	If England would lock the door
far di, vos zey faryogt der knut,	On those, who have been chased with whips,
un oyb dos folk zol hir fargisn,	And if the people here should blindly
farblendt, umshuldikes blut,—	Spill innocent blood,—
dan blaybt dem yidn in vaytshepl	Then the Jews in Whitechapel will still have
oyf yedn fal nokh dizer troyst,	In any case this one consolation,
az alts kumt fun a yidls kepl,	That everything comes from inside a Jew's head,
den levi yogt un marks farshtoyst.	Because Levy chases away and Marks banishes.[31]

The fear espoused here is of violence directed at the East End immigrant community. The term *yidls kepl* (Jew's head), which can be used as a compliment, in this context implies shrewdness or a swindler or a head that's up to no good.[32] Winchevsky showed the economic reasons behind anti-Semitism. On one side, he pointed at Jewish financiers and exploiters, condemning them as the reason why Jewish workers were hated. On the other side, he pointed toward nonunionized Jewish workers undercutting union gains in pay deals. His solutions were twofold: one was for Jewish workers to move out of densely populated Jewish areas, join unions, and work together with English workers. The other was to expose in the papers all incidents either of rich Jews exploiting non-Jewish workers or of any acts committed against the Jewish community or an individual.[33] This notits is highlighting Jewish bad behavior toward other Jews, but has little of the lightness or humor of previous examples. It displays and transmits fury and anxiety of imminent danger.

In summary, the notitsn offer a lens to see how the socialists encouraged immigrant workers to engage with English politics, and thus English life through including a Jewish perspective on the English news. However, through their radical opinions, they demand a critical and antiestablishment engagement. The concise nature of the poetic notitsn is key to their interest. They have a visual impact and stand out on the page, and the use of clever rhyme and rhythm invites their being read aloud. The sound bites are partial in their positions, offering one personal intervention into a political debate. Despite being an antireligious revolutionary internationalist, Winchevsky did not push total assimilation. Indeed, he is only too aware of being Jewish in England and of anti-Semitism. Rather, he suggests that the way forward is for the immigrant society to take its place critically in the English political landscape.

IN DI GASN: INSPIRING ANTHEMS

Music in public spaces can be a powerful medium of social order, creating a soundtrack for social action. Being in control of that soundtrack gives a structure for social activism.[34] The power of song, the memory of a melody, and the feeling it brings to a chorus of protesters adds piquancy and immediacy to the message contained within the lyric. The poems by Winchevsky that stood the test of time were those put to music and sung on union demonstrations. These were written as acts of resistance and protest for London Yiddish-speaking workers, and provided the background sounds to the struggle.[35]

The mid-to-late 1880s were busy with union activity, strikes, and marches. William Morris was publishing poems in *Commonweal*, the journal of the Socialist League (SL). Morris was writing poems to be sung on marches and for entertainment at the Social Democratic Federation (SDF) and SL events and was beginning to build up a collection of socialist activist songs.[36] Similar chants and songs were needed in Yiddish for immigrant marches and events, and Winchevsky provided them. In London the SDF and SL sang to Morris's lyrics, and from London to New York, protesting crowds sang to Winchevsky's lyrics. Winchevsky wrote for specific union protests and demonstrations. He was not standing on the sidelines but involved in the activism, writing for the Yiddish press, encouraging workers to join unions, and being a part of English socialist activism.

A sung version was the most common introduction for the worker to Winchevsky's poetry. The Russian mechanic and socialist writer Peysakh Novik described the first time he heard a poem by Winchevsky. He was working in a factory in Brisk (Belarus), and he heard the factory girls singing a song about the London newspaper the *Arbayter fraynd*:

Vos traybn di reder fun ale mashinen,	Who drives the wheels of every machine,
vos akern, zeyen un baken di broyt,	Who ploughs, sows and bakes the bread,
un kenen fundestvegn broyt nit gefinen,	And nevertheless cannot find any bread,
ven slek oder krankheyt zey shtirtst in a noyt.	When slack or sickness pushes them into want.[37]

Neither Novik nor the workers knew the song was written by Winchevsky, and they may have known about the London Yiddish newspaper only through the song's title. Novik was struck by the effect of the group singing: "The tune was haunting, solemn, and haunting. The machines knocked and the song carried, demanded, punished, and welcomed the *Arbayter fraynd*. . . . I heard this song many times in the factories. It was sung heartily and with feeling. At times a factory girl would get a tear in her eye. But after they finished singing the atmosphere, that was continuously oppressive, would simply become cleansed."[38]

Literary critic A. Litvak had a similar story to tell. He was so uplifted after hearing this song sung by factory girls, he wrote down the words as they sang them, wondering why the song had such power when it was just "activism in rhyme." He compared it to the energy generated from hearing workers sing repeatedly "working from eight to eight / For six rubles a day," and concluded that it was the intensity and fervor that created the power of the song.[39] Writing in 1911, literary critic Shaul Niger argued for the potential power of Winchevsky's sung verse: "The rhythm, the measuredness, the expression of intense experience, and condensed thought. For common people and for children rhythm is a game and a sort of spiritual cement, like music for dancing, that guides people, unites them, and makes them into a group, a collective. It is easy to have an effect on them with processions, marches, with music, with verse, and with rhythmic dancing speech. Better than writing editorials or proclamations about freedom, equality, and brotherhood—it is more purposeful to sing."[40]

These descriptions of the transformative power of rhythmic group singing are significant. When crowds come together on the strength of a common idea, there is an element of "emotional contagion." The sound is integral to the event, both mass chanting or singing, but also noise and rhythm of feet marching or machines whirring.[41] Nineteenth-century theories of crowds suggested that mood was transmitted through hypnosis, telepathy, and suggestibility. More recent theories argue that the atmosphere that is transmitted through the crowd physically gets into a person, changing the person's physical being.[42] Whether they were aware of theories of crowds, the socialists saw singing as important for activism. The poem "Tsu di raykhe" starts with these words:

Ir vundert zikh far vos ikh zing	You wonder why I sing
mit trern in di oygn	With tears in my eyes
fun layd un noyt un fun altsding. . . .	About suffering and need and everything. . . .
Ir fregt varum ikh zing amol	You ask why I sing sometimes
a lid vos makht nit freylekh?	A song that doesn't bring happiness?[43]

This poem suggests that Winchevsky saw himself as a singer, and although he called his output *lider*, which can mean poems or songs, he used the verb "sing" a number of times. However, in a later poem of 1891, "Mayne lider" (My poems), he had a different attitude:

Fun yidishe verter alt-modish,	From outdated Yiddish words,
fun eynfakhe reyd on a klang,	From simple speech without a rhyme,
fun tener oft venig melodish	From often unmelodious tones
farfas ikh mayn prostn gezang.	I compose my simple song.
Dokh makh ikh di lider tsum zingen nit,	But I do not write the poems to be sung,
a zifts iz far zey harmoniye,	A sigh is their harmony,
darum makht nit oys oyb zey klingen nit	So it doesn't matter if they do not resound
un oyb zey felt melodiye.	And if they lack melody.[44]

Here Winchevsky insists that he is not writing song lyrics.[45] This poem was reproduced in the introduction to Winchevsky's *Lider un gedikhte* (Collected poems), where Winchevsky admitted that although he had not written the poems to be sung, he was happy that they were sung by large crowds.[46] Despite Winchevsky's apparent ambivalence at being a poet of song, his poems were sung by crowds at demonstrations and rallies across the Jewish world throughout the 1880s and 1890s, and some were still sung decades later.

The Yiddish songs may have been inspired by English socialist songs written for parallel struggles. In 1885 William Morris wrote: "Things are going on very fast, and . . . my hopes of the great change coming speedily are much higher than they were a year ago."[47] He wrote two songs, "The March of the Workers" and "The Message of the March Wind," which offer hope that the time is right for change and that things are moving on. Winchevsky, responding to the same sense of hope, penned the song "Dray vekhter" (Three guards). The first guard is pessimistic about the world, the second believes the day will come and that he should hold firm, and the third feels the day is nearly here.[48]

CHAPTER 5

In 1932 the literary critic Isaac Greenberg, writing under the pen name A. Prints, claimed that "the *zeyde*'s political ear is strained and sensitive to every important development in the political and economic internal situation both at home and abroad."[49] In February 1886, the English socialist "march of the unemployed" led to two days of rioting, breaking the windows of clubs, and destroying shops. In May 1886, Winchevsky was inspired by the early news of the Haymarket demonstration in Chicago and the call to Chicago workers, to arm themselves and be ready for battle for the socialist revolution. The new impetus for revolutionary socialists caused great excitement about imminent change, leading Winchevsky to write "Es rirt zikh" (It's moving):[50]

Hert ir, kinder, vi es rirt zikh,	Have you heard, children, how it's moving,
vi es rirt zikh iberal?	How it's moving everywhere?
Vi der arbetsman mustirt zikh	How the worker prepares
tsu dem kamf mit kapital?	For the fight against capitalism?[51]

The repeated refrain, that things are "moving," creates both the excitement and the momentum of the song. The song's melody is not fast, and hundreds or thousands of Yiddish-speaking workers singing together at a walking pace would heighten the atmosphere where the sound would become part of the crowd.

However, the Chicago Haymarket demonstration did not end in socialist revolution, but in the death of five revolutionary worker leaders. The Bloody Sunday demonstration in Trafalgar Square on November 1887 left one demonstrator dead and scores injured. Hundreds were arrested, including William Morris, and this sobered the revolutionary optimism.[52] Winchevsky was angry at the revolutionaries in Morris's Socialist League for not walking hand in hand with the SDF. He spoke out against it in an article in the *Arbayter fraynd* titled "Di arbayter un zeyere firer" (The workers and their leaders). In it he reproached the socialist leaders for their lack of unity at such an important moment.[53] Marmor argues that when Winchevsky's writing demanded the oppressed working masses rise up and fight the tyrant, this was not revolutionary talk, but a call to take part in the protest and demonstrations of 1887.[54] The despair over the Bloody Sunday demonstration led Morris to write a memorial poem to the demonstrator Alfred Linnell who had died, and Winchevsky wrote almost no poetry in the next year.

By 1889, revolutionary excitement had returned. It inspired the Jewish socialists, trade union membership surged, and the Jewish tailors' strike was the first time that thousands of Jewish workers took to the streets in a general strike. Jewish and English trade unionists, revolutionaries, strikers, and shopkeepers worked together.[55] The main strike demand was for a twelve-hour working day, paid breaks, and restricted overtime. Within three weeks, 6,000 workers had come out on strike. The Master Tailors' Protective and Improvement Association made a tentative agreement and workers started returning to work, but at the last moment the masters refused to sign.[56] The English dock strike fund gave £100 to the strikers, and there were smaller contributions from English trade unions. Finally, in part as a response to the activist atheism of the socialists, and in part seeing unionization as an important part of anglicization, Lord Rothschild became involved, and Samuel Montagu put up the £100 necessary for the employers to resume talks. On October 3 an agreement was signed and demands were met. The English and Yiddish press gave daily accounts, but the *Jewish Chronicle* gave it little coverage, playing down the roles of union leaders Lyons and Wess and building up the role of the Anglo-Jewish community leaders.[57]

The poem "A bezem un a ker" (A broom and sweeping), written for the tailors' strike, imagined capitalism being swept away:

Dan vet mer keyn mitlman,	Then there will be no more middleman,
keyn parazit nit zayn!	No parasite!
Keyn mitlman, keyn kitlman, keyn titlman	No middleman, no clergyman, no titled man
nit zayn!	None![58]

This furious song portrays the anger at having middlemen and aristocrats, Rothschild and Montagu, as part of the workers' struggle in their attempt to gain the control and gratitude of the immigrant workers. The image of a broom reflects the socialists and anarchists working together to fight for changes in labor laws, even as they were moving further

CHAPTER 5

apart politically and their differences were about to lead to an anarchist takeover of the *Arbayter fraynd*.[59]

In 1890 the shoe and boot makers struck with Jews and gentiles working in close cooperation. Ten thousand workers came out on strike, demanding an end to outwork.[60] Winchevsky responded by producing the rallying cry "Der frayhayts-gayst" (The spirit of freedom):[61]

In di gasn,—tsu di masn	Into the streets,—to the masses
fun badrikte felker-rasn,	From oppressed human races,
ruft der frayhayts-gayst....	Calls the spirit of freedom....
Ikh kum lernen—arbet ern,	I come to teach—to honor work,
ern, akhtn un bagern,	Honor, care for, and demand,
arbet mit a tolk;	Structured work;
glik un fridn,—umgeshidn	Happiness and peace,—no separation
tsvishn haydn, kristn, yidn,	Between heathens, Christians, Jews,
tsvishn folk un folk.[62]	Between peoples.[63]

"Der frayhayts-gayst" was designed for the particular demands of the strike, as the reference to outwork, in the poem as "structured work" indicates. The poem encapsulated the internationalist desire for a socialism that did not differentiate by religion, only by class.[64] Feeling was high, and Winchevsky contributed to the body of socialist anthems by encouraging revolution and providing material to be sung on marches. In 1892 Winchevsky participated in socialist activity in both Jewish and English circles, trying to coordinate and unite union activity and encourage workers to strike and demonstrate as a way of taking control of the mechanisms of power.[65] The first edition of the *Veker* published the poem "A kamf-gezang" (A struggle-song). It began: *Viklt funander di fon di royte* (Unfurl the red flag), and contained reasons for Jewish activism:

Yidelekh, ir zayt bay ale natsyonen	Jews, among all the nations
geyrim un toyshvim gevezn tsuglaykh,	You were strangers and residents at the same time,
zayt itst bay zey in di frayhayts legyonen.	Be with them now in the freedom-legions.[66]

The biblical referencing of *geyrim un toyshvim* (strangers and residents) could have referred to the attempt to make Anglo-Jewish sweaters see the treatment of Jewish workers in sweatshops as a desecration of Judaism. Yet Winchevsky wrote for a transnational audience, and local references were often occluded or disappeared completely as he addressed the whole Yiddish-speaking world. As well as rousing march songs, Winchevsky produced visions of a different and equal world. In union action, women often struck independently of the men, and the poem "Tsvey veltn" (Two worlds), written in 1891, dreams of a time

Dort vu di froy iz a birgerin, tuendik	Where the woman is a citizen doing
zelbshtendik ir natirlekhe flikht....	Independently her natural duty....
Vu mayn un dayn zaynen verter fargesene,	Where mine and yours are forgotten words,
her un knekht—nemen, vos keyner farshteyt.	Ruler and slave—names that no one understands.[67]

And in one of his best-known songs, from 1892 and brought back to life in the Yiddish revival today, "Di tsukunft" (The future), a time is envisaged when

Es vet nit zayn a mayster,	There will be no masters,
nit di kroyn un nit der tayster,	Not the crown, not wealth,
nit dem zelners shverd....	Nor the soldier's sword....
Loz dos folk ...	Let the people ...
zikh nemen—nit farlangen—	seize—not demand—
rekht oyf der erd.	Justice in the world.[68]

Winchevsky produced powerful images of revolution, of hope, and of possibility. He may have touched the excitement of fighting for equality and imagining a postrevolutionary future. With these poems, written as song lyrics, the audience participated in creating the poem's fervor and atmosphere of a crowd moving together under a powerful political idea. Yet there were few gains, and years later, describing the strike fever in

London, Winchevsky mused: "We thought that slowly it would bring the socialist revolution. What a crazy thought!"[69]

CRITICS' VIEWS OF WINCHEVSKY'S POETRY

Throughout Winchevsky's literary life, he was the subject of self-imposed and external criticism and debate.[70] His early anxieties about his ability as a poet continued, and he was often dissatisfied with his poetry. This was reinforced by negative views from critics of Yiddish culture who particularly concentrated on two aspects. The first criticism focused on what they perceived as a lack of feeling in Winchevsky's poetry: that his poetry was written in a cold, conscious, and calculated way.[71] Even the *Jewish Chronicle* ploughed in with a criticism that the lack of feeling led to a lack of "imagination and colour."[72] Winchevsky's strongest critic, A. Litvak, argued that because Winchevsky was an intellectual who put ideas into his verse without feeling, his poetry lacked a lyrical flair.[73]

The second criticism constituted a deeper and more sustained critique concerning the quality of the poetry and whether it was accomplished enough to join the growing Yiddish literary canon. Litvak lambasted the simplicity of Winchevsky's verse, called the rhyme "childish," and saw it as *badkhones* (rhyming couplets of no poetic merit, used during a wedding), as pranking, easy to hear, singable, repeatable, and better spoken than read. He derided the poems as "similar to each other, the same content, the same tone, and often the same words," making the poem itself "shallow and banal." He described Winchevsky's poetic process as a recipe where Winchevsky "would come up with an idea, saturate it in sugar water, drip a few tears on it, chew it well, and then chop it into short lines—a dish for the Jewish masses."[74] Litvak's article created a furor among Winchevsky's supporters and added fuel to a literary debate that continued in print decades later.

Winchevsky's supporters repeated that it was precisely some of the negative criticism that made him such an important socialist poet and the *zeyde* of Jewish socialism. Prints [Greenberg] argued that it was indeed the simplicity and nonartistic and revolutionary content that influenced the worker. Rather than the bourgeois preoccupation with trees and flowers, the proletarian poet's laments were a protest motif.[75] Aaron Kushnirov claimed that those critics who derided Winchevsky's use of folklore elements, its fighting quality, and its high ideology as failings did so because they themselves were bourgeois. Indeed, had Winchevsky taken his inspiration from bourgeois writers rather than revolutionaries, those same critics would have embraced Winchevsky as a modernizer of Yiddish poetry.[76]

Although some critics were fans who wrote superlatives with an inability to see anything other than their idol the *zeyde*, more critical admirers saw Winchevsky as making a choice to eschew poetry in favor of activism.[77] They explored the lyrical aspects of his poetry in detail and traced it through its influences and what it influenced.[78] Far from having only a negative effect on the way people viewed his place in Yiddish literature, the continuing controversy about the quality of Winchevsky's verse may have attracted people back to Winchevsky, not only as the first proletarian poet but also as a first-class poet.[79] What none of the critics could argue with was his impact on the workers. Indeed, even Litvak could not deny the power of his verse. He conceded:

> Tens of thousands of Jewish workers were educated and revolutionized by Winchevsky's poems. . . . People sung them in the basements of Tsarist prisons . . . and got comfort and hope from them. In the sound of the march *In di gasn, tsu di masn* people went on demonstrations. . . . His poems were absorbed into the mass revolutionary energy. . . . Call it *badkhones*, call it whatever you want, but the effect of them was huge. For the literary community Winchevsky the writer was a meager member, but for the workers' movement his poems were a priceless treasure.[80]

Winchevsky's poetry in all its forms—satirical, sentimental, didactic, or utopian—emerges as a form of activism in the fight for a socialist revolution. However, although Winchevsky contributed extensively to Jewish socialist debate, his small socialist group ultimately had little influence on the London Jewish world. Despite some success in unionization and strikes, gains were rarely maintained, and Winchevsky's attempt to create an activist Jewish revolutionary movement in London was unsuccessful.

However, Winchevsky became a celebrity within the Jewish socialist world. Numerous articles were written about him, and meetings where he was to read his poetry were advertised with pop-star-style posters. If

CHAPTER 5

the poetry did not achieve its ostensible aims, did it achieve something else, some less tangible cultural effects that went beyond the polemical message it contained? Maybe the lasting success of the poetry was its cultural importance, becoming part of a popular socialist canon of songs that could be recited or sung by Yiddish-speaking Jews, whether political activists or not. Even today, several of his poems survive in Yiddish songbooks and recordings and are regularly sung as part of the Yiddish/Klezmer revival.[81]

Sex: Innuendo in the Immigrant Halls

I Maud, "How Jews Sit in a Yiddish Theater," *Bloffer*, no. 21 (November 1912). From the collections of the National Library of Israel. Although signed "I Maud," this is most likely the work of Zuni Maud, who cofounded and drew cartoons for the American satirical publication *Der kibitzer*. See http://www.museumoffamilyhistory.com/yt/lex/M/maud-zuni.htm.

6

Transforming Courtship

Ikh bin shoyn do nisht mer keyn griner	I am no longer a new immigrant
Megt ir gleybn mir.	Believe me.
Ir veys az do in London vi men klapt on in a tir,	You know that here is London, when you knock on a door,
kumt aroys a kleyne vayb, fardrey ikh ir dem kop,	Out comes a little wife. I turn her head,
kh'red ir on a bobemayse—az ikh zukh a dzhob.	I tell her a tale—that I'm looking for a job.
Ikh zukh a dzhob, oy oy a dzhob!	I'm looking for a job, oh, oh a job!
Un ven di mises zogt nisht,	And when the Mrs. says nothing,
veys ikh shoyn vos ikh hob tsu ton.	I already know what I have to do.[1]

Sitting in a Yiddish music hall in the East End of London in the early twentieth century, you would be listening to a varied program of songs, sketches, and acts, juxtaposing the serious and meaningful with the humorous and frivolous. There might be a rousing patriotic song of the Boer War followed by a cheeky chappy looking for a job in Whitechapel, full of double entendres. This might continue with a hilarious sketch of Eastern European shtetl life, and then a serious and shocking song appealing for money for families affected by the Kishinev pogrom. In the second show of the evening, there would be a few vulgar songs with sexual innuendo, playing to the lads in the gallery. And also juggling, whistling, or the rendition of a poem. The whole evening would be accompanied by

CHAPTER 6

Beki Goldstein and Joseph Markovitsh, ca. 1910. © Jewish Museum, London.

raucous laughter, shouting, eating, cries, sobbing, and all joining in well-known choruses.

Between 1898 and 1914, dozens of Yiddish songs were sung in the East End immigrant halls. Some were sung by visiting singers from Eastern Europe or America, but many were performed by home-grown, beloved local celebrities, including Arn Nager, Beki Goldstein, Rubin Doctor, Isaac Lubritsky, Joseph Sherman, and Joseph Markovitsh. Over eighty songs were written specifically by and for local performers. And over half of them have verses that relate in some way to sex and sexual relationships. They were all published in London around 1905. These are the songs that are the focus of this chapter and chapter 7.

Sexual contact and the roles of men and women were being debated and censored in the English public sphere. From the mid-1880s, a select group of radical, socialist, and feminist middle-class society intellectuals met as the "Men and Women's Club" and discussed matters pertaining to sex, sexuality, and the gender roles of men and women. Their debates were both initiated and intensified by sensational reports appearing in the media about underage sex and prostitution in London's East End.[2] The London lyrics relate to some of these new ideas and changing attitudes, but in particular they expose how features of developing relationships and sexual contact are changed by immigration.

The music-hall songs offer a wider view of sexual relations than the narrow religious definitions. They push for an engagement with modern life where there were more possibilities for sexual contact. Arrival in England brought the freedom to consider different forms of living, or at least let off steam and laugh at the thought of more sexual choice. The songs often link permissive attitudes and abusive sexual behavior to English charlatans. The anglicization of sexual practice did not constitute the sort of acculturation that Anglo-Jewry, immigrant socialists, or the immigrant orthodox would have liked. Songs with suggestive lyrics were pejoratively called *shund* (trash) by their critics, yet the music-hall songs pertaining to sex and relationships gave a platform, even if a comic one, for important ideas to be aired. They offered opportunities for the Yiddish music-hall audiences to be a part of a debate in the modern world.

This chapter examines how the lyrics portray premarital relationships: the reinvention of matchmaking, finding alternative dowries, courtship outside of more traditional Eastern European religious structures, and premarital sex. The songs do not offer a transparent window into sexual practice in the past. Yet they help us imagine a crucial space in the immigrant community, unexamined by Anglo-Jewish social historians.[3] Popular culture is of huge importance in reflecting the significance of sex in people's lives, and the songs show how people engaged with the complexity and sense of conflict around sex. Thus the songs enrich, transform, and nuance our current knowledge. The songs' tales are of an imagined society, yet they gave opportunities for audiences to actively construct and experiment with different possibilities of self-definition. The music halls became a space where new ideas could be tried out that may have been impossible in the real world outside.[4]

THE MUSIC-HALL ATMOSPHERE

Crucial to the success of the music hall was creating the right atmosphere for the entertainment to do its magic. Atmospheres are not passive properties of a space. Rather, they are actively created by the interaction between the space and the people and objects in it.[5] Atmospheres are not static, but constantly change as different interactions happen within them.[6] The making of the music-hall atmosphere can be seen as a collaboration, which included the performer's rendition of the song, the audience response, the suggestive lyrics, and the music-hall space itself. The resultant atmosphere of the halls encouraged courtship and sexual contact.

Collaboration between performer and audience is central to the mechanism used to transform openly crude music-hall songs into those where sex is less overt in the lyric, thus creating a sexual atmosphere more surreptitiously. Peter Bailey argues that "Knowingness," or insider knowledge, operates in this way: "The prime device lay in the 'things of suggestion.' . . . It was the compressed code of the double entendre and the innuendo that signalled complicity with an audience, investing language, tone and gesture with oblique but knowing conspiracies of meaning."[7] Meaning is created through the audience's collusion with the performer. The performer substitutes innuendo for explicit sexual references, knowing that the audience will understand what is being referred to. This is maintained by the performer insinuating with hand signs, nods, and winks, and the audience registers recognition through catcalls, shouts, or laughter. The performer can therefore use familiar, common language which allows shortcuts and understatement to create pathos and humor.[8]

The audience's insider knowledge of Yiddish culture and the experience of immigration into the small East End community added further nuances to sexual innuendo. Knowledge of Jewish perspectives on sex and courtship needed no translation. The impact of immigration on marriages and relationships was part of everyone's experience. The resulting atmosphere in the music hall was intimate, and although the music hall was a public place, the intimacy of shared understanding also made it a semiprivate space. The music hall was outside of immigrants' daily lives and existed only for the duration of the evening. It therefore became a place to lose oneself in fantasy and a laboratory to imagine different aspects of relating to one another.

The sexual atmosphere of the English music halls was of particular concern to religious conservative reformers. The reformer Mrs. Ormiston Chant of the Social Purity movement's National Vigilance Association campaigned against immorality. She directed her attack at who she deemed immoral women, who included prostitutes and female performers who she considered had lost their modesty and sense of shame. She decried performers' clothing, incidents of nudity, and indecent suggestiveness in the song lyrics, and encouraged the London County Council's Theatre and Music Halls Committee to inspect halls whenever possible and repress anything they saw as immoral.[9]

In order to avoid complaints about sexually explicit material in songs, many managers censored their own performers, fining or sacking them for risky allusions to extramarital sex. However, audiences were often sympathetic to allusions of sexual impropriety. Although lyrics or nudity were at times modified during an inspection, the censored version of the entertainment still contained the same content, but with further reliance on style, gesture, and insinuation. In some ways this led to more creative, subtle, and interesting songs because the words alone did not tell the story. The performance became paramount.[10]

Yiddish music halls seemed to get away with little censorship, but there were many critics of their crude and risqué lyrics. Orthodox immigrants saw the Yiddish theatre as a "nest of sin and blasphemy" containing immoral content and sexually promiscuous performers.[11] Anglo-Jews displayed anxiety about how the music halls impacted on the moral welfare of the immigrants.[12] And socialists writing in the Yiddish press were deeply ambivalent about the music halls, seeing them as a social problem and wanting workers to engage with higher culture.[13] It is possible that Yiddish lyrics were not censored by music-hall managers because they were less likely to cause offense outside the immigrant community. The Yiddish halls were not associated with many incidents of crime or those involving prostitutes, although there were a handful of incidents of immigrant gang violence that appeared in English newspapers.[14] The lyrics that refer to sex offer an intriguing insight into the changes that immigration brought to sexual relations, and how changing views of sex in the wider society were affecting the immigrant community.

COURTSHIP AND PREMARITAL SEX

For orthodox Jews in Eastern Europe, betrothal and marriage had been a tightly structured system organized by family and community but not including the prospective marriage partners. Parents, helped by a *shadkhn* (matchmaker), were involved in a decision based on uniting families and creating economic stability. The suitability of a prospective partner was judged by family lineage, Talmud scholarship, and money. Although character suitability may have been taken into account, sentimental reasons were not generally considered as important as creating a strong religious and economically viable unit for the purpose of bringing up a family. There were formal rituals of courtship in which the two young people would have had few (if any) opportunities to spend time alone together. The matchmaker suggested partners, the young people met under supervision, and the whole procedure was a family contract.[15] Even after a couple were engaged, they could still meet only under strict parental guidance, if indeed they met at all, before the marriage ceremony.

To support orthodox newlyweds, there were two economic systems set in place: the dowry and *kest*. The bride's dowry provided money to begin their new life, a trousseau, and domestic items for a new home. *Kest* was a system of support for orthodox families, whereby the bride's father provided food and lodging for a set number of years while his son-in-law continued Talmudic study, often in a *yeshive* (Jewish seminary).[16] These systems had worked well in Eastern European *shtetlekh* where everyone knew each other and lived life in community and according to its rules. In the larger towns—Lemberg, Lvov, Lodz, Warsaw, and Odessa—life was more easygoing with a greater influx of modern ideas. By the end of the nineteenth century, the challenges of modernity and the consequences of migration affecting the wider society were beginning to influence the system of arranged marriages. Still under parental control, the choice of marriage partner became more compassionate, with new marriage criteria including compatibility, affection, and mutual respect.[17] Young people were able to meet and get to know their betrothed. The changes to the structure of arranged marriages led to the development of courtship, which was a concept that had not been a part of traditional Jewish marriage mores. A space had opened up. Courtship brought possibilities for social contact and sexual feelings to develop between a young man and a young woman from their initial meeting to the first night of married life.[18]

The changes happening in Eastern Europe were often accelerated by immigration. In London, arranged marriages continued in orthodox circles, but they became less ubiquitous. Many single men, arriving alone, did not have family to support them, and as secularization grew, people began to make their own matches. Single people had to find ways to construct and define courtship without the old formal structures, new ways that not only aped their new country but created hybrid identities.[19] They needed places to meet and ways to finance courtship and marriage without the formality of a dowry. New ideas pertaining to women's role in sexual relationships and changing attitudes to physical contact between men and women put the redefinition of sexual mores clearly on the agenda.[20]

The search for a marriage partner was exacerbated by the mismatch in numbers of single Jewish immigrant men and women in London.[21] The high number of single men coming alone from Eastern Europe had left a dearth of marriageable-aged men in Eastern Europe, and a surfeit in the Yiddish-speaking diaspora. There was therefore greater competition for a bride among the immigrant population.

DANSING SKUL: LOCATIONS FOR COURTING

Whereas in the past supervised matchmaking took place in the home, as the system was changing or disappearing, the places for courtship also disappeared. Immigrants who had left the parental home and religious backgrounds behind them in Eastern Europe and were lodging in a room in London needed to find new places to meet a prospective marriage partner. For many immigrants it may have been the first time men and women regularly worked alongside each other in the workplace, having not had that degree of contact with the opposite sex outside of their family. Public locations provided places where men and women could mingle and make their own choices. Workingmen's clubs, friendly societies, and political organizations put on concerts, banquets, and socials, and the socialist and anarchist clubs tried to entice young people to socialism with frequent balls and benefits.[22] The bustling Jewish thoroughfares such as Whitechapel Road were popular courting grounds, and the Yiddish theatres and music halls served the same function.[23] The *London Standard* in 1902 reported how in the Yiddish music hall there were "scores of engaged couples dotted about," and "young Yiddish bucks too, in their smartest Sabbath attire and imitation 'joolery'; good-looking young Jewesses in the newest modes of Oxford Street, 'latest style, nineteen and eleven pence.'"[24]

Visitors to the London Yiddish stage remarked on the atmosphere there, which was more like a social club, where people went to chat

CHAPTER 6

rather than to watch a show. Four separate articles in the Yiddish and English press describe the atmosphere:

> Everyone talks, makes remarks to their friend about every word or arm lifted by the actors as if he felt he was in the [Petticoat] Lane on a Sunday rather than at the theatre.[25]
>
> The audience [is] noisy and demonstrative, as Jewish audiences invariably are everywhere. Everyone is talking, laughing and chattering.[26]
>
> The noise never stopped. It was not silenced, but only subdued, by the rise of the curtain.[27]
>
> The Jews . . . don't know how to sit in the Yiddish theatre; everyone shouts, brawls, and interrupts.[28]

The music halls were places where young, unmarried, and newly married could meet the opposite sex, relax, and feel sexy.[29] Yet the comments above describe sociability and do not mention the sexual nature of that contact.[30] A more caustic satirical comment was published on the front cover of the *Bloffer* of 1912, with a cartoon captioned "How Jews Sit in a Yiddish Theatre." Instead of seats, the stalls are made up of rows of beds with canoodling couples on each one.[31]

The music hall created a soundtrack for courtship. Hearing and singing popular songs created memories and associations. Two sing-along songs by Arn Nager fictionalize familiar local places, one a generic dancing school and the other the oft-frequented Victoria Park. These locations become music-hall caricatures for places where there is space for courtship and sexual dalliance. They blur the boundary between the real and the unreal, allowing the atmosphere of the songs to transfer into the music hall. The songs tell us less about the real-life places than about the ribaldry of the Yiddish music hall. They suggest that a function of these songs was to create a sexual atmosphere where physical contact became a possibility.

The title "Der dansing skul" sets up and heightens the expectation of the audience, and is used by Nager as an opportunity to make rhymed innuendos:

TRANSFORMING COURTSHIP

Ven di muzik shpilt azoy zis	When the music plays so sweetly
heybn di moydn—di hent	The girls lift up—their hands
ikh zog aykh es iz a prakht	I tell you it is magnificent
tsu farbrengen a nakht	To enjoy a night
nor in dansing skul.	Just in the dancing school.
. . .	. . .
Reytshel hot lib tsu shpringen hoykh	Rachel loves to jump high
in dem dansing skul	In the dancing school
biz zi hot bakumen a geshvolenem— fus	Until she got a swollen—foot
in dem dansing skul.	In the dancing school.[32]

These verses use typical schoolboy-style wordplay, where pauses in the lyric suggest a sexual word as a rhyming gag, but another word is used instead. The substituted word becomes the innuendo and produces the humor. The word *zis* (sweet), at the end of the first line quoted above, should rhyme at the end of the second line. However, instead of the expected word *fis* (legs), the word *hent* (hands) is used. Similarly the rhyme for the word *hoykh* (high) would be *boykh* (stomach or belly), but the word *fus* (foot) is used. The lyric conjures images of female bodies and sex, and indeed, the word *farbrengen*, meaning to go out on a date, can have sexual connotations. The humor works because of the way it is performed, with pauses by the singer and a glint in the eye, holding the gag as the audience joins in the joke by laughing. There is nothing subtle here, and just in case the double entendres are missed, the lines following those quoted continue: "She asked a doctor and he told her / That she was to become a mother soon." The combination of the evocation of a dance class in the lyric, the cheeky performance, and the audience response may not have created an atmosphere for serious courtship, but it created space for behavior considered unacceptable elsewhere in Jewish life. This song would have been sung at the late show and directed at intoxicated young adults, and its meaning would have gone over the heads of any children present.

At first glance, the suggestion of sexual activity in "Der dansing skul" is not culturally specific to being a Jewish immigrant in England. Yet Nager takes pains in his lyrics to transform the generic into an Anglo-immigrant dance class by referencing both England and Jews. The English location is established in two ways. First, there is a threepence entry fee, and second, there are a string of anglicisms including *mesh* (mash, slang for flirt) to rhyme with *kesh* (cash). There is also direct reference to this being a Jewish experience. In the verse following the one quoted earlier, the audience is addressed as "Oh Jews." The universal experience of flirting and sexual contact becomes specific to the Jewish Yiddish-speakers standing in the East End music hall. This local association gives a feeling of immediacy, of sharing, being together, and living in the present.

A second song that creates a fictional landscape from a familiar location is Arn Nager's "Viktorye park," already discussed in chapter 3 in relation to transnationalism. The real Victoria Park is on the northern edge of the East End and was constantly frequented by East End Jews.[33] Zangwill's 1892 evocation of the park in *Children of the Ghetto* offers a scene of serenity: "Victoria Park was *the* park to the Ghetto. A couple of miles off. Far enough to make a visit to it an excursion, it was a perpetual blessing to the Ghetto. . . . Esther loved the park in all weathers, but best of all in the summer, when the great lake was bright and busy with boats, and the birds twittered in the leafy trees and the lobelias and calceolarias were woven into wonderful patterns by the gardeners."[34] This floral and pictorial description stands in stark contrast to Nager's comic depiction of a sexually charged Victoria Park. The environment of the park is represented as sleazy rather than as a place for respectable courtship. The characters are humorous and there are lots of them, some named and some referred to by description only, such as young people "running breathless," "falling on the ground and knocking their teeth out," or "lying about snoring." There are others flirting: Yudke and Reytshel Tsvok are clad "she with a shoe, he a sock," a married couple walk together past a Jewish prostitute, and a canoodling couple rolling about in the grass "get married" in Victoria Park. The last verse pushes the song into a different realm, making explicit, crude jibes about sexual anatomy:

Dort geyt reb itsik vos raybt dem shmitsik	There goes Mr. Itzik, scraping his bow
zayn noz iz shpitsik vayl er heyst itsik	His nose is pointed, because he's called Itzik.
dort pedlt meyer mit foyle eyer	There, Meyer is peddling rotten eggs

TRANSFORMING COURTSHIP

dray far a tsveyer in viktorye park   Three for tuppence in Victoria Park.[35]

The word *shmitsik* or the more common *smitshik* in Lithuanian Yiddish means a bow for a stringed instrument, so Itzik is a street fiddler. However, *smitshik* is slang for a penis, and could be translated as "dick."[36] The word *raybn* also has double meanings. It literally means rub, or in this context scraping the bow on the fiddle. However, it is slang for sexual intercourse, equivalent to "screw," and *raybn zikh* is to masturbate.[37] The use of the word *noz* in the next line makes a connection to the expression *raybn a noz*, meaning "to give it to a person."[38] The "it" would need to be further determined, possibly with gestures, to make the meaning clear. The sexual connotations build to a crescendo where Meyer is peddling rotten *eyer* (eggs). *Eyer*, like "balls," is slang for testicles. Whether the unpleasant *eyer* belong to *Meyer* or he's peddling them, the humor is in bad taste, and similar to "Der dansing skul," is mainly addressed at entertaining the rowdiest of drunken young *patriotn* (fans).[39]

"Viktorye park" and "Dansing skul" do not evoke everyday pictures of real locations; rather, they are crafted backdrops to the narrative of the lyrics. They therefore create a distance for imagining sexy behavior. Yet courtship is not without dangers, and in an indeterminate room in "Gevald, gevald police!" (Help, help police!) a girl and boy are sitting at a table:

Plutsling nemt er zi arum	Suddenly he takes her up
un git ir a kush un a glet	And gives her a kiss and a caress
un klert nisht keyn zakh	And doesn't say anything
un shlept ir shoyn fun tish.	And drags her from the table.[40]

Consent becomes an issue, and the English police are called in to help. Images conjured by these songs set a ribald tone for couples listening, laughing, and joining in singing the choruses, with the lyrics in the London Yiddish music hall. The environment is created where a different, more tactile form of courtship becomes possible.

CHAPTER 6

AZOY GEYT DOS GELT AVEK: MATCHMAKING AND DOWRY

As the structures of arranged marriage disappeared, the system of matchmakers and dowries changed. Although young people may have been introduced to prospective partners by family, friends, or coworkers, many songs tell comic narratives of young people becoming their own matchmakers. No longer being given a dowry, and parents' financial support redefined on a more ad hoc basis, young people had to pay for courting out of their own pockets or find ways of making money to do so. The hope of economic improvement through immigration was hard to realize, and anxiety over money was acute. Nevertheless, after paying for board and lodgings or contributing to the family finances, some young unmarried people independently earning money did end up with a little disposable income.[41] This may have paid for a ticket to the Yiddish music hall, where matchmaking, money, and courtship were the butt of many jokes. Far from allaying any anxiety about money, songs often set up comic scenarios to laugh at the predicaments of young people.

The song "Azoy geyt dos gelt avek" (And so the money disappears) tells of young men going to great lengths to impress their girlfriends:

Er khanfet di meydlekh mit a kush mit a glet	He flatters the girls with a kiss, a caress
gliklekh iz er on an ek	He is endlessly happy
er koyft zey altsding tsu zeyer tualet	He buys them all sorts of toiletries
un azoy geyt di veydzhes avek.	And so the wages go away.
Un azoy geyt dos gelt avek	And so the money goes away
un dernokh dreyt zikh der moyekh.	And so your mind is spinning.
Men fort in kristl peles shpatsirn	You go to Crystal Palace
men hulyet az es iz a shrek.	And party so much, it's terrible.[42]

They borrow money from family members or pawn their belongings to buy jewelry and perfume and outings to Crystal Palace. Crystal Palace was one of the great Victorian attractions, with a huge glass and iron building from the Great Exhibition of 1851 and a park with statues, gardens, and exhibits. A trip there was clearly a way to make a good impression: it was a status symbol of empire combined with "alcohol, fashion, and spectacle."[43] By the 1880s it was mostly a proletarian pleasure-ground with fairground rides, sweets, coconut shies, swing boats, booze, and tea and cake.[44] It was glamorous, impressive, very English, and a good couple of bus rides away from the East End. It can be seen as a symbol of a changing status, moving toward becoming English. Yet "becoming" can be a precarious state. It was not only due to the merry-go-round that the young man's "mind is spinning" as his wages disappear on courtship. This scene is also an iconic image for the effects of immigration. For many young people, the two sexes mingling in the workplace and the absence of parents may have brought a sense of emancipation and new sexual freedom, but they also brought insecurity and bewilderment. The tension between displacement and acculturation can be creative, as this song attests, where the point of disjuncture left no familiar foothold, nothing was the same, and the free world made one's head spin in confusion and the need for readjustment.[45]

One option the songs posited for men who did not have enough money to get married was to find a girl who did: "I am looking for a girl with a dowry / I will marry her even if she's not in a hurry," sang Arn Nager in the song "Genendel." Without his own money, the suitor had to offer something else in his search for a wife. This suitor promised to work for his beloved Genendel, wash, cook, and bake for her, fuss over her, make her laugh, and treat her better than Rothschild if only she married him and put some money into his new business.[46] Part of the song's humor was in the role reversal in which the man chose to take on a traditionally female role of cooking and cleaning in return for financial help. Role reversal, uncommon in daily life, was not infrequent in the Yiddish music-hall songs, including an amount of cross-dressing, flagging up the tensions of being a male immigrant. It showed the anxiety of not being able to fulfill the traditional male role. For unmarried Jewish immigrant men searching for a bride, competition was fierce. Young women in the audience may have laughed at the fantastical idea that they, as women, had greater choice or, indeed, could have become as English as Rothschild.

For a working girl, building up her own dowry became particularly important, because having independent means could change her marriage prospects. The disruption of moving to England and settling into the new culture lost many women those vital years when they were deemed of marriageable age. In "Ver zukht a kale" (Who's looking for a bride?), the singer beyond her early adulthood sees herself as too old to be courted, so she has to have money to be able to find a husband. She writes an advertisement, clearly stating, "I'm looking for a husband and I have cash." Portraying a woman as her own matchmaker shows women's growing independence and reflects changes to women's role in the English sphere, where activist and independent women were campaigning for suffrage. For an immigrant man struggling for money, the fictional advertisement suggested in this song would have been an enticing prospect.[47]

Women's growing independence was regularly staged by female singers. Much of the humor that women performed subverted what was expected by displaying women in positions that were less usual than the lived life of the Jewish East End. One aspect of arranged marriages that caused much unhappiness for young women was when they were promised to older men by their parents. In two songs this distressing situation is subverted. In "Gevalt es iz a shlekhte tsayt" (Help it is a terrible time) and "Opgeklapte hoyshayne" (Beaten willows), young women go willingly into unions with elderly rich gentlemen as a way of getting enough money to spend on their younger lovers.[48] In the latter, the inversion does not spare the husband a good share of sexual humor. The title refers to the ritual of beating willow leaves on the festival of *hoyshane rabe*. The slang term "Opgeshlogene hoyshayne" means a person or thing that has had its day, and, in this case, the image of the bedraggled willow leaves comments on the elderly rich gentleman's lack of sexual prowess.[49] Subverting the narrative can be seen as offering young women in the audience a sort of wish fulfillment, a sense of being in control despite a match contracted by parents. The song combats the anxiety that she could be married off to someone a generation older than herself. Making fun of arranged marriages gave a space for women in the audience to be entertained with the prospect that they could change reality, before going back to the tensions of their daily lives.

Yet women's growing independence was not glorified. Popular on both sides of the Atlantic was the song "A boytshik ap to deyt" (An up-to-date boychik).[50] It tells the story of a young American immigrant, Lizi Klaf, who saves her wages for a dowry to get herself

A mesher, a tof	A dandy, a swell
a gu-gu, a blof	With goo-goo eyes, and assurance
a boytshikl vi in posek shteyt	A boychik, as it should be
a tentser, a brand	A dancer, a firebrand
an englishman	An Englishman
a boytshik ap to deyt.	An up-to-date boychik.[51]

A boychik, a word brought into American slang, is a warm, endearing term for a (usually Jewish) young man. However, it is ironic, and this song is brazenly overstepping Jewish cultural boundaries, because this boychik is an Englishman. An Englishman, in this context, is neither a Jewish immigrant nor an Anglo-Jew; here, he is a Christian. In addition, this Englishman is clearly middle class. Lizi's dowry has to be enough to claim a middle-class swell, enough to provide an enticement for a gentile to marry a Jew. This narrative is, however, a cautionary tale because all does not end well.

The increase in out-marriage was a huge source of concern. Many of the old established Sephardi community had assimilated through out-marriage, creating anxiety in the Anglo-Jewish establishment that the same would happen to the Ashkenazi community.[52] For the immigrant orthodox, the fear was that simply being in anglicized England was risky and could lead to young people's marrying out of Judaism. Marrying out of the community was not going to be sanctioned in this music-hall song, and this song had to have a bad ending or it would be condoning Lizi's choice. Gentiles appear in songs, but not as suitable husbands for Jewish girls. Here was a status quo that was less likely to be tampered with.

HAF PAST NAYN: PREMARITAL SEX

Although it was deemed unacceptable for unmarried men and women to have sexual relations before marriage, there is no specific Jewish religious law against it unless it is incestuous or adulterous.[53] Orthodox communities put safeguards in place to limit young people's contact with the opposite sex outside of their own family. With the disruption of immigration and an abandonment of religion, however, sex before marriage no longer had the same taboo attached to it. Indeed, the music hall encouraged and legitimized sexual contact.

Poster for the song "A boytshik ap to deyt," ca. 1902. © Jewish Museum, London. The song was sung by "our beloved character actor" Mr. S. Yozefzon and his wife Madame [Reytsh] Yozefzon. The text at the bottom of the poster lists other songs that the Yozefzons sung in London with the *grestn sukses* (greatest success).

TRANSFORMING COURTSHIP

Few music-hall songs alluding to premarital sex make any moral judgment. Rather, they tell comic tales, suggesting the possibility that sex was available outside marriage and that partners could be found in the Yiddish music hall. Nager offers a cheeky narrative in the song "Plezhur" (Pleasure). It offers advice to girls on how to find a husband.

Meydlekh far aykh—hob ikh a zakh a plezhur!	Girls, I've got something for you A pleasure!
Folg mayn plan—un nemt a man	Follow my plan—and get a husband
es iz a plezhur!	It is a pleasure!
Es iz laykht un gring—zo lang ir zayt ying	It is easy and simple—as long as you're young
dem plezhur!	The pleasure!
Un punkt tsum yor—krigt ir oyf shur	And within the year—you get, for sure
a plezhur.	A pleasure.[54]

Implied in Nager's song is the idea that if a girl does get pregnant, the boy will marry her. Nager's assumption was not a foolproof plan, as the Sarah Pyke House, which housed girls who had babies outside of marriage, attested.[55] The song "Plezhur" uses an anglicism as its title, which implies that this sort of pleasure is an English thing, so to do it makes one join English society. Or it could again be a warning about where anglicization can lead.

The link between sex and English society is alluded to in a number of songs. The narrative of "Haf past nayn" describes how a girl is "led astray by a charlatan." She desires marriage, but he will not agree until half past nine.[56] The term "half past nine" as a euphemism for sex was used in English music-hall songs, and is indeed the title of at least two.[57] The use of the same title in Yiddish serves to accentuate that "half past nine" is something foreign to the Jewish immigrant. It distances Jews from illegitimate sex in the wider culture. Even if Jews were (allegedly) "doing it," it is seen as an English thing to do. Similar to the song "A boytshik ap to deyt," this is a cautionary tale. A charlatan is not a Jew, and a charlatan is not someone to fall in love with.

CHAPTER 6

Markovitsh's song "Mazl" (Luck) makes the same case even more clearly. The second verse describes a couple who have prayed to God for children to no avail. The verse concludes:

Un irs a shvesterl mit a kurts kleydl	And a sister of hers, with a short dress,
on khasene, on khupe glat azoy	Without a wedding, without a wedding canopy, just like that
hot shoyn gehat a yingl mit a meydl	Has already had a boy and a girl
nu hot zi nit dos mazl fun a goy?	Does she not have the luck of the gentiles?[58]

The implication is that pregnancy outside of marriage is not a very Jewish thing, or at least if you behave that way, you're not behaving in a Jewish way. The statement, however tongue-in-cheek, suggests that there is luck to be had by throwing off religious mores and modernizing morality. However, this sort of luck is only for the English gentiles. The song reiterates to the laughing music-hall audience, as if they need reminding, that they are Jews and immigrants and that they live in a small, enclosed, Yiddish-speaking community, and they live their lives by Jewish customs.

There is a Janus quality to these songs, showing multistranded identity and being able to see both ways at the same time. The songwriters know enough about the old ways to know that the traditional immigrants in the audience would be appalled at their representation of sex in the lyrics. Yet they also know that those same immigrants know enough about the new ways not to see it as a malevolent attack on religion. For nonreligious immigrants there is a conceit that they are English enough to laugh at the old ways and Jewish enough to understand the moves toward newer ways. Enjoying the joke is a powerful statement of one's integration into English culture. The assertion of ethnic particularity is in Yiddish, but located in England. It gives the audience a foot in both worlds, old and new. The combination of old and new creates a new cultural artifact, a hybrid mixture sometimes called "ethnicization."[59] So these songs are not lamenting migration, but they are aware of the transition. Indeed, the audiences may go to the Yiddish music hall partly to remind themselves of that in a safe environment.

TRANSFORMING COURTSHIP

The London Yiddish music-hall songs pertaining to sex can be seen as symptomatic of a rapidly changing society. Although change was not confined to England, the London songs allude to changes brought on by immigration. In the traditional Jewish culture of Eastern Europe, religion had a privileged role and structured relationships, giving definition and containment to sexual contact. When these structures were removed, immigrants had to invent new sexual mores. The fall from the heights of Eastern European orthodoxy had left a big gap in people's lives, and the Yiddish music hall was happy to offer coarse humor and naughty fun at the expense of the orthodox and to the delight of the secular.

Although new forms of courtship provided fertile ground for humor, the songs' narratives rarely ended with a happy marriage. The music-hall songwriters may not have seen happy endings as entertaining or saucy-enough material for the music-hall audiences. The only description of the transition to marriage in these songs is Nager's "Malke, malke": "I finally married her, I am now her husband / But when I go out of the house, the lodger comes in."[60] To the music-hall audiences, marriage was portrayed as the end of lighthearted courtship and the beginning of difficulties. And it was marriage tensions that provided further opportunities for making comedy.

7

Marriage, Lodgers, and Transgressive Sex

Ver geyt do in di hoyzn di leydis ikh vet
der man shloft oyf der erd un der lodzher in bet
di moydn zaynen kalt vi ays
un dos iz a bavays
az london hot zikh ibergekert.

Who wears the trousers here? The ladies I bet
The husband sleeps on the floor and the lodger in the bed
The women are as cold as ice
And that is evidence
That London has turned upside down.[1]

Singing with sexual innuendo about being single held few risks. Courtship and marriage prospects were constant preoccupations for single people and their families, and weddings were joyful celebrations. Most humor was saved for marital strife. The more edgy music-hall material concerned areas of life that were not so openly discussed. Firstly, there was what happened after marriage, with the pressures of maintaining ongoing sexual relationships amid immigration, acculturation, and family concerns. The music hall delighted in suggesting all sorts of sexual dalliance, and continued to cultivate the sexual atmosphere through subtle and not-so-subtle references to extramarital sex. The most risqué material, however, was the dirty linen of the community, which was often tucked away and nuanced in the third line of a second verse. This material concerned sexual abuse, domestic violence, deserted wives, and Jewish prostitution.

Some of the Yiddish-speaking audience would have had arranged marriages in Eastern Europe, and some would have married in an East End *khevre*. There would be newly married couples at the halls and married men alone in London seeking entertainment as they saved money to bring their families from Eastern Europe. Although there was no equivalent in the London Yiddish press at this time, the problems that immigration posed for marriage were well documented in the American press. The column *A bintel brif* (A bundle of letters) in the New York Yiddish daily *Forverts* attests to the range of personal problems immigrants had with relationships as a direct consequence of moving to a new country: differences between husband and wife in religious observance, falling out of love, finding other partners, sexual problems, and being unable to deal with marriage as it changed in the new country.[2]

HELO, HELO: THE EXTRAMARITAL "LODGER" AND OTHER DALLIANCES

There is nothing to sing about marriages that run smoothly, and these stories do not regularly appear on the music-hall stage.[3] Of greater entertainment value is marital conflict, and the majority of sexual references in the London Yiddish music-hall songs implied that sex with the object of your desire was more fun as an extramarital affair. The songs repeatedly depict comic scenes of the lover creeping in and out of windows when the husband is away. This type of clowning was not new on the English music-hall scene, yet it moved into new territory in the Yiddish halls.[4]

Although in Jewish law sex between single people does not carry a prohibition, the prohibition of adultery is the seventh of the Ten Commandments. It was considered adultery if a married Jewish woman had sexual relations with any man other than her husband. For a Jewish man, however, it was considered so only if the sexual relations were with a married woman. Although frowned on by the rabbis, sexual relations between married men and single women were not considered adultery.[5] Immigrants, however, had to abide by English law, where any extramarital sex by men or women was considered adultery. Here, too, there were double standards. A man could divorce his wife for any one instance of infidelity, whereas a woman had to prove both adultery and a "matrimonial offense" such as cruelty, desertion, bigamy, or incest.[6]

There was also a nonmainstream niche alternative to marriage, an ideological choice propounded by the anarchists. They advocated free love and ridiculed girls who were tied to the religious forms they saw as nonsensical. Free love meant sexual relationships outside the legal structure of marriage, where the state could not interfere. The proponents of free love often held to the importance of honor and faithfulness and did not condone promiscuity, although conservative journalists sensationalized free love, claiming that it was dangerous and a threat to established society.[7]

Therefore, constant references to sex with married women in Yiddish music-hall songs may seem surprising, as if the songs are condoning it. For any woman feeling trapped in an unhappy marriage, hearing comedy about adultery may well have brought a mixed emotional response of laughter and reflection. Singing about it may have had a cathartic effect and allowed married people to laugh at the stresses of daily married life, difficulties, or inadequacies in their marriages, or enabled men to handle the emotions of missing wives they had left behind in Eastern Europe. One way the songs made fun of marriage and extramarital affairs was with the stock music-hall comic character of the lodger.

Vast numbers of people had lodgings in London, and as Jewish immigrants were greatly increasing the population of the East End, there was a decline in housing and a raising of rent. Streets of slums had been cleared and warehouses and factories erected.[8] Model blocks of flats were built in place of the slums; however, this provided fewer homes at higher rent.[9] Immigrants who wanted to live in the Yiddish-speaking enclave had to pay the higher rents and "key money," leading to people living in overcrowded buildings, sharing a few rooms, subletting, and taking in lodgers.[10] The stream of young male immigrants meant that there were plenty of lodgers to be had.

"The lodger" was a familiar stock character in English music-hall songs. "Our Lodger's Such a Nice Young Man," written in 1897 for the singer Vesta Victoria, tells of a naïve daughter describing how the family lodger helps everyone out, but in particular her mother.[11] A similar comic figure appears in Yiddish songs, where the lodger is mostly a source of flirtation and sexual dalliance for the married landlady.[12] In "Gevalt es iz a shlekhte tsayt" (Help it is a terrible time), a young wife of an older man has a lodger for "fun." In "Der dzhob" (The job), the husband goes out to work and the lodger rocks the (his) baby in the cradle. In "Aheym tsurik" (Back home), the lodger does not even pay rent, yet gets the best steak as well as sexual favors. In "Fri ov tshardzh" (Free of charge), the lodger gets the nicest room and finest bed, and when the husband leaves the house to buy the lodger some wine, the wife gets her "tiddle idl lomtom / totally free of charge." In "London hot zikh ibergekert" (London has turned upside down), the husband sleeps on the floor and the lodger in the bed. In all of these songs, the landlady gets the last laugh and the husband is the butt of the jokes.[13]

Yet not only the husband is mocked but also the lodger. Rather than the lodger being seen as seducer, he becomes objectified and a figure of fun, often naïvely responding to the greater experience of the landlady. In the hands of the Jewish songwriters, jibes were easily made at the expense of the young, male, naïve, orthodox immigrant. In "Freg keyn katshanes, es iz england" (Don't ask silly questions, this is England), the orthodox lodger with his hat and sidelocks is horrified when he is left alone in the room with a woman who is not part of his family, his landlady. The orthodox strictures against being alone with a woman were for just this reason, as she seduces him. The humor is directed at the lodger, who is seen as naïve, not only in matters of sex but in wanting to maintain the modesty of orthodox Jewish law in England. In these songs sexual misbehavior becomes an exemplification of the freedom of England.[14]

The sense these songs offer of the lodger being an unwilling plaything reflected an element of truth. Being a lodger was a precarious life in which the family held control of the day-to-day living arrangements, and the accommodation was very basic. The members of the Yiddish music-hall audience, mainly young, mainly male, may have felt that they were, indeed, powerless in their living arrangements. Zelig Oberman, a married orthodox man who came to London before his wife, relates in his East End memoir of his experience with his overly friendly landlady. She tried to make him take her to the pantomime at the Pavilion Theatre. He refused to go, but she was insistent. Oberman claims "the whole business became horrible."[15]

The frequency of the lodger appearing in song lyrics suggests that masculinity and power relations between husband and wife are affected by the migration experience. When the lodger cuckolds a husband, it is implied that through migration a man loses his potency. He works all hours in a sweatshop, but for such a low wage that he cannot support his family or pay the rent without the additional financial help from taking in a lodger. The man's inability to fulfill his role as husband and father means he has to give up everything, including his wife, in order to be successful as a breadwinner.[16] The lodger may hold a degree of power over the husband in these comic scenarios, yet the lodger is a worker, paying rent, and does not ultimately have the status ascribed to being the head of a household.

This situation is changed when the wife's affair is not with a lodger, but with her husband's boss. In Markovitsh's "Moyshe kum efn mir dem shlos" (Moses come and unlock it for me), the anxious wife is running around looking for her husband, who has left her because she has been accepting favors from his boss. She swears undying love to her husband as long as he comes back with the key for the boxes of expensive trinkets that her lover had given her.[17] Again, the husband is seen as powerless, but this time there is a class dimension. The lover may be a Jew, but he is also a boss, a master, and maybe a sweater. The husband is trapped. He cannot compete, for it would mean the loss of his livelihood. The only choice he is given in the narrative is to run away with the keys to the trinkets. The only way he can make his wife desire him is to take control over access to her lover's gifts.

This song was a part of the repertoire of Beki Goldstein. Goldstein was a favorite on the London Yiddish stage, here taking the role of a flustered, anxious, yet unfaithful wife. The audience's laughter would have been not only at the comic antics in the performance but also at watching their local celebrity performing them. The relationship between Goldstein and her fans, with their response of laughter and shouts, was crucial to the success of the performance. Goldstein colludes with them as she winks and nods, making fun of her wretched husband. In the English music hall, Jacky Bratton argues that music-hall representations of "disorderly women" added to the debate on the position of women against the background of the women's suffrage activism.[18] However, for working-class immigrant women, Goldstein's performance must have offered a foil to the harassed and exhausted wife, who would have guffawed at the idea that she could have enough time, amid homework, child-rearing, and looking after the family home, to have an affair.

Any female actors, such as Goldstein, performing on stage provided an extra frisson for their male fans, becoming a focus for men's sexual feelings in a way that was distanced and safe. The actor was public and visible to others, so not proprietary, and no one man had a monopoly on her attentions. The sexuality is carefully contained, and although the limits of what was acceptable behavior are tested, they are not transgressed.[19] The atmosphere is heightened when the material performed is of a sexual nature, and for female actors it was precarious because the limits were often transgressed in the fictional narratives. The charged feeling could resonate among the mixed audience of men and women.

Given the nature of this material, it is no surprise that the orthodox immigrant community of the East End railed against the Yiddish theatre and music hall and wanted to limit their activities. Yet the music-hall writers fought back. The tension between religious and secular appears in satirical songs that made merciless fun of the orthodox. "Laytudl laytudl day day" (vocalization such as tiddly om pom pom) was a comic ditty that lampooned halakhic (Jewish law) notions of what constitutes adultery and respect for rabbinic teachings. It was partly written, or at least adapted for an Anglo-immigrant audience, by East End publisher Yozef, here called Yoysef moykher-sforim.[20] The second of six verses tells of a woman who goes to her rabbi for advice. Her husband is demanding a divorce, in accordance with halakhic law, on account of her not having had any children.[21] As it is the rabbi's job to find a solution to this problem, he tells the woman not to worry, just to come into another room with him, and nine months later *laytudl laytudl day day*. This song satirizes rabbinic authority on a number of counts, creating a powerful subtext. Firstly, Hasidic rabbis would hold court for their congregation, where they would judge disputes with "divine inspiration." Secondly was the intimation of sexual abuse within the rabbinate. Finally, the song poured scorn on Jewish law that considered procreation as more important than love. No explanation would have been necessary for the insider humor to work.

Although most of the humor in these songs comes from the married woman having a lover, there are times where the narrative also has the husband, maybe unwillingly, taking a lover. In the song "Helo, helo" (Hello, hello), the husband takes a lover only because his wife is having an affair and he wants to stop her. He confronts her in the upwardly mobile area of Stamford Hill:

Shrayt zi, "oy ver iz zi?"	She shouts, "Oy, who is she?"
Zogt er, "kh'hob geton azoy vi di	He says, "I've done the same as you
vos zogstu mayn vaybele dertsi?	What do you say to that, my wife?
Helo, helo!"	Hello, hello!"[22]

Generally a married man having an affair is not considered funny unless his wife finds him and a row or a beating ensues publicly on the streets of London's Yiddishland. Here, the humor is in the adulterous woman getting her comeuppance, although the last laugh is only partially on the husband, because he is still a cuckold and simply clawing back a bit of his power. Yet the song makes a further statement. Setting the scene of adultery in Stamford Hill adds a class dimension because this verse contrasts with an earlier verse describing poverty in Whitechapel's working-class Commercial Street, implying that as one moves up in the world, morality goes awry.[23]

BRIVELEKH FUN RUSLAND: DESERTED WIVES

Many married men came to England months or years in advance of their wives and families, waiting until they had enough money to send for them. Some husbands used immigration as an excuse to escape family tensions and responsibilities, disappearing without a trace into a crowded London and abandoning their families back in Eastern Europe. Some took a second wife and started new families. The deserted wife in Eastern Europe was left without a breadwinner and without any knowledge of where her husband was. This had serious implications for an orthodox woman, because in Jewish law a wife cannot divorce her husband on her own accord; she has to be given a *get* (divorce papers) by her husband. Without being given a *get*, she cannot remarry. The religious authorities tried to trace the husband; however, this was not always easy. In Russia, a *ksube* (religious marriage contract) was the only official document required for a Jewish marriage. The lack of civil marriage documentation made it easier for men to desert their families. If the marriage had been contracted in Russia and the *ksube* had been lost, it was difficult to prove

MARRIAGE, LODGERS, AND TRANSGRESSIVE SEX

> איך זוך
>
> דיא אדרעסע פון מיין מאן אייזיק
> נארטמאן א רוסישער פון סאמאג. לעצ־
> טענס געוועןן אין מערטער־דוויליים,
> ווילס, אין הייזען פאבריק, יעצט אין
> א צוקער פאבריק, אדער אין מאנט־
> שעסטער. ווער עס וויים בישטע צוא
> מעלדען צוא חנה נארטמאן, 4, בע־
> טים גארדענס, קאמארשעל רויד, א.

Advertisement from the classifieds section of the *Idisher ekspres,* searching for a missing husband who had worked in trouser and sugar factories and may have moved to Manchester. © British Library Board, *Idisher ekspres*, 2 January 1904.

the validity of even the religious marriage and to track down the deserting husband.[24] If the husband could not be traced or proved dead, the wife is left an *agune*, a trapped woman. Without wages coming in, the wife and children would be forced onto charity or into prostitution.[25] The *Idisher ekspres*, in its classified section, had many people searching for lost relatives, some of these being deserted wives looking for their husbands.[26] In addition, the Eastern European press was full of appeals from abandoned women and their families and local rabbis pleading for the news of whereabouts of husbands.[27]

Markovitsh's song "Brivelekh fun rusland" (Letters from Russia) captures the desperation of this situation. The song is in the form of letters from Khaye-Sore, who has been deserted in Russia, to her husband who has come to London and disappeared. She hears nothing in return:

Nor ikh zits farshpart	But I sit imprisoned
ikh vart un vart un vart.	I wait and wait and wait.
fun der dire hot men mikh aroysgetribn	I have been thrown out of my flat
undzer moyshele iz shlaf	Our Moyshele is sick
ikh shray tsum himl aroyf	I cry to heaven above
un du vilst keyn entfer nit gebn.	And you don't want to give an answer.[28]

These lyrics were very close to this common experience in the immigrant community, and both the London Yiddish and Anglo-Jewish press publicized the situation.[29] Not only were women abandoned in Russia, but some families were abandoned in England while their husbands went on to America. The Board of Guardians was left to maintain the impoverished family, so it first checked that there was no collusion between husband and wife to try to get the financial support. As a deterrent, the board would attempt to trace the husband but not support the wife.[30] Charities went to considerable lengths to track down the husband rather than pay out.[31]

"Brivelekh fun rusland" narrates letters *from* Russia *to* London, making not only the husband but London the villain of the piece. London is the immoral place where the husband disappeared. In the second verse, Khaye-Sore tells us, "I have pawned everything / including your *tales* [prayer shawl]." The *tales* assumes symbolic significance that can represent an idea and be reinterpreted.[32] The husband identified the *tales* as a religious artifact that would be unnecessary in London. Thus the *tales* signifies not only religion but the abandonment of religion, and London was where you could abandon your religious practice as well as your wife. Khaye-Sore envies her husband's "London joy." London becomes the third party in the relationship, causing the split. The diaspora of London becomes a dangerous and evil place where lives are destroyed and new lives are remade. In desperation the final letter curses the husband: *Nem a mise meshine / in di goldene medine*. (The literal meaning is "Have an unnatural death in the golden country." Here the meaning is "Go to hell in England.")[33] Although the song clearly sides with Khaye-Sore's position, there is humor in these uncontrolled rhymed lines as she loses her temper, and the swear words *mise meshine* are contrasted with the mock-elevated term *goldene medine*, a phrase rarely used positively, and more often used about America.[34] Despite the tragic tale, England is shown as the future.

Markovitsh wrote other sentimental ballads that closely paralleled lived experience. The function of these songs in the music-hall program was to change the atmosphere quickly. The music-hall program would run a comic vulgar turn next to a serious and sad song. The fusion of laughter and tears became a hallmark of the Yiddish theatre and music hall, where audiences were expected to seamlessly move between emotions.[35]

NIT ZIKH ALEYN: DOMESTIC VIOLENCE

The juxtaposition of serious themes and pantomimic silliness can be seen particularly clearly in songs that describe domestic violence as a response to the immigrant experience. Domestic violence is dealt with both with gravitas and with humor, sometimes combining the two. Rabbinic exegesis offers different interpretations of Jewish law concerning what was termed "wife beating." There was a spectrum of opinions, from rabbis who saw domestic violence as wholly unacceptable and reason for divorce, to those who saw it as an acceptable punishment meted out by a man to his wife for "serious offenses." Even famous rabbis such as Caro and Maimonides saw "limited beatings" as a way to control the family.[36] Within the English working class there was an acknowledgment of the inevitability of violence between spouses, and that husbands had a right to use violence against their wives.[37]

Songs about domestic violence vary considerably in tone. The publisher Yozef was the author of "Er meynt yenem nit zikh aleyn" (He means that one, not himself). The song tells of domestic violence in the context of hypocrisy. It exposes a man who says one thing and does another. The man berates other men for their lack of honesty and generosity but does not set himself by the same standard. In the final verse, he condemns another man who curses his wife, yet the narrator goes home and beats his own wife. The lyrics are harsh:

On rakhmones shlogt er ir	Without mercy he hits her
oyf yedn trit shenkt der bandit	With every step, the bandit gifts
zayn shvabe froy petsh on a shir	His Swabian wife endless slaps[38]

Only the chorus line, "He means everyone except himself," moves the song into black humor. The word *shvabe* is an insult, and may have been used here as a swear word like "damned," or it may have got the audience sniggering at making fun of having a German origin.

Songs rarely touch on domestic violence unless it is to prove a point. In the song "A boytshik ap to deyt," discussed in chapter 6, there is an additional twist. Lizi Klaf saves her dowry to marry well, but the English "swell" she married does not prove a good husband, beating her *grin un gel* (equivalent to black and blue).[39] The song attributes this behavior to the new husband's being a gentile Englishman. The cautionary tale's message is simple: do not marry a fashionable, suave gentile because if you do, he'll do what an Englishman does: beat his wife. The fact that the song is a cautionary tale did not seem to lessen its popularity; it may, indeed, have contributed to it. The song is not suggesting that all gentiles beat their wives, but it does suggest that even music-hall songs exerted a cultural force to marry a Jew. The lyrics use the threat of domestic violence as a way of wielding community control. Englishness is referenced by a string of anglicized words, mostly slang: *mesher, toff, bloff,* and *ap to deyt*. The title word, *boytshik*, comes from the English word "boy" and the Slavic diminutive used in Yiddish, *tshik*. These anglicisms reinforce the idea that one must not be seduced by the temptation of the dominant culture. Unlike the hypocrisy of "Er meynt yenem nit zikh aleyn," where the behavior is shameful, here domestic violence is used to prove a point.

The immigrant community's status quo may not be rocked, but it can be criticized through comic subversion. When a wife beats her husband, it is portrayed as pantomime. In a verse of "Der dansing skul," a husband "endlessly" complains that "she hits me for no reason" and "tears pieces from my body." The slapstick humor comes from the seeming absurdity of a husband becoming a victim of domestic violence and crying like a child. To similar effect, the disempowered and cuckolded husband of the song "Vos geyst nisht aheym sore-gitl?" (Won't you come home Sore-Gitl?) threatens to beat his wayward wife with stock theatrical violence:

Ikh tsebrekh dir a beyn	I'll break your bones
hak oys dayne tseyn	Smash your teeth
makh fun dir a bild in a freym	And make you into a framed picture[40]

Yet he is ineffective, made to look like a child having a tantrum, and as such does not threaten any danger, other than his own sense of manhood. Both these songs use the theme of domestic violence to infantilize the husbands and create antiheroes.[41] Rather than make serious points, they show the emasculation of an immigrant man struggling to retain his sense of being the head of the household. Songs dealing with domestic violence within marriage open a space for naming bad behavior within the Yiddish-speaking community. They question the roles of men and women while offering a cathartic release for marriage tensions. These songs are edgy, even dangerous, and are a place to air dirty linen—not in the English public sphere, but in a semi-private immigrant space.

DER BAL-TOYVNIK: SEXUAL ABUSE

Although relationship difficulties could be laughed at in the music halls, the humor changed when sex became abusive. Many immigrants who had settled in London helped their extended families in Eastern Europe by bringing over relations to set them up with new lives in England. The song "Der bal-toyvnik" (The do-gooder), adapted by Nager for a London audience, tells a tale about hypocrisy. The ironically named Mr. Tsadik (Mr. Righteous), known and honored by the immigrant community, uses the pretext of doing good to fulfill his own sexual desires.[42] He pays for a female relation of his wife to come from Eastern Europe to England. She is indebted to him for the travel, board, and lodging and works for him for a slave-labor amount of one shilling a week.[43] The debt mounts with his gifts of clothes and shoes, and when he demands sexual favors, she is in no position to refuse. The righteousness of Mr. Tsadik is transformed into exploitation. Mr. Tsadik is a powerful man, and when pregnancy ensues, the do-gooder quietly calls a doctor who sorts it out. This song shames without naming, and challenges any idealized conception of immigrant life. This is not about sex between young people; it is about sexual exploitation, and possibly rape. Mr. Tsadik is not only a powerful man; he is married. Whatever foibles can be condoned among the young and single, this, in whatever Jewish terms, is serious.

OREM VEY: PROSTITUTION

When the *Pall Mall Gazette* published the "Maiden Tribute of Modern Babylon" in 1884, the report created a public furor, not only for its exposé of prostitution rings in London but also for its melodramatic reporting style. Melodrama was the genre generally associated with popular theatre and the music hall, rather than serious political agitation. The *Maiden Tribute* had subtitles such as "How Girls Are Bought and Ruined," "Why the Cries of the Victims Are Not Heard," and "You Want a Maid, Do

You?" In addition, the *Maiden Tribute* was touted by hawkers taunting young women to make money in the same way.[44] In the Yiddish theatre, story lines involving prostitution may have been dealt with seriously, but in the music halls prostitution was addressed with a light touch and with humor.[45]

Yet it was a very serious issue within the Jewish community. The Anglo-Jewish establishment believed that immigrants brought with them a level of vice and criminality that they had never seen before. The most worrying form of criminal activity involving prostitution was procuring for the white slave trade.[46] White slave trade procurers abducted young women and sold them to brothels across the world. In Galicia, the acute poverty and dearth of men to marry local Jewish girls made procurement easy, assisted by an unofficial wedding ceremony, known as a *shtile khupe* (silent/clandestine marriage). This marriage could take place in the home without a minister, simply with two witnesses, a ring, and a consecration blessing. Although these *shtile khupe*s were religiously correct, there was no registration documentation, and therefore no legal rights for the wives.[47] The *shtile khupe* enabled Jewish traffickers to pose as suitors, seduce young women into compromising situations, and court and marry them. The traffickers would then take their new wives to Europe and onward to other countries, where they would deny the marriage and force the women into prostitution.[48] The women could rarely be traced, although their families advertised in the classified section of the local Yiddish press.[49]

There were also procurers waiting at the London dockside for girls traveling alone, offering counterfeit assistance and luring them into East End brothels. The Jewish Association for the Protection of Girls and Women (JAPGW) was set up in 1885 by women from leading London Anglo-Jewish families to protect women and reduce the white slave trade by publicizing its existence and to make Eastern European communities aware of the dangers by advertising in Yiddish newspapers.[50] The JAPGW made a visible presence at the dockside, boarding ships to find women traveling alone or with male non–family members. JAPGW members escorted women to their addresses, and if these addresses were suspicious, they offered protection. Mile End's Charcroft House was a lodging house for "foreign Jewesses." Set up by Lady Battersea and Emma de Rothschild of the Anglo-Jewish establishment, Charcroft House

MARRIAGE, LODGERS, AND TRANSGRESSIVE SEX

```
יײַ׳ יײ׳                                ראבינאוויץ, זוכט איר סאנסאסני׳ סם
העגעדו                                          וויטשעפּעל.
, פּליאמ
ער, פּיײַ-    ── א שוועסטער ──                          גר א
יא מאקס     איך זוך מײַן שװעסטער, דושיינע               צוא
            בלאָק. 22 יאָהר אלט, א רוסישע                ֿפֿאַרי
25, H       פֿון רוסיען. לעצטענס געזעהען אײַן             ,4
── ── העגעזדו סט., בריק לײַן, וואו א פֿרויא
            האָט־ איהר צוגענומען. ווער עס ווייס
גרי און     ביטע צוא מעלדען אין 13, משאַאַט-              צוא
א גוטען     קאָר־ סטריט סטריט, בריק לײַן, איסט           א פּ
יגעננהי-    ────────                                     קימי
, ווערדען   עקסעלמאנס נייע                               געפּי
ֿסם גייט,   כשר רעסטאראנט                                 זעם
            31, וויל קם סטריט, קאָרנער ענגבורי            גוֿפֿאא
```

Advertisement from the classifieds section of the *Idisher ekspres*, searching for a missing sister, twenty-two years old, last seen taken in by a woman in a street near Brick Lane. © British Library Board, *Idisher ekspres*, 18 January 1904.

offered help to unmarried mothers and first-time "fallen women" who had chosen prostitution as a response to poverty.[51]

The world of Jewish prostitution was not infrequently sung about in the Yiddish music halls, although references are often tucked away and only alluded to by a word or two.[52] Yet key words could be easily spotted if you had insider knowledge, and the audience could pick up the clues. In Nager's "Viktorye park," among the host of roughly described characters is a reference to a Jewish prostitute:

Dort geyt khaye-ite a moyd fun lite	There goes Khaye-Ite, a young woman from Lithuania
zi iz di drite zi voynt in site.	She is the third; she lives in the city.[53]

Khaye-Ite's Jewishness is clearly shown in her name and her origin, and we are told that she is unmarried. That she is a prostitute is alluded to only indirectly in the lyric. The use of "the third" is surely a reference to Winchevsky's poem "Dray shvester" (Three sisters), where the third sister was the prostitute in Leicester Square. Although "Dray shvester" was written a decade earlier, it was a popular song, and as a creative reference point for Nager, it serves to reinforce the London backdrop of prostitution. The allusion to prostitution is reinforced by the reference to Khaye-Ite living

CHAPTER 7

"in the city." The City of London bordered the East End, although few if any Jewish immigrants lived there. Situated between the East End and the West End with the proximity to city businessmen, "living in the city" makes the connection to being a (possibly higher-class) prostitute. The class dimension is also hinted at by the wry comment about Khaye-Ite's *Litvak* (Lithuanian) origin. In an area of London where many of the immigrants were Polish Jews, this is a backhanded jibe. There was a tradition of *Litvak*s and Polish Jews insulting each other, in which the *Litvak*s saw themselves as more educated and saw Polish Jews as uncouth, and Polish Jews made fun of *Litvak*s. In this scenario, counterpointing (and rhyming) the words "city" and *lite* either gives Khaye-Ite's work as a prostitute elevated status or is trying to make a derogatory comment about *Litvak*s. Either way, there is something of a comic twist.

Folk song collector Derek Reid recounted his experience of hearing Bertha Jackson sing "Viktorye park," and how she showed the allusion to prostitution: "I should explain that some of my interpretations are taken from the subtleties of lift in the voice with which the singer—with a twinkle in her eye—implies sauce. Such things cannot be communicated on the written page."[54] The performer may have used a "twinkle" to get the desired response of acknowledging that Khaye-Ite was, indeed, a prostitute, but Nager does not make any social comment here other than creating a mixture of mainly Jewish characters to show the breadth of people using Victoria Park. The song shows that Victoria Park was a location for Jewish prostitution; however, the character of Khaye-Ite is drawn without the coarse descriptions of most of the other characters in the park.

Nager takes a different perspective in "Vos geyst nisht aheym soregitl?" (Won't you come home Sore-Gitl). Here the reference to prostitution is to a man's wife. The song is narrated by the husband, who is running around looking for her. In the first verse, he finds her in Regent Street flirting with other men. In the second, he is told that she likes a *gezunten goy* (a healthy gentile man):

In a publik hoyz iz dos geveyn	It was in a pub
ikh hob aleyn gezen	I myself saw them
vi er-mit-ir	How he and she
hobn getrunkn bir	Were drinking beer
gekusht zikh zeyer sheyn.	Kissing very nicely![55]

MARRIAGE, LODGERS, AND TRANSGRESSIVE SEX

The depiction of sexual behavior in this song is more open than in "Viktorye park." Although it does not state explicitly that Sore-Gitl is having sex for money, there are two references to prostitution. The first is the mention of Regent Street. Regent Street, in London's West End, was considered a place where prostitution was so common that no unaccompanied woman could be there at night for any other reason.[56] In 1887, there was a famous case where Elizabeth Cass, newly in London and working in the West End, was falsely arrested for soliciting in Regent Street.[57] Regent Street also conjures images of single young shopgirls in the large West End department stores, becoming independent, moving out of their parents' homes out from under the thumb of the patriarch, and making a little extra money through prostitution. This may have imperiled young women but also empowered them.[58] In a cartoon from 1871 entitled *An Awkward Encounter in Regent Street*, a respectable middle-class couple bump into a prostitute who is clearly on good terms with the husband.[59] Thus the reference to Regent Street is more than suggestive. It is clear to those in the know, although it may have gone over the heads of the newer immigrants.

The second reference to prostitution is Sore-Gitl's drinking and "making out" with a gentile man in a pub. This is inconceivably brazen behavior for a married Jewish woman, and such an outrageous suggestion simply adds to the comedy of the song.[60] The songsheet of "Vos geyst nisht aheym sore-gitl?" states the song should be sung to the tune of "Won't You Come Home Bill Bailey?," a popular ragtime tune by Hughie Cannon written in 1902. On one level, using a familiar American tune shows the powerful connection made to the popular culture of the West. However, the connection is not so simple. Martin Stokes argues that "musicians in many parts of the world have a magpie attitude toward genres, picked up, transformed, and reinterpreted in their own terms."[61] This rings true for this reappropriation of "Bill Bailey," as the changes to the original are significant to the immigrant experience. In "Bill Bailey," the wife tries to get her errant husband to come home, but in Nager's song, the male and female roles are inverted. This role reversal makes some claim to displaying the immigrant community as an "other," as a topsy-turvy world where men have a more subservient voice. The song's comedy lies in the weakness and inability of the husband to assert his rights. Not only does it play on men's fear of losing their

CHAPTER 7

position as head of the household, but in this scenario the reference to prostitution lies between a challenge to male power and a threat to the family.

A song that takes a more sinister angle is "Orem vey iz der mamen" (Poverty woe to Mother).[62] Also set in Victoria Park, it refers obliquely to the white slave trade and suggests significant Jewish involvement. The characters are men sitting on a bench smoking and pronouncing mocking comments on the world around them in an array of languages: Yiddish, German, English, Turkish, Russian, Romanian, French, Italian, Spanish, and Greek. These languages may refer to immigrant groups or sailors or international criminals. Whoever they are, they are a rather threatening group of men. They make fun of a young woman walking past dressed in the latest French fashion, laughing at her features and clothing. The final verse describes a rich "father" who lets his pretty "daughter" stand outside the *publik hoyz* flirting with gentile louts while he calculates her smiles and caresses to his advantage. The song is full of euphemisms, where *publik hoyz* could mean brothel, "father" would mean pimp, and "daughter" may imply child sex as well as trafficking. It is difficult to see the humor of this song on the page, yet the byline on the songsheet reads: "Sung by our beloved comic singer Rubin Dokter."[63] It can only be guessed at why child prostitution may be a subject for comedy, yet given the sensationalist media, it could be masquerading as a parody, or intended as shocking. The shock would not be that people were ignorant of the issue, but that it was not discussed in public. The difference between this song and previous references to prostitution is the ominous sense of danger, which would have had different meanings for men and women in the audience. Although the female characters in "Vos geyst nisht aheym sore-gitl" and "Viktorye park" seem to be in more independent positions, the women in "Orem vey is der mamen" are very clearly victims.[64]

A final allusion to prostitution is a rather chilling comic song. The narrative of the song "Rum to let" relates that lodgers are fed up with being insulted with a bad reputation and decide to go on strike. They give up being lodgers and get married, leaving the landladies bereft. So notices are put up advertising rooms to let with all sorts of incentives—eggs, fish, kisses, and a daughter in each room.[65]

MARRIAGE, LODGERS, AND TRANSGRESSIVE SEX

Rum to let, farlangt nor yunge boys	Room to let, desiring young boys
rum to let, khapt zey gikher oys. . . .	Room to let, grab them quickly. . . .
Ver es vil koyfn a bargen	Whoever wants to buy a bargain,
der zol koyfn dem gantsn set	Should buy the whole set
Ale tsuzamen farkoyf ikh holsel	I'll sell them all together wholesale
rum to let.	Room to let.

The song plays on the fear of one's daughters being molested. In the memoirs of Markovitsh, he relates how hard it was to find lodgings in London because he was a music-hall artist. It was assumed that he would seduce the daughters of the family. When Markovitsh told the man of one house that he was not a tightrope walker, but an educated man, the father responded: "That's even worse. You've got to be careful with these learned types. . . . They've got no sense of values—what we think is *treyf* [unclean], they think is kosher!"[66] "Rum to let" inverts this fear by using the daughters as bait to find lodgers.

The Yiddish music halls' songs of transgressive sex did different work from those of chapter 6. They created a context that allowed married members of the audience to disappear into a fantasy world, where humor could provide relief from married hardship, before returning to the daily tensions of their ordinary lives. It allowed matters such as marital abuse and prostitution to be discussed in an environment that welcomed cathartic responses in laughter and tears. Songs alluding to prostitution may have heightened the already sexualized atmosphere of the halls, especially if there were prostitutes in the audience allowing men to respond by seeing sex as a possibility.[67]

The immigrant music halls existed within the context of the English music halls. The songwriters wrote words to English tunes, were influenced by English lyrics and melodies, and were subject to English laws and inspections. The songwriters deliberately located their songs in Victoria Park and Regent Street, and referred to the problems of deserted wives and the white slave trade. Yet, at the same time, the Yiddish music

CHAPTER 7

hall was a closed community space using a private language. The use of local referencing provided a sense of community, of ownership, of sharing the experience and locating it in an internal space. Sex may be a universal experience, yet the anglicized Yiddish songs offered a way to engage with difficulties in the experience of sex for immigrants in London. In this community space, there was the opportunity to address edgy subjects, flaunting dirty linen in a semi-private space that was outside the English mainstream, and exposing internal problems that were a result of immigration to the "here" of the music hall in London and the "now" of being in an Anglo-immigrant audience.

Religion: Subverting Religious Motifs

"Matn toyre in vaytshepl" (The giving of the Torah in Whitechapel), *Bloffer*, no. 16 (May 1912). The tablets are inscribed with the words *shund* and *gele prese* (yellow press) and advertise a sensational news story. The caption reads: "*Moyshe* from Whitechapel gives the Jews a new Torah." From the collection of the National Library of Israel.

8

Religion as a Socialist Tool

Me gloybt az dray mit dray iz zibn	They believe that three and three is seven
Me zet darin	They even see
Zogar a zin	Sense in this
Kol-zman dos shteyt nor vu ge-shribn....	As long as it is written somewhere in the scriptures....
Ot hot got odemen fartribn	Now God drove Adam out
fun paradiz,	Of paradise,
un dizes iz	And this is
gants rikhtik vayl es shteyt geshribn.	Quite true because it is written in the scriptures.[1]

To the English outsider, Judaism may have seemed to unify all Jews living in England. However, from within the Jewish community, the nature of religious affiliation and practice was controversial. Adherence to particular orthodox strictures or radical opposition to religious ideas was hotly debated, often bringing conflict and antagonism that permeated both Anglo-Jewry and the East End immigrants.[2]

By the 1880s Anglo-Jewry was run by an elite hierarchy, who had created a Judaism that was both English and Jewish. They had developed anglicized synagogues, liturgy, and forms of clerical style and dress, and synagogue services were presented with decorum. The orthodox majority, led by the Chief Rabbinate and bound together in the United Synagogue, held control of the community with the remit to organize synagogues, burial, and charitable relief. Although these charitable wings supported the poorer sections of Anglo-Jewry, most working-class Jews could not afford the high synagogue fees.[3]

The religion of the Anglo-Jews stood in sharp contrast to the religion of the immigrants. The immigrant orthodox were from a different class and culture, and they brought their prayer customs with them from Eastern Europe. The immigrants' prayer was noisy, participatory, and informal, taking place in *khevres* (small community prayer rooms) rather than large synagogues. Khevres not only had prayers three times a day but also contained Torah study, classes, meetings, and *khadorim* for teaching boys the Bible and the Talmud in Yiddish.[4] During the 1880s khevres proliferated. Some were *landsmanshaftn*, named after towns the immigrants had come from; some were friendly societies or trade unions; and some were *shtiblekh* (Hasidic prayer rooms). The khevres used whatever makeshift accommodation they could find, leading to complaints about their cramped and dirty conditions.[5]

In an attempt to unite the larger khevres and immigrant synagogues and give them a voice within Anglo-Jewry, Samuel Montagu, Liberal Member of Parliament for Whitechapel, established the Federation of Synagogues in 1888. With Montagu's influence within Anglo-Jewry, the Federation was able to fight for immigrant needs through its voice on the Board of Deputies. By 1903 there were thirty-nine khevres and synagogues in the Federation. However, not all khevres wanted to join the Federation, and there was antagonism between the khevres and the United Synagogue about community control, which created bitter conflicts.[6] In addition there were tensions between the United Synagogue and the Federation of Synagogues as they vied for control of the orthodox East End.[7]

The socialists saw religious authority as a capitalist structure that upheld the class divide, and they opposed all religious practice. They were often Marxists, and argued that emancipation from capital would lead to emancipation from religion and religious oppression. In his early writings, Marx wrote of the difference between political and human emancipation. He argued that political emancipation may give civil rights but did not bring the emancipation of a person's faculties and religious ideas. Instead, a free country offered greater freedom to be religious. The only way to be truly emancipated would be for an individual to reject the comfort of religious fantasy, and see themselves as a social being, inseparable from political forces. This would lead to the abandonment of religious ideas, and true emancipation would be possible.[8]

At a mass meeting in Whitechapel in 1890, the socialist thinker Benjamin Feigenbaum pushed the atheist message in a powerful speech asking, "Is there a God?"[9] In the audience was a worker, Thomas Eyges, who was strongly influenced and became an anarchist: "To become a radical in those days, one had invariably first to abandon religious belief, to deny the existence of God. Then, as a matter of course, one became convinced of the uselessness of religious ceremonies, and then followed the abandonment of church or synagogue attendance. This was considered necessary in order to leave the mind free to consider life from a materialistic, rather than from a theological point of view."[10]

Those immigrants who converted to the ideas of socialism became part of a new community. They lost the structure of synagogue services, prayer, liturgical song, observance, study of religious texts, and an orthodox congregation. This was replaced with political events and meetings, theory and discussion, socialist anthems, activism, classes and cultural activities, and comrades.

Socialist and religious workers often came into conflict. Many young anarchists would tease and antagonize religious workers, provoking them by smoking demonstratively on the Sabbath outside East End synagogues and noisily attending annual Yom Kippur balls.[11] Even less religious workers felt their religion being profaned, and this caused greater animosity between the immigrant orthodox and the radical Left. The anger at the anarchists was exacerbated by the guilt many Jewish workers felt from being forced to work on the Sabbath. Other socialists were pragmatic, seeing winning workers to the socialist cause as more important than the anarchist pranks, and used a different approach, trying to put across scientific arguments against religious dogma.[12] They criticized the orthodox establishments for class exploitation and corruption and condemned religious theology and practice as superstitious and inequitable. But their aim, at least initially, was to involve workers in labor politics and so encourage their identification with the workers' struggle, anticipating that political conviction would expel religious practice in due course.

The atheist socialists' combative behavior was seen as incitement and fiercely opposed by the religious sectors of the community who united to fight them. Samuel Montagu tried to sabotage the socialists by putting the *Arbayter fraynd* out of circulation on a number of occasions. He also employed the charismatic preachers Dr. Mayer Lerner and Chaim Zundel Maccoby, the *magid* (Rabbi) of Kamenitzk, to preach against socialism and atheism in East End pulpits.[13]

Yet, despite differences, conflict, and a lack of understanding between sections of the community, religion had a particular unifying factor. There was much in common that stemmed from a knowledge of religious liturgy, text, rhythm of the Jewish year, festival customs, and general knowledge connected to Bible stories. Although different interpretations of religious texts often created different practice, the texts themselves were part of a shared language. These texts, biblical, Talmudic, and liturgical, were well known and gave inspiration, contexts, and structures to writers from different positions across the spectrum from orthodox to atheist. Nonreligious immigrants had almost invariably come from religious families, and many revolutionary socialists had been through a rigorous religious education, even rabbinical seminaries. Religious texts, terminology, and experience of the practice were part of the socialists' cultural identity, and could be used by them as understandable and familiar benchmarks from which to create a subtext of allusions and lay the basis of their critical comment.

In demanding a reexamination of the role of religion, socialist journalists used language from liturgy for effect, such as the headlines in the *Arbayter fraynd*: *Hine yom-hadin* (Today is the day of judgment) or *unetane tokef* (Let us voice the power), around the time of the High Holy Days.[14] These solemn words, central to the most intense days of prayer in the Jewish calendar, would have had a powerful effect when used out of context. Words from the liturgy acted as a marker or shorthand to describe a concept, while religion and God were reengineered to become socialist tools. The immigrant socialist poets both used and parodied religious texts, structures, and concepts as a part of their poetic vocabulary, allowing the reader to make connections between religious and socialist ideas. It could display the writers' knowledge of religious ideas and texts, to show that their rejection of religion was not from a position of ignorance. It included the religious worker in the creation of a broad workers' coalition. The use of familiar religious language by the socialists displayed the commonality of knowledge, if not of experience, between Jewish workers, whether currently religious or not.

One of Winchevsky's biographers, Abraham Bik, argues that socialists' use of religion "was not some intellectual cult of biblical themes, it was about using the religious terminology as a way of requisitioning workers to revolutionary ideas."[15] Indeed, just as the byline for the *Poylisher yidl* was from the Psalms, the *Arbayter fraynd* used a motto from the legendary rabbi Hillel: "If I am not for myself, who is for me? And if I am only for myself, what am I?"[16] This oft-used religious text, describing a humanitarian idea, became a socialist tract highlighting points of common philosophy in an attempt to show socialism to be the true religion. Although socialists may have inhabited an atheist and deeply antireligious stance, it did not necessarily lead them to abandon religious concepts that were helpful in promoting the socialist cause.

Socialist poetry with religious themes concentrated on three main areas. Some lyrics berated the inequity and corruption of rabbinical authority, conceptualizing it as part of the capitalist system. Other poetry scorned prayer and belief in God as antiquated and unscientific. It suggested that religious belief and practice served as an opiate that caused political inactivity and offered no way out of poverty. Thirdly, known religious ideas were used as a way of explaining socialist precepts.

RABINER, MASHINER: RELIGIOUS DIFFERENCES AND CLASS

Religious authority held huge power over the orthodox in both Anglo-Jewish and immigrant sections of the community, and the hierarchical structures in both were attacked by socialists. In the satirical poem of August 1888 "Rabiner un mashiner: A kontrast" (Rabbi and machinist: A contrast), Winchevsky singles out the Anglo-Jewish rabbinate for criticism and satire. This assault has less to do with the nature of religion and more to do with privilege, class, authority, paternalism, and control. The rabbi of the poem represents the Anglo-Jewish rabbinate of the United Synagogue, described as rich, lazy, working with words, and earning well.[17] The machinist represents the immigrant tailor who, by contrast, struggled to make in a year what the rabbi earned in a month, laboring with his hands, making what the rabbi used:

Ikh bin a mashiner,	I am a machinist,
du bist a rabiner—	You are a rabbi—
du handlst mit got,	You do business with God,
on zorg, on khlapot;	Without worry, without toil;
dayn eyntsike skhoyre	Your only merchandise
iz dayn bisl toyre,	Is your bit of Torah,
ven ikh zits un shtep,	While I sit and stitch,
farukt in a sklep. . . .	Bent over in a cellar. . . .
Du bist a rabiner,	You are a rabbi,
ikh bin a mashiner—	I am a machinist—
ven ikh zol zayn foyl,	If I am lazy,
ken ikh mit mayn moyl	I cannot make a living
nit makhn a lebn	With my words
mir vet men nit gebn	I will not be given high wages
mit mayn sheyn geshtalt	For my fine form
vi dir—groys gehalt.	As you are for yours.
Du bist a rabiner,	You are a rabbi,
ikh bin a mashiner—	I am a machinist—
ikh arbet—du zogst,	I work—you talk,
ikh makh—du farmogst;	I create—you own;
du paskenst a shayle	You rule on a religious problem
un lernst a vayle;	And study Torah for a while;
du shpilst zikh—ikh zorg,	You play—I worry,
du layst gelt, ikh borg.	You lend money, I borrow.[18]

The poem addresses themes that Winchevsky repeatedly wrote about: poverty, the worth of physical work, and the inequality of ownership. It stresses the difference between mental and physical work. These Marxist themes did not generally include a religious element, yet in "Rabiner un mashiner," the image of the rabbi posits rabbinical authority in the class hierarchy of the rich, and an exploiter of the worker. The rabbi becomes a symbol of the privilege of the rabbinate, setting him a class apart from the working tailor. The poem contrasts the jobs, showing the lack of connection between them. Each of the ten verses exposes how class division brings different aspects of inequality, in food, homes, and clothing. In particular the poem depicts the indifference, or even ignorance, of the rabbi to the tailor's plight. Class difference pits the Anglo-Jewish orthodox against both secular and religious immigrant workers. Religious workers were as affected by hardship as any other worker, and many were involved in union action. Many orthodox Jews did not see a conflict between praying in a khevre and fighting for improved working conditions, and small khevres would double up as meeting places for socialist and union meetings. Although the majority of religious workers did not subscribe to socialism, for some it was still seen as a useful framework for organizing worker protest.[19]

"Rabiner un mashiner" was likely to have been written in response to the ongoing debate about the nature of the sweating system and the role of immigrant labor. In March 1888 John Burnett, labor correspondent of the Board of Trade, published a report on sweating in the East End tailoring trade. Amid the report's analysis of the system and function of immigrant labor, he described the appalling conditions for workers in sweated workshops.[20] These conditions were condemned by Anglican and Catholic primates, and Jewish socialists agitated for Chief Rabbi Hermann Adler to follow suit. Adler refused, dismissing the dreadful working conditions as an exaggeration. The *Arbayter fraynd* decried him as an ally of the sweaters, citing connections between sweaters, capitalists, and the Anglo-Jewish religious leaders. The chief rabbi was condemned as someone who "believes in the sweating system more than God," and honorary officers of East End synagogues were called "sweaters."[21]

Unrest over labor conditions in the immigrant trades came to a head with the "Synagogue Parade" in 1889. On this tumultuous occasion, hundreds of Jewish workers marched to the Great Synagogue in Houndsditch, on the fringes of the City of London, and bordering the East End, where Adler was going to deliver a sermon to the unemployed and sweated labor.[22] In response to socialist demands for an eight-hour day, Adler mocked the East End workers by suggesting that he worked harder than they did and was also utterly exhausted by his toil.[23]

The socialists saw the sympathies of the Anglo-Jewish establishment as firmly lying with the masters and not with the workers. Winchevsky attempted to show that inequality was linked to corruption within the system and abuse of religious authority, and that the Anglo-Jewish clerics always took the side of masters and exploiters. Far from alienating religious immigrants, Winchevsky included them as workers. The religious immigrant workers were unlikely to have identified with the *rabiner* of the poem, since the Anglo-Jewish United Synagogue did not practice the strict religious Judaism they practiced and was not fighting their battles. Indeed, the *Jewish Chronicle* regularly campaigned against immigrant *khadorim* and khevres.[24] This gave the socialists and the workers a common target. The poem cleverly gave the religious immigrants no real choice, since they were hardly likely to think of themselves as middle-class orthodox Anglo-Jews and hence, notwithstanding their religiosity, were forced to place themselves in the ranks of the immigrant working class. Winchevsky's antagonism with Anglo-Jewish religious authority in his poems opened a door for orthodox immigrants to feel part of the workers' struggle. His barbs echoed their own frustrations, and they could see that Winchevsky was fighting against the type of religion that they were also against.

In Winchevsky's critique of class differences, he not only pitted Anglo-Jewry against the immigrant orthodox, he also attacked unequal behavior within immigrant religious structures. The poem "A khoydesh on arbayt" (A month without work), discussed in chapter 5, criticizes the ideas and modes of behavior in the immigrant khevres. They are also seen as places of inequality, where status could be conferred by virtue of pedigree or affluence rather than hard work. The poem establishes the importance of pride in being a worker:

Ikh bet nit bay keynem	I don't ask anyone
a titl, a sheynem	For a fine title
ikh vil keyn moyreyne nit zayn:	I won't be a teacher/rabbi:
Ikh vil a bavuster	I want to be known
als erlekher shuster,	As an honest cobbler,
als erlekher shnayder nor zayn.	As an honest tailor.[25]

The poem defines a worker as a cobbler or tailor, certainly not *moreynu*, a deferential term used for an immigrant rabbi. The poem demands pride

RELIGION AS A SOCIALIST TOOL

in being a productive worker. The fourth verse of the poem uses religious terminology to portray inequality in the synagogue system of "honors."

Ikh bet nit keyn shlishi,	I don't ask for a *shlishi*,
keyn maftir, keyn shishi,	No *maftir* no *shishi*,
ikh vil nit in mizrekh vant shteyn.	I don't want to stand at the eastern wall.

The meaning of this verse is transparent to synagogue-going Jews. The terms *shlishi* (third), *shishi* (sixth), and *maftir* (concluding) denote sections of Torah reading on a Sabbath when a member of the congregation is given an "honor" by being called up to the Torah to pronounce a blessing over some of the verses of that week's reading. There are usually eight honors, with those mentioned in the poem considered the most important. Anyone called up for an honor was expected to make a donation to the synagogue, and the amount of donation was announced to the congregation. To merit the distinction of the most important honors, a person would have to be wealthy enough to give a significant sum of money.[26]

Respect was also conferred by preferential seating. The reference to the *mizrekh vant* referred to the wall at the front of the synagogue, facing east toward Jerusalem, and near the ark containing the Torah scrolls. Seats there were reserved for the most respected synagogue members and officials, those who held authority in the community. Indeed, these were the people who would determine who received honors each Sabbath. A poor tailor sitting at the back of the khevre, earning barely enough to support his family, would have been excluded from this honors system even though he may have been as devout and deserving as wealthy members of the community.[27] By acknowledging this situation, Winchevsky's poem gives dignity to the religious worker who is not taking part in synagogue hierarchies and the honors system.

Religious language and ideas are used here as a way of explaining the dignity of work through a common synagogue experience. They identify how socialist principles can be used to challenge those religious structures that uphold inequality. In this way, the poem creates a space where the politically concerned religious immigrant worker could relate socialist thought to a religious context, perhaps not convincing enough to induce the reader or hearer to abandon religious practice as the author hoped, yet sufficient to extend the borders of who might be included within a very broad Left.

ARBAYTER KINNOUS: RELIGIOUS TEXT BECOMES SOCIALIST DOGMA

A penny pamphlet entitled *Kinnous oder arbayter klogelider* (Elegies or workers' laments) was published by the *Arbayter fraynd* printers in 1888.[28] It contains two long elegies about the life of the worker in London. The first elegy concerns sweating conditions in the East End, and the second focuses on the lack of unity among Jewish workers and on the need to stand united.[29]

The title word, as printed *Kinnous*, means dirges or elegies, and in standard Yiddish would be spelled *kines*. The earliest kines were laments commemorating the destruction of the Temples of Jerusalem. The most famous kine in the Bible is *Eykhe* (the Book of Lamentations), which is chanted to a mournful melody on the annual fast day of *Tisha B'av*. All religious men would be in synagogue, and familiar with the reading. *Eykhe* is made up of five chapters, and each chapter is a poem. The first four are written as acrostics with every verse starting with the next letter of the Hebrew alphabet, a common device in Hebrew prayer. Across time, a tradition developed of writing kines about later tragedies that befell the Jewish community, so that a history of Jewish sorrow and anti-Semitism can be viewed through them.

The socialist *Kinnous* of 1888 also use the acrostic form and continue the tradition of describing Jewish hardship, making extensive use of religious terminology and direct Hebrew quotations from *Eykhe*. Numerous religious concepts are referred to: the ritual expiation of sin before Yom Kippur, different levels of earth and hell, slavery in Egypt, and the biblical verse "You should love your neighbor as yourself."[30] The socialist *Kinnous* are carefully crafted, making religious allusions a direct part of the explanation of socialism. Verse five describes how, for immigrants to London, the tyrannical masters of Russia have been replaced by English gentile master sweaters who have thirty or forty slaves. The sweatshop masters are put here into the same category as the Russian tyrants.

RELIGION AS A SOCIALIST TOOL

Verse six takes the argument to a new level, by including biblical terminology. It begins with a rather peculiar statement demanding that we should recognize our own *sarey khamishim vesarey asares* (leaders of fifty and leaders of ten). This expression comes from a portion of the Torah about Yisro, the father-in-law of Moses. It was common for socialists to parody the Passover story where Moses leads the Children of Israel out of Egypt, and to include references to capitalism and the sweating system. Indeed, a reference to Egypt and slavery had already been made in this poem. However, in these *Kinnous*, it takes a new tack. In the Torah, Yisro, a Midianite (not a Jew), suggested to Moses that he delegate his authority and set up judges: leaders of thousands, hundreds, and *sarey khamishim vesarey asares*, leaders of fifty and ten. The socialist poem transfers talking about biblical judges to discussing leadership and hierarchy in London. The term *sarey khamishim vesarey asares* is so specific and so Jewish, it could not be used for English masters, so the phrase used the biblical concept of leadership as a way to explain Jewish involvement in sweating system abuses.

But it goes further. In response to the question of who the Jewish leaders are, the poem tells us their *yikhes* (pedigree). The Jewish sweaters come from families who were "bathhouse heaters, porters and domestic servants." Their parents worked in the service industries, not in production. They were upwardly mobile, ensuring that their children would not be workers, but would be masters, or as the poem suggests, Jewish tyrant masters. This idea is in keeping with socialist dogma, which differentiates between different types of work and which attacks upward mobility. The poem condemns the Jewish masters, and the strength of the condemnation is emphasized through the use of the biblical terminology. The biblical expression Judaizes the socialist concept and serves to draw the reader in before turning into a socialist tract. It therefore acts as fairly subtle manipulation. There is also a paradox in the use of these terms because in the Torah judges were chosen for their qualities of honesty and lack of greed. However, in the London context, the sweaters are characterized as dishonest and greedy.

The *Kinnous* are not tentative and do not hold back from offending the feelings of religious workers. Rather, they address them head on. They focus on some of the tricky feelings workers may have about their need

PRICE ONE PENNY.

קינות
אָדער

אַרבייטער קלאָגעלידער
KINNOUS

פֿערפֿאַסט פֿון

רעואל, יתר, יתרו, חובב, חבר, קני, פוטיאל.

עבדים משלו בנו, פרך אין מידם. (איכה)

LONDON.
Workers Friend Printing Office,
40, Berner Str., Commercial Road, London, E.
1888.

Cover of the *Kinnous oder arbayter klogelider* (Workers' laments), 1888. © British Library Board.

RELIGION AS A SOCIALIST TOOL

to compromise on religious observance. Verse seven describes how the workers toil for seven days without being given the Sabbath off:

Zibn teg arbaytn mir in gehenem-hatakhtn,	Seven days we work in hell,
shabes, undzer ru-tog, hobn mir oykh keyn tsayt vegn zikh tsu trakhtn.	On the Sabbath, our day of rest, we have no time to think about ourselves.
vayl shtendik iz shabes undzer mishpet, undzer yom-hadin,	Because the Sabbath is always our judgment, our day of judgment,
vos der sotn bay di veydzhes rekhnt oys undzere zind.	When Satan calculates our wages by our sins.

The familiar situation tells of having to work on the Sabbath to make a living. Yet for the religious it is a sin to work on the Sabbath, a sin that may come out in extra wages, but wages paid by Satan. The text draws on superstition and on the fear of the punishment for good and evil, and is layered with religious terms, concepts, and quotations. There is actually no mention of God in either of the two elegies. God is absent, but the notion of the divine is taken and inverted against religion, and shown as hypocritical. It is a brilliant example of how the poem undermines religion and at the same time expresses the inequality of capitalism. It makes the worker's kine utterly unlike an English socialist tract. The ideas are socialist, but so steeped in Jewish custom that they would be incomprehensible to an English socialist audience even in translation. They are totally *Jewish* texts, expressing a mainstream, socialist critique of religion and capitalism but specifically targeting the Jewish worker. As such, and notwithstanding the few specific references to England, the texts are transnational in that they would be understandable across the Jewish world.

These *Kinnous* are not simple parodies. They are deeply serious, thoughtful, and provocative attempts to subvert religious texts to socialist aims. Making the connection between an ancient form of religious text and the problems of the sweating system in London is a form of reengineering the religious elegy form. The seriousness of the *Kinnous* adds gravitas to the socialist subject matter, equating suffering under capitalism with previous eras of persecution. As well as showing connections, subverting a known text displays the differences and suggests, by example, ways to change and modernize.

The *Kinnous* are clever satires. They certainly show the authors' familiarity with Bible texts and with *Eykhe*, and a knowledge of religious debates. It is this that adds an element of humor to an otherwise serious text. On the front cover of the workers' kine, the authorship is attributed to Reuel, Yeser, Yisro, Khovav, Khever, Keini, and Putiel. These seven names are pseudonyms, and are an in-joke. The third name on the list is Yisro, whom we have already met, Moses's father-in-law, who suggested appointing judges. In a commentary to the Torah, the eleventh-century commentator Rashi lists seven names of Yisro: those used by the socialists as fictional authors of their *Kinnous*.

There is no obvious connection between Yisro and *Eykhe*. *Eykhe* is traditionally said to have been written by the prophet Jeremiah, but it was debated as to whether it was really the work of multiple authors. Possibly the implied meaning here is that the seven authors are really one person. Whatever the authors were saying in using the pseudonyms, these details are not as important as the Jewish socialist writers showing that they knew the texts well. They are showing off, or having a lot of fun at creating a clever text that has a serious meaning. They may have needed to confirm to the immigrant orthodox that they were part of the same culture, and that their political leanings came from choice, not from ignorance. They may, indeed, have known more about religious literature than the traditionally religious East End immigrant worker, and it is possible that some of the references would have gone over the heads of the workers who had less Jewish education than they had.

The use of a religious idea to make specific points about capitalism is also a part of the poem "310," written by Namerts (the pseudonym of Simon Friman) in 1889. The "310" of the title refers to a section of the Talmud that describes the number of worlds that the righteous orthodox are promised after death as a reward for good behavior on earth. Friman's poem is in the form of an argument between two characters: Capital and Work. Work claims that Capital has denied him the worlds of "mills and breweries and pleasure gardens" and left him one world of suffering, hunger, and cold. Capital tells Work it does not matter because he will get 310 worlds eventually. Work charges Capital with constantly trying to find new worlds through missionaries colonizing and looting other countries. Work warns Capital that it will rise out of the grave, out of the multiple worlds in heaven, and take over this one world on earth, leaving the 310 of the afterlife to Capital.³¹

Here, a Talmudic idea provides a bargaining tool in the debate about capitalism. It reprimands the rich for abusing the worker, yet at the same time it berates the religious workers for seeing the future as spiritually secure and so not needing to fight for the improvement of conditions in the present. It uses the concept of 310 to argue for revolution. In so doing, it belittles the religious concept and contends that one modern nonreligious world is more important than 310 religious worlds after death.

ALT UN YUNG: ATTACKING BELIEF IN GOD

God was considered to be an antipolitical concept, and religious practice an activity that mitigated against activism. The socialist poets attacked immigrant rabbis, whom they believed held the East End orthodox in thrall to superstitions and unscientific ideas, and workers who thoughtlessly believed them. These poems are not sensitive to the feelings of religious workers, and directly claim that belief in God and religious practice are outmoded ideas that have no place in a modern society. The poem "Alt un yung" by Izak Likhtnshvayg puts religious thought at one end of a continuum and scientific discovery at the other end. In the poem's narrative, the old outmoded heavens were full of the mysteries of God, angels, and paradise. It was a place where good and evil were rewarded. But now the modern heavens are open to the scientist who finds stars that make up other worlds where evil and righteousness have no part. The poem ends: "In the heavens there is no mediator / It is entirely different above / And the elders must hear / Though they don't want to believe it."³² The poem uses generational and scientific change as an argument for atheism. It allows for religion to be seen not as foolish but as old-fashioned and outdated. Science becomes the new philosophy that progressive generations need to take on. Faith can no longer be blind, as science affords answers.

Blind faith is also the butt of the attack in an untitled satirical poem by Winchevsky that uses the repeated last line of verses *es shteyt geshribn* (it is written in the scriptures). The poem mocks the way the orthodox defend illogical beliefs and behavior by claiming that it all comes from divine scriptures. The phrase may be used by the religious to explain their behavior, but it implies ignorance, because the exact location of chapter and verse of scriptures is not known. The use of *es shteyt geshribn* in this poem argues that the answer is not in the scriptures and that people use the expression as an excuse. The verses of the poem begin with stating that three plus three is seven, even is odd, straight is crooked. But having established some humorous examples, it moves to more serious claims: the world belongs to the rich, poverty has to exist, the Jews are a chosen people, and Jews have predestined partners and cannot choose their spouses. The variety of claims—political, religious, social—hit at different areas of workers' lives. The suggestion is that all of these areas need to be rethought, because the immediate reason is an abandonment of responsibility, a lazy claim, *es shteyt geshribn*. The main implication is that God is the most illogical concept and has no place in modern life.

A poem that gives a clearer statement of atheism is Bonfeld of Glasgow's "Reb yudl far got" (Mr. Jew before God). The poem tells of a poor man in a corner of a synagogue endlessly praying, weeping, and pleading with the creator of the bountiful and beautiful world not to forsake him. He begs for himself, for the Jewish people, and for relief from incessant anguish and poverty. The final line mockingly states: "And God answered thus—like the walls."[33] Its message is clear: activism will change conditions, not prayer; prayer is talking to the walls. Denying God was unlikely to draw religious workers to socialism, although it may have made less religious or newly socialist Jews feel supported for their choices.

Religious imagery and language used from a socialist perspective had a number of functions. Allusions to powerful liturgy grabbed attention and became shorthand for familiar ideas that did not have to be explained. The use of religious terminology shows that the socialists are not coming to atheism from a place of ignorance. Even if religious concepts were rejected, the structures of religious practice, literature, and knowledge were a part of their cultural makeup. The Yiddish language itself is suffused with religious terminology and conceits, creating a shared heritage that can communicate a message in the most straightforward way.

The reappropriation of religious ideas made them useful for the socialist cause. The socialists were not as interested in supporting religious immigrants as in converting them to radical politics and to an engagement with the modern world. Their use of religion, in this sense, was functional, with the sole aim of making revolutionary activists.

The socialists wanted to create a new community. Yet many workers were coming out of religious backgrounds and would have had divided loyalties. Some of those who became socialists would have been left with sentimental feelings for the old ways or harbored feelings of guilt for abandoning religious practice. Embedding religion into Jewish socialist dogma kept liturgical language close, kept a connection to biblical texts, and brought an old familiar mode into a new radical world.

9

Religion Updated and Improved

"Nisim" gresere un vunder	Great and wonderful "miracles"
zet men haynt a gantses yor . . .	Can be seen today the whole year . . .
Dankt dem himl far di "nisim,"	Thank heaven for the "miracles"
vos in "ist-end" kumen for.	That happen in the "East End."[1]

One type of noise that filled the streets of Whitechapel and Stepney three times daily, especially on the Sabbath and holy days, was the sound of prayer. Singing and mumbling would be heard coming from numerous small *khevres*, *shtiblekh*, and workplaces, as groups of men prayed during their breaks. Religious observance, however, was not homogenous in practice. Orthodoxy from the old country had a range of religious expressions, and the East End became a microcosm of Eastern European sects and factions, each with its own specific codes and styles.[2] In addition, there were immigrants who embraced the engagement with modernity and brought new ideas to their religious beliefs and practice. These divisions created diversity within the religious community and may indeed have brought a new vitality to Judaism in England, showing that religion mattered.[3] But it did not matter to everyone.

Although the socialists thought that religion was an apolitical belief that did not fit in with their principles, many workers lost their religious faith for less ideological reasons. The Jewish Board of Guardians and Russo-Jewish Committee had a policy of dispersing Jewish workers into non-Jewish trades as a way of lessening the crowded job market. However, this meant having to work on Saturday, rather than keeping the Sabbath. Additionally, exhausted workers from Jewish workshops wanted to sleep on the Sabbath morning rather than getting up early to pray, and in general there was growing religious indifference.[4] The *Jewish Chronicle* of 1903 reported a paper given by East End social worker and commentator Harry Samuel Lewis to a meeting of the West London Synagogue Association. Lewis expressed anxiety about the "decay of orthodoxy in East London": "It is a common saying amongst the foreign Jews that England is a 'freie Medinah' [free country]—a country where the restrictions of orthodoxy cease to apply.... As the Jew becomes anglicised, there is a risk that he may be de-Judaised. Unless he possess a reserve force of earnest conviction, he will be unable to retain a religious life which differs widely from that of the world around him."[5] This strongly worded paper, addressed to the Anglo-Jewish orthodox, decried the amount of voluntary Sabbath-breaking and the decline in regular synagogue attendance. Immigrant men may have arrived in London with their prayer shawls and phylacteries, but after a few months, when they had ceased being "new" immigrants, the religious items were discarded along with the practice. Lewis's fear was that losing the religious code would lead to more extensive moral degradation.

Music hall songs and satirical poetry often represent these changing times, describing and commenting on religious tensions. A major theme was how to relate religion to modern-day England, and either abandon religion or modernize orthodoxy to make it a part of daily life. The lyrics sometimes criticize Anglo-Jewish orthodoxy, yet mostly they concern immigrants' own religious practice. They lampoon the old-fashioned religion of the *heym*. They accuse England of being a place where religious observance is under threat, and they attempt to reshape the nature of religious practice. They use themes from festivals, liturgy, and religious philosophy to provide metaphors and frame ideas with humor and parody. The lyrics offer insight into concerns about religion at a popular level as they oppose, criticize, or celebrate both a changing religious life and a growing nonreligious cultural Judaism.

FREG KEYN KATSHANES: RELIGION IN THE HALLS

When religion was a theme in music-hall songs, it almost exclusively focused on narratives of the loss of religious practice in England. England is portrayed as a modern country of freedom and technological advance in stark contrast to the old homeland. With different degrees of sympathy, the songs voice different aspects of the experience of being a nonreligious Jew in England. The Yiddish music halls thus provided a place where nonreligious or nonpracticing Jews could meet like-minded people, and somewhere they may have attended more regularly than the synagogue.

The decline of religion was the theme of five London Yiddish music-hall songs discussed here, although the lyrics do not all exhibit the same concern and dismay with which Lewis wrote. Many immigrants going to the music hall would have only recently become nonreligious. For some, secularization would have been from ideological conviction, and the music hall could signify a sign of independence from religious strictures. For others, there may have been discomfort or guilt at abandoning religious mores, and the music hall bringing together similar people may have provided support. The music halls, however, were not only patronized by nonreligious Jews. The spectrum of observance meant that many Jews were partially observant. Jewish men and women may have felt attached to some of the religious mores, yet felt the loss of the prescribed religious code they had been a part of in Eastern Europe. Characters in music-hall songs put across these feelings of confusion, loss, and disorientation. Both the sadness at losing something precious as a result of immigration and the satire directed at religious ideas and authority were expressed in songs in both a serious and comic way.

Joseph Markovitsh's sentimental songs offer empathetic narratives of people complaining about the way religion had been discarded in London. In "Aheym tsurik" (Back home), the singer bemoans his decision to sell up and leave the old country after his wife dies, and move to live with his daughter and son-in-law in London.[6] He describes his despondency after his first few weeks in London:

Nishto keyn yontev, keyn shabes, keyn din	Here there are no festivals, no Sabbath, no law
ven ikh zing kol mekadesh klapt oybn di mashin.	If I sing "*Kol Mekadesh*," the machine is heard upstairs.
Men arbet um shabes, men neyt un men prest	They work on the Sabbath, sew and press

RELIGION UPDATED AND IMPROVED

men kokht do oykh shabes, men bakt un men frest.	They also cook here on the Sabbath, bake and gobble.
Dos yidishkeyt iz do tsu shand un tsu shpot	Here Judaism is held up to shame and ridicule
men lakht do fun frume, men gloybt nisht in got.	Here people laugh at the orthodox, and don't believe in God.
Mayn eydem, der knaker, der makher, der bos	My son-in-law, the big shot, the boss
roykhert um shabes a papiros.	Smokes a cigarette on the Sabbath.

Kol mekadesh is a prayer traditionally sung by the man of the house on a Friday night after coming in from synagogue, surrounded by the family just before the Sabbath meal. In "Aheym tsurik" the sound of the *Kol mekadesh* prayer is heard in counterpoint to noise not allowed on the Sabbath, those of the tailoring machines and cooking pots. Instead of sitting as a family to the Sabbath meal, people gobble like animals. It is not simply the act of breaking the religious rules of the Sabbath that the father complains about; it is the complete lack of interest in religious practice. In Lewis's *Jewish Chronicle* article quoted earlier, he warned: "It must often happen, however, that former convictions are replaced with indifference—indifference that not only extends to positive religion in the narrower sense but also to the obligations of moral rectitude."[7] And, indeed, in the third verse of "Aheym tsurik" there is a lodger jibe, showing extramarital sex as a symptom of the slippery slope caused by Sabbath-breaking. The tone of the song is light in its caricature of the family's loss of religion. The more serious ridicule is saved for the father, not for his orthodox practice, but for his antimodernization stance in eschewing freedom and democracy. The chorus runs as follows:

Aheym, aheym, aheym tsurik	Home, home, back home
moykhl, moykhl aykh dos glik	You can keep your joy
oyf hefker iz dos altsding do geshtelt	Everything here is chaotic.
Ikh bin mir a yid fun altn shtand	I am a Jew of the old ways
moykhl aykh dos fraye land	You can keep your free country
aheym aheym tsurik in der alter velt.	Home back home to the old world.

CHAPTER 9

The song polarizes the loss of religion into east and west, the old and the new, father and daughter. Although the verses show some sympathy for the father's dismay at the loss of religion, his rejection of the modernity of England transforms the father into a figure of fun, and he is no longer treated seriously.

This cannot be said for "Di tsvey doyres" (The two generations), another song by Markovitsh that engages with the themes of generational difference and the anglicization of religious practice.[8] This song, however, treats the subject seriously and with anger. It describes the way people with modern ideas forsake and scorn the old belief:

Fun altn dor lakht zikh der yunger oykh. . . .	The young also laugh at the old generation. . . .
alts vos alt iz hot bay zey keyn kheyn. . . .	Everything that is old has no charm for them. . . .
zey hobn shoyn far zey gants andere toyres	They have completely different codes of law,
andere klayzlekh, vi far zeyer tsayt	Other prayer rooms, up to date
men hast un men shpast	They hate and they jest
un men lakht un men makht	And they laugh and they make
fun dos yidishkayt an okh un vey	A travesty out of Judaism
fun got, fun gebot	Of God, of the commandments
fun gantsn religyon	Of the whole religion
alts iz a narishkeyt bay zey.	Everything is foolishness to them.

Markovitsh's narrator, as a symbol of the old orthodoxy, can only see the world in religious terms, revealed in his language. For him the youth may reject the actual Torah and prayer rooms, but they cannot be discarded as concepts because they structure his world. Instead, they are transformed into new versions that are contrary to their religious meaning. The final lines of the song mount a final attack: *Men khokhmet zikh un nokh di ale drokhim / shtarbn shtarbt men dokh a nar,* that after all the fooling about trying different ways in life, they (the youth) will die as fools. English mores are shown as foolish, but sympathy is unlikely to stay entirely with the song's narrator from a music hall full of those young people being berated.

Although the youth are shown to be the people losing their faith, the real culprit in these songs is repeatedly seen as England. The strong structures of Eastern European orthodoxy do not hold sway in England, and the lure of English culture is too strong. Arn Nager's song "Freg keyn katshanes!" (Don't ask silly questions!) suggests that the most foolish idea is the suggestion that one could come from Galicia as a hasidic Jew and remain so in England.[9] The title is a word play. *Katshanes* is not a common Yiddish word. The word means a stalk of a cabbage or an ear of corn, but is used in slang to mean blockhead, moron, or ham actor.[10] The title mimics the expression *freg nit keyn kashes*. The word *kashe* means a difficult question or Talmudic problem for which there is no easy answer, but the expression *freg nit keyn kashes* is slang for "Don't ask silly questions." The title, sung repeatedly in the chorus, plays with the similarity of the two phrases. On one hand, it can be seen to be poking fun at a religious concept by calling a difficult question on a piece of Talmudic law a "cabbage stalk," a foolish question. On the other hand, it implies that there is no answer to the question, or at least not a known or obvious one. The question the song poses is whether it is possible for an orthodox Hasidic immigrant to stay religious in London. The answer claims:

A kosherer yid, a tsadik iz do gor keyn metsie.	A kosher Jew, a pious man has no value here.
. . .	. . .
Yidishkayt, khsidishkayt hot do gor keyn kiem	Judaism, Hasidism does not exist here

The use of the word *do* (here) lays the blame of secularization on emigration to the free world. The chorus, spoken by the character of the anglicized neighbor, runs as follows:

Freg nit keyn katshanes, es iz england	Don't ask silly questions, this is England
vos toyg mir di tanes, es iz england	What's the use of complaining, this is England
ales iz kapoyer do geshtelt. . . .	Everything here is set up contrary . . .
A medinele mit minhogimlekh.	A little country with little customs.[11]

CHAPTER 9

England is shown as no place for the orthodox immigrant. England with its unfamiliar modes of behavior transforms Judaism into Anglo-Judaism. It is this anglicization of the religion by the Anglo-Jewish community that the orthodox immigrant finds so strange:

Shuln makht men do lehavdl poshet gor fun kloysters	People make synagogues here out of churches, as if you can make such a comparison
peysekh hit men op getray	They keep Passover loyally
teykef nokh dem seyder geyt men esn oysters	Immediately after the seder has finished, they eat oysters
anshtot afikoymen est men gor pay.	Instead of the dessert *matzah* after the seder they just eat pie.
Yonkiper zey haltn in eyn roykhn un fresn oy vay.	On Yom Kippur they constantly smoke and gobble, oh no.

The Anglo-Jews in the song "Freg keyn katshanes!" are framed in a Christian world which has churches and oysters and pie. This reflects the East End immigrants' baffled response to Anglo-Jewish United Synagogue formality with sermons in English, a solemn tone, begowned clerics, choral music, and stately architecture. They saw Anglo-Jewish concentration on anglicization as diluting Jewish religious practice. Indeed, in the East End, the chief rabbi was cheekily nicknamed "the West End *goy*."[12]

In this context, English foods are used in the song to show the incongruity of Englishness and Jewishness. Oysters are not kosher at any time and pie is not kosher on Passover. On Yom Kippur (the Day of Atonement), when Jews should be fasting, they are gobbling like animals. Using these food items in the narrative of this song suggests that it is not simply that Anglo-Jews have lapsed from religious practice. Worse, they have reinvented Jewish religious practice to make it English and resemble Christian practice. The song suggests not only a neglect of religious practice but a deliberate choice of not keeping Torah law, and flagrantly displaying that choice.

In the music hall, depictions of life were exaggerated for comic effect, athough had the Anglo-Jewish orthodox understood the Yiddish, they may not have found it so funny. The lyrics of these London songs can be seen as part of a continuing debate, expressing prevalent ideas and creating

RELIGION UPDATED AND IMPROVED

a space for people to engage with these ideas through entertainment. Yet the focus on England with its freedom to oust religion ignores the growing secularization occurring not only in the Western world but also in Eastern Europe. The song "Di velt is meshuge" (The world is mad) suggests that "what this dismal London has done" is a part of a world phenomenon:

Mit yorn tsurik gedenk ikh git	Years ago, I remember well
frum iz geven di gantse velt	All the world was religious
a baltfile a koshere yid. . . .	A leader of prayers, an orthodox Jew. . . .
Haynt farkert. . . .	Today it's the opposite. . . .
A yid gor on a bord	A Jew without any beard
eyn hultay	A libertine
a shkots. . . .	A prankster. . . .
un ikh vel shrayen gevalt	And I will shout help
az di velt iz meshuge.	Because the world is mad.[13]

London becomes a part of a wave of modernization sweeping the world. This is epitomized in the final verse, which refers to a German invention of a new machine with which *Flien zey mitakhes lemayle biz unter di shtern*, "They fly from below to up under the stars."[14] The implication is that new developments in technology run alongside the decline of religious practice. Instead of seeing God in the heavens, people are now searching for stars.

If religion is being questioned, then so is God. Markovitsh's song "Ikh bin a yidl fun der lite" (I am a Jew from Lithuania) tells the familiar story of a Jew escaping pogroms and economic hardship, only to find greater misfortune in London. Starving, the new immigrant pleads to God for help:

Derfar shtel ikh zikh davnen mit a groys fayer	So I stand and pray with great fire
riboyne shel oylem tate getrayer	God of the world, loyal father
a kashe tsu dir hob ikh a voyle	I have a tough question for you
nokh vos darfst du mikh mutshen az lebn lozt du mikh mimeyle?	Why do you need to torture me when you let me live life as a matter of course?

CHAPTER 9

Entfert rashe a teyrets got freg nisht ka shayles	Rashi gives a response: Don't ask God any questions
got ka kashes zolt ir nit fregn.	You shouldn't ask God difficult questions
Vorem ka entfer vet er nisht gebn	Because he won't give you an answer
er zitst zikh oybn un shvaygt zikh shtil	He sits in heaven and is silent
un do tut yeder vos er vil	And here everyone does whatever he likes
eyner baym tsveytn tsapt dos blit	One boss sheds another's blood
un er shvaygt un es art im nit	And he stays silent and doesn't care
nu freg ikh aykh tsi iz dos rekht?	So I ask you, is that just?[15]

Markovitsh locates God in the heavens, but the heavens above England are closed to entreaty. God remains silent. The England of the music halls has become a place of no religion and no God. No God to be a reminder not to eat oysters on Passover or have an affair with the lodger, but also no God to assuage the hunger of poverty.

These five songs portray the tension between religious and nonreligious Jews. They show immigrants trying to create a new way of being, trying to define what it means to be a nonreligious Jew in England. They portray characters who are secular as a positive choice, and celebrate being modern, new, up-to-date, English, young, not old-fashioned. They alleviate the fear of being an infidel by normalizing secularity as modernity. The songs are not generally judgmental, they tell stories, and often they lampoon all the characters. They portray London as a tempting experience, a place of change, that encourages a move away from the Eastern European religious past. The repetition of similar songs, poking fun at similar targets, raises the profile of being nonreligious and reinforces cultural rather than religious Judaism. In this way, some of these songs exemplify the denigration of religion that Lewis feared. The songs are a symptom of that decay. They normalize a particular type of anglicization that suggests that religion is not so important or necessary in England. The songs are part of establishing a new status quo celebrating a nonreligious, anglicized cultural reality.

SATIRIZING THE FESTIVALS

The most frequent type of religious critique in the London Yiddish lyrics is found in the satirical verse published in the mainstream Yiddish press. The writers were traditional or observant, and their writing sometimes included their own experience. They did not question religion as a belief; rather, they were insiders to the community, and criticized local religious wrangles as a participant. These poems are an attempt to create a modern observance that did not dilute practice, but kept its orthodox feel and anglicized it with current ideas and mores. These writers were deeply familiar with religious language, and at times, religious terminology was a key aspect of their poetic repertoire used for a range of subject matter, not necessarily connected to religious themes.

The poetry described in this section was mostly published in the *Idisher ekspres*, the *Tsayt*, and the *Bloffer*, written between 1906 and 1914.[16] The *Idisher ekspres* held a traditionally orthodox perspective, and as well as the main news, published news from local synagogues and *talmetoyres* and updates on the *shechita* controversy, and advertised religious artifacts and kosher foods. The *Tsayt* was a mainstream Jewish daily paper covering news from England and abroad of Jewish interest. It had readership from across the religious spectrum. The *Bloffer* was a fortnightly satirical magazine directed mainly at London's Yiddish-language cultural scene. It was broadly secular but assumed its audience had a basic level of religious participation or at least knowledge of religious Jewish mores. Avrom Margolin (Avreml), editor of the *Bloffer*, wrote regularly for all three papers, and is the author of around half of the lyrics considered in this section.

Avreml regularly used liturgy and biblical sources as intellectual ingredients in his poetry, publishing poems to coincide with Jewish festivals. Festivals and holy days provided rich pickings for the writer who could use their central ideas, historical stories, ritual, and liturgy, and relate them to current events and community foibles. Sometimes the link to the festival is tenuous, but religious structures are used to create a rich subtext. As each festival is different in character, satirical social comment could be focused as appropriate.

CHAPTER 9

Dr. Avrom Margolin (Avreml). From Steven Lasky, Museum of Family History, http://www.museumoffamilyhistory.com/yt/lex/M/margolin-a-dr.htm.

SIMKHES-TOYRE: CELEBRATING THE TORAH

Avreml's satire generally targets local personalities in the London Jewish community, either by openly naming them or under the guise of stereotypes. The 1912 poem "Di simkhes-toyre trinker" (The *simkhes-toyre* drinkers) tells of five Jewish "types" who are drinking a toast on the festival of *simkhes-toyre*.[17] *Simkhes-toyre* marks reaching the end of the weekly Torah readings, and starting again at the beginning of Genesis. The festival involves dancing with the Torah scrolls, and it is customary to toast them with a drink. The five verses of Avreml's poem ask why the actor, the Anglo-Jewish reverend, the usurer, the libertine, and the poet are drinking wine on *simkhes-toyre*. Avreml questions all of their motivations because he suggests that each has only a tangential link to the Torah. He argues that actors do not understand the text, usurers do not pray, and libertines mock the Torah. The answers he gives are that actors have the Torah to thank for art and cultural richness without which the Yiddish theatre would be diminished, the libertine youth owes the Torah his ability to think analytically, and the usurer toasts the laws in the Torah that allow him to charge interest from non-Jews.[18] The verse about the reverend, with due lack of reverence, questions why he would drink a toast to the Torah. Reverends were Anglo-Jewish ministers who would lead prayers and preach from the pulpit but were not learned in Jewish law. They were strongly looked down on by orthodox immigrants who had rebbes in their khevres who were experts in the intricacies of Talmudic law. The reverend was not called rabbi, a word reserved for the chief rabbi; he was a minister, and the poem mocks his lack of learning:[19]

Der "revrent" trinkt vayn simkhes-toyre . . .	The "reverend" drinks wine on simkhes-toyre . . .
Vos vil fun der "toyre" den er?	What does he want from the "Torah"?
A "posek" a prostn in droshe fartaytshn iz im dokh oft shver?	Is it often hard for him to interpret a simple "sentence"?
Der teyrets iz: reyshes, di "toyre" a "revrent" gut-kenen darf nit,	The response is: first, a "reverend" doesn't need to know the "Torah" well,
un tsveytns, hot lib er di toyre vayl er . . . makht a lebn dermit.	And second, he loves the Torah because he . . . makes a living from it.

The style of the poem is particularly fitted to celebrating the Torah because it is structured like a Talmudic argument. The Talmud, with its exegesis of Jewish law, has a coded format of question and response (*teyrets*). Using the Talmudic style for a poem about people who are mostly estranged from Talmudic Judaism poses questions about the relationship between modern Jews living in emancipated countries and an age-old religion. This satirical parody offers an analysis of modernity versus tradition, and questions the relationship of characters in the London diaspora to the old cultural norms. However, there is no simple duality between modernity and tradition because all of the nonreligious characters owe a debt to the Torah. Indeed, the poem shows a range of emerging Jewish diaspora cultures.

Just as actors were transnational carriers of culture, so the writers also inhabited transnational worlds, and at the time of writing this poem, Avreml was on a visit to Berlin. He traveled between London and Berlin, writing for American and London papers from wherever he was at the time. The poem "Di simkhes-toyre trinker" portrays tensions in diaspora culture, and the lack of specific London references implies that he was writing for a joint audience of London and Berlin. Underneath the title, Avreml dedicated the poem to the popular comic actor, his father-in-law Yankev (Jacob) Bleichman. Perhaps Avreml was honoring Bleichman, suggesting that he add this poem to his theatre repertoire, or perhaps he was reminding Bleichman of the biblical inspiration to his trade.[20] The inclusion of the dedication and the way Avreml's poetry constantly includes theatre culture indicate the position of entertainment as an important aspect of immigrant life.

SUKES: TABERNACLES

"A pekl nevies" (A bundle of prophecies), written in 1911, uses real names rather than "types."[21] The poem is based on a chapter from the prophet Ezekiel, which is read in a synagogue on the Sabbath in the middle of the festival of *Sukes*. The reading describes the end of time, when there will be a huge war to end all wars.[22] It prophesies the violent and bloody horrors that will happen as the world is turned upside down. The passage starts with the Hebrew phrase *Vehayo bayom hahu* (And it will happen on that day). Avreml's poem uses the same opening words in both Hebrew and Yiddish translation, before explaining:

Ven kumen vet meshiekh nor	When the Messiah will just come
vet zayn dos, vos ikh zog:	It will be like this, as I say:
gants "ist-end" mitn "vaytshepl"	All the "East End" and "Whitechapel"
vet vern umgekert,	Will be turned upside down,
un vunder veln dort geshen—	And wonders will happen there—
raboysay, shtoynt un hert!	Sirs, be amazed and listen!

RELIGION UPDATED AND IMPROVED

One sixty-six-line stanza describes the havoc that will be caused in the London Jewish community. Avreml conjures a mixture of eighteen famous or local personalities who were household names in the Jewish East End, and prophesies what will happen to them on that day. It reads like a Who's Who of movers and shakers in the community. There is the chief rabbi Hermann Adler and Claude Montefiore, the founder of Liberal Judaism. There is Shmuel Alman, the choirmaster and composer at the Great Synagogue in Duke's Place, and Ferdinand Shtoyb, the orchestra conductor at the Pavilion Theatre. There are Zionist leaders Theodore Herzl and Ahad Ha'am, and scholar Yankev-Meyer Zalkind.[23] Included is the playwright Jacob Gordin, actors Bleichman and Max Brin, music-hall artists Joseph Markovitsh and Arn Nager, and theatre critic and journalist Morris Myer. Also on Avreml's list are the missionary Tzvi Gutman; the anarchist leader Rudolf Rocker; Shteynvolf, who ran a Jewish restaurant; the "red rabbi" of the Kovne khevre; and Winston Churchill.[24]

As impressive as this list of people was the prophecy of the role they would play on the day of judgment. The chief rabbi would stand down, and questions and rulings would be taken to the secular Ahad Ha'am. Zalkind would become editor of the Anglo-Jewish newspaper the *Jewish World*. Rocker would leave anarchist ideology and become an inspector of kosher meat. Shmuel Alman (the classical composer and conductor) would take lessons from Shtoyb (the popular composer and conductor). The main Yiddish papers, the *Idisher ekspres* and the *Idisher zhurnal*, would switch to English, and the new editor would be Churchill. And so on.

The poem is full of in-jokes, lampooning the gap between the Anglo-Jews and the immigrants, religious and secular, high and low art, different political positions, scholarship, and journalism. It covers squabbles at the Wonderland Yiddish music hall and arguments about the quality of sensationalist Yiddish journalism. It mentions British colonial politics and possible Zionist colonies in Africa and America. The humor is fast and furious, rather like stand-up comedy. It is typical of the style Avreml uses when he writes for the *Bloffer*. He is not careful, not deferential, and names people indiscriminately. "A pekl nevies" is a parade of personalities putting religious, Zionist, anarchist, popular, and English on a par.

The poem uses a carefully crafted and subverted religious framework. There is a huge gap between the grave tone of Ezekiel's prophecy

CHAPTER 9

and Avreml's parody. Ezekiel does not add gravitas to Avreml's argument; rather, it helps Avreml ridicule both Jewish London and the prophetic text. The transfer of Ezekiel's prophecy of global disaster to Whitechapel questions the importance that locals put on local controversies. It suggests that parochial Whitechapel does not have to wait until the Messianic end of time because it is already an upside-down place full of conflicting ideologies and opinions. The final words of Avreml's poem deliberately mistranslate Ezekiel's words. Instead of repeating the Hebrew *Vehayo bayom hahu* (And it will happen on that day), Avreml writes in Yiddish: *gut vet zayn . . . in yenem tog'* (good will happen on that day). This gag ironically suggests that turning the East End world upside down would be a good thing. The critique Avreml is positing here, however, is too broad to be cutting, and is generally in good humor.

YONKIPER: THE DAY OF ATONEMENT

A stronger critique of religion is implied in Avreml's poem "Al-khet motivn" ("*Al-khet* themes"), written to coincide with Yom Kippur (*yonkiper* in standardized Yiddish) 1913.[25] *Al-khet* is the name of a prayer read repeatedly in synagogue during the long fast day. The prayer lists generalized sins that each individual has to atone for. Each line begins with the words "For the sin that I have committed" followed by the "set" sin. The poem starts with a cheeky opening gambit:

Ikh vil bay dir, got, nit oyf ale "al-khetn"	I don't want, God, to atone for any "sins"
oyf zind, vos ikh keynmol bin gor nit bagangen. . . .	For sins that I have never committed. . . .
Zol beser der rikhtiker nor "bal-aveyre"	Better the right "sinner"
antdekn zayn "khet" . . .	Reveal his "sin" . . .
anshtot dayn unshuldign, oremen poetl.	Instead of your poor, innocent little poet.

The rest of the poem uses the language of the al-khet prayer to tell groups of people which sins they should be atoning for. Here the butts of his humor are Anglo-Jewish reverends (again), Yiddish music-hall comedians, radicals, businessmen, preachers, and politicians. The poem, although light, contains sharp condemnation from a guilt-free poet who is, in effect, accusing them of the sin he proposes. The critique of religion is twofold. On one level the poet decries the generalization of the sins, suggesting that if people atone for sins they have not done, it hides those that they have committed. On another level the poem chooses to comment on the structures of Anglo-Jewry and on the quality of the rabbinate.

Reverends are attacked for "preaching for money," arguing that Anglo-Jewish ministers do their job only to earn a living, rather than from conviction.[26] On Yom Kippur, instead of being intermediaries and praying for atonement for the collective sins of their community, they are accused of *shoykhed* (bribery) and *bitui sfosayim* (vain or pointless speech). This may relate to specific local instances, or it may be a generalization mocking the Anglo-Jewish ministry. Socialists and anarchists are accused of not simply ignoring Yom Kippur, but deliberately eating on the day. They are ironically accused of sinning *bivli doas* (unintentionally). The radicals could not plead ignorance of orthodox ideas and practice. Indeed, on Yom Kippur they would have been dancing at the provocative Yom Kippur ball, while the synagogue-goers were beating their breasts to the al-khet prayer. Yiddish music-hall comedians are ordered to say the al-khet prayer for *nibl-pe* (speaking about sex or using sexual swear words) and *yeytser-hore* (giving in to the evil inclination). The term *nibl-pe* is not actually in the al-khet prayer. The prayer includes similar terms, such as *diber-pe* (offensive speech) and *tipshes-pe* (foolish talk), but neither of these sins were explicit enough for what Avreml wanted to say about music-hall performers' sexual banter and songs with crude lyrics. The term *yeytser-hore* refers to the evil inclination and can be used to mean bodily sins. In this instance it is probably referring to promiscuity.

Even those Jews who rarely went to synagogue would be likely to do so on Yom Kippur, which was regarded as the holiest of days in the Jewish calendar. Avreml could be sure that his liturgical references to al-khet would be familiar to the East End immigrant reader, more familiar than the more esoteric Talmudic or prophetic references he used in other poems. What would also be known are the solemnity and importance of the al-khet prayer, not generally a topic for humor. However, Avreml does not hold his punches. He is offensive and direct, and he implies that certain people are sinning and getting away with it. While they may not be breaking the law of the land, Avreml's accusation suggests that they are sins against the community.

The insults are moderated by the fact that Avreml targets the same types and individuals, and this creates a running gag in his satire. The cumulative structure serves to reinforce and emphasize Avreml's opinions, but it also reduces the power of the criticism. The volume of poetry with similar messages builds up into a consistent argument about difference, dissonance, and immorality in the Jewish community. By writing poems describing everyday situations in religious terms, Avreml showed where modernity can become a part of religious ideas. By doing so, he was arguing not that religion is outdated as a concept but that religious ideas and practice need rethinking and reinterpreting in modern London.

PEYSEKH: PASSOVER

"Mayn malke" (My queen) is set in a domestic arena on seder night, the first night of Passover in 1912. Avreml draws a traditional scene of a Jewish family where every husband is a king sitting on his throne surrounded by his "queen" and "princes" who minister to him. They are dressed in the ritual *kitlekh* (white robes) and fine clothes as they relate the story from the *hagode* narrative that recounts the exodus from Egypt. They tell of the plagues inflicted on the Egyptian people and of Pharoah's army that was drowned in the sea. The poem then turns to the first person and introduces the impoverished poet, whose wife "has no dresses and nothing to eat, but apart from that she is a queen, a countess." The final verse moans that his beautiful wife, however, will not let him be a king:

Zi hert mayne bafeln nit	She doesn't listen to my commands
un shenkt mir ale makes op,	And sends me lots of plagues,
un brekht di "koyses" oyf mayn kop,	And breaks the ritual "cups" of wine on my head,
zi iz a "sufrazhetke."	She is a "suffragette."[27]

In an amusing twist, the queen becomes the bearer of the plagues in order to attain her own freedom. The speaker becomes the dysfunctional husband, unable to make a living in London, similar to the emasculated singer of the Yiddish music-hall songs. Avreml invites the readership to laugh with him, and to question what sort of freedom this year's Passover will bring. There is a Passover tradition, informed by the seder liturgy, of personalizing the struggle for freedom.[28] So by engaging with the fight for votes for women, Avreml finds a place for Jewish religious tradition in the politics of contemporary England. Of course the surprise factor of the last line creates the humor and may have implied that immigrant Jewish women were not known for their suffragist activism.[29]

KHANIKE: THE FESTIVAL OF LIGHTS

Avreml was not the only poet to address local religious debate in the East End community. The anonymous poem "Haneyres halolu" (These candles) uses Hanukkah as a way of criticizing orthodox immigrant priorities in 1909. The title refers to the Hebrew prayer recited after lighting the Hanukkah candles praising God's wonders and miracles. The poem reminds the reader that Hanukkah is a time when we celebrate the history of the small group of brave Jewish fighters fighting against the large Greek army. The poem asks where heroism exists today in the immigrant community:

Aponim mir zenen danen andersh geven	Apparently then we were different
a folk fun giburim, fun gvure	A nation of heroes, of heroism
a yid iz geven oyfn shlakht feld a bren	A Jew on the battlefield had fervor
un nit nor gehit "matse shmure." . . .	And didn't only keep the commandment of *"shmure matzah." . . .*
Amol zenen yidn gegangen in krig	Once Jews went to war
farteydikt dem heylikn binyen!	Defending the holy temple!
Yetst hobn mir nor eyn eyntsign zig:	Now we only have one single victory:

ven mir davnen yedn tog mit a minyen....	That we pray every day in a minyan....
Mir hobn milkhomes yedn shabes in yor	We have wars every Sabbath of the year
nor alts in di shuln, di shuln.	But all of it [takes place] in the synagogues, the synagogues.[30]

The satire is directed at the immigrant orthodox for not seeing the wood for the trees. Compared with Hanukkah's heroism, the struggles of the orthodox immigrant community look petty. While the poem suggests that concern with trivia is unheroic behavior, the struggles the poem raises are not trivial. Preparing kosher *matzah* for Passover and praying in a quorum of ten men are basic tenets of orthodox Judaism. The poem suggests that these key elements of Judaism are belittled by turning into fierce synagogue battles. In the final lines of the poem, the speaker asks, "What will become of the Jews?" and the orthodox reply: "The Messiah will come." The poem berates the community for unthinking faith and small-minded behavior which does not resolve disputes.

SECULAR FESTIVITIES

Avreml's use of religious structures to make points about everyday life and politics can be seen as a way of incorporating modern life into an old religion. The opposite of this is where Jews make a new religion out of secularity. This is depicted on the satirical drawing heading up this section of the book. The reappropriation of religious structures is the theme of the poem "Moyshe un yakhne" (Moses and Yakhne) written in 1913.[31] The male name Moyshe and female name Yakhne are slang, *moyshe* being a derogatory term for the common ignorant herd, the uncouth fan who loves the vulgar spectacle, pop idols, cheap laughs, and music-hall gags. Yakhne additionally has the connotation of an indiscreet gossip.[32] The poem sets up a dichotomy between lowbrow popular culture and religion. It begins by addressing the *moyshe*s and *yakhne*s:

RELIGION UPDATED AND IMPROVED

Ir git dokh a "ton" in di fenster di hoykhe	You set a "tone" among the posh well-to-do
fun "pavilion" biz tsu "makhzike hadas."	From the "Pavilion" to the "Machzike Hadath."

The poem explains that everyone "dances like monkeys" to get the attention of the *moyshe*s and *yakhne*s from the libertine actors at the Pavilion Theatre to the staunchly orthodox at the *Machzike Hadath* synagogue. The anarchists, artists, and rabbis attempt to raise their basic literary, artistic, and moral standards. The charity boards worry about them; the missionaries want to ensure them for the world to come. The reverends want to purify their souls. But to little avail, because the *moyshe*s and *yakhne*s have their own religion:

Der "muzik hol" iz dokh bay aykh a "ganeydn"	The "music hall" is your "paradise"
der "shund-roman" iz bay aykh fun "khokhme" der kval	The "trash novel" is your font of "wisdom"
fun "poker" un "domino" shept ir taynugim	You draw pleasure from "poker" and "dominoes"
. . .	. . .
"hibru komedyens" zenen ayere neviim	"Hebrew comedians" are your prophets

The lines contain a precarious balance. On one side are the music halls, trash novels, poker, dominoes, and Hebrew comedians. On the other side are a range of religious concepts and terminology: paradise, wisdom, pleasure, and prophets. The *moyshe*s and *yakhne*s are seen to be swapping one culture for the other. But the popular culture they frequent is not only the Yiddish culture of the immigrant sphere. "Hebrew comedians" refers to actors portraying Jews in the English music halls. The Anglo-Jewish actors there were seen to propagate anti-Semitic stereotypes, and in an article in the *Tsayt* from 1914, the writer Y. Finkelstein deplored the way English audiences enjoy these stereotyped Jews. The article was furious because not only gentiles in the audience but "even the

Jews were strongly inspired by the 'Hebrew comedian's wisecracks and they drummed with their feet as if they wanted to hear it again."[33] Avreml's allusion to Hebrew comedians in the poem "Moyshe un yakhne" shows the muddied waters of anglicization, because it is the lowest form of English culture that is imbibed by the *moyshe*s and *yakhne*s.

Avreml's poem refers to three religious groups vying for the immigrants: the Anglo-Jewish rabbinate, the immigrant orthodox, and the Christian missionaries. None of them succeed here, and everyone is dancing to the tune of the most unthinking and vulgar in the immigrant society and of those who have no interest in religion. The *moyshe*s and *yakhne*s were more likely to be seen at the Yiddish theatre than in the synagogue. Indeed, Avreml argues that the music hall is their synagogue. In doing so he implies that religion is not entertaining enough to keep an audience.

DEM MELAMEDS GESHREY: ORTHODOX JOBS IN THE COMMUNITY

Internal religious structures of synagogues and schooling, kashres, and community institutions made many jobs available in the community, for the community. Working in these jobs could seem like being cushioned in a Yiddish-speaking bubble against the outside world. "Vos toygn di lider" (What good are poems), published in 1909, lists possibilities for employment within the community. The anonymous poet bemoans the difficulty of making money as a poet writing in Yiddish, and surveys other community jobs he could do that would pay better than a poet.[34] He could be a *mashgiyekh*, an inspector of foods for Passover that need to be made under special guidance. He could go around from house to house collecting money for the poor, proving he is genuine by showing a letter from a famous rabbi. He could study in a Jewish seminary paid for by the community. He could be a *memune*, a supervisor of a Jewish charity. He could amass gold ducats by being a *bal-nesnik*, a miracle worker divining through using the ritual cup that Jews use to wash their hands every morning. Or he could earn twenty-five shillings a week teaching "fifty bandits" in a dirty *kheyder*. The only downside of working in such jobs in the orthodox immigrant community is that you had to be orthodox yourself, and the poet complains that he would have to grow a beard.

"Vos toygn di lider" is a comic poem that argues that the community is, indeed, insular, paying more money to internal religious jobs that uphold the immigrant orthodox status quo than to a critical poet.

A serious complaint about working in the community comes up in an untitled poem with the first line *Dem melameds geshrey* (The teacher's cry). The poem concerns the need for Jewish education in addition to that provided in state schools. State schooling for the Jewish immigrants was provided both by the Jews' Free School (JFS) and by a system of nondenominational primary schools and Local Education Board schools. Many immigrant parents were reluctant to send their children to English schools because they associated state schools with a missionary purpose. The board schools that were largely Jewish therefore removed references to Christianity and appointed Jewish head teachers and teaching staff.[35] Yet even the JFS only taught basic Jewish religion classes, reduced further as government financial aid to the JFS was on condition they change the ratio of secular studies to Jewish studies.[36]

Religious immigrant parents were anxious that their children were not receiving a rigorous enough religious education. Even parents who were nominally religious and not regular synagogue attendees worried that their children would lose the cultural heritage that they no longer practiced themselves. Many parents had been educated in the *khadorim* and *talmetoyres* of Eastern Europe, where the standard of religious learning went beyond the Anglo-Jewish equivalent taught at the JFS and board schools. This anxiety was addressed within the immigrant community by setting up a system of East End khadorim and talmetoyres to run alongside regular schools. They taught Hebrew, Jewish texts, and prayers, with all teaching conducted in Yiddish. Financed entirely by the immigrants themselves, many small khadorim ran before and after school until late in the evenings and on Sundays. The Brick Lane Talmetoyre, set up in 1894, was connected to the large *Machzike Hadath* synagogue, and taught a thousand children, sixty to a class in a four-story building.[37]

The smaller, private khadorim for younger boys were taught by a rabbi or *melamed* and were often housed in kitchens and front rooms in cramped conditions for handfuls or dozens of boys. The earliest talmetoyre for older boys opened in Great Garden Street in 1881. Moses Angel, head teacher of the JFS, led a crusade against the use of Yiddish and the system of khadorim and talmetoyres, seeing them as obstacles to the JFS's process of anglicization. He tried to close them by demanding that the Jewish Board of Guardians inspect them. However, when they did so in 1881, apart from overcrowding, the reports were favorable. The system of khadorim, rather than diminishing, greatly increased with further waves of immigration.[38]

The untitled seventeen-verse poem starting *dem melameds geshrey* and published in 1906 reveals a tension within the religious school system, not between the Anglo-Jewish establishment and the immigrant orthodox but among the immigrants between the orthodox and the less observant traditional Jews. The poem, published in the *Idisher ekspres* in October 1906, questions the value each type of Jew puts on Jewish education, arguing that there was a lack of respect for religion teachers in the community and a consequent lack of respect for Judaism:

Bay undz yidn leyder	Unfortunately among us Jews
di ernste fun kheyder	The most serious in the *kheyder*
zaynen di melamdim aleyn.	Are the teachers themselves.
. . .	. . .
Ven es felt	When one is short of
a bisl kleyn gelt	A bit of change
eyn ovnt in teater tsu geyn	To go to the theatre one evening
di ershte svore	The first idea
dem kheyder a kapore	Is to sacrifice the *kheyder*
dos filt nor der melamed aleyn.	It is only the teacher that feels it.[39]

The poet, known only as *A fraynd fun melamdim* (A friend of teachers), is dismayed by less-orthodox parents' view of *kheyder* teaching as an add-on that can be sacrificed for any caprice. He argues in the poem that people see the teacher's livelihood as expendable, that they spend what the teacher earns in a week for a one-day holiday by the sea. Yet the teacher is dependent on private individuals paying him. The poem argues that anglicization has changed people's priorities, and that parents' desire for their children to go to *kheyder* is lip service. This leaves religion teachers relying on making a living out of those for whom the importance of Judaism is in decline.

The poet does not only berate parents; he also chastises the orthodox teachers, arguing that they must unite across institutions and modernize their teaching methods in order to gain respect. The final verse of the poem is a rousing cry:

Zet tsu makhn	Let it be that
men zol mer nisht lakhn	People should no longer laugh
fun di lerer fun toyre un religyon:	At the teachers of Torah and religion:
men zol gut bashitsn	One should protect well
mit koved bapitsn	Adorn with respect
di vos trogn di yidishe fon.	Those who carry the Jewish flag.

Judaism is portrayed as something precious that needed protecting. The agents of passing on religious knowledge were the teachers, but they could not do the job adequately without agreeing to modern teaching methods.[40] The poem is a double demand. It demands that religious and nominally religious parents treat the transmission of Judaism as seriously as their dedication to the process of anglicization. At the same time, it demands that Jewish teachers take modernization as seriously as the maintenance of Judaism. This was no lone complaint: in 1912 an *Idisher ekspres* article linked poor *kheyder* tuition to lack of family support for Jewish education and the popularity of lowbrow popular culture.[41]

IKH UN KRIST: CHRISTIANIZING JUDAISM

Although orthodox immigrants were keen to become a community acculturated to England, they were just as eager to distance themselves from the style of anglicization of the established Anglo-Jewish community. A *Bloffer* front cover picture from December 1912 entitled "Khanike un krismes" (Hanukkah and Christmas) depicts Santa Claus as a homely grandfather taking away a small child with the allure of trinkets. Matisyahu, the hero of the Hanukkah story, stands looking forlorn.[42] The subject of Jewish tradition disappearing into Christianity was addressed by satirists who turned their poetic attention onto the Anglo-Jewish community and criticized their lack of orthodoxy. The poem "Hepi nyu yir" (Happy New Year) is directed at the "rich uncles with stuffed bellies and empty hearts of our big London community." The title refers to the secular New Year, the turn of 1914, and airs acute anxiety about what anglicization is doing to Jewish practice:

A khanike likhtl in eyn hant	A Hanukkah light in one hand
oyf di lipn "maoz tsur"	On the lips "Maoz tsur"
in der tsveyter hant a yolke	In the second hand a Christmas tree
un a puding mit rozhinkes gor.	And a pudding made entirely of raisins.[43]

This form of anglicized Judaism, the poem tells us, "has subsumed the non-Jew" and the "spark of Judaism" will be forgotten forever.[44] This anxiety is different from that aired in the music halls about immigrants losing their orthodoxy in England. This poem argues that Anglo-Jews have become so assimilated that they have become Christianized, and that Judaism will not survive. It is a withering critique suggesting that one cannot be both Jewish and English, or rather Jewish and Christian at the same time.

The anxiety about the connection between Anglo-Jewish practice and Christianity is given specific detail in the poem "Di reformer." The title refers to Reform Judaism, which was established in England in 1842 in an attempt to modernize and anglicize Jewish religious practice. The Chief Rabbinate and many United Synagogue Jews saw Reform Judaism's reworking of parts of the liturgy and religious practice as heretical, and Reform was considered a threat to Anglo-Jewish power and authority.[45] In addition, they considered Reform practice as diluting the Jewish spirit by mimicking Christian practices too much. The poem "Di reformer," published in 1908, describes a new Reform synagogue where there is no rabbi but "a cheerful youth, a bachelor."[46] The cantor does not sing alone but is accompanied by an organ and a non-Jewish choir. People listen silently and with decorum, only opening their mouths for *kadish* and *yisker* (prayers demanding a congregation response). People do not wear *yarmelkes* (skullcaps) and, because the preacher preaches with an empty head, his words come out naked. The poem drives home the sterility of the environment of the new synagogue that is formal with ritual but that is not a Judaism that the author recognizes.

A number of poems allude to the flirtation between distinguished Anglo-Jews and Christianity. The 1912 poem "Mist" (Trash) refers to a priest disguising himself as a rabbi and luring Rothschild into a church to make a speech.[47] A poem of the following year, "Al-hanisim" (Because of the miracles) alludes to Claude Montefiore giving away a Christmas tree.[48] Claude Montefiore and Lily Montagu established Liberal Judaism in England in 1902 in a further attempt at anglicization of religious practice. Montefiore was a greatly respected, although controversial, thinker in the Anglo-Jewish community, incorporating Christian theology into his thinking.[49]

Part of this anxiety was fueled by missionary activity in the East End, which, although a constant feature, was not very successful. "Ikh un krist" (Myself and Christ) by Morris Gras in 1912 is a narrative tale in the form of a comic ballad, where a missionary bribes a Jew to become a Christian for a thousand pounds.[50] The Jew delightedly accepts, but is then caught out eating chicken one Friday night. With quick wit, the Jew explains that just as he was easily baptized with a drop of water turning him from a Jew to a Christian, so his Friday meal has been baptized changing from a hen into a fish. The humor of the poem showed the clever immigrant Jew who managed to fool the missionaries. The poem's critique of Anglo-Jewry was not that Jews would become Christians but that Judaism would become Christianized.

The songs and poems in this chapter argue for the need for transformation. Religious life was changing, and these lyrics can be seen as part of that change. The texts both engage with the debate around anglicization and reflect the changing positions that people held. All the poets can be seen to acknowledge the central influence and place of religion in the lives of the immigrants and how it is embedded in the Yiddish language. Through their poetry and satire, the poets and songwriters both reflect and influence the complex threads and tension between changing religious values. Whether the writers were trying to move away from Judaism or

CHAPTER 9

to establish a modern world, all the texts look forward. They may abandon religion but not the knowledge of it. They may decry the relevance of religious texts but still use them. They may eat on Yom Kippur but still know the meaning of the day and use that as an inspiration for poetry.

Conclusion

This book has told some of the tales contained within London's Yiddish lyrics. The lyrics were part of the political and cultural discourse about a range of subject matter, and writers articulated live contemporary debates that reflected the interests of their audience. In the accessibility of the style of the poetry and the performative elements of the songs, the texts offered alternative angles on those debates. The creative lyrics sometimes make clear points and sometimes offer surreptitious messages. Yet all advance controversial arguments, referencing pivotal discussions then current in national and community political life. Some interventions into these debates were ideological, some social, and some religious. Some were crucial and others less consequential, yet all were pertinent to the lives of the Yiddish-speaking immigrants to London.

The London lyrics were directed at, and referred to, both local and transnational audiences. The major focus was on the immigrant workers and inhabitants of the East End, and concerned personalities and events in Whitechapel and Stepney. Yet many of the lyrics were written with transferability in mind, and even if not consciously writing for a wider audience, writers knew that Yiddish-language material filtered across the Yiddish-speaking world. Even within the local perspective, many of the issues uncovered were general to the immigrant experience, and to the world of the struggling worker in any location. In this way the London of the lyrics becomes an exemplar of an idea, and a simple word change could transfer the text to a new country and generalize the experience. This mixture of local and transnational shows the importance of seeing London within a wider Jewish world. It changes the view of

CONCLUSION

London being a small and somewhat insignificant diaspora community to being an integral part of Ashkenaz.

The lyrics were all part of the process of acculturation. The texts promote English culture, modernity, and engagement with new ideas. Some of the ideas are controversial, some are mainstream, and some were seen as *shund* (trash). Whatever position the texts take on Englishness, they are looking forward and trying to take part in a wider popular culture.

DEBATE AND CULTURAL CONTROVERSY

The way the lyrics participate in debate looks different depending on the genre. Both Winchevsky and Nager wrote about prostitution, but from different angles. Winchevsky's lyrical ballads are open and clear and do not hide the subject matter or the political position. The poem "Dray shvester" argues that poverty can lead to prostitution and that society, not the individual, is the problem. The argument is not constructed as a polemic or a piece of journalism, but comes from the narrative of the poem, out of the mouths of the sisters selling their wares in Leicester Square. The poem is sentimental, but the point is political, unambiguous, and strong. This stands in contrast to the way Nager explored the same theme in his music-hall songs. In "Viktorye park" and "Vos geyst nisht ahem sore-gitl?," prostitution is alluded to by references to women "working in the city" or being out at night in Regent Street. The London audience may have grasped the insinuations immediately, yet the songs are light and comic and the innuendos are not lingered on. Nager's songs question sexual mores without making bold political statements. By hiding the references to prostitution in euphemisms, the songs flag the issue as a dangerous one not to be spoken about openly. Nager was making a choice. He knew Winchevsky's work, and even acknowledged a debt to "Dray shvester" in "Viktorye park." With different emphases, both Winchevsky's and Nager's interventions into the debate on prostitution through using stories were attempts to engage their audiences with ideas, and show connections between the immigrant community and the wider London world.

In another example, both Markovitsh and the writer working under the pseudonym Zimrey Ben Sloa addressed the subject of deserted wives. This was seen as an issue particularly affecting immigrants and debated

CONCLUSION

in the pages of both the Anglo-Jewish and Yiddish press. Markovitsh's sentimental music-hall song gives voice to the wife abandoned in Russia by her husband, who had escaped to London. The narrative shows the clear message that abandoning one's wife creates terrible hardship back in Eastern Europe. It is a moving song that demands a sympathetic response, yet does not put across any clear judgment in the telling of the story. Indeed, the audience is encouraged to both cry at the wife's misfortune and laugh at her loss of control in swearing at her husband. In contrast, a verse of "Der bloffer lakht" (The *Bloffer* laughs), which describes the same issue, has a much sharper, more critical edge. It may be amusing, but it is also angry and clearly judgmental. The satire is directed at shaming this behavior by drawing attention to the local aspects of the problem.

A further example concerns the tension between high art and popular culture and shows how the boundaries between the two are not straightforward. In "Moyshe un yakhne," Avreml attacks lowbrow popular culture by mocking audiences who are only looking for mindless entertainment. He suggests that these audiences lower the tone of the East End, and despite efforts to offer them higher culture, they religiously follow their pop stars and comic actors. Avreml accuses them of frequenting not only Yiddish music halls but the English music halls where Anglo-Jewish comedians uphold stage-stereotypes of Jews. Yet despite his disdain for the audiences, Avreml only gently mocked the writers, such as Nager, who were producing popular songs overflowing with crude innuendo. The debate about culture is not simple, and the popular songwriters were rarely music-hall consumers. Indeed, writers layered their verse with literary references and contributions to political debates and showed how the boundaries between high art and popular culture were entangled. This gray area can also be seen in Yozef's two "Hashiveynu nazad" parodies. The songs advertise the stars of the London music-hall stage and promote buying the coquettish songs that they sing. Yet the songsheet also advertises religious artifacts for use in prayer. Yozef was clearly addressing a wide audience of immigrants who may have sat on both sides of the popular culture debate.

These examples show that not only did popular cultural texts engage with contemporary debate but, depending on the genre and the writer, they had different approaches and different points to make. Writers were

CONCLUSION

not only concerned with getting messages across but in locating them within a context. The context may have been English politics or internal Jewish or immigrant politics, yet the points made about England often had wider implications and associations.

LOCAL AND TRANSNATIONAL

Between 1884 and 1914 most of the East End audience to Yiddish language culture would have been first-generation immigrants with Yiddish their mother tongue and second-generation immigrants who were bilingual in Yiddish and English. The immigrant community was steeped in the transnational experience of being in England and trying to find work in London's East End while bringing its cultural background and familial ties from the *heym* of Eastern Europe. It is therefore no surprise that the texts reflect this hybridity. But in this case, ideology is important to how that cultural mix is expressed in the texts.

The socialist poets were internationalists, and the message in their poetry was not confined to any locality or any cultural group. The socialist ideas knew no borders, and even when there was local content, such as a girl selling matches in the pouring rain in Cornhill, the message was a universal statement about society's refusal to deal with the issue of poverty. London's landmarks simply became a backdrop. Similarly, Winchevsky's "Der frayhayts-gayst," written for the 1890 Shoe and Boot Makers' strike, could be transferred to a workers' demonstration in Chicago, or sung in a sweatshop in Belarus.

Music-hall songs were also portable. They were written for particular singers who then owned their own repertoire. Indeed, songsheets sometimes included their photograph. When they traveled across the Yiddish-speaking world, they took their songs with them. Thus songwriters had to be pragmatic, making sure that local references in the lyrics could be easily changed. A song like "Azoy geyt dos gelt avek" could simply remove the reference to Crystal Palace. So local became transnational in transmission and in collaboration with new audiences.

The texts that traveled least were the satirical offerings in the *Bloffer* where references to local personalities were often detailed and personal. However, ideas were constantly pilfered between Yiddish papers, and the bad behavior exposed in the satirical verse was similar in other

CONCLUSION

Yiddish-speaking centers.[1] In all three genres there are lyrics that contained allusions to local, national, and transnational. The lyrics are built from the complex entanglements of being an Eastern European, a Jew, an immigrant, and a Yiddish speaker. They allude to ideologies, religious practice, and Russian and English literatures. They exhibit both the region of Ashkenaz and the links to the gentile worlds they are embedded within.

ANGLICIZATION

The London Yiddish lyrics were written in the language of the immigrants. It was an obvious choice for all the writers, but for the Jewish socialists it was also a pragmatic strategy. In the 1880s, Yiddish was considered a domestic rather than literary language, and not a language of progress and modernity where new ideas were being developed. Writing in Russian or German or English connected both writer and reader to a rich literary history, but the Yiddish literary tradition was still in an embryonic stage. The socialists chose Yiddish because their message was more important than the medium. Their version of acculturation was not directed at England per se, but about moving forward into a new political future. Just as using Yiddish was a pragmatic choice, so was engaging with English culture. They were not pursuing anglicization as much as addressing modernity. Winchevsky took pains to use a style of Yiddish the workers could understand, berating those such as William Morris for language that was too complex and poetic for uneducated readers. Similarly, Winchevsky references London politics and events to encourage workers to be activists where they are, in London.

The form of anglicization that emerges in music-hall songs is a force not for political change but for entertainment. Local references and anglicized language are very common, and there are numerous aspects of London life to make fun of and provoke laughter. Tired immigrant workers were not paying their hard-earned money to be given lectures or analysis. They went to the music halls seeking relaxation, an opportunity to meet the opposite sex, drink alcohol, hear their favorite stars, and learn some good songs to sing on the way out. The song lyrics propound different versions of Englishness that include possibilities for new sexual mores and are nonjudgmental about the decline of religion. The music

CONCLUSION

halls themselves were locations of anglicization, although they were seen by progressives and critics as the lowest form of popular entertainment. The music-hall songs promoted pleasure and gave audiences a sense of solidarity at being nonreligious Jews making their way in England. This type of anglicization was fiercely rejected by both the Anglo-Jewish and immigrant leaders.

Between 1900 and 1914 the satire that was being written and published in the *Bloffer*, *Tsayt*, and *Idisher ekspres* was directly engaging with anglicization. Most of it is critical of immigrant society. It criticizes the foibles of leaders of the community—their thoughtlessness, bad behavior, deception, corruption, and arrogance. The poems promote finding new ways of being Jews in England, not aping the Anglo-Jewish establishment with its middle-class English norms but instead finding a more progressive way, not imposing but creating new ways to be Jewish in London.

If anglicization was successful, London Yiddish lyrics would have slowly reduced and disappeared into English popular culture or Jewish popular culture written in English. This is, indeed, what happened over some decades as the number of first-language Yiddish speakers diminished. Although the Yiddish theatre continued, and at times blossomed, after World War II, and although *Di tsayt* continued being published until 1950, it was inevitable that there would never be enough Yiddish-speaking people to make up an ongoing audience. The success of the anglicization process meant not only the loss of a Yiddish popular culture in London but also a loss of access to that culture as historical evidence.

In the three genres of London Yiddish lyrics described in this book—poetry, song, and satire—writers engaged with their new lives in England. The texts serve as a critique of both Anglo-Jewry and aspects of the immigrant community, depending on the point of view of the author. Winchevsky was critical of immigrant master tailors. Avreml was critical of immigrants who abandoned Judaism. All of the writers understood that having to make a life in England was a compromise. It was a compromise of religion, culture, and language. It is this struggle that is reflected in the poems and songs as they portray the noise of Whitechapel in the complexity of religious and political debates and cultural controversy. The language itself reflects developing acculturation, as

CONCLUSION

anglicized words pepper the songs and satirical verse. The lyrics offer tantalizing glimpses into a rapidly changing immigrant culture. They act like a mirror, albeit a distorting mirror, through the desire to advertise, affect opinion, or entertain, yet they make the culture live. Knowledge of the performative element of the music-hall songs and the sung socialist choruses enhances the meaning by consideration of the locations of their performance. The shared insider knowledge created in the atmosphere of crowds and music halls exposes the live issues that concerned immigrant families and workers.

Although generally hidden and inaccessible today, the popular culture of the immigrant Jews in England can be used as a historical tool. It opens up aspects of the past that are hard to reach from other sources: the nature of entertainment, the socialists' use of humor and creativity in their determination to convince, the internal back-biting, and the intensely personal. Local Yiddish poetry and song offer perspectives from below, not institutional or elite perspectives. The lyrics can still draw one in with their comedy, their ideas, and their rhyming couplets. The techniques for humor, for diversion, and for sharp comment can still be piquant today. The songs and poems offer a new reading of Anglo-Jewish history through the compelling and vibrant Yiddish lyrics of London.

Notes

For the list of abbreviations, see page xvii.

Introduction

1. Morris Winchevsky, "London bay nakht," *PY*, 12 September 1884.
2. Yiddish newspapers, journals, songsheets, and songbooks are in the British Library; National Library of Israel, Jerusalem; YIVO library and archives, New York; Hebrew Union College, Cincinnati; and the Mazower private collection, London.
3. *Yidl* is the diminutive of the word *yid*, Jew, and may be a wordplay on the well-known enlightenment fiction *Dos poylishe yingl*.
4. Leonard Prager lists Yiddish songs and newspapers published in London. Prager, *Yiddish Culture in Britain: A Guide* (Frankfurt am Main: Peter Lang, 1990), 613–19; Prager, "A Bibliography of Yiddish Periodicals in Great Britain (1867–1967)," *Studies in Bibliography and Booklore* 9, no. 1 (Spring 1969): 3–32.
5. These phrases come from the songs "Vos geyst nisht aheym sore-gitl," *LK*, 16; "Dem nayem hashiveynu nazad," SG; *Gevald, gevald police*, performed by Fräulein Rubinstein (1905), from *Di Eybike Mame: Women in Yiddish Theater and Popular Song* (Mainz: Wergo, 2003), compact disc.
6. Anglicized Yiddish is sometimes referred to colloquially as "Cockney Yiddish." Some Yiddish words became incorporated into Cockney slang. See William Matthews, *Cockney, Past and Present: A Short History of the Dialect of London* (London: E. P. Dutton, 1938), 142.
7. Doris Sommer, *Bilingual Aesthetics: A New Sentimental Education* (Durham, NC: Duke University Press, 2004), xi–xii, 36–37. Sommer analyzes how bilinguals use multiple languages to create humor consciously and inadvertently.
8. This argument is proposed in detail by David Glover, who assesses how literature of fin-de-siècle England laid the ground and exposed ideas that led to the 1905 Aliens Act. David Glover, *Literature,*

Immigration, and Diaspora in Fin-de-Siècle England: A Cultural History of the 1905 Aliens Act (Cambridge: Cambridge University Press, 2012), 10.

9. Mike Sanders, *The Poetry of Chartism: Aesthetics, Politics, History* (Cambridge: Cambridge University Press, 2009), 13.
10. "Millions" of poems were published in the English press during Victoria's reign. Andrew Hobbs and Claire Januszewski, "How Local Newspapers Came to Dominate Victorian Poetry Publishing," *Victorian Poetry* 52, no. 1 (2014): 65–87.
11. Michael Aylward has collated a list of around a hundred Yiddish songs from records produced in London between 1904 and 1908. Those with local content include *Ich such a job*, performed by Yozef Sherman and the Pavilion Orchestra (London: Imperial, n.d.), vinyl 78; *Gevald, gevald police*.
12. David Mazower, "Kibbitzers, Coffee, and Kikhlekh," *Pakn Treger* 73 (Summer 2016): 21–24.
13. Sam Levenvirt, "London hot zikh ibergekert," *LK*, 129.
14. Aubrey Newman, *The United Synagogue, 1870–1970* (London: Routledge & K. Paul, 1976), 1–14. See also Michael Clark, *Albion and Jerusalem: The Anglo-Jewish Community in the Post-Emancipation Era, 1858–1887* (Oxford: Oxford University Press, 2009), 173–80. The Singer's Prayer Book of 1890 brought an updated translation.
15. Todd Endelman, *The Jews of Britain, 1656–2000* (Berkeley: University of California Press, 2002), 146; David Englander, "Booth's Jews: The Presentation of Jews and Judaism in 'Life and Labour of the London Poor,'" *Victorian Studies* 32, no. 4 (1989): 34; Geoffrey Alderman, *Modern British Jewry* (New York: Clarendon Press, 1992), 144.
16. Endelman, *Jews of Britain*, 178.
17. Alderman, *Modern British Jewry*, 76–86; Vivian Lipman, *Social History of the Jews in England: 1850–1950* (London: Watts, 1954), 27-9-50, 60–69.
18. The population of Jews in Britain was around 300,000 with substantial communities in Manchester and Leeds, and smaller ones in Liverpool, Glasgow, and Birmingham. Endelman, *Jews of Britain*, 127–30; Vivian Lipman, *A History of the Jews in Britain since 1858* (Leicester: Leicester University Press, 1990), 12, 45–46; Bernard Gainer, *The Alien Invasion: The Origins of the Aliens Act of 1905* (London: Heinemann, 1972), 3–6.
19. Vivian Lipman, *A Century of Social Service, 1859–1959: The Jewish Board of Guardians* (London: Routledge & Kegan Paul, 1959), 89, 78–79.

20. For the early days of the Federation, see Geoffrey Alderman, *The Federation of Synagogues, 1887–1987* (London: Federation of Synagogues, 1987), 1–41; Alderman, *Modern British Jewry*, 156–65.
21. Changes in Yiddish language cultural output can be seen to coincide with changes in generations of around sixteen years, starting in 1881. Benjamin Harshav, *Language in Time of Revolution* (Berkeley: University of California Press, 1993), 63. For background on Hasidic and *haskole* cultures of Eastern Europe, see David Biale, *Cultures of the Jews: A New History* (New York: Schocken Books, 2002), 802–46; Anthony Polonsky, *The Jews in Poland and Russia: 1881–1914* (Oxford: Littman Library of Jewish Civilization, 2010), 2:238–62.
22. The *LK* had at least eight issues, some collected into a volume of 150 songs, which is the version I reference. The *LLM* had at least two issues. Only incomplete copies with unclear pagination survive.
23. Prager, *Yiddish Culture*, 613–19.
24. Prager suggests the *LK* and the *LLM* were written around 1890, but this cannot be correct, as some of the writers would have been young children. More likely, the individual issues of the *LK* and the *LLM* were published 1898–1903 and the *LK* compilation around 1903. The songsheets are undated, but are from around the same time. See also Khone Shmeruk, "Dray londoner Yiddishe gasnlider fun far der ershter velt-milkhome," in *Studies in the Cultural Life of the Jews in England*, ed. Dov Noy and Issachar Ben-Ami (Jerusalem: Magnes, 1975), 114.
25. The *Bloffer* published thirty-nine issues between 1911 and 1913.
26. Avrom Margolin (1884–1961).
27. See particularly David Feldman, *Englishmen and Jews: Social Relations and Political Culture, 1840–1914* (New Haven, CT: Yale University Press, 1994), 185–257; Anne J. Kershen, *Uniting the Tailors: Trade Unionism amongst the Tailoring Workers of London and Leeds, 1870–1939* (London: F. Cass, 1995); William Fishman, *East End Jewish Radicals 1875–1914* (London: Duckworth, 1975); Bill Williams, *The Making of Manchester Jewry 1740–1875* (Manchester: Manchester University Press, 1985); Joseph Buckman, *Immigrants and the Class Struggle: The Jewish Immigrants in Leeds, 1880–1914* (Manchester: Manchester University Press, 1983).
28. Winchevsky's main biographers were Kalman Marmor, *Moris vintshevski, zayn lebn, virkn un shafn* (New York: Freiheit, 1928); Abraham Bik, *Moris vintshevski, troymer un kemfer* (Los Angeles: Arbeter Ring,

1956). His main critics were A. Litvak [Khayim Yankl Helfand], "Moris vintshevski, der onheyber," *Der veker*, 2 April 1932, 4–11; Nokhum Borukh Minkov, *Piyonern fun yidisher poezye in amerike: Dos sotsiale lid* (New York: O. fg., 1956), 7–85; Nakhman Mayzel, "Y. l. perets un moris vintshevski," *YK*, November 1950, 3–10. Winchevsky appears in other memoirs and fragments including Shaul Yanovski, *Ershte yorn fun yidishn frayhaytlekhn sotsialism* (New York: Fraye arbeter shtime, 1948), 136–85; Mordkhe Spektor, *Moment fotografyes* (Warsaw: A. Gitin, n.d.), 69–85. His fans included Yoel Entin writing a series of articles in the *Morgen dzurnal* in November 1943, Ber Grin (Isaac Greenberg)'s writing in *Morgen freiheit* between 1954 and 1962, and Leon Kobrin's memory of his first meeting with Winchevsky, "Der zeyde moris vintshevski, mayn ershte bagegenish mit im," *MF*, 3 June 1956.

29. See Melekh Epstein, *Profiles of Eleven: Profiles of Eleven Men Who Guided the Destiny of an Immigrant Society and Stimulated Social Consciousness among the American People* (Detroit: Wayne State University Press, 1965), 13–35; Rudolph Rocker and Colin Ward, *The London Years* (Nottingham: Five Leaves Press, 2005), 57–59; Fishman, *Radicals*, 138–44. Mentioning Winchevsky within large works include Lloyd Gartner, *The Jewish Immigrant in England, 1870–1914* (London: Simon Publications, 1973), 106–9; Nora Levin, *Jewish Socialist Movements: 1871–1917* (Oxford: Oxford University Press, 1978), 126–32; Jonathan Frankel, *Prophecy and Politics: Socialism, Nationalism, and the Russian Jews, 1862–1917* (Cambridge: Cambridge University Press, 1981), 29–50, 124–31; Sol Liptzin, *A History of Yiddish Literature* (New York: Jonathan David, 1985), 70–72.

30. For the way eros is portrayed in Jewish literature across time, see David Biale, *Eros and the Jews: From Biblical Israel to Contemporary America* (New York: BasicBooks, 1992), in particular chapter 7. For recent scholarship on the erotic and Yiddish poetry, see Zohar Weiman-Kelman, "Touching Time: Poetry, History and the Erotics of Yiddish," *Criticism* 59, no. 1 (forthcoming).

31. See Edward Bristow, *Prostitution and Prejudice: Jewish Fight against White Slavery, 1870–1939* (Oxford: Clarenden, 1982); Lara Marks, "Race, Class and Gender: The Experiences of Jewish Prostitutes and Other Jewish Women in the East End of London at the Turn of the Century," in *Women, Migration and Empire*, ed. Joan Grant (Stoke-on-Trent, UK: Trentham, 1996), 31–49; Paul Knepper, "British Jews and

the Racialisation of Crime in the Age of Empire," *British Journal of Criminology* 47, no. 1 (January 2007): 61–79; Lloyd Gartner, "Anglo-Jewry and the Jewish International Traffic in Prostitution, 1885–1914," *AJS Review* 7 (1982): 129–78; Susan L. Tananbaum, *Jewish Immigrants in London, 1880–1939* (London: Pickering and Chatto, 2014), 131–48.

32. See in particular Alderman, *Federation of Synagogues*; Bernard Homa, *A Fortress in Anglo-Jewry: The Story of the Machzike Hadath* (London: Shapiro, Vallentine, 1953); Bernard Homa, *Orthodoxy in Anglo-Jewry, 1880–1940* (London: Jewish Historical Society of England, 1969); Salmond Levin, "The Changing Pattern of Jewish Education," in *A Century of Anglo-Jewish Life*, ed. Salmond Levin (London: United Synagogue, 1971), 57–74; Newman, *United Synagogue, 1870–1970*.

33. The main source of information about Yiddish culture in Britain is Leonard Prager's invaluable lexicon. Prager, *Yiddish Culture*. Prager also wrote a number of articles on different aspects of Yiddish culture: "The Beginnings of Yiddish Fiction in England," in *Studies in the Cultural Life of the Jews in England*, ed. Dov Noy and Issachar Ben-Ami (Jerusalem: Magnes Press, Hebrew University, 1975), 245–310; "Paul Muni's Parents Sing at a London Yiddish Music Hall," in *Language and Civilization: A Concerted Profusion of Essays and Studies in Honour of Otto Hietsch*, vol. 2 (Frankfurt am Main: Peter Lang, 1992); "Der londoner farleger m. yozef," in *Oksforder yidish*, ed. Dovid Katz, vol. 2 (London: Harwood Academic Publishers, 1991); Prager, "Yiddish Periodicals." See also Shmuel Jacob Harendorf, *Theatre Caravans: Humorous Sketches* (London: Harendorf, 1954); Morris Myer, *Idish teater in london 1902–1942* (London: Naroditzki, 1943), and most recently, David Mazower's work, in particular, "Whitechapel's Yiddish Opera House: The Rise and Fall of the Feinman Yiddish People's Theatre," in *An East End Legacy: Essays in Memory of William J Fishman*, ed. Colin Holmes and Anne J. Kershen (Abingdon: Routledge, 2017), 155–87; David Mazower, *Yiddish Theatre in London* (London: Museum of the Jewish East End, 1987).

34. On London's popular culture, such as zoos to educate about imperialism, see Jonathan Schneer, *London 1900: The Imperial Metropolis* (New Haven, CT: Yale University Press, 1999), 97–106. For pleasure gardens, and broad London histories, see Jerry White, *London in the Nineteenth Century: "A Human Awful Wonder of God"* (London: Jonathan Cape, 2007); *London in the Twentieth Century* (London: Vintage Books, 2008). The histories of music halls are explored in detail in chapter 2.

35. Academic works on the Yiddish popular culture and the Jewish immigrant community of New York are numerous. See, for example, Nahma Sandrow, *Vagabond Stars: A World History of Yiddish Theater* (New York: Harper & Row, 1977); Joel Berkowitz and Barbara Henry, *Inventing the Modern Yiddish Stage: Essays in Drama, Performance, and Show Business* (Detroit: Wayne State University Press, 2012); Nina Warnke, "Immigrant Popular Culture as Contested Sphere: Yiddish Music Halls, the Yiddish Press, and the Processes of Americanization, 1900–1910," *Theatre Journal* 48, no. 3 (1996): 321–35; Judith Thissen, "Film and Vaudeville on New York's Lower East Side," in *The Art of Being Jewish in Modern Times*, ed. Barbara Kirshenblatt-Gimblett and Jonathan Karp (Philadelphia: University of Pennsylvania Press, 2013), 42–56; Edward Portnoy, "Freaks, Geeks, and Strongmen: Warsaw Jews and Popular Performance, 1912–1930," *TDR/The Drama Review* 50, no. 2 (2006): 117–35; Andrea Most, *Theatrical Liberalism: Jews and Popular Entertainment in America* (New York: New York University Press, 2013); Edna Nahshon, *New York's Yiddish Theater from the Bowery to Broadway* (New York: Columbia University Press, 2016). Bringing song into contemporary American Yiddish culture, see Abigail Wood, *And We're All Brothers: Singing in Yiddish in Contemporary North America* (Surrey: Ashgate, 2013).
36. A fabulous resource of around 200 Yiddish music-hall songs of the Lower East Side have been collected, published online, and recorded by Jane Peppler. Morris Rund, *American Yiddish Penny Songs: The Hebrew Union College Collection of Yiddish Broadsides, 1895–1922*, ed. Jane Peppler, 2015, http://www.yiddishpennysongs.com.
37. Abraham Simoronsky, "Di boyern krig mit england," songsheet, Vindeman.
38. Endelman, *Jews of Britain*, 145–50.
39. Eitan Bar-Yosef and Nadia Valman, "Between the East End and East Africa: Rethinking Images of 'the Jew' in Late Victorian and Edwardian Culture," in *"The Jew" in Late-Victorian and Edwardian Culture: Between the East End and East Africa*, ed. Eitan Bar-Yosef and Nadia Valman (Basingstoke: Palgrave Macmillan, 2009), 8, 3–9. Bar-Yosef and Valman analyze the ambivalence around anglicization and the variety of constructs of "the Jew" held by English society.
40. White believed that Jews undermined the confidence of working-class English people and that Jews should be English or go somewhere else. Glover, *Literature, Immigration*, 84–86. In responding to the pressure,

the Anglo-Jewish establishment had chosen anglicization rather than separatism. See David Englander, "Anglicized Not Anglican: Jews and Judaism in Victorian Britain," *Religion in Victorian Britain* 1 (1988): 252–68.

41. Israel Zangwill, "Anglicization" (1902), in *Nineteenth-Century Jewish Literature: A Reader*, ed. Jonathan Hess, Maurice Samuels, and Nadia Valman (Stanford, CA: Stanford University Press, 2013), 356–86.

42. "Di boyern krig mit england" was sung to the tune of "Break the News to Mother" by Charles K. Harris, an English music-hall song written in 1897. https://www.youtube.com/watch?v=45mw4IyliMA, accessed 19 September 2017. See also the songsheet W. Godwin and H. Wright, "Wishing the Boys Farewell" (London: Francis, Day & Hunter, 1900). Boer War propaganda in the English sphere also included plays and ballet; see Schneer, *London 1900*, 96–97.

43. On Anglo-Jewry's anglicization program, see Eugene C. Black, *The Social Politics of Anglo-Jewry: 1880–1920* (Oxford: Basil Blackwell, 1988), 71–156; Alderman, *Modern British Jewry*, 138–42. For anglicization by the immigrant community, see Feldman, *Englishmen*, 329–52.

44. Lipman, *Britain since 1858*, 29; *JC*, 14 September 1888, quoted in Gerry Black, *JFS: The History of the Jews' Free School, London since 1732* (London: Tymsder, 1998), 88.

45. *JC*, 9 May 1884, 11–12. Quoted in David Cesarani, *The Jewish Chronicle and Anglo-Jewry, 1841–1991* (Cambridge: Cambridge University Press, 1994), 78. Outside of formal education, Jewish girls' and boys' clubs were established to try to counter the rise of antisocial behaviors. The Jewish Lads Brigade (1895), the Brady St. Club (1896), and the Stepney Lads Club (1900) encouraged anglicization, fitness, and health, and preparing young women for marriage and motherhood. Tananbaum, *Immigrants in London*, 109–15; Feldman, *Englishmen*, 310; Robert Voeltz, "'A Good Jew and a Good Englishman': The Jewish Lads' Brigade, 1894–1922," *Journal of Contemporary History* 23 (1988): 119–20.

46. Feldman, *Englishmen*, 329–37. His arguments are applied to the following paragraphs. For the American context, see John Bodnar, *The Transplanted: A History of Immigrants in Urban America* (Bloomington: Indiana University Press, 1985), xvi–xx, 205–9. America, welcoming large numbers of newcomers, was more open to immigrants fitting congruent aspects of their heritage into the composite American

culture than the immigrants coming to the monocultures of Western Europe.

47. Feldman argues, "It was not the goal of anglicization that was rejected but its meaning that was disputed." Feldman, *Englishmen*, 336.
48. For competing arguments—Lucien Woolf's conception that Judaism had not suffered from modernity; Simon Dubnow's anxiety that modernity would lead to assimilation; and Zygmunt Bauman's view that modernity was a "doomed struggle," as Jews were too particularist to conform to a nation's view of uniformity—see David Feldman, "Was Modernity Good for the Jews?," in *Modernity, Culture, and "the Jew,"* ed. Bryan Cheyette and Laura Marcus (Stanford, CA: Stanford University Press, 1998), 171–76.
49. For the American context, see Warnke, "Popular Culture"; Alyssa Quint, "The Salon and the Tavern: Yiddish Folk Poetry of the Nineteenth Century," in *Inventing the Modern Yiddish Stage*, ed. Joel Berkowitz and Barbara Henry (Detroit: Wayne State University Press, 2012), 40–63.
50. Jerome Lawrence, *Actor, the Life and Times of Paul Muni* (London: W. H. Allen, 1975), 27.
51. The phrase "local London color" comes from Shmeruk, "Dray londoner gasnlider," 116.
52. "Strayk epidemye," *Tsayt*, 14 September 1913, 4.
53. Moshe Rosman, "Jewish History across Borders," in *Rethinking European Jewish History*, ed. Jeremy Cohen and Moshe Rosman (Oxford: Littman Library of Jewish Civilization, 2009), 28.
54. Ewa Morawska, "Immigrants, Transnationalism, and Ethnicization: A Comparison of This Great Wave and the Last," in *E Pluribus Unum? Contemporary and Historical Perspectives on Immigrant Political Incorporation*, ed. Gary Gerstle and John Mollenkopf (New York: Russell Sage Foundation, 2001), 175–79. On the differences between current and past migrations and the use of transnational theories, see Leo Lucassen, *The Immigrant Threat: The Integration of Old and New Migrants in Western Europe since 1850* (Urbana: University of Illinois Press, 2005), 6–20.
55. Daniel Soyer, "Transnationalism and Mutual Influence: American and East European Jewries in the 1920s and 1930s," in *Rethinking European Jewish History*, ed. Jeremy Cohen and Moshe Rosman (Oxford: Littman Library of Jewish Civilization, 2009), 202–3, 205. For a transnational perspective of American Yiddish culture in economic,

religious, and publishing contexts, see Ava F. Kahn and Adam D. Mendelsohn, eds., *Transnational Traditions: New Perspectives on American Jewish History* (Detroit: Wayne State University Press, 2014).

56. Debra Caplan splits transnationalism into structural, artistic, and economic strands, defining the artistic strand as "the global circulation of aesthetic ideas." She explains how the Vilna Yiddish theatre troupe was influenced by theatre aesthetics as they traveled to perform across the Yiddish world. Debra Caplan, "Nomadic Chutzpah: The Vilna Troupe's Transnational Yiddish Theatre Paradigm, 1915–1935," *Theatre Survey* 55, no. 3 (2014): 301–7.

57. Werner Sollors argues that the construction of an ethnic culture comes from the tension between the identity and culture one is born into and the one freely chosen. Werner Sollors, *Beyond Ethnicity: Consent and Descent in American Culture* (New York: Oxford University Press, 1986), 6.

58. Philip V. Bohlman, "When Migration Ends, When Music Ceases," *Music and Arts in Action* 3, no. 3 (2011): 148–65. An example of Bohlman's ideas can be seen in Parvati Nair, "Voicing Risk: Migration, Transgression and Relocation in Spanish/Moroccan Rai," in *Music National Identity and the Politics of Location: Between the Global and the Local*, ed. Ian Biddle and Vanessa Knights (Hampshire, UK: Ashgate, 2013), 65–77.

59. Manuel Peña, *The Texas-Mexican Conjunto: History of a Working-Class Music* (Austin: University of Texas Press, 1985), 13; Su Zheng, *Claiming Diaspora: Music, Transnationalism, and Cultural Politics in Asian/Chinese America* (Oxford: Oxford University Press, 2010), 28.

60. Nadia Kiwan and Ulrike Hanna Meinhof, "Music and Migration: A Transnational Approach," *Music and Arts in Action* 3, no. 3 (2011): 7–8.

61. See, for example, Gayatri Gopinath, "'Bombay, UK, Yuba City': Bhangra Music and the Engendering of Diaspora," *Diaspora: A Journal of Transnational Studies* 4, no. 3 (1995): 304.

62. Slobin calls this intersection an embedded local subculture, an overarching regional superculture and a transregional interculture. Mark Slobin, *Subcultural Sounds: Micromusics of the West* (Hanover, NH: University Press of New England, 1993), 11–12. See also Thomas Turino, *Music as Social Life: The Politics of Participation* (Chicago: University of Chicago Press, 2008).

63. Diaspora has been a focus of other disciplines not covered here. Sociologist Stuart Hall stressed the need to see cultural identity as a

never-complete process that is incorporated into artistic forms of representation. He argued that the diaspora experience is defined by its heterogeneity, diversity, and hybridity rather than by any essentialist or purist idea. These differences are the transformative power by which the diaspora identities are "constantly producing and reproducing themselves anew." Stuart Hall, "Cultural Identity and Cinematic Representation," *Framework* 36 (January 1989): 68, 78.

64. Rebecca Kobrin, *Jewish Bialystok and Its Diaspora* (Bloomington: Indiana University Press, 2010), 1–13. These theories connect with ideas of glocalization (ideas that combine both global and local considerations), which have a tangential relevance to this argument. See John Connell and Chris Gibson, *Sound Tracks: Popular Music, Identity, and Place* (London: Routledge, 2003); Lisa Lowe, "Heterogeneity, Hybridity, Multiplicity: Marking Asian American Differences," *Diaspora: A Journal of Transnational Studies* 1, no. 1 (1991): 24–44; Timothy Craig and Richard King, eds., *Global Goes Local: Popular Culture in Asia* (Vancouver: University of British Columbia Press, 2002).

65. For the growing divisions in Eastern European religious mores, see Stephen Sharot, *Judaism: A Sociology* (London: David & Charles Newton Abbot, 1976), 104.

1. Immigrant Labor, Political Activism, and Socialist Poetry

1. Joseph Markovitsh, "Aheym tsurik," unpublished manuscript, MPC. Black Lion Yard refers to the location for hiring casual labor, similar to that at the corner of Goulston Street (see the song "Hashiveynu nazad" in chapter 3).
2. Vivian Lipman, *A History of the Jews in Britain since 1858* (Leicester: Leicester University Press, 1990), 56–61.
3. L. Kahan, "Tsum fertsn-yorikn yubileum," written for the United Ladies Tailors and Mantle Workers Association, London, 17 November 1902, songsheet.
4. For Jews and the sweating system, see Todd Endelman, *The Jews of Britain, 1656–2000* (Berkeley: University of California Press, 2002), 130; David Feldman, "The Importance of Being English: Jewish Immigration and the Decay of Liberal England," in *Metropolis, London: Histories and Representations since 1800*, ed. David Feldman and Gareth Stedman-Jones (London: Routledge, 1989), 66.
5. Rudolph Rocker and Colin Ward, *The London Years* (Nottingham: Five Leaves, 2005), 89–90; Endelman, *Jews of Britain*, 135.

6. James Schmiechen, *Sweated Industries and Sweated Labor: The London Clothing Trades, 1860–1914* (London: Croom Helm, 1984), 3. Factories had more rigorous inspections than workshops, so workshop masters would ensure they had less than the fifty-worker limit. Ibid., 135–49.
7. Some division of labor was due to new power-driven machinery used in factories which needed less labor. David Feldman, *Englishmen and Jews: Social Relations and Political Culture, 1840–1914* (New Haven, CT: Yale University Press, 1994), 193–94.
8. Andrew Godley, *Jewish Immigrant Entrepreneurship in New York and London, 1880–1914: Enterprise and Culture* (Basingstoke, UK: Palgrave, 2001), 100–101.
9. Winchevsky wrote in his memoirs: "You can't say 'slack' in Yiddish. The dictionary says 'unemployment,' but it means simply 'hunger.' I know what it means. My acquaintance with it is more than theoretical." Winchevsky, *Erinerungen, gezamelte verk* (New York: Freiheit, 1927), 10:261.
10. Gareth Stedman Jones, *Outcast London: A Study in the Relationship between Classes in Victorian Society* (Oxford: Penguin Books, 1971), 43.
11. The English busy season was February and March, October and November. All trades, seasonal or not, had a slack period after the Christmas consumer boom. Ibid., 34–35.
12. Ellen Ross, "'Fierce Questions and Taunts': Married Life in Working Class London, 1870–1914," in Feldman and Stedman-Jones, *Metropolis, London*, 224.
13. Endelman, *Jews of Britain*, 133; Anne J. Kershen, *Uniting the Tailors: Trade Unionism amongst the Tailoring Workers of London and Leeds, 1870–1939* (London: F. Cass, 1995), 114–15.
14. Harold Pollins, *Economic History of the Jews in England* (Rutherford, NJ: Fairleigh Dickinson University Press, 1982), 152; Jonathan Frankel, *Prophecy and Politics: Socialism, Nationalism, and the Russian Jews, 1862–1917* (Cambridge: Cambridge University Press, 1981), 121; Schmiechen, *Sweated Industries*, 107; C. Russell and Harry Samuel Lewis, *The Jew in London: A Study of Racial Character and Present-Day Conditions* (London: T. Fisher Unwin, 1900), 84.
15. Bernard Gainer, *The Alien Invasion: The Origins of the Aliens Act of 1905* (London: Heinemann, 1972), 31; Pollins, *Economic History*, 153; Schmiechen, *Sweated Industries*, 187.
16. These positions are argued by Eugene C. Black, *The Social Politics of Anglo-Jewry: 1880–1920* (Oxford: Basil Blackwell, 1988), 200; Feldman, *Englishmen*, 246–51.

17. Beatrice Potter, "The Tailoring Trade and the Jewish Community," in *Life and Labour: East London*, ed. Charles Booth (London: Williams and Norgate, 1889), 1:232–33; Gainer, *Alien Invasion*, 17.
18. Bill Williams, "'East and West' in Manchester Jewry, 1880–1914," in *The Making of Modern Anglo Jewry*, ed. David Cesarani (London: B. Blackwell, 1990), 21.
19. From Jewish Board of Guardians minutes quoted in Geoffrey Alderman, *Modern British Jewry* (New York: Clarendon, 1992), 116.
20. David Cesarani, *The Jewish Chronicle and Anglo-Jewry, 1841–1991* (Cambridge: Cambridge University Press, 1994), 71.
21. Geoffrey Alderman, *The Federation of Synagogues, 1887–1987* (London: Federation of Synagogues, 1987), 8. After 1890 the shelter and the board worked along parallel lines, helping immigrants and transmigrants alike. Alderman, *Modern British Jewry*, 116–17.
22. Wess was a Lithuanian Jew, coming to London in 1881. William Fishman, *East End Jewish Radicals, 1875–1914* (London: Duckworth, 1975), 172. Details of the 1889 strike ibid., 169–90; Kershen, *Uniting the Tailors*, 135–39; Feldman, *Englishmen*, 216–21.
23. Feldman, *Englishmen*, 227.
24. David Schloss, "The Jew as a Workman," in *The Nineteenth Century* 29 (1891): 99–108. From David Englander, ed., *A Documentary History of Jewish Immigrants in Britain, 1840–1920* (Leicester: Leicester University Press, 1994), 145.
25. Pollins, *Economic History*, 162–63.
26. Kershen, *Uniting the Tailors*, 127.
27. Morris Winchevsky, "Der frayhayts-gayst," *AF*, 27 June 1890.
28. See Frankel, *Prophecy*, 31–41; Rocker and Ward, *London Years*, 57–65; Fishman, *Radicals*, 114–24.
29. Rocker and Ward, *London Years*, 50–56; Fishman, *Radicals*, 97–134; Frankel, *Prophecy*, 29–41.
30. Rocker and Ward, *London Years*, 57; Paul Buhle and Dan Georgakas, *The Immigrant Left in the United States* (Albany: State University of New York Press, 1996), 22; Nora Levin, *Jewish Socialist Movements: 1871–1917* (Oxford: Oxford University Press, 1978), 132.
31. Winchevsky, editorial, *PY*, 25 July 1884.
32. The modern Yiddish press dated back to the 1860s in Odessa, with Alexander Tsederboym's *Kol mevaser* (A voice of tidings) published as a Yiddish supplement to the Hebrew newspaper *HaMelitz* (The advocate). It serialized the first works of Sholem Yankev Abramovitsh

(Mendele). Later, Sholem Aleichem was serialized in the *Yidishes folksblat* (Jewish people's paper) in St. Petersburg in 1885. Nathan Cohen, "The Yiddish Press and Yiddish Literature: A Fertile but Complex Relationship," *Modern Judaism* 28, no. 2 (May 2008): 149–51.
33. Fishman, *Radicals*, 151. For details of the *Poylisher yidl*, see ibid., 141–51.
34. Lloyd Gartner, *The Jewish Immigrant in England, 1870–1914* (London: Simon Publications, 1973), 112.
35. Endelman, *Jews of Britain*, 139.
36. A secular antireligious worker became known as a "Berner-Streeter." Gartner, *Jewish Immigrant*, 112.
37. Rocker and Ward, *London Years*, 58.
38. *AF*, 15 July 1885. Quoted in Kershen, *Uniting the Tailors*, 130.
39. Frankel, *Prophecy*, 118–19.
40. Report of discussion at International Workingmen's Club, 1888. *AF*, 6 September 1889. From Feldman, *Englishmen*, 218.
41. Kahan, "Tsum fertsn-yorikn yubileum."
42. Winchevsky's SDF membership card (1893) and delegate card for the International Workers' Socialist Congress in Zurich (1893) are in the YIVO archives (Kalman Marmor Collection).
43. Ian Watson, *Song and Democratic Culture in Britain: An Approach to Popular Culture in Social Movements* (New York: Croom Helm, 1983), 9; Richard Middleton, "Popular Music of the Lower Classes," in *The Romantic Age, 1800–1914*, ed. Nicholas Temperley (London: Athlone, 1981), 73, 135.
44. Laurence Senelick, "Politics as Entertainment: Victorian Music-Hall Songs," *Victorian Studies* 19, no. 2 (1975): 152–53; Middleton, "Popular Music," 70–71; Watson, *Democratic Culture*, 19.
45. C. Alexander McKinley, *Illegitimate Children of the Enlightenment: Anarchists and the French Revolution, 1880–1914* (New York: P. Lang, 2008), 130.
46. For an overview of poetry during this period, see Sol Liptzin, *A History of Yiddish Literature* (New York: Jonathan David, 1985), 73–97; Irving Howe, Ruth R. Wisse, and Khone Shmeruk, *The Penguin Book of Modern Yiddish Verse* (New York: Viking, 1987).
47. Isaac Meir Dik, who wrote solely in Yiddish, was seen as a "scribbler and dilettante." David Fishman, *The Rise of Modern Yiddish Culture* (Pittsburgh: University of Pittsburgh Press, 2005), 6.
48. For the influence of the biblical prophets on Winchevsky's early Hebrew poetry, see Abraham Bik, *Moris vintshevski, troymer un kemfer*

(Los Angeles: Arbeter Ring, 1956), 12–16. For the influence of Russian meter, see Benjamin Harshav, *Language in Time of Revolution* (Berkeley: University of California Press, 1993), 66. For the influence of Dickens and Victorian conventions in Winchevsky's early writing, see Ronald Sanders, *The Downtown Jews: Portraits of an Immigrant Generation* (New York: Dover Publications, 1987), 143.

49. Literary critic Bialostotski called Zunzer's verse "fine, intelligent, moral-enlightenment *badkhones* about good and bad." B. Y. Bialostotski, "In di gasn—tsu di masn," *Veker*, 24 June 1922. See also Alyssa Quint, "The Salon and the Tavern: Yiddish Folk Poetry of the Nineteenth Century," in *Inventing the Modern Yiddish Stage*, ed. Joel Berkowitz and Barbara Henry (Detroit: Wayne State University Press, 2012), 44–54; Liptzin, *History of Yiddish Literature*, 48.

50. The "sweatshop" or "proletarian" poets were Morris Winchevsky (1856–1932), Morris Rosenfeld (1862–1923), Dovid Edelshtadt (1866–92), and Joseph Bovshover (1873–1915).

51. A. Litvak [Khayim Yankl Helfand], "Moris vintshevski, der onheyber," *Der veker* (2 April 1932), 4–11.

52. The YIVO archive includes hundreds of articles about Winchevsky and posters advertising him reading at socialist events in America.

53. Chris Waters, *British Socialists and the Politics of Popular Culture, 1884–1914* (Manchester: Manchester University Press, 1990), 3, 13; Peter Bailey, *Leisure and Class in Victorian England: Rational Recreation and the Contest for Control, 1830–1885* (London: Routledge & Kegan Paul, 1978), 48–49; Dave Russell, *Popular Music in England, 1840–1914: A Social History* (Manchester: Manchester University Press, 1987), 43–44.

54. Russell, *Popular Music*, 50.

55. There were brass bands and orchestras; however, choral singing was seen as the most political form of music making. Ibid., 52; Stephen Yeo, "A New Life: The Religion of Socialism in Britain, 1883–1896," *History Workshop* 4 (1977): 6.

56. *Clarion*, 12 December 1895. Quoted in Russell, *Popular Music*, 53–54.

57. Tonic Sol-fa was also used by temperance movement choirs. It aimed to be morally uplifting and a distracting pastime to replace drink and gambling. Charles Edward McGuire, "Music and Morality: Tonic Sol-Fa, the Temperance Movement, and the Oratorios of Edward Elgar," in *Chorus and Community*, ed. Karen Ahlquist (Urbana: University of Illinois Press, 2006), 111–19. Socialist and conservative

choirs used the same methods of Victorian part-harmony and sol-fa, with reformers wanting to maintain the status quo and the socialists wanting to overthrow it. Waters, *British Socialists*, 101, 128.

58. Waters, *British Socialists*, 107, 121; Yeo, "New Life," 29. A substantial repertoire had been earlier developed by Chartists, who used poetry as integral to political action. Their poetry affirmed shared values, contributed to Chartist debate and strategy, and articulated the movement's identity. Mike Sanders, *The Poetry of Chartism: Aesthetics, Politics, History* (Cambridge: Cambridge University Press, 2009), 11.
59. Morris Winchevsky, "Dos lid funem hemd," *PY*, 29 August 1884.
60. An advertisement for an anarchist choir. *AF*, 18 September 1903, 6.
61. Ruth Livesey, *Socialism, Sex, and the Culture of Aestheticism in Britain, 1880–1914* (Oxford: Oxford University Press/British Academy, 2007), 1–10.
62. Jacky Bratton argues that ballads written for causes were dull, as they used only popular forms to preach to the workers. Bratton, *The Victorian Popular Ballad* (London: Macmillan, 1975), 145.
63. Morris Winchevsky, "Vilyem moris: an erinerung," *Forverts*, 3 October 1897, 3.
64. Ibid.
65. Abraham Cahan, *Bleter*, 3:21. Quoted in Kalman Marmor, *Moris Vintshevski, zayn lebn, virkn un shafn* (New York: Freiheit, 1928), 395.
66. Steven Cassedy, *To the Other Shore: The Russian Jewish Intellectuals Who Came to America* (Princeton, NJ: Princeton University Press, 1997), xxi, 17–18.
67. Leonard Prager, "The Beginnings of Yiddish Fiction in England," in *Studies in the Cultural Life of the Jews in England*, ed. Dov Noy and Issachar Ben-Ami (Jerusalem: Magnes Press, Hebrew University, 1975), 250. See also Harshav, *Language in Time of Revolution*, 66.
68. McKinley, *Illegitimate Children*, 130; Yeo, "New Life," 20. Laura Mason argues: "Songs overleapt boundaries between politics, entertainment, and the market, to become one of the most easily used means of communication." Laura Mason, *Singing the French Revolution: Popular Culture and Politics, 1787–1799* (Ithaca, NY: Cornell University Press, 1996), 2.
69. A. L. Lloyd, *Folk Song in England* (London: Panther Books, 1969), 380.
70. McKinley, *Illegitimate Children*, 131. Many disaffected Americans identified with "The Marseillaise," so that whistling it while walking

down a street was a political comment. Simon Newman, *Parades and the Politics of the Street: Festive Culture in the Early American Republic* (Philadelphia: University of Pennsylvania Press, 2000), 177–78.
71. Thomas B. Eyges, *Beyond the Horizon: The Story of a Radical Emigrant* (Boston: Group Free Society, 1944), 78.
72. Morris Winchevsky, "Di marseyese," *LK*, 118; *Lider un gedikhte* (New York: Maisel, 1910), 129; *Gezamelte verk:* lider (New York: Astoria Press, 1927), 71–72; *Di fraye harfe* (Warsaw: Ferlags drukeray, 1907), 33–34; *Der londoner arbayter zinger* (London: Arbayter fraynd drukeray, 1894), 11–12.
73. A. Prints [Isaac Greenberg], "Vintshevskis lider," *MF*, 27 March 1932.
74. Rocker and Ward, *London Years*, 26–27; Fishman, *Radicals*, 219.
75. Eyges, *Horizon*, 79.
76. On William Morris and the Berner Street Club, see ibid., 79–83; Gartner, *Jewish Immigrant*, 127–28; Fishman, *Radicals*, 192–94.
77. Shaul Yanovski, *Ershte yorn fun yidishn frayhaytlekhn sotsyalism* (New York: Fraye arbeter shtime, 1948), 182–83.
78. *AF*, 13 June 1890. For an overview of the relationship between the English and Yiddish socialists, see Rocker and Ward, *London Years*, 101–5.
79. Rocker and Ward, *London Years*, 84. In 1900 the publication of the *Arbayter fraynd* was interrupted for a period due to financial trouble, and Rocker set up the intellectual cultural periodical *Zherminal*, which came out monthly between 1901 and 1903 and then periodically until 1909.
80. Bal Metufl, "Aroyf un arop," *IE*, 13 July 1904.
81. The radical Right counterpublic, made up of different groups on the right, argued for restriction to "steer British society onto a fresh course." David Glover, *Literature, Immigration, and Diaspora in Fin-de-Siècle England: A Cultural History of the 1905 Aliens Act* (Cambridge: Cambridge University Press, 2012), 103. For arguments of right-wing groups, see ibid., 103–18.
82. Endelman, *Jews of Britain*, 159; Israel Finestein, *Jewish Society in Victorian England: Collected Essays* (London: Vallentine Mitchell, 1993), 205–6.
83. *Royal Commission on Alien Immigration* (q.1,641, q.1,724) in Feldman, "Importance," 72–73.
84. Feldman, "Importance," 58; Feldman, *Englishmen*, 269.

85. William Eden Evans-Gordon, *The Alien Immigrant* (Memphis, TN: General Books, 2010), 24–29.
86. Alderman, *Modern British Jewry*, 135; Endelman, *Jews of Britain*, 160.
87. Gainer, *Alien Invasion*, 63.
88. Endelman, *Jews of Britain*, 173.
89. *JC*, 15 July 1904, 21.
90. On the relaxation of the rules of the act, see Glover, *Literature, Immigration*, 164–66.
91. Pollins, *Economic History*, 162–63.
92. Rocker and Ward, *London Years*, 106–11; Donald Rumbelow, *The Houndsditch Murders and the Siege of Sidney Street* (Stroud, Gloucestershire, UK: History Press, 2009), 15–29, 69–85, 123–39. For how anarchism and anti-alienism was portrayed in fiction and verse, see Glover, *Literature, Immigration*, 171–86.
93. Feldman, *Englishmen*, 272, 290, 361–66.
94. Gerry Black, *JFS: The History of the Jews' Free School, London since 1732* (London: Tymsder, 1998), 95–97; Feldman, *Englishmen*, 327, 239–43.
95. Gidley argues that diasporic memory of the homeland made immigrants react swiftly. Ben Gidley, "Diasporic Memory and the Call to Identity: Yiddish Migrants in Early Twentieth Century East London," *Journal of Intercultural Studies* 34, no. 6 (7 May 2013): 662–63. There are at least three London composed songs to raise money for those affected by pogroms. Goldberg, "Di barimte lid fun kishinyever pogrom," *SG*; Yozef Semilson, "Dos troyerike lid funem keshenever pogrom," *SY*; Yozef, "Der odeser pogrom," *LK*, 123.
96. Stuart A. Cohen, *English Zionists and British Jews: The Communal Politics of Anglo-Jewry, 1895–1920* (Princeton, NJ: Princeton University Press, 1982), 73–75; Ben Gidley, "The Ghosts of Kishinev in the East End: Responses to a Pogrom in the Jewish London of 1903," in *The "Jew" in Late-Victorian and Edwardian Culture: Between the East End and East Africa*, ed. Eitan Bar-Yosef and Nadia Valman (Basingstoke: Palgrave Macmillan, 2009), 131–43.

2. London Yiddish Music-Hall Culture

1. Nit ka Yold (Arn Nager), "Mayn meshugas," *Bloffer*, no. 1 (October 1911): 12.
2. David Mazower, *Yiddish Theatre in London* (London: Museum of the Jewish East End, 1987), 16.
3. Ibid., 11. Mazower lists plays performed in London: satirical comedies *Shmendrik* (1877) and *The Two Kuni Lemels* (1980); biblical romantic

operettas such as *Shulamis* (1880), and serious dramas on biblical themes such as *Bar Kochba* (1887).

4. Nahma Sandrow, *Vagabond Stars: A World History of Yiddish Theater* (New York: Harper & Row, 1977), 98–99. Sandrow relates how the actor David Kessler, who regularly visited London, was generally hoarse in the fourth act of a play after yelling through the first three.

5. In Goldfaden's opera, *Shulamis*, the song "The Vow" is a duet that forwards the plot, but the song "Almonds and Raisins" is a popular lullaby totally unrelated to the plot. Nahma Sandrow, "Romanticism and the Yiddish Theatre," in *Yiddish Theatre: New Approaches*, ed. Joel Berkowitz (Oxford: Littman Library of Jewish Civilization, 2003), 50. See also Sandrow, *Vagabond Stars*, 127; Mazower, *Yiddish Theatre*, 12; Leonard Prager, *Yiddish Culture in Britain: A Guide* (Frankfurt am Main: Peter Lang, 1990), 51.

6. Jacob Gordin and Ruth Gay, "Inventing a Yiddish Theater in America," in *The Jewish King Lear: A Comedy in America*, ed. Ruth Gay and Sophie Glazer (New Haven, CT: Yale University Press, 2007), 90.

7. Nina Warnke, "The Child Who Wouldn't Grow Up: Yiddish Theatre and Its Critics," in Berkowitz, *New Approaches*, 204. Sandrow uses the term "high *shund*" to describe the melodrama-operettas set in "exotic lands" in "courts of sultans and emperors." "The plots wandered on and on, providing twists and thrills; comedians turned somersaults and made vulgar puns." Sandrow, *Vagabond Stars*, 111–12.

8. Joel Berkowitz, "This Is Not Europe, You Know: The Counter-Maskilic Impulse of American Yiddish Drama," in *Yiddish in America: Essays on Yiddish Culture in the Golden Land*, ed. Edward Shapiro (Scranton, PA: Weinberg Judaic Studies Institute, University of Scranton, 2008), 144–46.

9. Nina Warnke, "Immigrant Popular Culture as Contested Sphere: Yiddish Music Halls, the Yiddish Press, and the Processes of Americanization, 1900–1910," *Theatre Journal* 48, no. 3 (1996): 323–24.

10. Sandrow, *Vagabond Stars*, 108.

11. "Idisher teater in london," *PY*, 15 August 1884. For many illiterate immigrants, theatre was their introduction to world literature, from Yiddish translations of Shakespeare, Ibsen, Tolstoy, Dumas, Sardou, and Strindberg and the classic Yiddish writers Sholem Aleichem, Sholem Ash, Y. L. Peretz, and Jacob Gordin. Bernard Mendelovitch, *Memories of London Yiddish Theatre* (Oxford: Oxford Centre for Postgraduate Hebrew Studies, 1990), 1.

12. David Mazower, email correspondence, 23 June 2015.
13. Joel Berkowitz and Barbara Henry, eds., *Inventing the Modern Yiddish Stage: Essays in Drama, Performance, and Show Business* (Detroit: Wayne State University Press, 2012), 9–10.
14. David Mazower, "Stories in Song: The Melo-Deklamatsyes of Joseph Markovitsh," in Berkowitz, *New Approaches*, 127–37. Markovitsh had to satisfy the "conflicting demands of the audience, his fellow actors, the highbrow critics, and his own artistic conscience." Ibid., 120.
15. Berkowitz, "Not Europe," 146.
16. Morris Winchevsky, *Erinerungen* (New York: Freiheit, 1927), 174–75.
17. Prager gives examples of the Berner Street Club of the anarchists, the Mantle Makers dramatic club, and the Arbeter Ring. Prager, *Yiddish Culture*, 50–51.
18. Shmuel Jacob Harendorf, "Yidish teater in england," in *Yidn in england: shtudyes un materyaln 1880–1940* (New York: YIVO, 1966), 228.
19. Sandrow, *Vagabond Stars*, 71.
20. Mendelovitch, *Memories*, 1.
21. Mazower, *Yiddish Theatre*, 13.
22. Henry Irving (1838–1905) was possibly the most famous classical English actor on the Victorian stage.
23. Jacob Adler and Lulla Rosenfeld, *A Life on the Stage: A Memoir* (New York: Knopf, 1999), 256.
24. Lloyd Gartner, *The Jewish Immigrant in England, 1870–1914* (London: Simon Publications, 1973), 260.
25. *PY*, 25 July 1884, 2–3. Other reviews were similarly uncomplimentary. Describing the play "Di mames zindl" (The mother's sin): "Of the women, Madame Chisik excelled, but more for her singing than her acting, because she hadn't learned the words well." *PY*, 22 August 1884, 7. These unsigned reviews were probably by Winchevsky. See Winchevsky, *Erinerungen*, 206.
26. For example, *PY*, 8, 15, 27 August 1884; 7 November 1884.
27. Harendorf, "Yidish teater," 233. Adler's acting and music schools were advertised weekly, *PY*, from 5 September 1884. The acting school advertisement stated: "Mr Adler the famous Yiddish actor needs young men and women to learn stagecraft. Come every day 8–3 to 9 Raven Row E or in person in the Yiddish Dramatic Club."
28. Boaz Young, *Mayn lebn in teater* (New York: Yidisher kultur farband, 1950), 51. Young describes hearing the actors Mr. and Mrs. Gradner singing on stage at the Princes Street Club just before leaving on tour.

Their song stayed in his mind as he later worked at the tailor's machine, and its power brought tears to his eyes remembering them. Ibid., 52.
29. Adler was paid £3 10/week, '"more than enough to keep him in style.'" Mazower, *Yiddish Theatre*, 13.
30. Lulla Rosenfeld, *Bright Star of Exile: Jacob Adler and the Yiddish Theatre* (New York: Crowell, 1977), 165; Harendorf, "Yidish teater," 233.
31. Myer Landa, *The Jew in Drama* (New York: KTAV, 1969), 284.
32. Young, *Mayn lebn*, 53–54. Rosenfeld relates how Dinah Shtettin from a religious family left home at sixteen and became a chorus girl, living with the Gradners. When her father found out, Jacob Adler intervened, calling the theatre an honorable profession. Dinah was also in love with Adler, and as his protégé, it set up rivalries. Rosenfeld, *Bright Star*, 181.
33. Orthodox immigrants sometimes went to Yiddish theatre for the melodies and the pride the plays instilled in Jewish history. Landa, *Jew in Drama*, 284.
34. Harendorf, "Yidish teater," 233.
35. Ibid., 235–36.
36. Sandrow, *Vagabond Stars*, 72.
37. Harendorf, "Yidish teater," 234.
38. Adler and Rosenfeld, *Life on Stage*, 257.
39. The Princes Street Club manager Abraham Smith claimed the accident had been deliberately caused by the jealousy of the manager of the Russian National Club in Lambeth Street. Mazower, *Yiddish Theatre*, 14–15. The *JC* editor Asher Myers suggested the fire was caused by isolationism, and proved that people should not go to the Yiddish theatre. David Cesarani, *The Jewish Chronicle and Anglo-Jewry, 1841–1991* (Cambridge: Cambridge University Press, 1994), 78.
40. "Max Rosenthal: The Forbes-Robertson of the Yiddish Stage," *Jewish World* 30 (November 1900): 151.
41. "A Yiddish Theatre for London," *JC*, 4 April 1902.
42. Arn Nager, "Der program fun morgen oyf der nakht," *LK*, 92–93.
43. Prager, *Yiddish Culture*, 447–48.
44. M. Yozef, "A finfter hashiveynu nazad," SY.
45. Leonard Prager, "Paul Muni's Parents Sing at a London Yiddish Music Hall," in *Language and Civilization; A Concerted Profusion of Essays and Studies in Honour of Otto Hietsch* (Frankfurt am Main: Peter Lang, 1992), 1:428–71. For Muni's time in London, see Jerome

Lawrence, *Actor, the Life and Times of Paul Muni* (London: W. H. Allen, 1975), 25–27.
46. Mazower, *Yiddish Theatre*, 16.
47. Peter Bailey, *Leisure and Class in Victorian England: Rational Recreation and the Contest for Control, 1830–1885* (London: Routledge & Kegan Paul, 1978), 29; Martha Vicinus, *The Industrial Muse: A Study of Nineteenth Century British Working-Class Literature* (London: Croom Helm, 1974), 238.
48. David Craig, *The Real Foundations; Literature and Social Change* (Oxford: Oxford University Press, 1974), 89.
49. There were four types of English halls: West End aristocratic variety theatre; smaller, less aristocratic West End; large, bourgeois halls in less fashionable parts and suburbs; and minor halls of the poor districts. *Harpers New Monthly Magazine*, 1891. Quoted in Steve Attridge, *Nationalism, Imperialism, and Identity in Late Victorian Culture: Civil and Military Worlds* (Basingstoke: Palgrave Macmillan, 2003), 20.
50. Gareth Stedman Jones, "Working-Class Culture and Working-Class Politics in London, 1870–1900: Notes on the Remaking of a Working Class," *Journal of Social History* 7, no. 4 (1974): 490; Dagmar Kift, *The Victorian Music Hall: Culture, Class, and Conflict* (Cambridge: Cambridge University Press, 1996), 176. Bailey describes the halls as having features of "the pleasure-garden-cum-promenade, the pub, club and parlour, the marketplace-cum-fairground, the street, the betting shop, the brothel and the dance hall," and at times also had elements of "the lecture room and the school." Peter Bailey, "Custom, Capital and Culture in the Victorian Music Hall," in *Popular Culture and Custom in Nineteenth-Century England*, ed. Robert D. Storch (London: Croom Helm, 1982), 204.
51. Bailey, "Custom, Capital, Culture," 197; Anthony Bennett, "Music in the Halls," in *Music Hall: Performance and Style*, ed. Jacky Bratton and Ann Featherstone (Milton Keynes, UK: Open University Press, 1986), 6–9.
52. Jacky Bratton describes the work of Jenny Hill, who played sympathetic portrayals of working-class girls: a waitress, a serving girl, street saleswomen and downtrodden mothers, disillusioned wives, and elderly women. Jacky Bratton, "Jenny Hill: Sex and Sexism in the Victorian Music Hall," in *Music Hall: Performance and Style*, ed. Jacky Bratton and Ann Featherstone (Milton Keynes, UK: Open University

Press, 1986), 92–106. For female music hall "types," see also Jane Traies, "Jones and the Working Girl: Class Marginality in Music-Hall Song 1860–1900," in *Music Hall: Performance and Style*, ed. Jacky Bratton and Ann Featherstone (Milton Keynes, UK: Open University Press, 1986), 31–36.

53. Landa, *Jew in Drama*, 275.
54. Y. Finkelstein, "Hibru komedyes: 'Artistn' vos makhn a lebn fun bashmutsikn dos idishe folk," *Tsayt*, 22 January 1914, 2. An arsonist (*fayermakher*) was an anti-Semitic stereotype of a Jew used in the English music halls. See Edward Marshall, "Ambivalent Images: A Survey of Jewish Involvement and Representation in the British Entertainment Industry, 1880–1980" (unpublished PhD thesis, Royal Holloway, University of London, 2010), 68; Henry Chance Newton, *Cues and Curtain Calls: Being the Theatrical Reminiscences of H. Chance Newton ("Carados" of the Referee)* (Devon, UK: John Lane, 1927), 256–57; Christie Davies, "Exploring the Thesis of the Self-Depreciating Jewish Sense of Humor," in *Semites and Stereotypes: Characteristics of Jewish Humor*, ed. Avner Ziv and Anat Zajdman (Westport, CT: Greenwood, 1993), 38–39. This stereotype can also be seen in anti-Semitic postcards of the time, such as "Faule Fische und Makes," from ca. 1901, University of Minnesota, "Center for Holocaust and Genocide Studies," accessed 26 June 2015, http://www.chgs.umn.edu/histories/otherness/otherness1-3.html.
55. For an examination of how Jews were portrayed by Hebrew comedians, see Marshall, "Ambivalent Images," 63–72. Stock characters had a powerful impact, and Jewish characters from melodrama moved into theatre and fiction. David Glover, *Literature, Immigration, and Diaspora in Fin-de-Siècle England: A Cultural History of the 1905 Aliens Act* (Cambridge: Cambridge University Press, 2012), 87–99.
56. Stedman Jones, "Working-Class Culture," 490; Dagmar Kift, *The Victorian Music Hall: Culture, Class, and Conflict* (Cambridge: Cambridge University Press, 1996), 176.
57. Dave Russell, "Varieties of Life: The Making of the Edwardian Music Hall," in *The Edwardian Theatre: Essays on Performance and the Stage*, ed. Michael Booth and Joel Kaplan (Cambridge: Cambridge University Press, 1996), 78.
58. Barry J. Faulk, *Music Hall & Modernity: The Late-Victorian Discovery of Popular Culture* (Athens: Ohio University Press, 2004), 13.

59. Vicinus, *Industrial Muse*, 258; Jacky Bratton, *The Victorian Popular Ballad* (London: Macmillan, 1975), 157; Bailey, "Custom, Capital, Culture," 201.
60. Blanchard Jerrold, *London: A Pilgrimage* (London, 1872; repr. New York, 1970), 167. Quoted in Peter Bailey, "Conspiracies of Meaning: Music-Hall and the Knowingness of Popular Culture," *Past and Present* 144 (1994): 143.
61. The chairman could be bribed to produce lengthier or nicer introductions. Vicinus, *Industrial Muse*, 252.
62. Bailey, "Conspiracies," 161. Bailey's research on "knowingness" has been held in high regard by scholars. See in particular Patrick Joyce, *Visions of the People: Industrial England and the Question of Class 1848–1914* (Cambridge: Cambridge University Press, 1993), 223; Dave Russell, *Popular Music in England, 1840–1914: A Social History* (Manchester: Manchester University Press, 1987), 153; Russell, "Varieties of Life," 75; Attridge, *Nationalism, Imperialism*, 23–24.
63. Doris Sommer argues that there may be irritation on not getting the bilingual joke, yet the appreciating of one's imperfect comprehension allows for greater democracy. Doris Sommer, *Bilingual Aesthetics: A New Sentimental Education* (Durham, NC: Duke University Press, 2004), 36.
64. "Londonized" is my term. In a talk on London jokes in the eighteenth century, Simon Jarrett described how the use of London slang identified who were the "assimilated Londoners," creating an "in-group" and a larger "out-group" of newcomers. Simon Jarrett, "A Welshman Coming to London, and Seeing a Jackanapes . . ." (Conference, London and the Nation, Birkbeck, University of London, 10 July 2015).
65. Joseph Markovitsh, "50 yor," *IS*, 20 November 1953, 2.
66. Ibid., 27 November 1953, 2.
67. Joseph Markovitsh, "A kholem," *IS*, 4 December 1953.
68. Ibid.
69. "A Music-Hall in the East End," *The Standard*, 28 October 1902. This review was reprinted in the *JC* in the same week, with the comment that it was a "somewhat unsympathetic" portrayal. "A Yiddish Music-Hall in the East End," *JC*, 31 October 1902.
70. Leib Shalom Kreditor, "Yidish teater in london: shtrikhn un episodn," in *Hundert yor yidish teater*, ed. Y. Klinger (London: Lett Printers, 1962), 14.

71. Henry Chance Newton, "Music-Hall London," in *Living London: Its Work and Its Play, Its Humour and Its Pathos, Its Sights and Its Scenes*, ed. George Sims (New York: Cassell, 1902), 225. For Jewish freak shows in Warsaw, see Edward Portnoy, "Freaks, Geeks, and Strongmen: Warsaw Jews and Popular Performance, 1912–1930," *TDR/The Drama Review* 50, no. 2 (2006): 117–35.
72. "A Visit to the Yiddish Music Hall," *JC*, 8 February 1907.
73. Ibid.
74. Nager, "Program fun morgen."
75. Penelope Summerfield, "The Effingham Arms and the Empire: Deliberate Selection in the Evolution of Music Hall in London," in *Popular Culture and Class Conflict, 1590–1914: Explorations in the History of Labour and Leisure*, ed. Eileen Yeo and Stephen Yeo (Sussex, UK: Harvester Press, 1981), 209.
76. The expense of building repairs could be prohibitive for small halls, forcing them to close. Susan Pennybacker, "'It Was Not What She Said, but the Way That She Said It': The London County Council and the Music Halls," in *Music Hall: The Business of Pleasure*, ed. Peter Bailey (Milton Keynes, UK: Open University Press, 1986), 127–28.
77. Dave Russell, "'We Carved Our Way to Glory': The British Soldier in Music Hall Song and Sketch, c. 1880–1914," in *Popular Imperialism and the Military 1850–1950*, ed. John MacKenzie (Manchester: Manchester University Press, 1992), 53.
78. Stedman Jones, "Working-Class Culture," 494–95; Bailey, "Custom, Capital, Culture," 198.
79. Laurence Senelick, "Politics as Entertainment: Victorian Music-Hall Songs," *Victorian Studies* 19, no. 2 (1975): 150.
80. Bailey, "Custom, Capital, Culture," 196; Papers of the Select Committee on Theatres and Places of Entertainment (HC 1892 [240], 440–42). Quoted in Pennybacker, "Not What She Said," 129.
81. Bratton, *Victorian Ballad*, 156.
82. Kift, *Victorian Music Hall*, 168.
83. Pennybacker, "Not What She Said," 128, 130–35.
84. Warnke, "Popular Culture," 321–31. For American vaudeville, also see Edna Nahshon, *New York's Yiddish Theater from the Bowery to Broadway* (New York: Columbia University Press, 2016), 240–55.
85. Eyner vos iz dort geveyn, "Der idisher teater," *IE*, 25 December 1901.
86. Talmud, tractate Megillah (7b).

87. Ahuva Belkin, "The 'Low' Culture of the Purimshpil," in Berkowitz, *New Approaches*, 29.
88. Eyner, "Der idisher teater," *IE*, 7 May 1902.
89. Avreml, "Di ani-maamins fun bloffer," *Bloffer*, no. 5 (December 1911): 10.
90. Morris Myer, *Yidish teater in london 1902–1942* (London: Naroditzki, 1943), 31.
91. For early years of the Bund, see Nora Levin, *Jewish Socialist Movements: 1871–1917* (Oxford: Oxford University Press, 1978), 261–79; Jonathan Frankel, *Prophecy and Politics: Socialism, Nationalism, and the Russian Jews, 1862–1917* (Cambridge: Cambridge University Press, 1981), 171–246.
92. *JC*, 6 August 1909, 20.
93. Joseph Chaim Brenner, *Out of the Depths*, trans. David Patterson (San Francisco: Westview, 1992), 353–448.
94. *Bloffer*, no. 6 (December 1911).
95. "From the East End," *JC*, 6 August 1909, 20.
96. L. Izraeli, "Repertuar fun idishn teater," *IE*, 21 February 1912.
97. Kh. T., "Di idishe bine in london," *IE*, 9 July 1913, 4.
98. *Bloffer*, no. 1 (October[?] 1911).
99. "A Word to the Public," *Idisher zhurnal*, 14 March 1912, repr. in Mazower, *Yiddish Theatre*, 70. The article asks the audience to behave well, sit quietly, only applaud at appropriate times, not to whistle or eat; states that ladies should take off hats; and prohibits children under eight years old.
100. "Brilliant talent . . . one of the most notable operatic triumphs in this country . . . the most highly trained singers and musicians . . . with an accuracy, a precision, and a perfect mastery, astonishing in its excellence." "Rigoletto in Yiddish: A Notable Triumph," *JC*, 19 April 1912, 32–33.
101. *IE*, 17 and 24 April 1912, 2.
102. For an account of the Feinman theatre, see David Mazower, *Yiddish Theatre*.
103. L. Izraeli, "Di pavilyen: Ir repertuar un personel," *IE*, 28 February 1912, 2.
104. Ibid.; Leon Kussman, "Faynman—yidish folks teater (batrakhtungn vegn 'templ')," *IE*, 26 June 1912, 2.

3. The Transnational Scope

1. Y. Goldman, "Dos lid 'goles rusland,'" Songsheet Malimzon, MPC.

2. The term "messy" is used by Lisa Lowe to describe the lack of uniformity in Asian American poetry and fiction. Lowe, "Heterogeneity, Hybridity, Multiplicity: Marking Asian American Differences," *Diaspora: A Journal of Transnational Studies* 1, no. 1 (1991): 27.
3. For theory around layering transnational ideas into a "network of networks," see Nina Glick Schiller and Ulrike Hanna Meinhof, "Singing a New Song? Transnational Migration, Methodological Nationalism and Cosmopolitan Perspectives," *Music and Arts in Action* 3, no. 3 (2011): 25.
4. For the *JC* letters page on unity, see the discussion of Winchevsky's poem "Akhdes" in chapter 8.
5. For the theory of supercultures and subcultures, see Mark Slobin, *Subcultural Sounds: Micromusics of the West* (Hanover, NH: University Press of New England, 1993), 87–89.
6. Martin Stokes, *Ethnicity, Identity, and Music: The Musical Construction of Place* (Oxford: Berg, 1994), 19.
7. For an introduction to the different centers of Yiddish theatre, see Nahma Sandrow, *Vagabond Stars: A World History of Yiddish Theater* (New York: Harper & Row, 1977), 70–90.
8. Nadia Kiwan and Ulrike Meinhof call these "*spatial* hubs." They argue that artists are facilitated through a range of hubs. These include "*human* hubs"—individuals like the artists themselves—and "*institutional* hubs" set up to support migrant musicians. Kiwan and Meinhof, "Music and Migration: A Transnational Approach," *Music and Arts in Action* 3, no. 3 (2011): 7–8.
9. *Landsmanshaftn* supported transnational movement between America and Eastern Europe. See Daniel Soyer, "Transnationalism and Mutual Influence: American and East European Jewries in the 1920s and 1930s," in *Rethinking European Jewish History*, ed. Jeremy Cohen and Moshe Rosman (Oxford: Littman Library of Jewish Civilization, 2009), 202–5. Soyer focuses on support and does not include culture in his analysis. See also Ben Gidley's argument of how *landsmanshaftn* in London supported associational politics and kept diasporic memory alive. Gidley, "Diasporic Memory and the Call to Identity: Yiddish Migrants in Early Twentieth Century East London," *Journal of Intercultural Studies* 34, no. 6 (7 May 2013): 650–53.
10. George Lipsitz, *Dangerous Crossroads: Popular Music, Postmodernism, and the Poetics of Place* (New York: Verso, 1994), 4.

11. See Philip V. Bohlman, *The Music of European Nationalism: Cultural Identity and Modern History* (Santa Barbara, CA: ABC-CLIO, 2004), 55.
12. Thomas Turino, *Music as Social Life: The Politics of Participation* (Chicago: University of Chicago Press, 2008), 210.
13. Goldfaden wrote musical operas from the 1870s to the early 1900s. Avrom Goldfaden, *Hashivenu Nasad: Kehr Uns Zurik*, arr. Kammen (New York: Hebrew Publishing Company, 1921); *Di idishe bine* (Brooklyn: Hebrew Publishing Company, 1897), 203–4. The title is so unfamiliar it is translated into more straightforward Yiddish as a subtitle.
14. Lamentations 5:21. The poetry of the Book of Lamentations tells of the destruction of the Temple of Jerusalem by the Babylonians in 586 B.C. It is read in synagogue on the fast day of Tisha B'av, which commemorates the destruction of the Temples of Jerusalem.
15. A verse from the original is reprinted in Ruth Rubin, *Voices of a People: The Story of Yiddish Folksong* (Philadelphia: Jewish Publication Society of America, 1979), 374. Also *Hashiveynu nazad*, performed by David Roitman (St. Petersburg: Musique Internationale, 1970?), 33⅓ rpm vinyl.
16. "Dem nayem hashiveynu nazad," SG. Reprinted in Khone Shmeruk, "Dray londoner gasnlider fun far der ershter velt-milkhome," in *Studies in the Cultural Life of the Jews in England*, ed. Dov Noy and Issachar Ben-Am (Jerusalem: Magnes, 1975), 117–19. Also called "Hashiveynu nazad" in *LK*, 156–57.
17. Note the rhyme *fayt* and *gayt* is in the Polish-Yiddish dialect.
18. *Yoykelte* is translated as a non-Jewish woman in the glossary of anglicisms in Arye-Meyer Kayzer, *Bay undz in vaytshepl: mayses un mayselekh* (London: Naroditski, 1944), 172.
19. The way bilingual immigrants use the mixture of languages is explored by Sommer, who argues that the multiple codes can last for generations. Doris Sommer, *Bilingual Aesthetics: A New Sentimental Education* (Durham, NC: Duke University Press, 2004), 175.
20. Lloyd Gartner, *The Jewish Immigrant in England, 1870–1914* (London: Simon Publications, 1973), 24–26; Vivian Lipman, *A Century of Social Service, 1859–1959: The Jewish Board of Guardians* (London: Routledge & Kegan Paul, 1959), 93; David Cesarani, *The Jewish Chronicle and Anglo-Jewry, 1841–1991* (Cambridge: Cambridge University Press, 1994), 70.

21. Yozef, "A ferter hashiveynu nazad," *LLM*, 14; Yozef, "A finfter hashiveynu nazad," SY.
22. Little Turner Street no longer exists, but was nearly opposite what is present-day Turner Street.
23. Leonard Prager, *Yiddish Culture in Britain: A Guide* (Frankfurt am Main: Peter Lang, 1990), 614.
24. This song is probably from 1901–2, when Salli and Philip Weisenfreund were in London. The other names probably refer to Karl Gutentag, Joseph Sherman, and Morris Akselrod.
25. *Di idishe bine.*
26. Prager notes how changing the meaning of *hashiveynu nazad* in each verse generates the humor. Leonard Prager, "Der londoner farleger m. yozef," in *Oksforder yidish*, ed. Dovid Katz (London: Harwood Academic Publishers, 1991), 2:195.
27. *Dem nayem hashiveynu nazad*, performed by Esther Djzaldovsky (ca. 1950; Toronto: Unpublished recording by Chaim Neslen, n.d.), cassette tape; Chaim Neslen, interviewed by Vivi Lachs, 25 April 2009.
28. "Hashiveynu nazad," *Bloffer*, no. 34 (May 1913).
29. David Mazower, *Yiddish Theatre in London* (London: Museum of the Jewish East End, 1987), 15.
30. Morris Winchevsky, "London bay nakht," *PY*, 12 September 1884; "London bay nakht oder di lempelekh" ("London at night" or "The streetlights"), *Arbayter lider* (London: Lidz internatsionale arbayter bildungs klub, n.d.), 13–15. Prager suggests the date is 1894. Prager, *Yiddish Culture*, 125.
31. Ivan Miatlev, 1796–1844.
32. Nokhum Borukh Minkov, *Piyonern fun yidisher poezye in amerike: dos sotsiale lid* (New York: O. fg., 1956), 63.
33. Morris Winchevsky, *Erinerungen* (New York: Freiheit, 1927), 176.
34. Kalman Marmor, *Moris Vintshevski, zayn lebn, virkn un shafn* (New York: Freiheit, 1928), 119.
35. Morris Winchevsky, "Di lempelekh," SY.
36. Gayatri Gopinath writes how "multiple diasporas intersect both with one another and with the national spaces that they are continuously negotiating and challenging." Gopinath, "'Bombay, UK, Yuba City': Bhangra Music and the Engendering of Diaspora," *Diaspora: A Journal of Transnational Studies* 4, no. 3 (1995): 304.

37. This type of adaptation is common. "Ot azoy neyt a shnayder" (This is how a tailor stitches) was an Eastern European work song from the beginning of the eighteenth century, with verses added after union action of the 1880s when conditions of work changed. Ruth Rubin, *Jewish Folk Songs: In Yiddish and English* (New York: author, 1989), 50. London Jews sing the song with the word "penny" rather than "guilder." They would not necessarily have known that this was a substitution.
38. Louis Gilrod, "A het oder a get," *Lider magazin*, vol. 3, New York: n.d., *LK*, 6–7.
39. "Gevalt es iz a shlekhte tsayt," *Idisher bine*, 214–16; SY.
40. "Azoy geyt dos gelt avek," *LK*, 52; SG; *Yidishe teater lider* (New York: Hebrew Publishing Company, 1901), 42–43.
41. "The Jewish Athletic-Association," *JC*, 15 January 1909, 6.
42. Jerry White, *Rothschild Buildings: Life in an East End Tenement Block 1887–1920* (London: Routledge & Kegan Paul, 1980), 185.
43. Eugene C. Black, *The Social Politics of Anglo-Jewry: 1880–1920* (Oxford: Basil Blackwell, 1988), 231.
44. Charles Poulsen, *Victoria Park: A Study in the History of East London* (London: Stepney Books: Journeyman Press, 1976), 94–101.
45. Stokes, *Ethnicity, Identity*, 3.
46. Arn Nager, "Viktorye park," *LLM*, 15.
47. For this use of the term and for its etymology, see Online Etymology Dictionary, "kike," accessed 20 October 2016, http://www.etymonline.com/index.php?allowed_in_frame=0&search=kike.
48. The characters may allude to real people. Nager wrote for the *Bloffer* under the pseudonym *Nit ka yold* (Nobody's dupe). Satire there named people in opinionated comments. See, for example, *Bloffer*, no. 13 (April 1912): 5.
49. Vivi Lachs, "Revolution in Anglo-Yiddish Poetry: Morris Winchevsky's Strategies to Revolutionise the Jewish Immigrants to Britain, 1884–1894," *Studies in Ethnicity and Nationalism* 14, no. 1 (2014): 17.
50. Dan Miron, "The Literary Image of the Shtetl," *Jewish Social Studies* 1, no. 3 (Spring 1995): 4.
51. Andy Bennett, "Music, Space and Place," in *Music, Space and Place: Popular Music and Cultural Identity*, ed. Sheila Whiteley, Andy Bennett, and Stan Hawkins (Aldershot: Ashgate, 2004), 3.
52. *Victoria Park*, performed by Bertha Jackson (London: Unpublished recording by Derek Reid, 1978), cassette tape. Jackson was ninety years

old in 1978 and remembered learning it as an eight-year-old, which would date the song to around 1896. Derek Reid, "Six Yiddish Street Songs of East London," in *Proceedings of the First International Conference on Jewish Music 1994*, ed. Steve Stanton (London: City University, 1997), 105–6.

53. John Connell and Chris Gibson, *Sound Tracks: Popular Music, Identity, and Place* (London: Routledge, 2003), 191.
54. Avrom Vevyorke, *Di idishe prese un dos idishe teater in london* (London: M. Susman, n.d.).
55. "Der bloffer lakht," *Bloffer*, no. 4 (November 1911); nos. 5 and 6 (December 1911); no. 12 (March 1912); no. 13 (April 1912). Numbers 4–6 were written under the pen name Zimri ben salu, who is a biblical character who appears in the Old Testament in Numbers 25:10–15. He is killed by the leader Pinchas as a punishment for openly having a sexual relationship with a Mideonite (non-Jewish) woman.
56. As taken from the definitions from Lesley Brown, *The New Shorter Oxford English Dictionary on Historical Principles* (Oxford: Clarendon, 1993), 249. See also the American-Yiddish vaudeville song translated as "Bluff! Bluff! Bluff!" Edna Nahshon, *New York's Yiddish Theater from the Bowery to Broadway* (New York: Columbia University Press, 2016), 247.
57. See under entry for Kusman. Prager, *Yiddish Culture in Britain*, 388. Beinfeld and Bochner translate the noun *blof* as "bluff, fraud." Solon Beinfeld and Harry Bochner, *Comprehensive Yiddish-English Dictionary* (Bloomington: Indiana University Press, 2013), 174.
58. "Der bloffer lakht," *Bloffer*, no. 13 (April 1912): 16.
59. *Bloffer*, no. 4 (November 1911): 12.
60. *Bloffer*, no. 12 (March 1912): 8.
61. *Bloffer*, no. 6 (December 1911): 16; ibid., no. 4 (November 1911).
62. For the dispute on the Jewish hospital, see Gerry Black, *Lord Rothschild and the Barber: The Struggle to Establish the London Jewish Hospital* (London: Tymsder, 2000), 67–76.
63. See ibid., 52–82.
64. *Bloffer*, no. 5 (December 1911): 11; *Bloffer*, no. 6 (December 1911).
65. *Bloffer*, no. 6 (December 1911).
66. See, for example, *IS*, 2 January 1904.
67. *Bloffer*, no. 12 (March 1912).
68. *Bloffer*, no. 5 (December 1911).
69. This verse may refer to Morris Myer, journalist and editor of the *Tsayt*, who was the butt of other satirical pieces in the *Bloffer*.

4. Debates and Ballads

1. Morris Winchevsky, *Der blinder fidler*, LG, 188.
2. Biographical details are mostly from Morris Winchevsky, *Erinerungen* (New York: Freiheit, 1927); Kalman Marmor, *Moris Vintshevski, zayn lebn, virkn un shafn* (New York: Freiheit, 1928); Melekh Epstein, *Profiles of Eleven: Profiles of Eleven Men Who Guided the Destiny of an Immigrant Society and Stimulated Social Consciousness among the American People* (Detroit: Wayne State University Press, 1965), 13–35; Rudolph Rocker and Colin Ward, *London Years* (Nottingham: Five Leaves, 2005), 57–59; William Fishman, *East End Jewish Radicals, 1875–1914* (London: Duckworth, 1975), 138–44.
3. For Winchevsky's early Hebrew poems, see Abraham Bik, *Moris vintshevski, troymer un kemfer* (Los Angeles: Arbeter Ring, 1956); A. R. Malakhi, "Moris vintshevski (tsu zayn zibetsik yorikn yubileum)," *Tsukunft*, September 1926, 501–4; A. R. Malakhi, "Moris vintshevski (tsu zayn 75-yorikn yubileum)," *Tsukunft*, November 1930, 768–60.
4. Winchevsky's biography comes from Epstein, *Profiles of Eleven*, 18–48.
5. Winchevsky was also active in English socialist circles. Nathan Ausubel, "The Story of Yiddish," *MF*, 11 August 1947. A small amount of writing appeared in the SDF's *Justice* and *Today* and the SL's *Commonweal*. Epstein, *Profiles of Eleven*, 33. He wrote under the pseudonym Jim from Bethnal Green, and translated his story *Grishke's roman* into English, which was published in the *London Sun* in 1893 and later in Morris Winchevsky, *Stories of the Struggle* (Chicago: Charles H. Kerr, 1908), 3. See also Marmor, *Lebn*, 138–39, 154.
6. The "meshugener filozof" column was variously called "Di tseshlogene gedanken fun dem meshugenem filozof" (Crazy ramblings of the mad philosopher) and "Bilder un verter fun a meshugenem filozof" (Pictures and words from a crazy philosopher). They are collected together in Morris Winchevsky, *Der meshugener filozof in england* (New York: Forward Association, 1920).
7. Nineteenth-century revolutionary poetry has been understood as functioning to provoke a "rupture," which forces the reader to contemplate an alternative existence. Pauline Johnson, *Marxist Aesthetics (Routledge Revivals): The Foundations within Everyday Life for an Emancipated Consciousness* (London: Taylor & Francis, 2013), 100. The

term "cognitive rupture" comes from Mike Sanders, *The Poetry of Chartism: Aesthetics, Politics, History* (Cambridge: Cambridge University Press, 2009), 10. Sanders's analysis of poetry from the Chartist movement argues that the political and aesthetic were "thoroughly imbricated practices. Sanders, *Poetry of Chartism*, 3.

8. A. Litvak [Khayim Yankl Helfand], "Moris vintshevski, der onheyber," *Der veker*, 2 April 1932, 4–8. Although *badkhones* means rhyming couplets used by a wedding jester, in Litvak's criticism it could be translated as "doggerel." For Zunzer, see chapter 2.

9. Bik, *Troymer, kemfer*, 5–34; Abraham Bik, "Moris vintshevski, der liriker," *YK*, August–September, 1956, 11–15; Marmor, *Lebn*, 379–93. The critic A. Litvin argued that revolutionary workers' songs, including those of Winchevsky, affect both spirit and aesthetics, and as such are located between folk poetry and modern Yiddish poetry. A. Litvin, "Di revolutsyonere lid un di folks-lid—di ershte revolutsyonere lid—a mitl fun agitatsye," in *Idishe literatur*, ed. M. Levitan (Kiev: kultur lige, 1928), 1:318–20.

10. Morris Winchevsky, *Mayn arbeter-muze*, *YK*, May 1952, 43. First published as *Frayn un lebn* (1912).

11. Jonathan Frankel, *Prophecy and Politics: Socialism, Nationalism, and the Russian Jews, 1862–1917* (Cambridge: Cambridge University Press, 1981), 130.

12. *PY*, 15 August 1884. Quote from Winchevsky, *Erinerungen*, 174.

13. Adler's rendition was advertised. *PY*, 15, 22, and 29 August 1884. The poem was published in *Di idishe bine* (Brooklyn: Hebrew Publishing Company, 1897, 398–400), which underlines its performative nature and shows the strong connection between the workers' songs and the Yiddish stage.

14. Winchevsky, *Erinerungen*, 175.

15. Nokhum Borukh Minkov, *Piyonern fun yidisher poezye in amerike: Dos sotsiale lid* (New York: 1956), 19.

16. The poetry was reproduced in collections of his own poetry and of socialist poetry including *Gezamelte verk: lider*; *LG*; *Di fraye harfe*; *Der londoner arbayter zinger*; *Freiheit: revolutsyonere lider un shirim* (Geneva: Bund Publishers, 1905).

17. Shakhne Epshteyn, "Moris vintshevski (tsu zayn 60-sten geburtstog)," *Tsukunft*, December 1916, 1045.

18. Marmor, *Lebn*, 157–58, 163–64.

19. Philip Krantz, "Winchevsky," editorial, *AF*, 15 July 1885.

20. For an examination of Winchevsky's inclusive politics, see Vivi Lachs, "The Yiddish Veker in London: Morris Winchevsky; Building a Broad Left through Poetry 1884–1894," *Socialist History*, no. 45 (2014): 1–24.
21. Dovid Edelshtadt, "Tsum meshugenem filozof," *AF*, March 1890.
22. Rocker and Ward, *London Years*, 61–62.
23. Edelshtadt, *Mayn muze*, quoted in Marmor, *Lebn*, 172.
24. Morris Winchevsky, "An d. edelshtat" (To D. Edelshtadt), quoted ibid.
25. This move "symbolized the new status acquired by New York and the relative decline of London." Frankel, *Prophecy*, 119.
26. Morris Winchevsky, "Parti politik," *FV*, July 1892, 57.
27. Marmor, *Lebn*, 158–59.
28. Litvak, "Vintshevski, der onheyber," 6.
29. Marmor, *Lebn*, 172–73.
30. Morris Winchevsky, "Akhdes," *AF*, 29 August 1890.
31. "The Authorised Daily Prayer Book," *JC*, 1 August 1890, 7.
32. Elkan Levy, "The New West End Synagogue, 1879–2004" (lecture, July 11, 2004), www.newwestend.org.uk/visitors/history-and-architecture.html.
33. Even to Anglo-Jewry, the Singer's Prayer Book was a compromise, with different elements of the community considering it too moderate or too traditional. Michael Clark, *Albion and Jerusalem: The Anglo-Jewish Community in the Post-Emancipation Era, 1858–1887* (Oxford: Oxford University Press, 2009), 180.
34. "Unity, not Uniformity," *JC*, 7 February 1890, 6.
35. *JC*, 7 February 1890, 11–12; 9 May 1890, 13; 27 June 1890, 15–16; 25 July 1890, 19–20.
36. Between World Wars I and II, "Akhdes" became the basis of the popular song "Ale Brider." This version created a community cohesion song about unity, cutting out all allusions to local politics and religion. Mlotek calls "Ale Brider" a "folklorised version," quoting Litvin in *Di tsayt* (n.d.) that the song "was the most popular folk song that was sung in the old country mostly at Bundist parties"; Eleanor Gordon Mlotek, *Mir trogn a gezang!: The New Book of Yiddish Songs* (New York: Workmen's Circle Education Department, 1989), 160–61. The only surviving recording is *Alle Brider*, performed by Rhoda Cohn and Mary Feldman, from *Children Sing! Kinder Zingen* (New York: Metro, 1947), 33⅓ rpm vinyl. This song remains popular today, made famous by the Klezmatics. Their upbeat version added equality politics with

verses about women and homosexuality. *Ale Brider*, performed by the Klezmatics, from *Shvaygn=Toyt* (Round Rock: Piranha Records, 1989), compact disc.

37. Winchevsky, *LG*, 8. Based on these ballads, literary critic A. Prints called Winchevsky "the singer of need and loneliness of the London masses." A. Prints, "Vintshevskis lider," *MF*, 27 March 1932.
38. Morris Winchevsky, *LG*, 145–200.
39. Minkov, *Piyonern*, 20–21.
40. Prints, "Vintshevskis lider."
41. Winchevsky, "Tsum nayem yor," *AF*, 3 January 1890. When reproduced in the *Siluetn*, the title was changed to "Der alter man un der nayer yor," *LG*, 182–83.
42. Morris Winchevsky, "Nor dos nit," *AF*, 30 January 1891. This poem is not in the *Siluetn*.
43. Morris Winchevsky, "Oremer yosel," *Tsukunft*, 16 January 1885. Retitled in the *Siluetn* as "Der yoseml" (The little orphan), *LG*, 152–53.
44. Morris Winchevsky, "A meydele in der siti," *Tsukunft*, 27 March 1885.
45. A version of this song substitutes "Leicester" with "Manchester." Manchester was the second largest immigrant community in England. Manchester Square is in Marylebone, London, although not known for its prostitutes. *Dray shvester*, performed by Zelig Shnadover (n.d.; Mexico City: Unpublished recording by Itzik Gottesman, n.d.), mp3.
46. Morris Winchevsky, "Dray shvester," *FV*, October 1891.
47. See William Stead, "The Maiden Tribute of Modern Babylon: The Report of Our Secret Commission," *Pall Mall Gazette*, 4 July 1885. See also Edward Bristow, *Prostitution and Prejudice: The Jewish Fight against White Slavery, 1870–1939* (Oxford: Clarendon, 1982), 37–38, 40–42.
48. For an alternative interpretation of the song, see Marc Miller, *Representing the Immigrant Experience: Morris Rosenfeld and the Emergence of Yiddish Literature in America* (Syracuse, NY: Syracuse University Press, 2007), 72.
49. Morris Winchevsky, *Dray shvester: Three Sisters*, arr. Henry Lefkowitch, New York: Metro Music, 1932. Dovid Katz called "Dray Shvester" Winchevsky's most famous poem. Dovid Katz, *Words on Fire: The Unfinished Story of Yiddish* (New York: Basic Books, 2004), 327. There have been six known recordings of "Dray shvester": *Die Drei Schwesters*, performed by Morris Goldstein (New York: Brunswick, 1928), 78 rpm vinyl; *Die Drei Schwestern*, performed by Morris

Goldstein (New York: Victor, 1928), vinyl 78; *Dray Shvester*, performed by Klezmer Klub, from *Whitechapel, mayn Vaytshepl* (London: Klub Records, 2009), compact disc; *Dray Shvester*, performed by Metropolitan Klezmer, from *Surprising Finds* (New York: Rhythm Media Records, 2003), compact disc; *Drei Schwester*, performed by Simon Osovitsky (Tel Aviv: Galton, n.d.), 33⅓ rpm vinyl; *Dri Shvester*, performed by Pincus Lawenda (New York: Banner, ca. 1945), 33⅓ rpm vinyl. Also *In england is do a shtot lester*, sung by Sonia Shtern (unpublished recording: 1955, YIVO archives), mp3; *Dray shvester*, sung by Zelig Shnadover (Mexico City: unpublished recording by Itzik Gottesman, n.d.), mp3. Winchevsky wrote an English translation: "Three Sisters," unpublished manuscript, YIVO archives, n.d.
50. This quote comes from a House of Lords select committee report in 1881. Quoted in Jerry White, *London in the Nineteenth Century: "A Human Awful Wonder of God"* (London: Jonathan Cape, 2007), 306–7.
51. Morris Winchevsky, "Oyfn strend," *LG*, 198.
52. Morris Winchevsky, "Rent," *AF*, 15 December 1885.
53. Morris Winchevsky, "Di farfroyene," *AF*, 23 January 1891.
54. Bik, *Troymer, kemfer*, 22–26.
55. Karsten Troyke, personal email correspondence with author, 2008.
56. Morris Winchevsky, "Di oreme maria," *AF*, 25 October 1889.
57. Charles Booth, *Charles Booth's London: A Portrait of the Poor at the Turn of the Century, Drawn from His "Life and Labour of the People in London,"* ed. Albert Fried, Richard M. Elman, and Raymond Williams (London: Hutchinson, 1969), xx–xxiv.

5. Making Socialist Activists

1. Morris Winchevsky, "In kamf," *FV*, October 1891. For a translation into English rhymed couplets, see Aaron Kramer, "Four Yiddish Proletarian Poets: 1. Morris Winchevsky," *Jewish Life*, May 1950, 24–25.
2. For example, the fifth anniversary celebration of the *Arbayter fraynd*, *AF*, 13 June 1890.
3. Morris Winchevsky, "Tsum arbayter fraynd," *Freiheit*, 1905, 10–11 (dated 1885).
4. Ruth Rubin, "History of an American Yiddish Folk Song," *Jewish Quarterly* 2, no. 2 (Autumn 1954): 151–60.
5. Morris Winchevsky, "Tsu di arbayter: nokh a tsuruf," *AF*, 27 February 1891.

6. Morris Winchevsky, "More shkhoyre," *FV*, September 1892.
7. Morris Winchevsky, "Vi di raykhe layt lebn," *Veker*, 1892–93. The words "sweater" and "pawnbroker" are in the diminutive form, adding irony to the meaning.
8. Morris Winchevsky, "Akhdes," *AF*, 29 August 1890.
9. The reference to coupons is time specific, because in 1897 the Board of Guardians saw the system of coupons as wasteful and abolished it in favor of cash. Vivian Lipman, *Social History of the Jews in England: 1850–1950* (London: Watts, 1954), 117. The reference may also have overtones of coupons used in the Stock Exchange.
10. Editorial, *PY*, July 1884.
11. Morris Winchevsky, "A khoydesh on arbayt," *PY*, 31 October 1884.
12. Morris Winchevsky, *Erinerungen* (New York: Freiheit, 1927), 261.
13. Ruth Livesey, *Socialism, Sex, and the Culture of Aestheticism in Britain, 1880–1914* (Oxford: Oxford University Press/British Academy, 2007), 38–39. Livesey bases her argument on Wilde's *The Soul of Man under Socialism* (1891), Morris's "aesthetic continuum," *News from Nowhere* (1890). Also, Gerard Manley Hopkins's poem "Harry Ploughman" was published in 1887.
14. Winchevsky, *Erinerungen*, 262.
15. Krantz justified difficult material by arguing: "Readers, especially Jewish readers, need food for thought. All Jews can study the Talmud, since eventually they need to understand God; so the *Arbayter fraynd* should not surpass their level of comprehension either." *AF*, 15 October 1885. Quoted in Karin Hofmeester, *Jewish Workers and the Labour Movement: A Comparative Study of Amsterdam, London and Paris (1870–1914)* (Aldershot, UK: Ashgate, 2004), 127. Winchevsky considered that short, clear paragraphs would increase accessibility to the ideas and therefore be a "good medium to awaken the masses." Winchevsky, *Erinerungen*, 207, 211.
16. Irving Howe called Winchevsky a "journalist in verse." Irving Howe and Kenneth Libo, *World of Our Fathers* (London: Phoenix, 2000), 425.
17. *FV*, May 1891. Note that none of the notitsn have titles.
18. This refers to the Jewish community already being able to get free schooling from Jewish schools such as the Jews' Free School.
19. *FV*, August–September 1891.
20. Ibid.
21. *FV*, July 1892. Primrose-women were members of the Primrose League, an organization set up in 1883 to campaign for the Conservatives.

22. David Feldman, *Englishmen and Jews: Social Relations and Political Culture, 1840–1914* (New Haven, CT: Yale University Press, 1994), 277–78.
23. Edward, second child and eldest son of Victoria and Albert, was nicknamed "Bertie."
24. *FV*, July 1891.
25. Max Weinreich, *History of the Yiddish Language* (New Haven, CT: Yale University Press, 2008), 234–35.
26. David Glover, *Literature, Immigration, and Diaspora in Fin-de-Siècle England: A Cultural History of the 1905 Aliens Act* (Cambridge: Cambridge University Press, 2012), 82–86.
27. Morris Winchevsky, "A kleyner volkn oyfn himl," *PY*, 3 October 1884, 1–2. The corner of Brick Lane and Commercial Road was the central thoroughfare of Jewish Whitechapel. Marmor described Winchevsky as "alarmist"; Kalman Marmor, *Moris Vintshevski, zayn lebn, virkn un shafn* (New York: Freiheit, 1928), 103–4.
28. "Rikblik oyf dos alte yor." *PY*, 26 September 1884. Thomas de Torquemada was the leader of the Spanish inquisition, and Haman is the villain of the Purim story who attempted to kill the Jews of Persia. The Tiszaeszlár Affair of 1882–83 was a trial for blood libel in Austria which led to anti-Semitic pogroms.
29. Kalman Marmor, *lebn, virkn un shafn*, 104.
30. *FV*, July 1891.
31. Ibid.
32. Thanks to my Facebook buddies who discussed the associations behind the usage of the term *Yidls kepl*—Judy, Ross, Daniel, Esther, Michael, Itzik, and Miryem-Khaye.
33. Winchevsky, "Kleyner volkn," 1–2.
34. Tia DeNora, *Music in Everyday Life* (Cambridge: Cambridge-Obeikan, 2000), 16–17. Mervyn Busteed suggests that for migrant groups, if songs contain ideas about group identity, then singing or humming them is in itself an act of resistance. Mervyn Busteed, "Songs in a Strange Land—Ambiguities of Identity amongst Irish Migrants in Mid-Victorian Manchester," *Political Geography* 17, no. 6 (1998): 600–601.
35. Some sung poems were published with sheet music. Morris Winchevsky, *Dray shvester: Three Sisters*, arr. Henry Lefkowitch, (New York: Metro Music, 1932). "Dray shvester," "Es s rirt zikh," and "Der frayhayts-gayst" were published in Moshe. Beregovski and

Itzik Fefer, *Yidishe folks-lider* (Kiev: Melukhe-farlag, 1938), 76–77, 68–69, 88–90. These three songs and "Tsum arbeter fraynd" and "A bezem un a ker" were republished in Moshe Beregovskiĭ and Mark Slobin, *Old Jewish Folk Music: The Collections and Writings of Moshe Beregovski* (Syracuse, NY: Syracuse University Press, 2000), 126–28. One leaflet for the Synagogue Parade of 1889 announced that it would "proceed with music." This would have almost certainly included Winchevsky's anthems. Harold Pollins, *Economic History of the Jews in England* (Rutherford, NJ: Fairleigh Dickinson University Press, 1982), 157.

36. Nicholas Salmon, "The Communist Poet-Laureate: William Morris's 'Chants for Socialists,'" *Journal of the William Morris Society* 14 (2001): 31, 37–38. These songs were collected and published as *Chants for Socialists*.
37. Morris Winchevsky, "Tsum arbayter fraynd," *Freiheit*, 1905. Poem dated 1885.
38. Peysakh Novik, *Moris vintshevski—di lebedike traditsye (tsu zayn 100ste geboyrntog)*, YK, January 1957, 31.
39. A. Litvak [Khayim Yankl Helfand], "Di rol fun der revolutsyoner lid in der arbeter-bavegung," in *Idishe literatur*, ed. M. Levitan (Kiev: kultur lige, 1928), 1:322–23.
40. Shmuel Niger, *Moris vintshevski: tsu zayn 70 yorikn geburtstog*. Press cutting, YIVO. Title missing, 1926. Ben Yakir saw the poetry's inherent sing-ability as "a sign of true folk poetry." Ben Yakir, "A lang dervartenes bukh," *Tsukunft*, February 1911, 94.
41. Martin Stokes, "Music, Affect and Political Action" (lecture, Royal Holloway, 5 February 2013).
42. Teresa Brennan, *The Transmission of Affect* (Ithaca, NY: Cornell University Press, 2014), 1, 53–55.
43. Morris Winchevsky, "Tsu di raykhe," *Tsukunft*, 6 February 1885.
44. Morris Winchevsky, "Mayne lider," *AF*, 13 February 1891.
45. Sh. Zinger noticed the "humility" of this poem, arguing that Winchevsky was too hard on himself, thus supporting his critics: "Even in this [poem] the fine rhythm of Yiddish song is apparent. They are not 'insufficient' and 'unmelodic' as he himself would have." Zinger, *Moris vintshevski (tsu zayn hundertstn geboyrntog), Der fraynd*, September–October 1956.
46. Morris Winchevsky, *LG*, 8. Here the poem is titled *Mayne folkslider*.

47. Letter from Morris to socialist activist Frederick Pickles, October 1885. Quoted in Livesey, *Culture of Aestheticism*, 45.
48. Morris Winchevsky, "Dray vekhter," *AF*, 15 November 1885.
49. A. Prints [Isaac Greenberg], "Vintshevskis lider," *MF*, 27 March 1932.
50. Marmor, *Lebn*, 134.
51. Morris Winchevsky, "Es rirt zikh," *AF*, 12 December 1886. Abraham Bik argued that the ubiquitous word *kamf* (fight) was a "holy metaphor": "For Winchevsky the word *kamf* has a direct relationship to strivings to be the awakener from slavery and the caller to great deeds of heroism. It is, actually, for him a synonym for heroism. '*Kamf*' is that which transforms the slave into a hero and makes him dream in everyday truth." Bik, *Moris vintshevski, troymer un kemfer* (Los Angeles: Arbeter Ring, 1956), 16–17.
52. Livesey, *Culture of Aestheticism*, 45.
53. Marmor, *Lebn*, 136–37.
54. Ibid., 140–41.
55. Feldman, *Englishmen*, 216–17; Harry Kelly, introduction to Thomas B. Eyges, *Beyond the Horizon: The Story of a Radical Emigrant* (Boston, MA: Group Free Society, 1944), 16. See also William Fishman, *East End Jewish Radicals, 1875–1914* (London: Duckworth, 1975), 164–82.
56. Fishman, *Radicals*, 172. A poster in English headlined "The Strike Still Continues" hangs in the Jewish Museum, London.
57. David Cesarani argues that the *JC* held an ambivalent position on the strike. On one hand, it treated socialists and anarchists with contempt and horror, and on the other hand, it supported Jews to unionize so that they "fend off allegations in the anti-alien press that there were thousands of immigrant anarchists or criminals in the East End." Cesarani, *The Jewish Chronicle and Anglo-Jewry, 1841–1991* (Cambridge: Cambridge University Press, 1994), 80.
58. Morris Winchevsky, "A bezem un a ker," *AF*, 11 October 1889.
59. In a front cover poem about anarchists, the author has Rudolf Rocker and a group of anarchists all holding brooms. The illustrative cartoon shows Rocker sweeping with a broom on top of a globe. *Bloffer*, no. 3 (November 1911): 1.
60. David Feldman argues that the Jewish and gentile communities had significant contact during the early years of immigration, and gives examples from union activism: Feldman and Stedman, "Mr Lewinstein Goes to Parliament: Reflections on the Historiography and History of Jewish Immigration to London," unpublished paper, 2017.

61. For years this song was sung on May 1 demonstrations. Winchevsky even translated it into Hebrew. Marmor, *Lebn*, 153.
62. The word *lern* is probably *lernen*, to teach, possibly used in this form as a rhyme.
63. Morris Winchevsky, "Der frayhayts-gayst," *AF*, 27 June 1890.
64. After the Kishinev pogrom of 1903, Winchevsky accepted aspects of Jewish nationalism. See A. Litvak [Khayim Yankl Helfand], "Moris vintshevski, der onheyber," *Der veker*, 2 April 1932, 7. Itshe Goldberg claimed Winchevsky felt stuck in the middle, attacked from both sides, socialist and nationalist. Goldberg, "A bezem un a ker," *YK*, March 1967.
65. Marmor, *Lebn*, 172–73.
66. Morris Winchevsky, "A kamf-gezang," *Veker*, 23 December 1892.
67. Morris Winchevsky, "Tsvey veltn," *FV*, May 1891.
68. Morris Winchevsky, "Di tsukunft," *Freiheit*, 26–27 (dated 1892).
69. Winchevsky, *Erinerungen*, 264.
70. To revisit the parallels between Winchevsky and William Morris, Morris also suffered from severe criticism for his socialist poetry. Critics saw his work as crude propaganda or simply did not relate to it as poetry. Salmon, "Communist Poet-Laureate," 36.
71. Shmuel Niger, "Moris vintshevski (tsu zayn 70 yorikn geburtstog)," *Der tog*, 5 September 1926.
72. Yankev Hodess, "'Yiddish Literature': The Writings of Morris Winchevsky," *Jewish Chronicle Books and Bookmen Supplement*, 30 January 1914, 8.
73. Litvak [Khayim Yankl Helfand] was a leader in the Bund and one of their "most influential and prolific Yiddish writers" as well as an editor of and contributor to the Yiddish socialist press. YIVO online encyclopedia, yivoencyclopedia.org/article.aspx/Litvak_A.
74. A. Litvak [Khayim Yankl Helfand], "Moris vintshevski, der onheyber," *Der Veker*, 2 April 1932, 4–11.
75. A. Prints [Isaac Greenberg], "Vintshevskis lider," *MF*, 27 March 1932.
76. Aaron Kushnirov, "Der zeyde fun der yidishe poezye," *MF*, 16 March 1947, 6.
77. See Yoel Entin, "Veg keyn amerike hot gefirt durkh london," *Morgen dzurnal*, 14 November 1943; Ber Grin (Isaac Greenberg)'s in *MF* 1954 and 1962; Leon Kobrin, "Der zeyde moris vintshevski, mayn ershte bagegenish mit im," *MF*, 3 June 1946.

78. In particular in the work of Bik, *Troymer, kemfer*, 23–32; Nokhum Borukh Minkov, *Piyonern fun yidisher poezye in amerike* (New York: O. fg. 1956), 22–32; Ben-Yakir, "A lang ervartetes bukh," *Tsukunft*, February 1911, 92–93.
79. Moyshe Katz. "Der zeyde Moris vintshevski," *MF*, 12 August 1956, 10.
80. Litvak [Khayim Yankl Helfand], "Moris vintshevski, der onheyber," 6.
81. Recent publications of Winchevsky's songs include "Dray shvester" in Aharon Vinkovetzky, Abba Kovner, and Sinai Leichter, *Anthology of Yiddish Folksongs* (Jerusalem: Magnes Press, Hebrew University, 1985), 3:213–14; "Es rirt zikh" in Aharon Vinkovetzky, Abba Kovner, and Sinai Leichter, *Anthology of Yiddish Folksongs* (Jerusalem: Magnes Press, 1987), 4:35–36; "Di tsukunft" in Eleanor Gordon Mlotek and Joseph Mlotek, *Songs of Generations: New Pearls of Yiddish Song* (New York: Workmen's Circle, 2004), 86–87. Recordings include the versions of *Dray Shvester* quoted earlier; *Di tsukunft*, performed by Adrienne Cooper, from *In Love and Struggle* (New York: YIVO, 1999), compact disc. *Di tsukunft* is taught in Yiddish songschools today. The most lasting cultural aspect may be the song "Ale Brider." Most recently, London's Great Yiddish Parade is reviving Winchevsky's activist anthems and singing them on the streets of London. See "The Great Yiddish Parade" on Facebook, https://www.facebook.com/groups/thegreatyiddishparade/.

6. Transforming Courtship

1. *Ich such a Job*, performed by Yozef Sherman and the Pavilion Orchestra (London: Imperial, n.d.), 78 rpm vinyl.
2. Lesley Hall, *Sex, Gender and Social Change in Britain since 1880* (New York: Palgrave Macmillan, 2000), 30; Lucy Bland, *Banishing the Beast: English Feminism and Sexual Morality, 1885–1914* (London: Penguin, 1995), 5–15; Judith R. Walkowitz, "Science, Feminism and Romance: The Men and Women's Club 1885–1889," *History Workshop Journal* 21 (1986): 38; Judith R. Walkowitz, *City of Dreadful Delight: Narratives of Sexual Danger in Late-Victorian London* (Chicago: University of Chicago Press, 1992), 135–36.
3. Scholarship on sex is limited to issues surrounding prostitution and the white slave trade, in particular in the work of Edward Bristow, *Prostitution and Prejudice: The Jewish Fight against White Slavery, 1870–1939* (Oxford: Clarendon, 1982); Lara Marks, "Race, Class and

Gender: The Experiences of Jewish Prostitutes and Other Jewish Women in the East End of London at the Turn of the Century," in *Women, Migration and Empire*, ed. Joan Grant (Stoke-on-Trent, UK: Trentham, 1996), 113–37; Paul Knepper, "British Jews and the Racialisation of Crime in the Age of Empire," *British Journal of Criminology* 47, no. 1 (January 2007): 61–79; Lloyd Gartner, "Anglo-Jewry and the Jewish International Traffic in Prostitution, 1885–1914," *AJS Review* 7 (1982): 129–78. This will be considered in more detail in chapter 7. There are references to Anglo-Jewish support for unmarried mothers and the anarchist position on free love in Susan L. Tananbaum, *Jewish Immigrants in London, 1880–1939* (London: Pickering and Chatto, 2014), 138–41; Rudolph Rocker and Colin Ward, *The London Years* (Nottingham: Five Leaves, 2005), 42. The missing scholarship in social history concerns the daily lives of the immigrant community.

4. Patrick Joyce, *Visions of the People: Industrial England and the Question of Class 1848–1914* (Cambridge: Cambridge University Press, 1993), 224.
5. Gernot Böhme, "Atmosphere as the Fundamental Concept of a New Aesthetics," *Book Eleven* 36, no. 1 (1993): 121.
6. Quoted in Ben Anderson, "Affective Atmospheres," *Emotion, Space and Society* 2, no. 2 (2009): 79.
7. Peter Bailey, "Conspiracies of Meaning: Music-Hall and the Knowingness of Popular Culture," *Past and Present* 144 (1994): 138–70, 158.
8. Ibid., 144–46.
9. Bland, *Banishing the Beast*, 114–17. Chant's most notorious attack was against the presence of prostitutes in the audience of the West End music halls. Penelope Summerfield, "The Effingham Arms and the Empire: Deliberate Selection in the Evolution of Music Hall in London," in *Popular Culture and Class Conflict, 1590–1914: Explorations in the History of Labour and Leisure*, ed. Eileen Yeo and Stephen Yeo (Sussex, UK: Harvester, 1981), 219.
10. Jacky Bratton, *The Victorian Popular Ballad* (London: Macmillan, 1975), 155–57; Susan Pennybacker, "'It Was Not What She Said, but the Way That She Said It': The London County Council and the Music Halls," in *Music Hall: The Business of Pleasure*, ed. Peter Bailey (Milton Keynes, UK: Open University Press, 1986), 127–28.
11. Shmuel Jacob Harendorf, "Yidish teater in england," in *Yidn in england: shtudyes un materyaln 1880–1940* (New York: YIVO, 1966), 232–33.

12. For example, 22 May 1908, 24; Harry Samuel Lewis, "East End Judaism—Need and Possibilities of Reform," *JC*, 20 February 1903.
13. Nina Warnke, "Immigrant Popular Culture as Contested Sphere: Yiddish Music Halls, the Yiddish Press, and the Processes of Americanization, 1900–1910." *Theatre Journal* 48, no. 3 (1996): 321–35, 321. Warnke's article examines socialists' attitude to the Lower East Side Yiddish halls.
14. The East End was terrorized by the rival Bessarabian and Odessan gangs, who frequented the music halls, including a murder outside the York Minster music hall. *ELO*, 29 November 1902. Jerome Lawrence describes how gangs "defeated" Salli and Philip Weisenfreund's ability to run the hall. Lawrence, *Actor, the Life and Times of Paul Muni* (London: W. H. Allen, 1975), 27. Also see James Morton, *East End Gangland & Gangland International Omnibus* (London: Timewarner Paperbacks, 2003), 47–49. In another incident, an "alleged riot" in the Manor Theatre in Hackney, two Jewish tailors arguing over the quality of different theatres, ended with chairs ripped up and thrown around. *ELO*, 10 May 1902. For crime in the immigrant community, see Colin Holmes, "East End Crime and the Jewish Community, 1887–1911," in *The Jewish East End 1840–1939* (London: Jewish Historical Society of England, 1981).
15. Sydney Weinberg, *The World of Our Mothers: The Lives of Jewish Immigrant Women* (Chapel Hill: University of North Carolina Press, 1988), 23–24.
16. *Kest* was not only to allow the newly married man to study but also to let the couple save enough to establish an independent home. Chae-Ran Freeze, *Jewish Marriage and Divorce in Imperial Russia* (Hanover, NH: University Press of New England [for] Brandeis University Press, 2002), 30–31.
17. Ibid., 11–12. This change was partly due to resistance by children to arranged partners. Despite parents' opposition, children would run away from home or convert to Christianity to marry the partner of their choice. Ibid., 16–17. For the changes in community control in villages and towns, see Stephen Sharot, *Judaism: A Sociology* (London: David & Charles Newton Abbot, 1976), 103–4. For middle-class women, remaining single became an option. Naomi Shepherd, *A Price below Rubies: Jewish Women as Rebels and Radicals* (London: Weidenfeld & Nicholson, 1993), 212–14.

18. Seidman's recent book analyzes the changes in Jewish marriage mores due to modernization and secularization. She explores the role of literature in that transformation. Naomi Seidman, *The Marriage Plot: Or, How Jews Fell in Love with Love, and with Literature* (Stanford, CA: Stanford University Press, 2016), 166–67.
19. Seidman argues that Jewish secularity not only was an expression of acculturation and the "triumph of Jewish continuity but was the place where these ideas were negotiated. Naomi Seidman, "Religion/Secularity," in *The Routledge Handbook of Contemporary Jewish Cultures*, ed. N. Valman and L. Roth (London: Routledge, 2015), 157.
20. What constituted attraction for men and women had been more fluid. A pale Talmud scholar would be seen as a good match for a woman who would be the primary breadwinner. Seidman, *Marriage Plot*, 180.
21. Vivian Lipman, *A History of the Jews in Britain since 1858* (Leicester: Leicester University Press, 1990), 49.
22. In Eastern Europe the Bund activities offered a place for single men and women to meet and develop romantic ties through political bonds. However, political activism did not equate with libertinism. "Although the 'sexual revolution' and family question were central to the radical movements, some parties felt obliged to regulate relationships. The unprecedented intermingling of the sexes impelled the Bund . . . not only to reject the idea of sexual license espoused by some radicals but also to uphold a strict code of morality that essentially mirrored the norms of traditional Jewish society." Freeze, *Jewish Marriage*, 23–24.
23. "The Whitechapel Road in those days [1909] was an extraordinary corso. The East End youngsters paraded up and down, the girls, according to fashion, in blue velvet, the boys all in brown, from hat to shoes, their white panama canes alone providing a colour contrast." Charles Landstone, "Edwardian Vignettes: A Visit to the Pavilion Theatre," *JC*, 27 November 1970.
24. "A Music-Hall in the East End," *The Standard*, 28 October 1902.
25. Eyner vos iz dort geveyn, "Der idisher teater," Part 1: 25 December 1901. The "lane" referred to is Petticoat Lane in Whitechapel.
26. "Music-Hall in the East End."
27. Landstone, "Edwardian Vignettes."
28. Eyner vos iz dort geveyn, "Der idisher teater," *Idisher ekspres*, 7 May 1902.
29. For men working in male-only environments, cooped up all day, the evening at a music hall where they were cramped in the halls with

smoke, drink, and women would have made a "giddy" setting. Martha Vicinus, *The Industrial Muse: A Study of Nineteenth Century British Working-Class Literature* (London: Croom Helm, 1974), 249–50.

30. There were often two music-hall shows a night. The earlier performance, intended for families and children, omitted the saucier material. A *JC* review of an early showing at the Princess' music hall commented on its purity and lack of suggestive material. The early showing had an audience of only a hundred, but the later performances had five hundred. "A Visit to the Yiddish Music Hall," *JC*, 8 February 1907.

31. *Bloffer*, no. 21 (November 1912): cover. Image is reproduced just before this chapter.

32. Arn Nager, "Der dansing skul," *LK*, 107.

33. Victoria Park was so popular that it was called the "Polish Brighton," and the tram or bus heading there the "Polish Express." Eugene C. Black, *The Social Politics of Anglo-Jewry: 1880–1920* (Oxford: Basil Blackwell, 1988), 231.

34. Israel Zangwill and Meri-Jane Rochelson, *Children of the Ghetto: A Study of a Peculiar People* (Detroit: Wayne State University Press, 1998), 165. Zangwill can be seen as a PR man for the immigrants, producing an idealized and romanticized version of the 1870s.

35. Arn Nager, "Viktorye park," *LLM*, 15. The published version has three verses. Reid recorded two verses from Bertha Jackson. He was sent a third verse (different from the published version) by an unnamed man who had heard the Jackson recording on the radio. Derek Reid, "Six Yiddish Street Songs of East London," in *Proceedings of the First International Conference on Jewish Music 1994*, ed. Steve Stanton (London: City University, 1997), 111.

36. Itsik smitchik is part of a vocabulary of crude names. Michael Wex, *Born to Kvetch: Yiddish Language and Culture in All of Its Moods* (New York: St. Martin's, 2005), 204; email correspondence with Vivi Lachs, 23 December 2016.

37. Solon Beinfeld and Harry Bochner, *Comprehensive Yiddish-English Dictionary* (Bloomington: Indiana University Press, 2013), 646.

38. Alexander Harkavy, *English-Yiddish Dictionary: Yiddish-English Dictionary* (New York: Schocken Books, 1988), 476.

39. For an analysis of the behavior of music-hall fans within an American context, see Nina Warnke, "*Patriotn* and Their Stars: Male Youth

Culture in the Galleries of the New York Yiddish Theatre," in *Inventing the Modern Yiddish Stage: Essays in Drama, Performance, and Show Business*, ed. Joel Berkowitz and Barbara Henry (Detroit: Wayne State University Press, 2012), 169–77.
40. "Gevald, gevald police!"
41. By 1911 English women were delaying marriage until age twenty-five or twenty-six, so that they could work longer. This gave them more time to save for their dowries, and after contributing to the family income they had some degree of independence. James Schmiechen, *Sweated Industries and Sweated Labor: The London Clothing Trades, 1860–1914* (London: Croom Helm, 1984), 70.
42. "Azoy geyt dos gelt avek," *LK*, 52; SG.
43. Peter Gurney, "'A Palace for the People?' The Crystal Palace and Consumer Culture in Victorian England," in *Victorian Prism: Refractions of the Crystal Palace*, ed. James Buzard, Joseph Childers, and Eileen Gillooly (Charlottesville: University of Virginia Press, 2007), 139.
44. Jerry White, *London in the Nineteenth Century: "A Human Awful Wonder of God"* (London: Jonathan Cape, 2007), 270–71.
45. The terminology of disjuncture and displacement is developed in Philip V. Bohlman, "When Migration Ends, When Music Ceases," *Music and Arts in Action* 3, no. 3 (2011): 57.
46. Arn Nager, "Genendel," *LK*, 122.
47. "Ver zukht a kale," *LK*, 111.
48. "Gevalt es iz a shlekhte tsayt," SY; Y. Finklshteyn, "Opgeklapte hoyshayne," SM.
49. Beinfeld and Bochner, *Yiddish Dictionary*, 258.
50. The song was published in London and New York, and there is a songsheet sketch between the characters of the song. *Lizi klaf*, SY, ca. 1898. *Lizzie Clough* performed by Bertha Jackson (London: Unpublished recording by Derek Reid, 1978), cassette tape.
51. S. Yozefzon, "A boytshik ap to deyt," SM.
52. The *JC* wrote virulently against marrying out. Henry de Worms had to resign his presidency of the Anglo Jewish Association when he sanctioned his daughter's Anglican wedding. Arthur Cohen, not orthodox, resigned the presidency of the Board of Deputies when his daughter out-married. Michael Clark, *Albion and Jerusalem: The Anglo-Jewish Community in the Post-Emancipation Era, 1858–1887* (Oxford: Oxford University Press, 2009), 203.

53. Rachel Biale, *Women and Jewish Law: The Essential Texts, Their History, and Their Relevance for Today* (New York: Schocken Books, 1995), 190.
54. Arn Nager, "Plezhur," *LLM*, 9–10.
55. Paul Knepper, "British Jews and the Racialisation of Crime in the Age of Empire," *British Journal of Criminology* 47, no. 1 (January 2007): 67–69.
56. "Haf past nayn," SG, MPC.
57. Charles Collins, "Half Past Nine on My Wedding Day," sung by the English comic Nellie Wallace. Here the bride is looking forward to her wedding night as "We're going to blow out the candles at half past nine." Peter Davison, *Songs of the British Music Hall* (London: Oak Publications; distributed by Music Sales Corp., 1971), 220–23. See also Wal Pink and George Le Brunn, *Half-Past Nine* (New York: T. B. Harms, 1893).
58. Joseph Markovitsh, "Mazl," *LLM*.
59. For ethnicization, see Ewa Morawska, "Immigrants, Transnationalism, and Ethnicization: A Comparison of This Great Wave and the Last," in *E Pluribus Unum? Contemporary and Historical Perspectives on Immigrant Political Incorporation*, ed. Gary Gerstle and John Mollenkopf (New York: Russell Sage Foundation, 2001), 178–79. For hybridity, see Mercedes Dujunco, "Hybridity and Disjuncture in Mainland Chinese Popular Music," in *Global Goes Local: Popular Culture in Asia*, ed. Timothy Craig and Richard King (Vancouver: University of British Columbia Press, 2002), 28.
60. Arn Nager, "Malke, malke," *LK*, 115.

7. Marriage, Lodgers, and Transgressive Sex

1. Sam Levenvirt, "London hot zikh ibergekert," *LK*, 129.
2. Isaac Metzker, *A Bintel Brief: Sixty Years of Letters from the Lower East Side to the Jewish Daily Forward* (New York: Schocken Books, 1971), 65–70.
3. There are numerous love songs outside of the music-hall repertoire— both folk songs and theatre songs. These can be found in almost all Yiddish folksong collections.
4. The popular comic-strip character Ally Sloper portrays a cartoon of a "minor deviant" who, although married, plays the field. He operates "on the fringes of legality." This cartoon character, drawn to be read, seemed to have more freedom than the cartoon-style characters depicted in the English music hall. Peter Bailey, "Ally Sloper's

Half-Holiday: Comic Art in the 1880s," in *History Workshop Journal*, vol. 16 (n.p.: Oxford University Press, 1983), 11.
5. In Jewish law polygamy was allowed, though forbidden by later rabbis. Rachel Biale, *Women and Jewish Law: The Essential Texts, Their History, and Their Relevance for Today* (New York: Schocken Books, 1995), 183–84.
6. Lesley Hall, *Sex, Gender and Social Change in Britain since 1880* (New York: Palgrave Macmillan, 2000), 10–12. See also Marjorie Levine-Clark, "From 'Relief' to 'Justice and Protection': The Maintenance of Deserted Wives, British Masculinity and Imperial Citizenship, 1870–1920," *Gender & History* 22, no. 2 (2010): 303–8.
7. *AF*, 23 November 1889. Quoted in Lloyd Gartner, *The Jewish Immigrant in England, 1870–1914* (London: Simon Publications, 1973), 117. See also Hall, *Sex, Gender*, 130, 59. Anarchist leader Rudolph Rocker described in his memoirs how in 1898 he and his partner, Milly Witkop, were stopped from entering the United States because they had no marriage certificate. See Rudolph Rocker and Colin Ward, *The London Years* (Nottingham: Five Leaves, 2005), 42.
8. Geoffrey Alderman, *Modern British Jewry* (New York: Clarendon, 1992), 126.
9. For an example of the Four Per Cent Industrial Dwellings Company's model housing scheme, see Jerry White, *Rothschild Buildings: Life in an East End Tenement Block 1887–1920* (London: Routledge & Kegan Paul, 1980), 4–30.
10. David Feldman, *Englishmen and Jews: Social Relations and Political Culture, 1840–1914* (New Haven, CT: Yale University Press, 1994), 182. The housing shortage was exacerbated by the fact that immigrants worked mainly as unskilled labor in workshops with irregular hours, so requiring both workers and masters to live in the East End, and masters often used a room in the house as a workshop. Ibid., 174, 179.
11. Fred Murray and Laurence Barclay, "Our Lodger's Such a Nice Young Man." Peter Davison, *Songs of the British Music Hall* (London: Oak Publications; distributed by Music Sales Corp., 1971), 135. Other popular English music-hall songs of the period included "Flanigan the Lodger," B. W. Hitchcock, 1885, sung by Pat Rooney; "We Saved It for the Lodger," Lester Barnett and Felix McGlennon, 1889; "The Wife, the Lodger and I," Harry Wincott and Harry Leighton, 1902.

12. The English word "lodger" is used in these songs, but would be translated as "boarder" for an American audience. In Louis Gold's repertoir, the lyrics of the song "Mayn vayb" (My Wife) read *"border (lodzher),"* offering alternate lyrics for different locations.
13. "Gevalt es iz a shlekhte tsayt," SY; Arn Nager, "Der dzhob," *LK*, 9–11; Joseph Markovitsh, "Aheym tsurik," unpublished manuscript, MPC; "Fri ov tshardzh," *LLM*, 12–13.
14. Arn Nager, "Freg keyn katshanes," *LLM*, 9–10.
15. Zelig Oberman, *In mayne teg* (London: Narod, 1947), 92.
16. Wage earning was a precarious position, and if the husband was not earning, his position as head of the household could be contested. Ellen Ross, "'Fierce Questions and Taunts': Married Life in Working-Class London, 1870–1914," in *Metropolis London: Histories and Representations since 1800*, ed. David Feldman and Gareth Stedman-Jones (London: Routledge, 1989), 224.
17. Joseph Markovitsh, "Moyshe kum efn mir dem shlos," *LK*, 93–95.
18. Jacky Bratton, "Beating the Bounds: Gender Play and Role Reversal in the Edwardian Music Hall," in *The Edwardian Theatre: Essays on Performance and the Stage*, ed. Michael Booth and Joel Kaplan (Cambridge: Cambridge University Press, 1996), 109.
19. Peter Bailey, "Parasexuality and Glamour: The Victorian Barmaid as Cultural Prototype," *Gender & History* 2, no. 2 (1990): 148–49.
20. Yozef, "Laytudl laytudl day day," SY, NLI. Prager calls the first verses of this song "vulgar and stupid." Leonard Prager, "Der londoner farleger m. yozef," in *Oksforder yidish*, ed. Dovid Katz, vol. 2 (London: Harwood Academic Publishers, 1991), 196.
21. Halakhic law allows a man to sue for divorce if there are no children after ten years of marriage. ChaeRan Freeze, *Jewish Marriage and Divorce in Imperial Russia* (Hanover, NH: University Press of New England [for] Brandeis University Press, 2002), 138–40.
22. *Hello, Hello*, ca. 1898, performed by Bertha Jackson (London: Unpublished recording by Derek Reid, 1978), cassette tape.
23. Whitechapel is in the heart of the East End Yiddish ghetto. Stamford Hill was one location of upward mobility, around four miles north of the East End.
24. David Englander, "Stille Huppah (Quiet Marriage) among Jewish Immigrants in Britain," *Jewish Journal of Sociology* 34, no. 2 (1992): 90–93.
25. Lara Marks, "Race, Class and Gender: The Experiences of Jewish Prostitutes and Other Jewish Women in the East End of London at

the Turn of the Century," in *Women, Migration and Empire*, ed. Joan Grant (Stoke-on-Trent, UK: Trentham, 1996), 44–45.
26. See, for example, *IS*, 2 January 1904.
27. Gartner, *Jewish Immigrant*, 168–71.
28. Joseph Markovitsh, "Brivelekh fun rusland," *LK*, 31. This song should not be confused with Solomon Smulewitz, "A brivele fun rusland," 1912.
29. For many years the American *Forverts* published a "Gallery of Vanished Men," and a national desertion bureau was set up in New York. Sydney Weinberg, *The World of Our Mothers: The Lives of Jewish Immigrant Women* (Chapel Hill: University of North Carolina Press, 1988), 110. See also Reena Sigman Friedman, "'Send Me My Husband Who Is in New York City': Husband Desertion in the American Jewish Immigrant Community 1900–1926," *Jewish Social Studies* 44, no. 1 (1982): 1–18. Also see C. Russell and Harry Samuel Lewis, *The Jew in London: A Study of Racial Character and Present-Day Conditions* (London: T. Fisher Unwin, 1900), 188–91.
30. The Jewish Board of Guardians and the Russo-Jewish Committee would not aid deserted wives if the marriage had been set up as a scam. However, numerous small charities helped. Lloyd Gartner, "Women in the Great Jewish Migration," *Jewish Historical Studies: Transactions of the Jewish Historical Society of England* 40 (2005): 131. The Jewish Board of Guardians' sickness and emergency benefits included deserted wives together with young widows, orphans, deserted children, and women with husbands in jail or an asylum. Vivian Lipman, *A Century of Social Service, 1859–1959: The Jewish Board of Guardians* (London: Routledge & Kegan Paul, 1959), 117–18.
31. For the issue of deserted wives within the English community, see Marjorie Levine-Clark, "From 'Relief' to 'Justice and Protection': The Maintenance of Deserted Wives, British Masculinity and Imperial Citizenship, 1870–1920," *Gender & History* 22, no. 2 (2010): 302–21.
32. Reinterpreting cultural objects happens with resistance. Manuel Peña, *The Texas-Mexican Conjunto: History of a Working-Class Music* (Austin: University of Texas Press, 1985), 13.
33. In standard Yiddish this would say *in der goldener medine*, but the published song uses the quoted version.
34. Mark Slobin, *Tenement Songs: The Popular Music of the Jewish Immigrants* (Urbana: University of Illinois Press, 1996), 157.

35. Anna Tselniker describes the attitude of her father, Meier Tselniker, that the Yiddish theatre should have "*a zing, a lach un a trer* (a song, a laugh and a tear). If they don't hear a song, have a good laugh and cry their eyes out, all at the same time, they don't get their money's worth." Anna Tselniker, *Three for the Price of One* (London: Spiro Institute, 1991), 9.
36. Biale, *Women and Jewish Law*, 93–95.
37. Ross, "Fierce Questions," 233.
38. M. Yozef, "Er meynt yenem nit zikh aleyn," *LK*, 32. The word *shvabe* (German) is pejorative.
39. The literal meaning is "green and yellow."
40. Arn Nager, "Vos geyst nisht aheym sore-gitl?"
41. David Biale argues that *haskole* (enlightenment) literature made unmarried men into antiheroes trapped between passivity and sexual entanglements. Biale, *Eros and the Jews: From Biblical Israel to Contemporary America* (New York: BasicBooks, 1992), 171. The married antihero of the music-hall songs is set up as a comic buffoon but fulfills a psychological role of comfort at seeing someone worse off than yourself.
42. Isaac Reingold, Nager (adapted), "Der bal-toyvnik," *LK*, 8–9. Reingold was a prolific poet and lyricist. Nager's adaptation is close to the original, changing some words and currency to British equivalents.
43. Carl Meyer and Clementina Black consider the very worst wages for East End women in 1909 were one penny an hour, which would make around six shillings a week. Meyer and Black, *Makers of Our Clothes: A Case for Trade Boards, Being the Results of a Year's Investigation into the Work of Women in London in the Tailoring, Dressmaking, and Underclothing Trades* (London: Duckworth, 1909), 71. See also Susan L. Tananbaum, *Jewish Immigrants in London, 1880–1939* (London: Pickering and Chatto, 2014), 151–53.
44. William Stead, "The Maiden Tribute of Modern Babylon: The Report of Our Secret Commission," *Pall Mall Gazette*, 4–13 July 1885. Sensational writing also appeared in the Yiddish press. The *Teglikher ekspres* (The daily express) front covers reproduced English drawings of murders including a sexual element: "Cartwright was a beautiful factory girl. She died defending her chastity" (12 August 1897). Articles included "Married His Sister and Committed Suicide" (2 August 1897). In the *Idisher vokhentlikher zhurnal*, a melodramatic story in 1906 described an East End gang member tyrannizing street women

who were too scared to testify in court (9 January 1907). For the use of melodrama in the *Maiden Tribute*, see Judith R. Walkowitz, *City of Dreadful Delight: Narratives of Sexual Danger in Late-Victorian London* (Chicago: University of Chicago Press, 1992), 81–94.

45. Yiddish plays include Avrom Goldfaden's *Di kishufmakherin* (1879) and *Meshiekhs tsaytn* (1891), Perets Hirschbein's *Miriam*, and Scholem Asch's famous *Got fun nekome* (1907). Ben Furnish comments how these plays affected larger discourses outside the theatre; Furnish, "'It's Both Hot and Incredibly Innocent': A Century of Sex on the American Jewish Stage," in *Jews and Sex*, ed. Nathan Abrams (Nottingham: Five Leaves, 2008), 149–51.

46. Scholarship includes Edward Bristow, *Prostitution and Prejudice: The Jewish Fight against White Slavery, 1870–1939* (Oxford: Clarendon, 1982); Marks, "Race, Class and Gender"; Paul Knepper, "British Jews and the Racialisation of Crime in the Age of Empire," *British Journal of Criminology* 47, no. 1 (January 2007): 61–79; Lloyd Gartner, "Anglo-Jewry and the Jewish International Traffic in Prostitution, 1885–1914," *AJS Review* 7 (1982): 129–78; Tananbaum, *Immigrants in London*.

47. Englander, "Stille Huppah," 91. See also the fictional prank where a *shtile khupe* led to unfortunate repercussions. Israel Zangwill and Meri-Jane Rochelson, *Children of the Ghetto: A Study of a Peculiar People* (Detroit: Wayne State University Press, 1998), 117–20.

48. Bristow, *Prostitution, Prejudice*, 85–108. Bristow gives an international view of Jewish involvement in the white slave trade. For Anglo-Jews' attempts to fight against the trade, see ibid., 236–45.

49. See the classified notices in *IE*, for example, 5 January 1900; 8 April 1902; 21 February 1904.

50. The JAPGW was originally called the Jewish Ladies Society for Preventive and Rescue Work but changed its name in 1897 when men got involved with the organization. Lipman, *Social Service*, 247–48. In 1890 notices were published in Jewish newspapers in Eastern Europe "warning young girls from leaving their homes by the advice of strangers or under the care of strangers." Gartner, "International Traffic," 143.

51. See Knepper, "Racialisation of Crime," 61–79; Lara Marks, "The Luckless Waifs and Strays of Humanity: Irish and Jewish Immigrant Unwed Mothers in London, 1870–1939," *Twentieth Century British History* 3, no. 2 (1992): 124–26. Charcroft House later moved to Shepherd's Bush. See also Marks, "Race, Class and Gender," 31–50; Eugene C.

Black, *The Social Politics of Anglo-Jewry: 1880–1920* (Oxford: Basil Blackwell, 1988), 232–35; Tananbaum, *Immigrants in London*, 138–41.
52. Performances in English on this theme packed London music halls. Bristow, *Prostitution, Prejudice*, 41.
53. Arn Nager, "Viktorye park."
54. Derek Reid, "Six Yiddish Street Songs of East London," in *Proceedings of the First International Conference on Jewish Music 1994*, ed. Steve Stanton (London: City University, 1997), 106.
55. Arn Nager, "Sore gitl?"
56. Jerry White, *London in the Twentieth Century: "A Human Awful Wonder of God"* (London: Jonathan Cape, 2007), 312–13.
57. Lucy Bland, *Banishing the Beast: English Feminism and Sexual Morality, 1885–1914* (London: Penguin, 1995), 119.
58. Pamela Cox and Annabel Hobley, *Shopgirls: The True Story of Life behind the Counter* (London: Random House, 2014), 54–60.
59. "An Awkward Encounter in Regent Street," *The Day's Doings*, 24 June 1871, Mary Evans Picture Library, reproduced in Jeremy Paxman, *The Victorians: Britain through the Paintings of the Age* (London: BBC Books, 2010), 126.
60. Sima Beeri suggests that *publik hoyz* can also refer to a brothel in the Lithuanian Yiddish dialect.
61. Martin Stokes, *Ethnicity, Identity, and Music: The Musical Construction of Place* (Oxford: Berg, 1994), 16.
62. "Orem vey iz der mamen," S. *Orem vey* is hard to translate, as it is a wordplay. *Oy vey* means "Oh dear," but the word *oy* is substituted by *orem*, which means poor.
63. Rubin Dokter was in London writing songs and performing vaudeville until 1910. See David Mazower, "London–New York, or the Great British Yiddish Theatre Brain Drain," https://yiddishstage.org/london-new-york-or-the-great-british-yiddish-theatre-brain-drain, accessed 24 November 2016.
64. The German Jewish feminist movement, the Judischer Frauenbund, was set up in 1904 by feminist activist writer Bertha Pappenheim. The feminists saw women as enslaved by pimps or poverty and viewed all prostitutes as white slaves even if no traffickers were implicated. Marion Kaplan, "Prostitution, Morality Crusades and Feminism: German-Jewish Feminists and the Campaign against White Slavery," in *Women's Studies International Forum*, vol. 5 (Amsterdam: Elsevier, 1982), 622.

65. Arn Nager, "Rum to let," *LK*, 103.
66. Joseph Markovitsh, "50 yor," *IS*, 4 December 1953.
67. Peter Bailey, "Conspiracies of Meaning: Music-Hall and the Knowingness of Popular Culture," *Past and Present* 144 (1994): 161.

8. Religion as a Socialist Tool

1. Morris Winchevsky, no title, in the *Meshugener filozof* column, *AF*, 28 November 1890.
2. For an overview of the differences in religious practice, see Bernard Homa, *Orthodoxy in Anglo-Jewry, 1880–1940* (London: Jewish Historical Society of England, 1969), 8–24. Scholarship has concentrated on conflict arising from the cultural clash between the two sections of the community and the ensuing battles around *shechita*, *kashres*, marriage, and burial.
3. Aubrey Newman, *The United Synagogue, 1870–1970* (London: Routledge & K. Paul, 1976), 1–14; Geoffrey Alderman, *The Federation of Synagogues, 1887–1987* (London: Federation of Synagogues, 1987), 9–10; Michael Clark, *Albion and Jerusalem: The Anglo-Jewish Community in the Post-Emancipation Era, 1858–1887* (Oxford: Oxford University Press, 2009), 173–79.
4. Potter describes *khevres* as "self-creating, self-supporting and self-governing communities; small enough to generate public opinion and the practical supervision of private morals, and large enough to stimulate charity, worship and study by communion and example." Charles Booth, *Life and Labour of the People of London*, vol. 3, 1st ed. (London, 1902), 172.
5. Geoffrey Alderman, *Modern British Jewry* (New York: Clarendon, 1992), 142–45, 158.
6. The Federation gave greater status and representation to the immigrant religious within an Anglo-Jewish context. It created a position from which to bargain on issues around burial and *shechita*. For the early days of the Federation, see Alderman, *Federation of Synagogues*, 1–41; Alderman, *Modern British Jewry*, 156–65; Todd Endelman, *Jews of Britain, 1656–2000* (Berkeley: University of California Press, 2002), 175–80.
7. This United Synagogue scheme planned to build an all-encompassing East End center for the immigrants with a 1,200-seat synagogue, meeting hall, study center, Jewish court, provident society, and savings bank. It came to nothing amid opposition from some Anglo-Jews as

well as being at odds with immigrants' desires. Endelman, *Jews of Britain*, 178.
8. Karl Marx and David McLellan, *Early Texts* (California: Barnes & Noble, 1971), 80–90.
9. Thomas B. Eyges, *Beyond the Horizon: The Story of a Radical Emigrant* (Boston, MA: Group Free Society, 1944), 76–78.
10. Ibid., 75.
11. *JC*, 23 September 1904; David Feldman, *Englishmen and Jews: Social Relations and Political Culture, 1840–1914* (New Haven, CT: Yale University Press, 1994), 335.
12. Nora Levin, *Jewish Socialist Movements: 1871–1917* (Oxford: Oxford University Press, 1978), 133.
13. Samuel Montagu saw the *AF* as the gravest threat to Judaism because it constantly verbally assaulted religion and its institutions. William Fishman, *East End Jewish Radicals, 1875–1914* (London: Duckworth, 1975), 155–57. Rocker describes attempts at sabotaging the *AF* by Anglo-Jewish leaders. On one occasion, the back cover text, "Workers do your duty, spread the *Arbayter fraynd!*" was changed to "destroy." On another occasion a printer was paid off and escaped to America. Another printer was bribed, stopping the *AF* without warning from May 1887 for three months. Rudolph Rocker and Colin Ward, *The London Years* (Nottingham: Five Leaves, 2005), 61.
14. *AF*, 31 August 1888; 14 September 1888. These are familiar words from key parts of the liturgy on Rosh Hashanah and Yom Kippur. The translation of *unetane tokef* is from Jonathan Sacks, *Koren Sacks Yom Kippur Mahzor* (Jerusalem: Koren Publishers, 2012), 843.
15. Abraham Bik, *Moris vintshevski, troymer un kemfer* (Los Angeles: Arbeter Ring, 1956), 10.
16. Rabbi Hillel, *Pirkei Avos* 1:14. Hillel (110 B.C.–A.D. 10) was one of the most influential rabbis in Jewish history in the development of the Talmud.
17. The Yiddish word *rabiner* was used to refer to the German rabbinate and so, by extension, the Anglo-Jewish rabbinate. Rabbis from the immigrant orthodox community were generally called *rebbe* or *rov*.
18. Morris Winchevsky, "Rabiner un mashiner: A kontrast," *AF*, 17 August 1888.
19. Alderman, *Federation of Synagogues*, 14–15.
20. The report related the decline of the skilled English craftsman to subcontracting by Jewish middlemen, leading to thousands of destitute

Jewish immigrants working in sweating conditions. Sheila Blackburn, *A Fair Day's Wage for a Fair Day's Work?: Sweated Labour and the Origins of Minimum Wage Legislation in Britain* (Aldershot: Ashgate, 2007), 44. This analysis was contested by sociologists Beatrice Potter and David Schloss, who were concerned to contradict the link between the middleman subcontractor and sweating conditions. Feldman, *Englishmen*, 187.

21. *AF*, 2–9 March 1888. Quoted in Feldman, *Englishmen*, 133.
22. Harold Pollins, *Economic History of the Jews in England* (Rutherford, NJ: Fairleigh Dickinson University Press, 1982), 157; Nancy Green and P. Altman, *Jewish Workers in the Modern Diaspora* (Berkeley: University of California Press, 1998), 137–39.
23. *JC*, 22 February 1889, 6–7.
24. David Cesarani, *The Jewish Chronicle and Anglo-Jewry, 1841–1991* (Cambridge: Cambridge University Press, 1994), 76.
25. Morris Winchevsky, "A khoydesh on arbayt."
26. Oberman went to considerable lengths to gain respect in his khevre by *shnodering* (donating) a higher sum for his *aliye* than would be expected for the honor. Zelig Oberman, *In mayne teg* (London: Narod, 1947), 116–7.
27. This system of honors was also in place in Anglo-Jewish synagogues.
28. Reuel, yeser, yisro, khovav, khever, keini, and putiel, *Kinnous oder arbayter klogelider* (London: Worker's Friend Printing Office, 1888). The nonstandard spelling of *Kinnous* is the published transliteration.
29. Parodies of prayers and religious observance were a common strategy for the antireligious movement that started in London in 1885. Stephen Sharot, *Judaism: A Sociology* (London: David & Charles Newton Abbot, 1976), 105. Parodies were particularly made of Passover haggadahs. See "Tsvishn shpil un parodye—fun 1865 biz 1918," accessed 1 July 2015, http://zeltenebikher.blogspot.co.uk/2015/04/1865-1818.html. On the Soviet "Red Haggadah," see Anna Shternshis, *Soviet and Kosher: Jewish Popular Culture in the Soviet Union, 1923–1939* (Bloomington: Indiana University Press, 2006). Later poets, such as Perets Markish, also created a "fusion of blasphemy and sacral form," "overcoding" his poetry with imagery taken from liturgy, the Bible, and Jewish history. Seth Wolitz, "A Yiddish Modernist Dirge: Di Kupe of Perets Markish," *Modern Jewish Studies Annual* 6 (1987): 64.
30. Leviticus 19:18.
31. Namerts (Simon Friman), "310," *AF*, 15 May 1889.

32. Izak Likhtnshvayg, "Alt un yung," *AF*, 25 September 1896.
33. Bonfeld, "Reb yudl far got," *AF*, 24 July 1896.

9. Religion Updated and Improved

1. Avreml, "Al-hanisim," *Tsayt*, 26 December 2013.
2. Stephen Sharot, *Judaism: A Sociology* (London: David & Charles Newton Abbot, 1976), 103–4. See Zelig Oberman's arduous quest for a place to pray in London suiting his Hasidic background. Oberman, *In mayne teg* (London: Narod, 1947), 91, 98–100, 107.
3. David Englander, "Anglicized Not Anglican: Jews and Judaism in Victorian Britain," *Religion in Victorian Britain* 1 (1988): 270.
4. C. Russell and Harry Samuel Lewis, *The Jew in London: A Study of Racial Character and Present-Day Conditions* (London: T. Fisher Unwin, 1900), 119–20; Lloyd Gartner, *The Jewish Immigrant in England, 1870–1914* (London: Simon Publications, 1973), 192–93; Todd Endelman, *The Jews of Britain, 1656–2000* (Berkeley: University of California Press, 2002), 146–47.
5. Harry Samuel Lewis, "East End Judaism—Need and Possibilities of Reform," *JC*, 20 February 1903. Lewis was a social worker dealing with family and youth issues in the East End. He coauthored *The Jew in London* with Russell and Lewis. He was particularly interested in loss of faith.
6. Joseph Markovitsh, "Aheym tsurik," unpublished manuscript, n.d. The title implies going or moving back home.
7. Lewis, "East End Judaism."
8. Joseph Markovitsh, "Di tsvey doyres," *LLM*, 11.
9. Arn Nager, "Freg keyn katshanes!," *LLM*, 9–10.
10. Solon Beinfeld and Harry Bochner, *Comprehensive Yiddish-English Dictionary* (Bloomington: Indiana University Press, 2013), 592. The spelling in the dictionary would be *katshenes*. The long *a* used in the song as *katshanes* makes it rhyme with *tanes*.
11. It is hard to translate diminutives in Yiddish. Diminutives do not necessarily mean "little." In this instance, it may mean strange or different. It could be affectionate or mocking.
12. Endelman, *Jews of Britain*, 146. See also David Englander, "Booth's Jews: The Presentation of Jews and Judaism in 'Life and Labour of the London Poor,'" *Victorian Studies* 32, no. 4 (1989): 34; Geoffrey Alderman, *Modern British Jewry* (New York: Clarendon, 1992), 144.
13. "Di velt iz meshuge," *SY*. Notice that nonstandard *git* rhymes with *yid*.

14. This probably refers to the Zeppelin airship, developed by the German Count Ferdinand von Zeppelin in the early twentieth century.
15. Joseph Markovitsh, "Ikh bin a yidl fun der lite," *LK*, 106.
16. Two poems were published in periodicals; the one-off *Purim zhurnal* of 1910 and the popular weekly magazine the *Fonograf.*
17. Avreml, "Di simkhes-toyre trinker," *IE*, 2 October 1912.
18. Laws forbidding Jews to take interest on loans to other Jews are from Exodus 22:24 and Deuteronomy 23:20121. This issue is explored in Louis Jacobs, *The Jewish Religion: A Companion* (Oxford: Oxford University Press, 1995).
19. See Alderman, *Modern British Jewry*, 93–94.
20. See Museum of Family History, "Lives in the Yiddish Theatre," accessed 26 June 2015, http://www.museumoffamilyhistory.com/yt/lex/B/bleichman-jacob.htm.
21. Avreml, "A pekl nevies," *Bloffer*, no. 3 (November 1911): 5–6.
22. Ezekiel 38:18–39:9.
23. Zalkind was a British orthodox rabbi and a friend of Rudolf Rocker. He tried to reconcile religion with anarchism and Zionism. Yankev-Meyer Zalkind, Online Yiddish Lezicon, accessed 2 January 2017, http://yleksikon.blogspot.co.uk/2016/07/yankev-meyer-zalkind-j-m-salkind.html.
24. In the poem, they are referred to by their surnames only.
25. Avreml, "Al-khet motivn," *Tsayt*, 10 October 1913.
26. The humor has an edge because it was a source of controversy that Anglo-Jewish ministers were badly paid. Alderman, *Modern British Jewry*, 93–94.
27. Avreml, "Mayn malke," *Bloffer*, no. 13 (April 1912).
28. The seder liturgy asks people to see themselves as if they had personally come out of Egypt.
29. It should be noted that in November 1912 the Jewish League for Woman Suffrage was established. See Linda Gordon Kuzmack, *Woman's Cause: The Jewish Woman's Movement in England and the United States, 1881–1933* (Columbus: Ohio State University Press, 1990), 134–42.
30. "Haneyres halolu," *IE*, 15 December 1909.
31. Avreml, "Moyshe un yakhne," *Tsayt*, 14 November 1913.
32. See Beinfeld and Bochner, *Yiddish Dictionary*, 421, 336.
33. Y. Finkelstein, "Hibru komedyes," 2.
34. "Vos toygn di lider," *IE*, 28 September 1909.

35. At its height the JFS had 5,700 pupils and the Old Castle Street School had 1,500 Jewish pupils. Suzanne Kirsch Greenberg, "Anglicization and the Education of Jewish Immigrant Children in the East End of London," in *Jewish History: Essays in Honour of Chimen Abramsky*, ed. Ada Rapoport-Albert and Steven J. Zipperstein (London: Peter Halban, 1988), 115–16, 149; Gerry Black, *JFS: The History of the Jews' Free School, London since 1732* (London: Tymsder, 1998), 118; Benjamin J. Lammers, "The Citizens of the Future: Educating the Children of the Jewish East End, ca. 1885–1939," *Twentieth Century British History* 19, no. 4 (2008): 398.
36. Gartner, *Jewish Immigrant*, 222–34.
37. *JC*, 24 February 1905. Quoted in Nancy Green and P. Altman, *Jewish Workers in the Modern Diaspora* (Berkeley: University of California Press, 1998), 196.
38. Gartner, *Jewish Immigrant*, 233–34. Later talmetoyres included Commercial Road in 1898, Bethnal Green, and Dalston. Salmond Levin, "The Changing Pattern of Jewish Education," in *A Century of Anglo-Jewish Life*, ed. Salmond Levin (London: United Synagogue, 1971), 65; Black, *JFS*, 126; Susan L. Tananbaum, *Jewish Immigrants in London, 1880–1939* (London: Pickering and Chatto, 2014), 92–96.
39. Untitled (Dem melamed geshrey), *IE*, 17 October 1906.
40. On the push to modernize talmetoyres, see Tananbaum, *Immigrants in London*, 98–99.
41. B. Verbi, "Teater krizis," *IE*, 19 June 1912, 2.
42. *Bloffer*, no. 23 (January 1912).
43. "Hepi nyu yir," *IE*, 31 December 1913.
44. *Ma yafit* (How beautiful) is the title and first words of a Friday night song that Polish Jews used to sing to a melody that was popular with Eastern European nobles. A *ma yafit yid* is someone who abases himself to non-Jews with flattery and groveling. Yitzkhok Niborski, *Verterbukh fun loshn-koydesh shtamike verter in yidish* (Paris: Bibliotech Medem, 1999), 151.
45. Israel Finestein, *Anglo-Jewry in Changing Times: Studies in Diversity, 1840–1914* (London: Vallentine Mitchell, 1999), 24–26.
46. M. R. "Di reformer," *Fonograf*, 17 January 1908.
47. "Mist," *Bloffer*, no. 9 (January 1912).
48. Avreml, "Al-hanisim," *Tsayt*, 26 December 1913. Al-Hanisim refers to a Hebrew prayer added on certain festivals.

49. For Montefiore's ideas on Judaism and Christianity, see Daniel Langton, *Claude Montefiore: His Life and Thought* (London: Vallentine Mitchell, 2002).
50. Moris Gros, "Ikh un krist," *Bloffer*, no. 18 (June 1912).

Conclusion

1. Avrom Vevyorke, *Di idishe prese un dos idishe teater in london* (London: M. Susman, n.d.).

Bibliography

Primary Sources

ARCHIVES
Bibliotheque Medem, Paris
British Library, London
Klau Library, Hebrew Union College, Cincinnati
Mazower Private Collection, London
National Library of Israel, Jerusalem
New York Public Library, Dorot Jewish Division
YIVO library and archive, New York
    Kalman Marmor collection
    Leon Kussman collection
    Territorial collection: England

NEWSPAPERS, MAGAZINES, AND JOURNALS
All titles were published in London, unless otherwise stated.
Der arbayter fraynd
Der bloffer
East London Observer
Der Fonograf
Forverts (New York)
Di fraye velt
Der fraynd (Russia)
Der idisher ekspres
Der idisher vokhentlikher zhurnal
Di idishe shtime
The Jewish Chronicle
Jewish Life
Jewish World
Morgen freiheit (New York)
Der morgen zhurnal (New York)

BIBLIOGRAPHY

Der poylisher yidl
The Standard
Der teglikher ekspres
Der tog
Di tsayt
Di tsukunft
Tsukunft (New York)
Der veker
Der veker (New York)
Yidishe kultur (New York)

SONG AND POETRY COLLECTIONS

Arbayter lider. London: Lidz internatsionale arbayter bildungs klub, n.d.
Beregovski, Moshe, and Itzik Fefer. *Yidishe folks-lider.* Kiev: Melukhe-farlag, 1938.
Di fraye harfe. Warsaw: Ferlags drukeray, 1907.
Freiheit: Revolutsionare lider un shirim. Geneva: Bund, 1905.
Di idishe bine. Brooklyn: Hebrew Publishing Company, 1897.
Der londoner arbayter zinger. London: Arbayter fraynd drukeray, 1894.
Der londoner kupletist. London: London aktyoren gezelshaft, ca. 1903.
Der londoner lider magazin. London: n.d., ca. 1900.
Mlotek, Eleanor Gordon. *Mir trogn a gezang: The New Book of Yiddish Songs.* New York: Workmen's Circle, 1982 (1977).
Mlotek, Eleanor Gordon, and Joseph Mlotek. *Songs of Generations: New Pearls of Yiddish Song.* New York: Workmen's Circle, 2004.
Reuel, yeser, khovav yisro, keini khever, un putiel. *Kinnous oder arbayter klogelider.* London: Worker's Friend Printing Office, 1888. British Library.
Rund, Morris. *American Yiddish Penny Songs: The Hebrew Union College Collection of Yiddish Broadsides, 1895–1922.* Edited by Jane Peppler. 2015. http://www.yiddishpennysongs.com.
Vinkovetzky, Aharon, Abba Kovner, and Sinai Leichter. *Anthology of Yiddish Folksongs.* Vol. 3. Jerusalem: Magnes Press, Hebrew University, 1985.
———. *Anthology of Yiddish Folksongs.* Vol. 4. Jerusalem: Magnes Press, Hebrew University, 1985.
Winchevsky, Morris. *Gezamelte verk: lider.* Vol. 2. New York: Astoria, 1927.
———. *Lider un gedikhte.* New York: Maisel, 1910.
Yidishe teater lider. New York: Hebrew Publishing Company, 1901.

AUDIO RECORDINGS

Ale Brider. Performed by the Klezmatics. From *Shvaygn=Toyt.* Round Rock: Piranha Records, 1989, compact disc.

BIBLIOGRAPHY

Alle Brider. Performed by Rhoda Cohn and Mary Feldman. From *Children Sing! Kinder Zingen.* New York: Metro, 1947, 33⅓ rpm vinyl.

Dray Shvester. Performed by Klezmer Klub. From *Whitechapel, mayn Vaytshepl.* London: Klub Records, 2009, compact disc.

Dray shvester. Performed by Metropolitan Klezmer. From *Surprising Finds.* New York: Rhythm Media Records, 2003, compact disc.

Dray shvester. Performed by Zelig Shnadover. N.d. Mexico City: Unpublished recording by Itzik Gottesman, n.d., mp3.

Drei Schwester. Performed by Simon Osovitsky. Tel Aviv: Galton, n.d., 33⅓ rpm vinyl.

Die Drei Schwestern. Performed by Morris Goldstein. New York: Victor, 1928, 78 rpm vinyl.

Die Drei Schwesters. Performed by Morris Goldstein. New York: Brunswick, 1928, 78 rpm vinyl.

Dri Shvester. Performed by Pincus Lawenda. New York: Banner, ca. 1945, 33⅓ rpm vinyl.

Gevald, gevald police. Performed by Fräulein Rubinstein. 1905. From *Di Eybike Mame: Women in Yiddish Theater and Popular Song.* Mainz: Wergo, 2003, compact disc.

Hashiveinu nazad. Performed by David Roitman. St. Petersburg: Musique Internationale, 1970?, 33⅓ rpm vinyl.

Hashivenu nazad. Performed by Klezmer Klub. From *Whitechapel, mayn Vaytshepl.* London: Klub Records, 2009, compact disc.

Hello, Hello. Performed by Bertha Jackson. London: Unpublished recording by Derek Reid, 1978, cassette tape.

Ich such a Job. Performed by Yozef Sherman and the Pavilion Orchestra. London: Imperial, n.d., 78 rpm vinyl.

Lizzie Clough. Performed by Bertha Jackson. London: Unpublished recording by Derek Reid, 1978, cassette tape.

Der nayem hashiveynu nazad. Performed by Esther Djzaldovsky, ca. 1950. Toronto: Unpublished recording by Chaim Neslen, n.d., cassette tape.

Di Tsukunft. Performed by Adrienne Cooper. From *In Love and Struggle.* New York: YIVO, 1999, compact disc.

Victoria Park. Performed by Bertha Jackson. London: Unpublished recording by Derek Reid, 1978, cassette tape.

Victoria Park. Performed by Klezmer Klub. From *Whitechapel, mayn Vaytshepl.* London: Klub Records, 2009, compact disc.

BIBLIOGRAPHY

SHEET MUSIC

Godwin, W., and H. Wright. "Wishing the Boys Farewell." London: Francis, Day & Hunter, 1900.

Goldfaden, Avrom. *Hashivenu Nasad: Kehr Uns Zurik*, arranged by Kammen. New York: Hebrew Publishing Company, 1921.

Pink, Wal, and George Le Brunn. *Half Past Nine*. New York: T. B. Harms & Co., 1893.

Winchevsky, Morris. *Dray shvester: Three Sisters*, arranged by Henry Lefkowitch. New York: Metro Music, 1932.

WEBSITES

Museum of Family History. "Lives in the Yiddish Theatre: Jacob Bleichman." Accessed 28 September 2017. http://www.museumoffamilyhistory.com/yt/lex/B/bleichman-jacob.htm.

———. "Lives in the Yiddish Theatre: Dr. A. Margolin." Accessed 28 September 2017. http://www.museumoffamilyhistory.com/yt/lex/M/margolin-a-dr.htm.

Online Etymology Dictionary. "kike." Accessed 20 October 2016. http://www.etymonline.com/index.php?allowed_in_frame=0&search=kike.

Online Yiddish Lezicon. "Yankev-Meyer Zalkind." Accessed 2 January 2017. http://yleksikon.blogspot.co.uk/2016/07/yankev-meyer-zalkind-j-m-salkind.html.

University of Minnesota. "Center for Holocaust and Genocide Studies." Accessed 26 June 2015. http://www.chgs.umn.edu/histories/otherness/otherness1-3.html.

"Yiddish Penny Songs." Accessed 19 September 2017. http://www.yiddishpennysongs.com.

Zeltenbikher. "Tsvishn shpil un parodye—fun 1865 biz 1918." Accessed 1 July 2015. http://zeltenebikher.blogspot.co.uk.

MEMOIRS

Adler, Jacob, and Lulla Rosenfeld. *A Life on the Stage: A Memoir*. New York: Knopf, 1999.

Eyges, Thomas B. *Beyond the Horizon: The Story of a Radical Emigrant*. Boston, MA: Group Free Society, 1944.

Kobrin, Leon. "Der zeyde moris vintshevski, mayn ershte bagegenish mit im." *MF*, 3 June 1946.

Markovitsh, Joseph. "Fun mayne 50 yor in england." *Di idishe shtime*, 21 installments, 13 November 1953–9 April 1954.

Mendelovitch, Bernard. "Memories of London Yiddish Theatre." Oxford: Oxford Centre for Postgraduate Hebrew Studies, 1990.

BIBLIOGRAPHY

Oberman, Zelig. *In mayne teg.* London: Narod, 1947.
Rocker, Rudolph, and Colin Ward. *The London Years.* Nottingham: Five Leaves, 2005.
Rosenfeld, Lulla. *Bright Star of Exile: Jacob Adler and the Yiddish Theatre.* New York: Crowell, 1977.
Winchevsky, Morris. *Erinerungen.* New York: Freiheit, 1927.
Yanovski, Shaul. *Ershte yorn fun yidishn frayhaytlekhn sotsyalism.* New York: Fraye arbeter shtime, 1948.
Young, Boaz. *Mayn lebn in teater.* New York: Yidisher kultur farband, 1950.

OTHER PRIMARY TEXTS

Aleichem, Sholem. "London, farvos brenstu nisht." In *Motl peysi dem khasns,* 174–82. New York: Farlag Matones, 1970.
Ausubel, Nathan. "The Story of Yiddish." *MF,* 11 August 1947.
Ben-Yakir. "A lang ervartetes bukh." *Tsukunft* (February 1911): 91–98.
Berlin, Nosn. *Di emese velt; oder eyn rayze in gehenem* (London: 1886).
Bialostotski, B. Y. "In di gasn - tsu di masn." *Der veker,* 24 December 1922: 14–16.
Booth, Charles. *Life and Labour of the People of London.* Vol. 3. 1st ed. London, 1902.
Brenner, Joseph Chaim. *Out of the Depths.* Translated by David Patterson. San Francisco: Westview, 1992.
Entin, Yoel. "Veg keyn amerike hot gefirt durkh london." *Morgen dzhurnal,* 14 November 1943.
Epshteyn, Shakhne. "Moris vintshevski (tsu zayn 60stn geburtstog)." *Tsukunft* (December 1916): 1043–46.
Eyner Vos iz Dort Geveyn. "Der idisher teater." *Idisher ekspres,* 25 December 1901.
Eyner Vos iz Dort Geveyn. "Der idisher teater." *Idisher ekspres,* 7 May 1902.
Finkelshteyn, Y. "Hibru komedyes: 'artistn' vos makhn a lebn fun bashmutsikn dos idishe folk." *Tsayt,* 22 January 1914.
"From the East End." *Jewish Chronicle,* 6 August 1909.
Goldberg, Itshe. "A bezem un a ker." *Yidishe kultur* (March 1967): 21–28.
Hodess, Jacob. "'Yiddish Literature': The Writings of Morris Winchevsky." *Jewish Chronicle—Books and Bookmen Supplement,* 30 January 1914, 8.
Izraeli, L. [Leon Kussman]. "Di pavilyen: ir repertuar un personel." *Idisher ekspres,* 28 February 1912.
———. "Repertuar fun idishn teater." *Idisher ekspres,* 21 February 1912.
Katz, Moyshe. "Der zeyde Moris vintshevski." *Morgen freiheit,* 12 August 1956, 10.
Katznellenbogen, Jacob Shalom. *A vinter nakht: in der ist-end fun london.* Translated by A. B. Higer. London: Mazin, 1908.

BIBLIOGRAPHY

Kayzer, Arye-Meyer. *Bay undz in vaytshepl: mayses un mayselekh*. London: Naroditski, 1944.

Kramer, Aaron. "Four Yiddish Proletarian Poets: 1. Morris Winchevsky." *Jewish Life*, May 1950, 23–25.

Kushnirov, Aaron. "Der zeyde fun der yidishe poezye." *Morgen freiheit*, 16 March 1947, 6.

Kussman, Leon. "Faynman—yidish folks teater (batrakhtungen vegn 'templ')." *Idisher ekspres*, 19 and 21 June 1912; 26 June 1912.

Landstone, Charles. "Edwardian Vignettes: A Visit to the Pavilion Theatre." *Jewish Chronicle*, 27 November 1970.

Levy, Amy, and S. Bernstein. *Reuben Sachs*. Ontario: Broadview, 2006.

Litvak, A. [Khayim Yankl Helfand]. "Di rol fun der revolutsyoner lid in der arbeter-bavegung." In *Idishe literatur*, edited by M. Levitan. Vol. 1, 321–24. Kiev: Kultur-lige, 1928.

———. "Moris vintshevski, der onheyber." *Der veker*, 2 April 1932, 4–11.

Litvin, A. "Di revolutsyonere lid un di folks-lid—di ershte revolutsyonere lid—a mitl fun agitatsye." In *Idishe literatur*, edited by M. Levitan. Vol. 1, 317–20. Kiev: Kultur-lige, 1928.

Malakhi, A. R. "Moris vintshevski (tsu zayn zibetsik yorikn yubileum)." *Tsukunft*, September 1926, 501–4.

———. "Moris vintshevski (tsu zayn 75-yorikn yubileum)." *Tsukunft*, November 1930, 758–60.

"Max Rosenthal: The Forbes-Robertson of the Yiddish Stage." *Jewish World*, 30 November 1900.

Metzker, Isaac. *A Bintel Brief: Sixty Years of Letters from the Lower East Side to the Jewish Daily Forward*. New York: Schocken Books, 1971.

Meyer, Carl, and Clementina Black. *Makers of Our Clothes: A Case for Trade Boards, Being the Results of a Year's Investigation into the Work of Women in London in the Tailoring, Dressmaking, and Underclothing Trades*. London: Duckworth, 1909.

"A Music-Hall in the East End." *The Standard*, 28 October 1902.

Niger, Shmuel. "Moris vintshevski: tsu zayn 70 yorikn geburtstog." *Der tog*, 5 September 1926.

Novik, Peysakh. "Moris vintshevski: di lebedike traditsye." *Yidishe kultur*, January 1957, 28–34.

"Rigoletto in Yiddish: A Notable Triumph." *Jewish Chronicle*, 19 April 1912.

Spektor, Mordkhe. *Moment fotografyes* (Warsaw: A. Gitin, n.d.).

Stead, William. "The Maiden Tribute of Modern Babylon: The Report of Our Secret Commission." *Pall Mall Gazette*, 4–13 July 1885.

T., Kh. "Di idishe bine in london." *Idisher ekspres*, 9 July 1913.

BIBLIOGRAPHY

Verbi, B. "Teater krizis." *Idisher ekspres*, 19 June 1912.
"A Visit to the Yiddish Music Hall." *Jewish Chronicle*, 8 February 1907.
Winchevsky, Morris. "A kleyner volkn oyfn himl." *Poylisher yidl*, 3 October 1884.
———. "Idisher teater in london." *Poylisher yidl*, 15 August 1884.
———. "Mayn arbeter-muze." *Yidishe kultur*, May 1952, 42–45.
———. *Der meshugener filozof in england*. New York: Forward Association, 1920.
———. *Stories of the Struggle*. Chicago: Charles H. Kerr, 1908.
———. "Vilyem moris: an erinerung." *Forverts*, 3 October 1897.
"A Yiddish Music-Hall in the East End." *Jewish Chronicle*, 31 October 1902.
"A Yiddish Theatre for London." *Jewish Chronicle*, 4 April 1902.
Zangwill, Israel. "Anglicization." In *Nineteenth-Century Jewish Literature: A Reader*, edited by Jonathan Hess, Maurice Samuels, and Nadia Vaiman, 356–86. Stanford, CA: Stanford University Press, 2013.
Zangwill, Israel, and Meri-Jane Rochelson. *Children of the Ghetto: A Study of a Peculiar People*. Detroit: Wayne State University Press, 1998.

Secondary Sources

Alderman, Geoffrey. *The Federation of Synagogues, 1887–1987*. London: Federation of Synagogues, 1987.
———. *Modern British Jewry*. New York: Clarendon, 1992.
Anderson, Ben. "Affective Atmospheres." *Emotion, Space and Society* 2, no. 2 (2009): 77–81.
Attridge, Steve. *Nationalism, Imperialism, and Identity in Late Victorian Culture: Civil and Military Worlds*. Basingstoke: Palgrave Macmillan, 2003.
Bailey, Peter. "Ally Sloper's Half-Holiday: Comic Art in the 1880s." *History Workshop Journal* 16: 4–32. N.p.: Oxford University Press, 1983.
———. "Conspiracies of Meaning: Music-Hall and the Knowingness of Popular Culture." *Past and Present* 144 (1994): 138–70.
———. "Custom, Capital and Culture in the Victorian Music Hall." In *Popular Culture and Custom in Nineteenth-Century England*, edited by Robert D. Storch, 180–208. London: Croom Helm, 1982.
———. *Leisure and Class in Victorian England: Rational Recreation and the Contest for Control, 1830–1885*. London: Routledge & Kegan Paul, 1978.
———. "Parasexuality and Glamour: The Victorian Barmaid as Cultural Prototype." *Gender & History* 2, no. 2 (1990): 148–72.
Bar-Yosef, Eitan, and Nadia Valman. "Between the East End and East Africa: Rethinking Images of 'the Jew' in Late Victorian and Edwardian Culture." In *"The Jew" in Late-Victorian and Edwardian Culture: Between the East End*

and East Africa, edited by Eitan Bar-Yosef and Nadia Valman, 1–27. Basingstoke: Palgrave Macmillan, 2009.

Beinfeld, Solon, and Harry Bochner. *Comprehensive Yiddish-English Dictionary*. Bloomington: Indiana University Press, 2013.

Belkin, Ahuva. "The 'Low' Culture of the Purimshpil." In *Yiddish Theatre: New Approaches*, edited by Joel Berkowitz, 29–43. Oxford: Littman Library of Jewish Civilization, 2003.

Bennett, Andy. "Music, Space and Place." In *Music, Space and Place: Popular Music and Cultural Identity*, edited by Sheila Whiteley, Andy Bennett, and Stan Hawkins, 2–7. Aldershot: Ashgate, 2004.

Bennett, Anthony. "Music in the Halls." In *Music Hall: Performance and Style*, edited by Jacky Bratton and Ann Featherstone, 1–22. Milton Keynes, UK: Open University Press, 1986.

Berkowitz, Joel. "Introduction: Writing the History of the Yiddish Theatre." In *Yiddish Theatre: New Approaches*, edited by Joel Berkowitz, 1–25. Oxford: Littman Library of Jewish Civilization, 2003.

———. "This Is Not Europe, You Know: The Counter-Maskilic Impulse of American Yiddish Drama." In *Yiddish in America: Essays on Yiddish Culture in the Golden Land*, edited by Edward Shapiro, 135–65. Scranton, PA: Weinberg Judaic Studies Institute, University of Scranton, 2008.

Berkowitz, Joel, and Barbara Henry, eds. *Inventing the Modern Yiddish Stage: Essays in Drama, Performance, and Show Business*. Detroit: Wayne State University Press, 2012.

Biale, David. *Cultures of the Jews: A New History*. New York: Schocken Books, 2002.

———. *Eros and the Jews: From Biblical Israel to Contemporary America*. New York: BasicBooks, 1992.

Biale, Rachel. *Women and Jewish Law: The Essential Texts, Their History, and Their Relevance for Today*. New York: Schocken Books, 1995.

Bik, Abraham. "Moris vintshevski, der liriker." *YK*, August–September 1956, 11–15.

———. *Moris vintshevski, troymer un kemfer*. Los Angeles: Arbeter Ring, 1956.

Black, Eugene C. *The Social Politics of Anglo-Jewry: 1880–1920*. Oxford: Basil Blackwell, 1988.

Black, Gerry. *JFS: The History of the Jews' Free School, London since 1732*. London: Tymsder, 1998.

———. *Lord Rothschild and the Barber: The Struggle to Establish the London Jewish Hospital*. London: Tymsder, 2000.

Blackburn, Sheila. *A Fair Day's Wage for a Fair Day's Work? Sweated Labour and the Origins of Minimum Wage Legislation in Britain*. Aldershot: Ashgate, 2007.

BIBLIOGRAPHY

Bland, Lucy. *Banishing the Beast: English Feminism and Sexual Morality, 1885–1914*. London: Penguin, 1995.

Bodnar, John. *The Transplanted: A History of Immigrants in Urban America*. Bloomington: Indiana University Press, 1985.

Bohlman, Philip V. *The Music of European Nationalism: Cultural Identity and Modern History*. Santa Barbara, CA: ABC-CLIO, 2004.

———. "When Migration Ends, When Music Ceases." *Music and Arts in Action* 3, no. 3 (2011): 148–65.

Böhme, Gernot. "Atmosphere as the Fundamental Concept of a New Aesthetics." *Book Eleven* 36, no. 1 (1993): 113–26.

Booth, Charles. *Charles Booth's London: A Portrait of the Poor at the Turn of the Century, Drawn from His "Life and Labour of the People in London."* Edited by Albert Fried, Richard M. Elman, and Raymond Williams. London: Hutchinson, 1969.

Braber, Ben. *Jews in Glasgow 1879–1939: Immigration and Integration*. London: Vallentine Mitchell in association with EJPS, 2007.

Bratton, Jacky. "Beating the Bounds: Gender Play and Role Reversal in the Edwardian Music Hall." In *The Edwardian Theatre: Essays on Performance and the Stage*, edited by Michael Booth and Joel Kaplan, 86–110. Cambridge: Cambridge University Press, 1996.

———. "Jenny Hill: Sex and Sexism in the Victorian Music Hall." In *Music Hall: Performance and Style*, edited by Jacky Bratton and Ann Featherstone, 92–110. Milton Keynes, UK: Open University Press, 1986.

———. *The Victorian Popular Ballad*. London: Macmillan, 1975.

Brennan, Teresa. *The Transmission of Affect*. Ithaca, NY: Cornell University Press, 2014.

Bristow, Edward. *Prostitution and Prejudice: The Jewish Fight against White Slavery, 1870–1939*. Oxford: Clarendon, 1982.

Brown, Lesley. *The New Shorter Oxford English Dictionary on Historical Principles*. Oxford: Clarendon, 1993.

Buckman, Joseph. *Immigrants and the Class Struggle: The Jewish Immigrants in Leeds, 1880–1914 Joseph Buckman*. Manchester: Manchester University Press, 1983.

Buhle, Paul, and Dan Georgakas. *The Immigrant Left in the United States*. Albany: State University of New York Press, 1996.

Busteed, Mervyn. "Songs in a Strange Land—Ambiguities of Identity amongst Irish Migrants in Mid-Victorian Manchester." *Political Geography* 17, no. 6 (1998): 627–65.

Caplan, Debra. "Nomadic Chutzpah: The Vilna Troupe's Transnational Yiddish Theatre Paradigm, 1915–1935." *Theatre Survey* 55, no. 3 (2014): 296–317.

BIBLIOGRAPHY

Cassedy, Steven. *To the Other Shore: The Russian Jewish Intellectuals Who Came to America.* Princeton, NJ: Princeton University Press, 1997.

Castles, Stephen, and Mark J. Miller. *The Age of Migration: International Population Movements in the Modern World.* New York: Palgrave Macmillan, 2003.

Cesarani, David. *The Jewish Chronicle and Anglo-Jewry, 1841–1991.* Cambridge: Cambridge University Press, 1994.

Clark, Michael. *Albion and Jerusalem: The Anglo-Jewish Community in the Post-Emancipation Era, 1858–1887.* Oxford: Oxford University Press, 2009.

Cohen, Nathan. "The Yiddish Press and Yiddish Literature: A Fertile but Complex Relationship." *Modern Judaism* 28, no. 2 (May 2008): 149–72.

Cohen, Stuart A. *English Zionists and British Jews: The Communal Politics of Anglo-Jewry, 1895–1920.* Princeton, NJ: Princeton University Press, 1982.

Connell, John, and Chris Gibson. *Sound Tracks: Popular Music, Identity, and Place.* London: Routledge, 2003.

Cox, Pamela, and Annabel Hobley. *Shopgirls: The True Story of Life behind the Counter.* London: Random House, 2014.

Craig, David. *The Real Foundations; Literature and Social Change.* Oxford: Oxford University Press, 1974.

Craig, Timothy, and Richard King, eds. *Global Goes Local: Popular Culture in Asia.* Vancouver: University of British Columbia Press, 2002.

Davies, Christie. "Exploring the Thesis of the Self-Depreciating Jewish Sense of Humor." In *Semites and Stereotypes: Characteristics of Jewish Humor*, edited by Avner Ziv and Anat Zajdman, 29–46. Westport, CT: Greenwood, 1993.

Davison, Peter. *Songs of the British Music Hall.* London: Oak Publications; distributed by Music Sales Corp., 1971.

DeNora, Tia. *Music in Everyday Life.* Cambridge: Cambridge-Obeikan, 2000.

Dujunco, Mercedes. "Hybridity and Disjuncture in Mainland Chinese Popular Music." In *Global Goes Local: Popular Culture in Asia*, edited by Timothy Craig and Richard King, 25–39. Vancouver: University of British Columbia Press, 2002.

Endelman, Todd. *The Jews of Britain, 1656–2000.* Berkeley: University of California Press, 2002.

Englander, David. "Anglicized Not Anglican: Jews and Judaism in Victorian Britain." *Religion in Victorian Britain* 1 (1988): 235–73.

———. "Booth's Jews: The Presentation of Jews and Judaism in 'Life and Labour of the London Poor.'" *Victorian Studies* 32, no. 4 (1989): 551–72.

———, ed. *A Documentary History of Jewish Immigrants in Britain, 1840–1920.* Leicester: Leicester University Press, 1994.

———. "Stille Huppah (Quiet Marriage) among Jewish Immigrants in Britain." *Jewish Journal of Sociology* 34, no. 2 (1992): 85–109.

BIBLIOGRAPHY

Epstein, Melekh. *Profiles of Eleven: Profiles of Eleven Men Who Guided the Destiny of an Immigrant Society and Stimulated Social Consciousness among the American People*. Detroit: Wayne State University Press, 1965.

Evans-Gordon, William Eden. *The Alien Immigrant*. 1903. Reprint, Memphis, TN: General Books, 2010.

Faulk, Barry J. *Music Hall & Modernity: The Late-Victorian Discovery of Popular Culture*. Athens: Ohio University Press, 2004.

Feldman, David. *Englishmen and Jews: Social Relations and Political Culture, 1840–1914*. New Haven, CT: Yale University Press, 1994.

———. "The Importance of Being English: Jewish Immigration and the Decay of Liberal England." In *Metropolis: London; Histories and Representations since 1800*, edited by David Feldman and Gareth Stedman-Jones, 56–84. London: Routledge, 1989.

———. "Mr Lewinstein Goes to Parliament: Reflections on the Historiography and History of Jewish Immigration to London." Unpublished paper, 2017.

———. "Was Modernity Good for the Jews?" In *Modernity, Culture, and "the Jew,"* edited by Bryan Cheyette and Laura Marcus, 171–87. Stanford, CA: Stanford University Press, 1998.

Feldman, David, and Gareth Stedman Jones, eds. *Metropolis: London; Histories and Representations since 1800*. London: Routledge, 1989.

Finestein, Israel. *Anglo-Jewry in Changing Times: Studies in Diversity, 1840–1914*. London: Vallentine Mitchell, 1999.

———. *Jewish Society in Victorian England: Collected Essays*. London: Vallentine Mitchell, 1993.

Fishman, David. *The Rise of Modern Yiddish Culture*. Pittsburgh: University of Pittsburgh Press, 2005.

Fishman, William. *East End Jewish Radicals, 1875–1914*. London: Duckworth, 1975.

Frankel, Jonathan. *Prophecy and Politics: Socialism, Nationalism, and the Russian Jews, 1862–1917*. Cambridge: Cambridge University Press, 1981.

Freeze, ChaeRan. *Jewish Marriage and Divorce in Imperial Russia*. Hanover, NH: University Press of New England [for] Brandeis University Press, 2002.

Friedman, Reena Sigman. "'Send Me My Husband Who Is in New York City': Husband Desertion in the American Jewish Immigrant Community, 1900–1926." *Jewish Social Studies* 44, no. 1 (1982): 1–18.

Furnish, Ben. "'It's Both Hot and Incredibly Innocent': A Century of Sex on the American Jewish Stage." In *Jews and Sex*, edited by Nathan Abrams, 150–61. Nottingham: Five Leaves, 2008.

Gainer, Bernard. *The Alien Invasion: The Origins of the Aliens Act of 1905*. London: Heinemann, 1972.

Gartner, Lloyd. "Anglo-Jewry and the Jewish International Traffic in Prostitution, 1885–1914." *AJS Review* 7 (1982): 129–78.

———. *The Jewish Immigrant in England, 1870–1914*. London: Simon Publications, 1973.

———. "Women in the Great Jewish Migration." *Jewish Historical Studies: Transactions of the Jewish Historical Society of England* 40 (2005): 129–39.

Gidley, Ben. "Diasporic Memory and the Call to Identity: Yiddish Migrants in Early Twentieth Century East London." *Journal of Intercultural Studies* 34, no. 6 (7 May 2013): 650–64.

———. "The Ghosts of Kishinev in the East End: Responses to a Pogrom in the Jewish London of 1903." In *The "Jew" in Late-Victorian and Edwardian Culture: Between the East End and East Africa*, edited by Eitan Bar-Yosef and Nadia Valman, 98–112. Basingstoke: Palgrave Macmillan, 2009.

Glover, David. *Literature, Immigration, and Diaspora in Fin-de-Siècle England: A Cultural History of the 1905 Aliens Act*. Cambridge: Cambridge University Press, 2012.

Godley, Andrew. *Jewish Immigrant Entrepreneurship in New York and London, 1880–1914: Enterprise and Culture*. Basingstoke, UK: Palgrave, 2001.

Gopinath, Gayatri. "'Bombay, UK, Yuba City': Bhangra Music and the Engendering of Diaspora." *Diaspora: A Journal of Transnational Studies* 4, no. 3 (1995): 303–21.

Gordin, Jacob, and Ruth Gay. "Inventing a Yiddish Theater in America." In *The Jewish King Lear: A Comedy in America*, edited by Ruth Gay and Sophie Glazer, 73–106. New Haven, CT: Yale University Press, 2007.

Gottlieb, Jack. *Funny, It Doesn't Sound Jewish: How Yiddish Songs and Synagogue Melodies Influences Tin Pan Alley, Brodway, and Hollywood*. Albany: State University of New York Press, 2004.

Green, Nancy, and P. Altman. *Jewish Workers in the Modern Diaspora*. Berkeley: University of California Press, 1998.

Gurney, Peter. "'A Palace for the People'? The Crystal Palace and Consumer Culture in Victorian England." In *Victorian Prism: Refractions of the Crystal Palace*, edited by James Buzard, Joseph Childers, and Eileen Gillooly, 138–50. Charlottesville: University of Virginia Press, 2007.

Hall, Lesley. *Sex, Gender and Social Change in Britain since 1880*. New York: Palgrave Macmillan, 2000.

Hall, Stuart. "Cultural Identity and Cinematic Representation." *Framework* 36 (January 1989): 68–81.

Harendorf, Shmuel Jacob. *Theatre Caravans: Humorous Sketches*. London: Harendorf, 1954.

———. "Yidish teater in england." In *Yidn in england: shtudies un materialn 1880–1940*, 225–48. New York: YIVO, 1966.

BIBLIOGRAPHY

Harkavy, Alexander. *English-Yiddish Dictionary: Yiddish-English Dictionary.* New York: Schocken Books, 1988.

Harshav, Benjamin. *Language in Time of Revolution.* Berkeley: University of California Press, 1993.

Heskes, Irene, and Lawrence Marwick. *Yiddish American Popular Songs, 1895 to 1950: A Catalog Based on the Lawrence Marwick Roster of Copyright Entries.* Washington, DC: Library of Congress, 1992.

Hobbs, Andrew, and Claire Januszewski. "How Local Newspapers Came to Dominate Victorian Poetry Publishing." *Victorian Poetry* 52, no. 1 (2014): 65–87.

Hodess, Jacob. "Tsu der geshikhte fun der english-yidisher prese." In *Yidn in england: Shtudyes un materyaln 1880–1940*, 40–71. New York: YIVO, 1966.

Hofmeester, Karin. *Jewish Workers and the Labour Movement: A Comparative Study of Amsterdam, London and Paris (1870–1914).* Aldershot, UK: Ashgate, 2004.

Holmes, Colin. "East End Crime and the Jewish Community, 1887–1911." In *The Jewish East End 1840–1939*, 109–23. London: Jewish Historical Society of England, 1981.

Homa, Bernard. *A Fortress in Anglo-Jewry: The Story of the Machzike Hadath.* London: Shapiro, Vallentine, 1953.

———. *Orthodoxy in Anglo-Jewry, 1880–1940.* London: Jewish Historical Society of England, 1969.

Howe, Irving, and Kenneth Libo. *World of Our Fathers.* London: Phoenix, 2000.

Howe, Irving, Ruth R. Wisse, and Khone Shmeruk. *The Penguin Book of Modern Yiddish Verse.* New York: Viking, 1987.

Jacobs, Louis. *The Jewish Religion: A Companion.* Oxford: Oxford University Press, 1995.

Johnson, Pauline. *Marxist Aesthetics (Routledge Revivals): The Foundations within Everyday Life for an Emancipated Consciousness.* London: Taylor & Francis, 2013.

Joyce, Patrick. *Visions of the People: Industrial England and the Question of Class 1848–1914.* Cambridge: Cambridge University Press, 1993.

Kahn, Ava F., and Adam D. Mendelsohn, eds. *Transnational Traditions: New Perspectives on American Jewish History.* Detroit: Wayne State University Press, 2014.

Kaplan, Marion. "Prostitution, Morality Crusades and Feminism: German-Jewish Feminists and the Campaign against White Slavery." In *Women's Studies International Forum* 5: 619–27. Amsterdam: Elsevier, 1982.

Katz, Dovid. *Words on Fire: The Unfinished Story of Yiddish.* New York: Basic Books, 2004.

Kershen, Anne J. *Uniting the Tailors: Trade Unionism amongst the Tailoring Workers of London and Leeds, 1870–1939*. London: F. Cass, 1995.
Kift, Dagmar. *The Victorian Music Hall: Culture, Class, and Conflict*. Cambridge: Cambridge University Press, 1996.
Kirsch Greenberg, Suzanne. "Anglicization and the Education of Jewish Immigrant Children in the East End of London." In *Jewish History: Essays in Honour of Chimen Abramsky*, edited by Ada Rapoport-Albert and Steven J. Zipperstein, 111–26. London: Peter Halban, 1988.
Kisch, Egon Erwin, and Harold B. Segel. *Egon Erwin Kisch, the Raging Reporter: A Bio-Anthology*. West Lafayette, IN: Purdue University Press, 1997, 224–25.
Kiwan, Nadia, and Ulrike Hanna Meinhof. "Music and Migration: A Transnational Approach." *Music and Arts in Action* 3, no. 3 (2011): 3–20.
Knepper, Paul. "British Jews and the Racialisation of Crime in the Age of Empire." *British Journal of Criminology* 47, no. 1 (January 2007): 61–79.
Knudsen, Jan Sverre. "Music of the Multiethnic Minority: A Postnational Perspective." *Music and Arts in Action* 3, no. 3 (2011): 77–91.
Kobrin, Rebecca. *Jewish Bialystok and Its Diaspora*. Bloomington: Indiana University Press, 2010.
Kreditor, Leib Shalom. "Yidish teater in London: Shtrikhn un episodn." In *Hundert yor yidish teater*, edited by Y. Klinger. London: Lett Printers, 1962.
Kuzmack, Linda Gordon. *Woman's Cause: The Jewish Woman's Movement in England and the United States, 1881–1933*. Columbus: Ohio State University Press, 1990.
Lachs, Vivi. "Revolution in Anglo-Yiddish Poetry: Morris Winchevsky's Strategies to Revolutionise the Jewish Immigrants to Britain, 1884–1894." *Studies in Ethnicity and Nationalism* 14, no. 1 (2014): 1–19.
———. "The Yiddish Veker in London: Morris Winchevsky; Building a Broad Left through Poetry 1884–1894." *Socialist History* 45 (2014): 1–24.
Lammers, Benjamin J. "The Citizens of the Future: Educating the Children of the Jewish East End, c. 1885–1939." *Twentieth Century British History* 19, no. 4 (2008): 393–418.
Landa, Myer. *The Jew in Drama*. New York: KTAV, 1969.
Langton, Daniel. *Claude Montefiore: His Life and Thought*. London: Vallentine Mitchell, 2002.
Lawrence, Jerome. *Actor, the Life and Times of Paul Muni*. London: W. H. Allen, 1975.
Levin, Nora. *Jewish Socialist Movements: 1871–1917*. Oxford: Oxford University Press, 1978.
Levin, Salmond. "The Changing Pattern of Jewish Education." In *A Century of Anglo-Jewish Life*, edited by Salmond Levin, 57–74. London: United Synagogue, 1971.

BIBLIOGRAPHY

Levine-Clark, Marjorie. "From 'Relief' to 'Justice and Protection': The Maintenance of Deserted Wives, British Masculinity and Imperial Citizenship, 1870–1920." *Gender & History* 22, no. 2 (2010): 302–21.

Levy, Elkan. "The New West End Synagogue, 1879–2004." Lecture, 11 July 2004. Accessed 26 June 2013. http://www.newwestend.org.uk/docs/EDLlecture.pdf.

Lipman, Vivian. *A Century of Social Service, 1859–1959: The Jewish Board of Guardians*. London: Routledge & Kegan Paul, 1959.

———. *A History of the Jews in Britain since 1858*. Leicester: Leicester University Press, 1990.

———. *Social History of the Jews in England: 1850–1950*. London: Watts, 1954.

Lipsitz, George. *Dangerous Crossroads: Popular Music, Postmodernism, and the Poetics of Place*. New York: Verso, 1994.

Liptzin, Sol. *A History of Yiddish Literature*. New York: Jonathan David, 1985.

Livesey, Ruth. *Socialism, Sex, and the Culture of Aestheticism in Britain, 1880–1914*. Oxford: Oxford University Press/British Academy, 2007.

Lloyd, A. L. *Folk Song in England*. London: Panther Books, 1969.

Lowe, Lisa. "Heterogeneity, Hybridity, Multiplicity: Marking Asian American Differences." *Diaspora: A Journal of Transnational Studies* 1, no. 1 (1991): 24–44.

Lucassen, Leo. *The Immigrant Threat: The Integration of Old and New Migrants in Western Europe since 1850*. Urbana: University of Illinois Press, 2005.

Marks, Lara. "The Luckless Waifs and Strays of Humanity: Irish and Jewish Immigrant Unwed Mothers in London, 1870–1939." *Twentieth Century British History* 3, no. 2 (1992): 113–37.

———. "Race, Class and Gender: The Experiences of Jewish Prostitutes and Other Jewish Women in the East End of London at the Turn of the Century." In *Women, Migration and Empire*, edited by Joan Grant, 31–50. Stoke-on-Trent, UK: Trentham, 1996.

Marmor, Kalman. *Moris Vintshevski, zayn lebn, virkn un shafn*. New York: Freiheit, 1928.

Marx, Karl, and David McLellan. *Early Texts*. Paladin, CA: Barnes & Noble, 1971.

Mason, Laura. *Singing the French Revolution: Popular Culture and Politics, 1787–1799*. Ithaca, NY: Cornell University Press, 1996.

Matthews, William. *Cockney, Past and Present: A Short History of the Dialect of London*. London: E. P. Dutton, 1938.

Mazower, David. "Kibbitzers, Coffee, and Kikhlekh." *Pakn Treger*, no. 73 (Summer 2016): 21–24.

———. "London–New York, or the Great British Yiddish Theatre Brain Drain," 20 November 2016. Accessed 24 November 2016. https://yiddishstage.org/london-new-york-or-the-great-british-yiddish-theatre-brain-drain.

BIBLIOGRAPHY

———. "Stories in Song: The Melo-Deklamatsyes of Joseph Markovitsh." In *Yiddish Theatre: New Approaches*, edited by Joel Berkowitz, 119–37. Oxford: Littman Library of Jewish Civilization, 2003.

———. "Whitechapel's Yiddish Opera House: The Rise and Fall of the Feinman Yiddish People's Theatre." In *An East End Legacy: Essays in Memory of William J Fishman*, edited by Colin Holmes and Anne J. Kershen, 155–87. Abingdon: Routledge, 2017.

———. *Yiddish Theatre in London*. London: Museum of the Jewish East End, 1987.

McGuire, Charles Edward. "Music and Morality: John Curwen's Tonic Sol-Fa, the Temperance Movement, and the Oratorios of Edward Elgar." In *Chorus and Community*, edited by Karen Ahlquist, 111–38. Urbana: University of Illinois Press, 2006.

McKinley, C. Alexander. *Illegitimate Children of the Enlightenment: Anarchists and the French Revolution, 1880–1914*. New York: P. Lang, 2008.

McLellan, David. *Karl Marx: His Life and Thought*. St Albans, Hertfordshire, UK: Paladin, 1976.

Middleton, Richard. "Popular Music of the Lower Classes." In *The Romantic Age, 1800–1914*, edited by Nicholas Temperley, 63–81. London: Athlone, 1981.

Miller, Marc. *Representing the Immigrant Experience: Morris Rosenfeld and the Emergence of Yiddish Literature in America*. Syracuse, NY: Syracuse University Press, 2007.

Minkov, Nokhum Borukh. *Piyonern fun yidisher poezye in amerike: dos sotsiale lid*. New York: O. fg., 1956.

Miron, Dan. "The Literary Image of the Shtetl." *Jewish Social Studies* 1, no. 3 (Spring 1995): 1–43.

Morawska, Ewa. "Immigrants, Transnationalism, and Ethnicization: A Comparison of This Great Wave and the Last." In *E Pluribus Unum? Contemporary and Historical Perspectives on Immigrant Political Incorporation*, edited by Gary Gerstle and John Mollenkopf, 175–212. New York: Russell Sage Foundation, 2001.

Morton, James. *East End Gangland & Gangland International Omnibus*. London: Time Warner Paperbacks, 2003.

Most, Andrea. *Theatrical Liberalism: Jews and Popular Entertainment in America*. New York: New York University Press, 2013.

Myer, Morris. *Yidish teater in london 1902–1942*. London: Naroditzki, 1943.

Nahshon, Edna. *New York's Yiddish Theater from the Bowery to Broadway*. New York: Columbia University Press, 2016.

Nair, Parvati. "Voicing Risk: Migration, Transgression and Relocation in Spanish/Moroccan Rai." In *Music National Identity and the Politics of Location:*

Between the Global and the Local, edited by Ian Biddle and Vanessa Knights, 65–80. Hampshire, UK: Ashgate, 2013.
Newman, Aubrey. *The United Synagogue, 1870–1970*. London: Routledge & K. Paul, 1976.
Newman, Simon. *Parades and the Politics of the Street: Festive Culture in the Early American Republic*. Philadelphia: University of Pennsylvania Press, 2000.
Newton, Henry Chance. *Cues and Curtain Calls: Being the Theatrical Reminiscences of H. Chance Newton ("Carados" of the Referee)*. London: John Lane, 1927.
———. "Music-Hall London." In *Living London: Its Work and Its Play, Its Humour and Its Pathos, Its Sights and Its Scenes*, edited by George Sims, 222–28. New York: Cassell, 1902.
Niborski, Yitzkhok. *Verterbukh fun loshn-koydesh-shtamike verter in yidish*. Paris: Bibliothèque Medem, 1999.
Paxman, Jeremy. *The Victorians: Britain through the Paintings of the Age*. London: BBC Books, 2010.
Peña, Manuel. *The Texas-Mexican Conjunto: History of a Working-Class Music*. Austin: University of Texas Press, 1985.
Pennybacker, Susan. "'It Was Not What She Said, but the Way That She Said It': The London County Council and the Music Halls." In *Music Hall: The Business of Pleasure*, edited by Peter Bailey, 120–40. Milton Keynes, UK: Open University Press, 1986.
Pollins, Harold. *Economic History of the Jews in England*. Rutherford, NJ: Fairleigh Dickinson University Press, 1982.
Polonsky, Anthony. *The Jews in Poland and Russia: 1881–1914*. Vol. 2. Oxford: Littman Library of Jewish Civilization, 2010.
Portnoy, Edward. "Freaks, Geeks, and Strongmen: Warsaw Jews and Popular Performance, 1912–1930." *TDR/The Drama Review* 50, no. 2 (2006): 117–35.
Potter, Beatrice. "The Tailoring Trade and the Jewish Community." In *Life and Labour: East London*, edited by Charles Booth, 209–40. Vol. 1. London: Williams and Norgate, 1889.
Poulsen, Charles. *Victoria Park: A Study in the History of East London*. London: Stepney Books: Journeyman Press, 1976.
Prager, Leonard. "The Beginnings of Yiddish Fiction in England." In *Studies in the Cultural Life of the Jews in England*, edited by Dov Noy and Issachar Ben-Ami, 245–310. Jerusalem: Magnes Press, Hebrew University, 1975.
———. "A Bibliography of Yiddish Periodicals in Great Britain (1867–1967)." *Studies in Bibliography and Booklore* 9, no. 1 (Spring 1969): 3–32.
———. "Der londoner farleger m. yozef." In *Oksforder yidish*, edited by Dovid Katz, 175–98. Vol. 2. London: Harwood Academic Publishers, 1991.

———. "Paul Muni's Parents Sing at a London Yiddish Music Hall." In *Language and Civilization; A Concerted Profusion of Essays and Studies in Honour of Otto Hietsch*, 428–71. Vol. 1. Frankfurt am Main: Peter Lang, 1992.

———. *Yiddish Culture in Britain: A Guide*. Frankfurt am Main: Peter Lang, 1990.

Prints, A. [Isaac Greenberg]. "Vintshevskis lider." *Morgn freiheit*, 27 March 1932.

Quint, Alyssa. "The Salon and the Tavern: Yiddish Folk Poetry of the Nineteenth Century." In *Inventing the Modern Yiddish Stage*, edited by Joel Berkowitz and Barbara Henry, 40–63. Detroit: Wayne State University Press, 2012.

Reid, Derek. "Six Yiddish Street Songs of East London." In *Proceedings of the First International Conference on Jewish Music 1994*, edited by Steve Stanton, 102–14. London: City University, 1997.

Rosman, Moshe. "Jewish History across Borders." In *Rethinking European Jewish History*, edited by Jeremy Cohen and Moshe Rosman, 15–29. Oxford: Littman Library of Jewish Civilization, 2009.

Ross, Ellen. "'Fierce Questions and Taunts': Married Life in Working-Class London, 1870–1914." In *Metropolis London. Histories and Representations since 1800*, edited by David Feldman and Gareth Stedman-Jones, 219–44. London: Routledge, 1989.

Roth, Cecil. *A History of the Jews in England*. Oxford: Clarendon, 1949.

Rubin, Ruth. "History of an American Yiddish Folk Song." *Jewish Quarterly* 2, no. 2 (Autumn 1954): 51–60.

———. *Jewish Folk Songs: In Yiddish and English*. New York: author, 1989.

———. *Voices of a People: The Story of Yiddish Folksong*. Philadelphia: Jewish Publication Society of America, 1979.

Rumbelow, Donald. *The Houndsditch Murders and the Siege of Sidney Street*. Stroud, Gloucestershire, UK: History Press, 2009.

Russell, C., and Harry Samuel Lewis. *The Jew in London: A Study of Racial Character and Present-Day Conditions*. London: T. Fisher Unwin, 1900.

Russell, Dave. *Popular Music in England, 1840–1914: A Social History*. Manchester: Manchester University Press, 1987.

———. "Varieties of Life: The Making of the Edwardian Music Hall." In *The Edwardian Theatre: Essays on Performance and the Stage*, edited by Michael Booth and Joel Kaplan, 61–85. Cambridge: Cambridge University Press, 1996.

———. "'We Carved Our Way to Glory': The British Soldier in Music Hall Song and Sketch, c. 1880–1914." In *Popular Imperialism and the Military 1850–1950*, edited by John MacKenzie, 50–79. Manchester: Manchester University Press, 1992.

Sacks, Jonathan. *Koren Sacks Yom Kippur Mahzor.* Jerusalem: Koren Publishers, 2012.

Salmon, Nicholas. "The Communist Poet-Laureate: William Morris's Chants for Socialists." *Journal of the William Morris Society* 14 (2001): 31–40.

Samuel, Raphael. *Theatres of Memory: Past and Present in Contemporary Culture.* London: Verso, 1996.

Sanders, Mike. *The Poetry of Chartism: Aesthetics, Politics, History.* Cambridge: Cambridge University Press, 2009.

Sanders, Ronald. *The Downtown Jews: Portraits of an Immigrant Generation.* New York: Dover Publications, 1987.

Sandrow, Nahma. "Romanticism and the Yiddish Theatre." In *Yiddish Theatre: New Approaches*, edited by Joel Berkowitz, 47–59. Oxford: Littman Library of Jewish Civilization, 2003.

———. *Vagabond Stars: A World History of Yiddish Theater.* New York: Harper & Row, 1977.

Schiller, Nina Glick, and Ulrike Hanna Meinhof. "Singing a New Song? Transnational Migration, Methodological Nationalism and Cosmopolitan Perspectives." *Music and Arts in Action* 3, no. 3 (2011): 21–39.

Schmiechen, James. *Sweated Industries and Sweated Labor: The London Clothing Trades, 1860–1914.* London: Croom Helm, 1984.

Schneer, Jonathan. *London 1900: The Imperial Metropolis.* New Haven, CT: Yale University Press, 1999.

Seidman, Naomi. *The Marriage Plot: Or, How Jews Fell in Love with Love, and with Literature.* Stanford, CA: Stanford University Press, 2016.

———. "Religion/Secularity." In *The Routledge Handbook of Contemporary Jewish Cultures*, edited by N. Valman and L. Roth, 151–161. London: Routledge, 2015.

Senelick, Laurence. "Politics as Entertainment: Victorian Music-Hall Songs." *Victorian Studies* 19, no. 2 (1975): 149–80.

Sharot, Stephen. *Judaism: A Sociology.* London: David & Charles Newton Abbot, 1976.

Shepherd, Naomi. *A Price below Rubies: Jewish Women as Rebels and Radicals.* London: Weidenfeld & Nicholson, 1993.

Shmeruk, Khone. "Dray londoner yiddishe gasnlider fun far der ershter veltmilkhome." In *Studies in the Cultural Life of the Jews in England*, edited by Dov Noy and Issachar Ben-Ami, 113–23. Jerusalem: Magnes, 1975.

Shternshis, Anna. *Soviet and Kosher: Jewish Popular Culture in the Soviet Union, 1923–1939.* Bloomington: Indiana University Press, 2006.

Slobin, Mark. *Subcultural Sounds: Micromusics of the West.* Hanover, NH: University Press of New England, 1993.

———. *Tenement Songs: The Popular Music of the Jewish Immigrants.* Urbana: University of Illinois Press, 1996.

Sollors, Werner. *Beyond Ethnicity: Consent and Descent in American Culture.* New York: Oxford University Press, 1986.

Sommer, Doris. *Bilingual Aesthetics: A New Sentimental Education.* Durham, NC: Duke University Press, 2004.

Soyer, Daniel. "Transnationalism and Mutual Influence: American and East European Jewries in the 1920s and 1930s." In *Rethinking European Jewish History*, edited by Jeremy Cohen and Moshe Rosman, 201–20. Oxford: Littman Library of Jewish Civilization, 2009.

Stedman Jones, Gareth. *Outcast London: A Study in the Relationship between Classes in Victorian Society.* Oxford: Penguin Books, 1971.

———. "Working-Class Culture and Working-Class Politics in London, 1870–1900: Notes on the Remaking of a Working Class." *Journal of Social History* 7, no. 4 (1974): 460–508.

Stokes, Martin. *Ethnicity, Identity, and Music: The Musical Construction of Place.* Oxford: Berg, 1994.

Summerfield, Penelope. "The Effingham Arms and the Empire: Deliberate Selection in the Evolution of Music Hall in London." In *Popular Culture and Class Conflict, 1590–1914: Explorations in the History of Labour and Leisure*, edited by Eileen Yeo and Stephen Yeo, 209–40. Sussex, UK: Harvester, 1981.

Szeintuch, Yechiel. "Bre'i ha'ashmodai." *Hulyot* 6 (2000): 402–4.

Tananbaum, Susan L. *Jewish Immigrants in London, 1880–1939.* London: Pickering and Chatto, 2014.

Thissen, Judith. "Film and Vaudeville on New York's Lower East Side." In *The Art of Being Jewish in Modern Times*, edited by Barbara Kirshenblatt-Gimblett and Jonathan Karp, 42–56. Philadelphia: University of Pennsylvania Press, 2013.

Traies, Jane. "Jones and the Working Girl: Class Marginality in Music-Hall Song 1860–1900." In *Music Hall: Performance and Style*, edited by Jacky Bratton and Ann Featherstone, 23–48. Milton Keynes, UK: Open University Press, 1986.

Tselniker, Anna. *Three for the Price of One.* London: Spiro Institute, 1991.

Turino, Thomas. *Music as Social Life: The Politics of Participation.* Chicago: University of Chicago Press, 2008.

Vevyorke, Avrom. *Di idishe prese un dos idishe teater in London.* London: M. Susman, n.d.

Vicinus, Martha. *The Industrial Muse: A Study of Nineteenth Century British Working-Class Literature.* London: Croom Helm, 1974.

Voeltz, Robert. "'A Good Jew and a Good Englishman': The Jewish Lads' Brigade, 1894–1922." *Journal of Contemporary History* 23 (1988): 119–27.

BIBLIOGRAPHY

Walkowitz, Judith R. *City of Dreadful Delight: Narratives of Sexual Danger in Late-Victorian London.* Chicago: University of Chicago Press, 1992.

———. "Science, Feminism and Romance: The Men and Women's Club 1885–1889." *History Workshop Journal* 21 (1986): 37–59.

Warnke, Nina. "The Child Who Wouldn't Grow Up: Yiddish Theatre and Its Critics." In *Yiddish Theatre: New Approaches*, edited by Joel Berkowitz, 201–16. Oxford: Littman Library of Jewish Civilization, 2008.

———. "Immigrant Popular Culture as Contested Sphere: Yiddish Music Halls, the Yiddish Press, and the Processes of Americanization, 1900–1910." *Theatre Journal* 48, no. 3 (1996): 321–35.

———. "*Patriotn* and Their Stars: Male Youth Culture in the Galleries of the New York Yiddish Theatre." In *Inventing the Modern Yiddish Stage*, edited by Joel Berkowitz and Barbara Henry, 161–83. Detroit: Wayne State University Press, 2012.

Waters, Chris. *British Socialists and the Politics of Popular Culture, 1884–1914.* Manchester: Manchester University Press, 1990.

Watson, Ian. *Song and Democratic Culture in Britain: An Approach to Popular Culture in Social Movements.* New York: Croom Helm, 1983.

Weiman-Kelman, Zohar. "Touching Time: Poetry, History and the Erotics of Yiddish." *Criticism* 59, no. 1 (forthcoming 2018).

Weinberg, Sydney. *The World of Our Mothers: The Lives of Jewish Immigrant Women.* Chapel Hill: University of North Carolina Press, 1988.

Weinreich, Max. *History of the Yiddish Language.* New Haven, CT: Yale University Press, 2008.

Wex, Michael. *Born to Kvetch: Yiddish Language and Culture in All of Its Moods.* New York: St. Martin's, 2005.

White, Jerry. *London in the Nineteenth Century: "A Human Awful Wonder of God."* London: Jonathan Cape, 2007.

———. *London in the Twentieth Century.* London: Vintage Books, 2008.

———. *Rothschild Buildings: Life in an East End Tenement Block 1887–1920.* London: Routledge & Kegan Paul, 1980.

Williams, Bill. "'East and West' in Manchester Jewry, 1880–1914." In *The Making of Modern Anglo Jewry*, edited by David Cesarani, 15–33. London: B. Blackwell, 1990.

———. *The Making of Manchester Jewry 1740–1875.* Manchester: Manchester University Press, 1985.

Wolitz, Seth. "A Yiddish Modernist Dirge: Di Kupe of Perets Markish." *Studies in Yiddish* 9, no. 6 (1987): 56–72.

Wood, Abigail. *And We're All Brothers: Singing in Yiddish in Contemporary North America.* Surrey: Ashgate, 2013.

Yeo, Stephen. "A New Life: The Religion of Socialism in Britain, 1883–1896." *History Workshop* 4 (1977): 5–56.

Zheng, Su. *Claiming Diaspora: Music, Transnationalism, and Cultural Politics in Asian/Chinese America*. Oxford: Oxford University Press, 2010.

Zinger, Sh. D. "Moris vintshevski (tsu zayn hundertstn geboyrntog)." *Der fraynd* (September–October 1956): 5–6.

Zylbercwaig, Zalmen. *Leksikon fun yidishn teater*. New York: Farlag Elisheva, 1931.

UNPUBLISHED THESES AND CONFERENCE PAPERS

Jarrett, Simon. "A Welshman Coming to London, and Seeing a Jackanapes . . ." London and the Nation Conference. Birkbeck, University of London, 10 July 2015.

Kinderman, Martin. "My Love She Dwells in London Town: Conceptions of Urban Love in Amy Levy's Poetry." Literary London Society Annual Conference. London, 22 July 2015.

Marshall, Edward. "Ambivalent Images: A Survey of Jewish Involvement and Representation in the British Entertainment Industry, 1880–1980." Unpublished PhD thesis. Royal Holloway, University of London, 2010.

Stokes, Martin. "Music, Affect and Political Action." Lecture. Royal Holloway, 5 February 2013.

Glossary

Ashkenaz. In this book, used to mean the Yiddish-speaking world.

Bund. Jewish socialist labor organization founded in Vilnius in 1897, organizing workers' action and secular educational and cultural activities. Members of the Bund promoted the use of Yiddish.

Hasidic. Pertaining to Hasidism, a religious sect founded in the mid-eighteenth century in Poland.

Heym. Homeland.

Kashres. Kosher.

Khevre. Small community organizations, consisting of prayer rooms in the informal Eastern European style of prayer. They also provided community support.

Kheyder (pl. *khadorim*). Religious schooling for younger boys, taking place after school and on Sundays.

Kunst. High art.

Kupletn. Rhyming couplets.

Machzike Hadath. Strictly orthodox large East End immigrant synagogue.

Melamed. Teacher in a *kheyder* or *talmetoyre*.

Shadkhn. Matchmaker.

Shechita. Ritual slaughter of animals for kosher food.

Shtibl. Small Hasidic prayer room.

GLOSSARY

Shund. Literally, "trash." Derogatory term used for popular culture.

Simkhes-toyre. Festival celebrating the Torah. Last day of *Sukes*.

Sukes. Festival of Tabernacles. Occurs in the autumn.

Talmetoyre. Religious schooling for older boys taking place after school and on Sundays.

Torah. Five books of Moses.

Veker. Awakener.

Yom Kippur. Day of Atonement. The most solemn fast day of the Jewish year.

Zeyde. Grandfather.

Appendix 1

Location of the London Yiddish Lyrics

SOCIALIST POETRY

Most socialist poetry in this book is by Morris Winchevsky (MW). Many of the poems are reproduced in collections. This list gives the original sources when known.

Notitsn do not have titles, so they are listed as *Notis*, followed by the first few words. The Yiddish newspapers and pamphlets in this section are located in the British Library and the National Library of Israel.

Poem	Author	Publication	Date	Page(s) where text is cited
"Akhdes"	MW	*AF*	29 August 1890	98–102, 113, 259n36
"Alt un yung"	Izak Likhtnshvayg	*AF*	25 September 1896	189
"An d. edelshtat"	MW	*AF*	Quoted Marmor *Leben*, 172	97
"A bezem un a ker"	MW	*AF*	11 October 1889	127, 264n35
"Der blinder fidler"	MW	*LG*	1910	91
"Dray shvester"	MW	*FV*	October 1891	104–7, 167, 220
"Dray vekhter"	MW	*AF*	15 November 1885	125
"Es rirt zikh"	MW	*AF*	12 June 1886	34, 126, 267n81, 265n51
				(Continued)

APPENDIX 1

Poem	Author	Publication	Date	Page(s) where text is cited
"Di farfroyrene"	MW	*AF*	23 January 1891	106
"Der frayhayts-gayst"	MW	*AF*	27 June 1890	128, 222, 263n35
"In kamf"	MW	*FV*	October 1891	109
"A kamf-gezang"	MW	*Veker*	23 December 1892	128–29
"A khoydesh on arbayt"	MW	*PY*	31 October 1884	xvi, 113–14, 182–83
"Kinnous oder arbayter klogelider"	Reuel, Yeser, Yisro, et al.	*Workers' Friend*	1888	184–88
"Di lempelekh"	MW	*SY (MPC)*	n.d.	79
"Dos lid funem hemd"	MW	*PY*	29 August 1884	33
"London bay nakht"	MW	*PY*	12 September 1884	77–79, 102
"Mayne lider"	MW	*AF*	13 February 1891	125
"Mayn muze"	Dovid Edelshtadt		Quoted Marmor *Leben*, 172	96
"A meydele in der siti"	MW	*Tsukunft*	27 March 1885	103–4, 106
"More shkhoyre"	MW	*FV*	September 1892	111–12
"Nor dos nit"	MW	*AF*	30 January 1891	103
Notits—"der liberale zogt"	MW	*FV*	July 1892	118–19
Notits—"ven england"	MW	*FV*	July 1891	121–22
Notits—"ven mentshn"	MW	*FV*	July 1891	119–20
Notits—"zey gibn a peni"	MW	*FV*	August–September 1891	117–18
Notits—"zey tseylen"	MW	*FV*	May 1891	115–17
"Di oreme maria"	MW	*AF*	25 October 1889	107–8
"Oremer yosel"	MW	*Tsukunft*	16 January 1885	103, 106
"Oyfn strend"	MW	*LG*	1910	105–6

LOCATION OF THE LONDON YIDDISH LYRICS

Poem	Author	Publication	Date	Page(s) where text is cited
"Parti politik"	MW	*FV*	July 1892	97–98
"Rabiner un mashiner"	MW	*AF*	17 August 1888	179–82
"Reb yudl far got"	Bonfeld of Glasgow	*AF*	24 July 1896	190
"Rent"	MW	*AF*	15 December 1885	106
"Rikblik oyf dos alte yor"	MW	*PY*	26 September 1884	121
"310"	Namerts [Simon Friman]	*AF*	15 May 1889	188–89
"Tsu di arbayter (nokh a tsuruf)"	MW	*AF*	27 February 1891	111–12
"Tsu di raykhe"	MW	*Tsukunft*	6 February 1885	124–25
"Di tsukunft"	MW	*Freiheit*	1905 (dated 1892)	129, 267n81
"Tsum arbayter fraynd"	MW	*Freiheit*	1895 (dated 1885)	110–11, 264n35
"Tsum fertsn-yorikn yubileum'"	L. Kahan	Songsheet NLI	1902	24
"Tsum meshugenem filozof"	Dovid Edelshtadt	*AF*	March 1890	96
"Tsum nayem yor"	MW	*AF*	3 January 1890	103
"Tsvey geslekh"	MW	*PY*	15 August 1884	94, 102
"Tsvey veltn"	MW	*FV*	May 1891	129
"Untitled (Me gloybt)"	MW	*AF*	28 November 1890	175
"Vi di raykhe layt lebn"	MW	*Veker*	23 December 1892	112

APPENDIX 1

MUSIC-HALL SONGS

This lists all written lyrics mentioned in the text and footnotes, including different versions. Recordings are mentioned only if there was no surviving text for that song. For complete references of recordings, refer to the bibliography. Different spellings for the same song reflect those of the titles in the publications.

Title of song	Writer	Publication/ page numbers	Location	Page(s) where text is cited
"Aheym tsurik"	Markovitsh	Unpub. manuscript	MPC	157, 194–96
"Azoy geyt di gelt avek"	n.k.	SG	MPC	As below
"Azoy geyt dos gelt avek"	n.k.	LK, 52	NLI	80, 146–47, 222
"Azoy geyt dos gelt avek"	n.k.	Yidishe teater lider, 42–3	YIVO	As above
"Der bal-toyvnik"	Nager (adapted from Isaac Reingold)	LK, 8–9	NLI	79, 165
"Di barimte lid funem kishinyever pogrom"	Goldberg	SG	MPC	243n95
"Di boyern krig mit england"	Avrom Simironsky	S (unknown)	MPC	11, 233n42
"A boytshik ap to deyt"	Yozefson	SM	MPC	148–50, 163–64
"Brivelekh fun rusland"	Markovitsh	LK, 31	NLI	161–62
"Der dansing skul"	Nager	LK, 107	NLI	142–44, 164
"Der dzhob"	Nager	LK, 9–11	NLI	157
"Er meynt yenem nit zikh aleyn"	Yozef	LK, 32	NLI	163–64
"A ferter hashiveynu nazad"	Yozef	LLM, 14	NLI	70, 74–76
"A finfter hashiveynu nazad"	Yozef	SY	MPC	70, 74–76
"Freg keyn katshanes"	Nager	LLM, 9–10	NLI	157, 197–98

314

LOCATION OF THE LONDON YIDDISH LYRICS

Title of song	Writer	Publication/page numbers	Location	Page(s) where text is cited
"Fri ov tshardzh"	n.k.	*LLM*, 12–13	MPC	157
"Genendel"	Nager	*LK*, 122	NLI	147
"Gevald, gevald police"	n.k.	Compact disc		145
"Gevalt es iz a shlekhte tsayt"	n.k.	SY	MPC	80, 148, 156–57
"Gevalt es iz a shlekhte tsayt"	n.k.	*Idishe bine*, 214–16	YIVO	As above
"Haf past nayn"	n.k.	SG	MPC	151
"Hashiveynu nazad" (same text as "Dem nayem hashiveynu nazad")	n.k.	*LK*, 156–57	NLI	See under "Dem nayem"
"Helo, Helo"	n.k.	Unpub. Compact disc	Reid	159 60
"A het oder a get"	Adapted for Beki Goldstein	*LK*, 6–7	NLI	66, 79–80
"A het oder a get"	Louis Gilrod	*Lider magazin* (NY) vol. 13	YIVO	79–80
"Ich such a job"	n.k. singer: Sherman	Vinyl		228n11
"Ikh bin a yidl fun der lite"	Markovitsh	*LK*, 106	NLI	199–200
"A kholem"	Markovitsh	*IE*, 27 November 1953		52
"Laytudl laytudl day day"	Yozef	SY	NLI	159, 275n20
"Dos lid 'goles rusland'"	Y. Goldman	Songsheet Malimzon	MPC	67
"Lizi klaf" (sketch)	Yozef	SY	MPC	272n50
"Lizzie Clough" ("a boytshik ap to deyt")	S. Yozefzon	Unpub. Compact disc	Reid	See under "A boytshik"

(*Continued*)

APPENDIX 1

Title of song	Writer	Publication/ page numbers	Location	Page(s) where text is cited
"London hot zikh ibergekert"	Sam Levenvirt	*LK*, 129	NLI	5, 154, 157
"Malke, malke"	Nager	*LK*, 115	NLI	153
"Mazl"	Markovitsh	*LLM*	MPC	152
"Moyshe kum efn mir dem shlos"	Markovitsh	*LK*, 93–95	NLI	158
"Dem nayem hashiveynu nazad" (see also "Hashiveynu nazad")	n.k.	Schmeruk, "Dray londoner gasnlider," 117–19		70, 71–74, 76
"Der odeser pogrom'"	Yozef	*LK*, 123	NLI	243n95
"Opgeklapte hoyshayne"	Finklshteyn	SM	MPC	148
"Orem vey iz der mamen"	n.k.	S-Ikbo moley	MPC	170
"Plezhur"	Nager	*LLM*, 9–10	MPC	151
"Der program fun morgen oyf der nakht"	Nager	*LK*, 92–93	NLI	46
"Rum to let"	Nager	*LK*, 103	NLI	170–71
"Dos troyerike lid fun keshenever pogrom"	Yozef Semilson	SY	MPC	243n95
"Tsvey doyres"	Markovitsh	*LLM*, 11	MPC	196
"Di velt iz meshuge"	n.k.	SY	MPC	199
"Ver zukht a kale"	n.k.	*LK*, 111	NLI	148
"Viktorye park"	Nager	*LLM*, 15	NLI	81–83, 144–45, 167–68
"Vos geyst nisht aheym sore-gitl"	Nager	*LK*, 16	NLI	164, 168–70

LOCATION OF THE LONDON YIDDISH LYRICS

SATIRICAL VERSE

Avreml (Avrom Margolin) is the editor of the *Bloffer*. Most other authors are also pseudonyms. The *Bloffer* is found in NLI and the *Idisher ekspres* and the *Tsayt* are found in the BL.

Title	Author	Publication and page number	Date	Page where text is cited
"Al-hanisim"	Avreml	*Tsayt*, 4	26 December 2013	217
"Al-khet motivn"	Avreml	*Tsayt*, 4	10 October 1913	206–8
"Di ani-maamins fun bloffer"	Avreml	*Bloffer*, no. 5, 10	December 1911	58
"Aroyf un arop"	Bal metufl	IE	13 July 1904	36
"Der bloffer lakht"	Zimri ben Salu	*Bloffer*, no. 4, 12	November 1911	84–87
"Der bloffer lakht"	Zimri ben Salu	*Bloffer*, no. 5, 11	December 1911	As above
"Der bloffer lakht"	Zimri ben Salu	*Bloffer*, no. 6, 16	December 1911	As above
"Der bloffer lakht"	Zimri ben Salu	*Bloffer*, no. 12, 8	March 1912	As above
"Der bloffer lakht"	Zimri ben Salu	*Bloffer*, no. 13, 6	April 1912	As above
"Haneyres halolu"	n.k.	IE, 4	15 December 1909	209–10
"Hashiveynu nazad"	n.k.	*Bloffer*, no. 34, 12	May 1913	76
"Hepi nyu yir"	n.k.	IE	31 December 1913	216
"Ikh un krist"	Moris Gros	*Bloffer*, no. 18, 11	June 1912	217
"Mayn malke"	Avreml	*Bloffer*, no. 13, 6	April 1912	208–9
"Mayn meshugas"	Nit ka yold	*Bloffer*, no. 1	October 1911	40
"Mist"	L.A.L.A.	*Bloffer*, no. 9, 9	January 1912	217
"Moyshe un yakhne"	Avreml	*Tsayt*, 4	21 November 1913	210–12, 221
"A pekl nevies"	Avreml	*Bloffer*, no. 3, 5–6	November 1911	204–6
"Di reformer"	M. R.	Fonograf, 10	17 January 1908	216 (*Continued*)

APPENDIX 1

Title	Author	Publication and page number	Date	Page where text is cited
"Di simkhes-toyre trinker"	Avreml	*IE*	2 October 1912	202–4
"Strayk epidemye"	n.k.	*Tsayt*, 4	14 September 1913	15
Untitled ("Dem melameds geshrey")	n.k.	*IE*	17 October 1906	213–15
"Vos toygn di lider"	n.k.	*IE*	28 September 1909	212–13

Appendix 2

London Immigrant Personalities

These biographies of personalities mentioned in the book are mostly drawn from Prager, *Yiddish Culture in Britain* (P) and Zylbercweig, *Leksikon fun yidishn teater* (Z).

Adler, Jacob: Born 1877, Odessa. Had a long career as actor and manager, becoming a famous star across the Yiddish world and seen as the king of the Yiddish stage. Lived in London 1883–87, where he established the Russian Hebrew Workman's Club and later the Princes Street Club. He also set up a Yiddish drama and music school. (P, 101–2; Rosenfeld, *Bright Star*; Morris Myer, *Idish teater in london*, 253)

Akselrod, Morris: Born 1879, Jassy, Romania. Actor in London from 1901 touring the United Kingdom and abroad. Nicknamed "The Jewish Dan Leno." His wife, Mine, also performed in the Yiddish theatre. (P, 105–6)

Alman, Shmuel: Born 1877, Russia. Came to London in 1903 to study at the Guildhall School of Music. Became choirmaster at the Great Synagogue, Duke's Place, composing liturgical music. He translated Verdi's *Rigoletto* into Yiddish, to be performed at the Faynman Yiddish Theatre. (P, 109–10)

Avreml: See Margolin, Avrom.

Bleichman, Yankev (Jacob): Born 1870, Fokshan, Romania. Well-known comic actor performing across Europe from the 1880s. A frequent visitor to London. Father-in-law of Avrom Margolin. (Z, 1:181. For a translation of Z, see http://www.museumoffamilyhistory.com/yt/lex/B/bleichman-jacob.htm.)

Brin, Max: Born 1884. Character actor in London, 1909. (P, 174)

Finkelshteyn, Y: Wrote articles for the Yiddish press and is the author of the song "Opgeklapte hoyshayne." (P, 239)

Friman, Simon (Namerts): Born 1862, Lithuania. Came to London 1889. Writer for the socialist press and theatre. (P, 254)

Goldstein, Beki: Born 1877, Mlavo, Poland. Came to London 1901. A character actress on the London Yiddish stage and touring across the Yiddish-speaking world. Married Joseph Markovitsh. (P, 287; Z, 2:377)

Gutentag, Karl: Born 1878. Romantic actor in Poland, touring, performed in London, where he met and married Yiddish actress Berte Akselrod. (P, 301)

Gutman, Tsvi: Born 1865, Russia. Converted to Christianity and worked in the Mildmay Mission in London from 1891 with responsibility for Jewish immigrants. (P, 301)

Izraeli, L.: See Kussman, Leon.

Krantz, Philip: Born 1858. Lived in London 1883–90. Was the first editor of the *Arbayter fraynd* 1883–89. (P, 382)

Kussman, Leon (L. Izraeli): Born 1884. Journalist in London from 1911 and editor of the *Bloffer* from 1913. He wrote articles for the *Idisher ekspres* under the pen name L. Izraeli. He moved to New York in 1913 and worked on the *Morgen dzhurnal*. (P, 388–89)

Lubritski, Isaac: Born ca. 1859 in Vishegrod, Poland. He was a popular *badkhn* (wedding jester), and continued this work on emigrating to London. He was a prompter in the Pavilion Theatre, where his children acted. He also wrote songs and articles under the pseudonym Izak Badkhn. (P, 426–27; Z, 2:1014)

Margolin, Avrom (Avreml): Born 1884, Russia. Studied medicine in Berlin but did not practice for long. He married the actor Clara Bleichman (daughter of Yankev Bleichman) and they settled in London. Was a doctor in the British army. Became a writer and edited the *Bloffer* in 1912. Went to the United States after the war and worked for the Forverts. (P, 437–38; Yechiel Szeintuch, "Bre'i ha'ashmodai," *Khulyot* 6 [2000]: 402–4)

Markovitsh, Joseph: Born 1882? Ukraine. Came to London around 1900 already a professional singer. He sang, acted, and wrote songs and plays for the London Yiddish music hall and theatre. (P, 439; Z, 2:1265–66; Mazower, "Stories in Song")

Myer, Morris: Born 1879, Romania. Lived in London from 1902. Writer, translator, theatre critic, and editor of the *Idisher zhurnal* and *Di tsayt*. (P, 443)

Nager, Arn: Born 1880. Actor, singer, writer, composer of burlesques and melodramas performed in London. He may have run a music hall in Berner Street, East London. He wrote for the *Bloffer* and many of his songs (17 known) were published in songbooks and songsheets. (P, 478; Z, 2:1384–86)

Namerts: See Friman, Simon.

Rocker, Rudolf: Born 1873, Mainz, Germany. Came to England in 1894. Learned Yiddish and became the leader of the London Jewish anarchists, writing, giving lectures, and editing the *Arbayter fraynd* from 1898. (Rocker and Ward, *London Years*)

Sherman, Joseph (Yozef): Born 1875, Romania, and worked with Goldfaden. He came to London around 1901 as a comedian and later played vaudeville in English. (P, 585–86)

Shtoyb, Ferdinand: Born 1862, Czechoslovakia. Arrived in London 1881. Pianist and cellist at the Strand Theatre. In 1886 worked with Jacob Adler's troupe as piano accompanist and as orchestra conductor at the Pavilion Theatre. (P, 602)

Weisenfreund, Salli and Philip: Arrived in London from Poland around 1901. Salli sang in music halls and Philip managed the York Minster music hall. Moved to America 1902. Parents of Paul Muni. (P, 675; Z, 1:672–73)

Winchevsky, Morris: Born 1856, Lithuania. Lived in London 1879–94. Edited and wrote for the London Yiddish press, sometimes under the pseudonyms Ben Nets (BN) or Leopold Benedict (LB). He wrote a regular column as the *meshugener filozof* in the *Arbayter fraynd* and the *notitsn* in the *Fraye velt*.

Yozef, M.: East End printer and publisher. Published Yiddish songsheets and composed his own songs. Sometimes called Yozef mokher sforim. He was an active Zionist. (Prager, *Farleger*, 179–97)

Index

Adler, Hermann, 28, 181, 205
Adler, Jacob, 43–45, 246n29, 246n32, 319; acting schools, 245n27; and Winchevsky, 94
Adler, Nathan, 43, 45, 101
adultery, 155–60
Agudah Hasozialistim Chaverim, 28
Ahad Ha'am, 205
Akselrod, Morris, 75, 254n24, 319
Aliens Act (1905), 18, 37, 227n8
Aliens bill (1911), 38
Aliens Defence Committee, 38
Alman, Shmuel, 205, 319
alrightnik, 26–27, 44
America: artistes, 47, 136; deserted wives, 276n29; *landsmanshaftn*, 252n9; language, 275n12; Marseillaise, 241n70; publications, 133, 155; references in texts, 15, 148–49, 162, 205; songs and versions, 11, 75, 79–80, 83, 111, 169; transmigrants and migrants, 7, 45, 73, 81, 162, 233n46; Winchevsky in America, 240n52; Yiddish-speaking diaspora, 69
anarchists, 13, 35, 44, 141; and the *Arbayter fraynd*, 128; in art, 265n59; associated with crime, 37–38, 265n57; disputes with socialists, 26, 35, 97, 128; free love, 156, 274n7;

Kishinev pogrom, 39;
Marseillaise, 34; in poetry, 15, 87, 101, 127, 205, 207, 211; and religion, 177, 207, 211, 284n23; and Winchevsky, 95–97. *See also* Rocker, Rudolf
Angel, Moses, 12, 213
anglicization, 11–13, 94, 200, 223–24; by Anglo-Jewry, 36, 44, 127, 214, 233n40, 233n45; by the immigrants, 51, 234n47; poetry as a force for anglicization, 14, 68, 200; and sex, 137, 151; in texts, 196, 198, 212, 214–17; and Winchevsky, 94
anglicized Yiddish, 14, 51, 70; cockney-Yiddish, 227n6; words from texts, 2, 72, 114, 164, 119
anthems, 4, 23, 31, 34, 122–29, 267n81. *See also* Marseillaise
anti-alienism, 23–24, 36–39, 119–21. *See also* anti-Semitism
anti-Semitism, 11, 36–37, 42, 58, 87, 263n28; and stereotypes of "The Jew," 50, 83, 211, 248n54; and Winchevsky, 120–22, 184. *See also* anti-alienism; pogroms
Arbayter fraynd, Der, 8, 28, 30, 92, 126, 242n79; advertising choirs, 35; anarchist take-over, 96, 101, 128; complexity of articles, 114–15,

INDEX

Arbayter fraynd, Der (*continued*)
262n15; front cover, 65; nonpartisan, 95–98; sabotage, 178, 281n13; *Tsum arbayter fraynd*, 110, 123; using religious motifs, 178–79; West-End goy, 181; Yanovsky, Saul, 35
Aseyfes khakhomim, 92
Ashkenaz, 16, 69, 74, 79, 220, 309
Ashkenazi, 5, 6, 149
assimilation, 11, 13, 122, 149, 216, 234n48; Londonized, 249n64
Association for Preventing the Immigration of Destitute Aliens, 36
atheism, 10, 127, 177–79, 189–90
Authorized Daily Prayer Book, 99
Avreml. *See* Margolin, Avrom

Baccarat affair, 119–20
badkhones, 93, 130–31, 240n49, 258n8
Bailey, Peter, 51, 138, 247n50, 273n4
Becker, Simcha, 27
Berkowitz, Joel, 42
Berner Street Club, 30, 34–35, 239n36, 245n17
Bialystok, 17–18
Bible (Torah), 92, 101, 178, 184, 282n29; authorized prayer book, 99; bible study, 176, 180; biblical language, 10, 185; Eykhe, 184–85; Ezekiel, 204–6; in poems, 180, 188, 202–4, 215; scrolls, 70, 202; synagogue reading, 183, 202, 310. *See also* Talmud
Bik, Abraham, 93, 106, 179, 239n48, 265n51
Bleichman, Yankev (Jacob), 204–5, 319
Bloffer, Der, 9, 60–63, 201, 224, 229n29, 316; anglicization, 222; *Der bloffer lakht*, 84–87, 221; covers of, 60–62, 133, 142, 173, 215–16; style,
63, 205; writers, 320, 321. *See also* Margolin, Avrom (Avreml)
Bloody Sunday (1887), 34, 126
board schools, 13, 213
Bonfeld of Glasgow, 190
Booth, Charles, 108
Bratton, Jacky, 158, 241n62, 247–48n52
Brecht, Bertolt, 107
Brenner, Joseph, 59–60
Brin, Max, 205
British Brothers' League, 36–37
Broder, Berl, 31
Bund, 8, 59, 98, 266n73, 270n22, 309
Burnett, John, 181

Cahan, Abraham, 33, 41, 46, 89
Cannon, Hughie, 169
Cass, Elizabeth, 169
Chance Newton, Henry, 53
Chant, Ormiston, 138–39
Charcroft House, 166–67, 278n57
charity, 85, 113, 161, 211–12, 280n4
chartists, 241n58, 258n7
Chief Rabbinate, 6, 45, 175, 216. *See also* Adler, Hermann; Adler, Nathan
children: anglicisation, 13, 53; child labour, 3, 23; child prostitution, 2, 161, 170–71; deserted children, 276n30; hunger, 78, 94; in music halls, 143, 251n99, 271n30; no children, 159, 275n21; out of wedlock, 152; songs and games, 27, 37, 80, 118, 124, 215; working children, 2, 102–8. *See also* schooling
choirs, 32–33, 216, 240–41n57, 241n60; socialist choirs, 4, 30, 35. *See also* Alman, Shmuel
Christianity: book of common prayer, 99; Christianity in schools,

324

213; Christianizing Judaism, 198, 215–17; conversion, 11; marrying a Christian, 12, 149, 151, 164, 269n17; missionaries, 28, 212; noise on the Sabbath, 36; working together, 128
Churchill, Winston, 36–38, 205
Clarion, 32–33
Clarion Vocal Union, 32
Commercial road, 62, 74, 121, 263n27, 285n38; Princess' Hall, 47, 49
Conservative party, 80, 118–19, 262–63n21
courtship, 141–47. See also dowry; matchmakers
cross-dressing, 50, 54, 147

deserted wives, 86, 160–62, 171, 220–21, 276n30. See also missing people
Dokter, Rubin, 170, 279n63
domestic violence, 163–65
dowry, 140–41, 147–49, 163

Edelshtadt, Dovid, 96–97
Evans-Gordon, William, 11, 36
Evening News, 121
Eyges, Thomas, 34–35, 177

Federation of Synagogues, 7, 13, 101, 176
Feigenbaum, Benjamin, 177
Feinman Yiddish People's Theatre, 3, 62–63
Feldman, David, 36, 234n48, 237n7
festivals: Hanukkah, 120, 209–10, 215–16; Passover, 75, 185, 198, 208–9, 212, 282n29; Purim, 57–58, 62, 120, 263n28, 284n16; Rosh Hashanah, 178, 281n14; Simkhes Toyre, 202–4, 310; Sukes, 204, 310;

Yom Kippur, 62, 177, 184, 198, 206–7, 281n14, 310
Finkelshteyn, Y., 50, 211, 320
Fonograf, Der, 59, 284n16
Forverts, 33, 41, 89, 155, 276n29, 320
Fraye velt, Di, 8, 92, 96–97, 115–16
Friman, Simon (Namerts), 188, 320

Gallop, Konstantin, 35, 96
gambling, 3, 5, 112, 240n57; Baccarat affair, 119–20; Winchevsky's poem, 94
gentiles: anglicisation, 11–12; baking plays, 41, 55; marrying a gentile, 149, 152, 164; as seducer or pimp, 49, 52, 170, 279n64; as sexual beings, 168–69; wider society, 15, 16, 52, 77; work, 85, 128, 184, 265n60
Gilrod, Louis, 79–80
Gladstone, William, 2
Goldfaden, Avrom, 14, 32, 40, 253n13; *Hashiveynu nazad*, 70–77; in London, 42, 46, 321; poet, 94, 244n5
Goldstein, Beki, 2, 8, 80, 158–59, 320; images, 66, 136
Gordin, Jacob, 41, 42, 59, 205
Gras, Morris, 217
Great Exhibition (1851), 146
Great Synagogue in Houndsditch, 181
Gutentag, Karl, 75, 320
Gutman, Tsvi, 205, 320

hasidism, 100, 159, 197, 309; *shtiblekh*, 176, 283n2
haskole, 31, 277n41
Haymarket demonstration, Chicago, 126
Hebrew comedians, 50, 83, 211–12

INDEX

Hebrew Dramatic Club, 43–45, 94, 245n28, 246n39, 319
Hebrew language, 31, 60, 213, 238n32; language of prayers, 70–71, 184, 204, 206, 209, 285n48; and Winchevsky, 92, 94, 239n48, 257n3, 266n61
Henry, Barbara, 42
Herzl, Theodore, 205
Hillel, Rabbi, 179, 281n16
House of Commons Select Committee on Immigration, 36
House of Lords Select Committee on the Sweating System, 36
Housing, 27, 73, 156, 274nn9–10; model dwellings, 80, 156, 274n9; rent and key money, 2, 37, 106, 156–58

Idisher ekspres, Der, 9, 57, 63, 201, 205, 215; advertisements: gramophone records, 4; missing people, 161, 167; music-hall repertoire, 58; poetry and satire, 59, 60, 224
Izraeli, L. *See* Kussman, Leon

Jewish Association for the Protection of Girls and Women (JAPGW), 166, 278n50
Jewish Board of Guardians, 6–7, 27, 114, 192, 214; coupons and loans, 26, 113, 262n9; deserted wives, 162, 276n30; strategies re. immigration, 73, 78
Jewish Chronicle: on the authorised prayer book, 99; on Becker's shelter, 27; on decay of orthodoxy, 193, 195; on the Jews Free School, 12; on *khadorim* and *khevres*, 182; on lack of unity, 68, 101; on marrying out, 272n52; on the tailor's strike, 127, 265n57; on Victoria Park, 80; on Winchevsky's poetry, 130; on Yiddish, 46, 59; on Yiddish music hall, 53–55, 60, 249n69, 271n30; on Yiddish theatre, 62, 246n39
Jewish League for Woman Suffrage, 284n29
Jewish World, 46, 205
Jews' Free School, 12, 213–14, 285n35
Judischer Frauenbund, 279n64

Kayzer, Jenya, 44
Kessler, David, 244n4
khadorim and *talmetoyres*, 7, 12–13, 212–15, 285n38, 309–10; Anglo-Jewish antagonism, 182; attached to khevres, 176; Idisher *Ekspres* updates, 201
khevres, 6–7, 68, 176, 192, 282n26, 309; Akhdes, 99–100; Beatrice Potter's description, 280n4; Machzikhe Hadath, 13; rabbis, 26, 203, 205; and socialists, 38, 181–83
kheyder. *See khadorim* and *talmetoyres*
Kishinev pogrom, 39, 135, 266
knowingness, 51, 138. *See also* Bailey, Peter
Kobrin, Leon, 230n28
Kobrin, Rebecca, 17–18
Krantz, Philip, 30, 35, 94, 115, 262n15, 320
kupletn. *See* rhyming couplets
Kussman, Leon (L. Izraeli), 60, 62–63

Landa, Myer, 49, 246n33
landsmanshaftn, 26, 68–69, 176, 252n9
Lasalle, Ferdinand, 30

INDEX

Lerner, Mayer, 178
Levy-Lawson, 121
Lewis, Harry Samuel, 193–95, 200, 283n5
Liberal Judaism, 205, 217
Liberal Party, 7, 11, 36–37, 118, 176
Lieberman, Aaron, 28, 92
Litvak, A. (Khayim Yankl Helfand), 93, 124, 130–31
Litvaks, 168
lodgers, 50, 56, 139; boarder, 80, 275n12; danger to daughters, 170–71; decay of religion, 200; English music hall, 274n11; housing, 25, 140–41; unfaithful landlady, 84, 153–58, 195
London County Council, 55–57; Theatre and Music Halls Committee, 139
Londoner kupletist, Der, 8, 55, 74–75, 80; images vi, 48, 66
Londoner lider magazin, Der, 8
Londoner siluetn, 102–8
Londonised Yiddish, 51, 72, 249n64
London places: Berner Street, 2, 106, 321; Black Lion Yard, 23, 236n1; Commercial street, 160; Cornhill, 2, 103–4, 222; Crystal Palace, 2, 80, 146–47, 222, 272n43; Leicester Square, 104–5, 167, 220; Mile End, 166; Oxford Street, 53, 141; Petticoat Lane, 142, 72; Regent Street, 2, 168–69, 171, 220; Stamford Hill, 160, 275n23; the Thames, 25. *See also* Commercial road; Victoria Park; Whitechapel Road
London Standard, 53, 249n69
Lower East Side, 57, 69, 79, 96, 232n36. *See also* New York
Lubritski, Isaac, 46, 136, 320

Maccoby, Chaim Zundel, 178
Machzike Hadath, 13, 210–11, 213, 309
Maiden Tribute of Modern Babylon, 104–5, 165–66, 277n44
Manor Theatre, 47, 269n14
Mansion House Fund, 7
Margolin, Avrom (Avreml), 9, 221, 224, 316, 320; biblical imagery, 201–9, 210–12; pictures, 60–61, 202
Markovitsh, Joseph, 8, 42, 136, 171, 320; in Avreml's poem, 205; songs: on deserted wives, 161–62, 220–21; on decay of religion, 194–96, 199–200; on immigration, 51–53; on sex outside of marriage, 152, 158
Marks, Harry, 121
Marmor, Kalman, 79, 93, 94, 98, 126, 263n27
marriage, 139–41, 154–65; free love, 156; out-marriage, 12, 149–52; *shtile khupe*, 166. *See also* adultery; lodgers
Marseillaise, 34, 241–42n70
Marxism, 95, 110–11, 176, 180
Master Tailors' Protective and Improvement Association, 127
matchmakers, 139–41, 148
Mazin. *See* printers
Men and Women's Club, 136
Mendelovitch, Bernard, 43, 244n11
Meshugener filozof, 92, 96, 98, 257n6, 321
Metropolitan Board of Works, 78
Miatlev, Ivan, 78–79, 254n31
Miron, Dan, 82–83
missing people: husband, 161, 276n29; sister, 167; wife, 86
Montagu, Lily, 217
Montagu, Samuel, 27, 28, 127–28; Federation of Synagogues, 7, 176; sabotaging the *Arbayter fraynd*, 178, 281n13

327

INDEX

Montefiore, Claude, 205, 217
Morris, William, 81, 125, 126, 223, 266n70; Berner Street club, 35; socialist aesthetic, 33, 114; Socialist League, 31, 123
Muni, Paul, 47
music: brass bands, 81, 240n55; broadside ballads, 31; carried by musicians, 8, 16–17, 49, 69, 222; folk song, 31–32, 47; in music-hall, 46–49, 51–52, 142, 145; and place, 80–83, 171, 225; and power, 122–26; religious melodies, 184, 285n44; reworked melodies, 47, 55, 79–80, 83, 114, 169; and socialism, 31–35, 42–44, 125–26; in theatre, 40; transnational, 76–77, 252n8; Yiddish parodies, 70–71, 74. See also anthems; choirs
music halls: English halls, 47, 55–57, 137–39, 151, 171, 247n49; repertoire, 12, 47–50, 52–54, 58, 63, 222; sex, 155–56; stock characters, 49, 158; Yiddish halls, 46–49, 52–57. See also cross-dressing; Hebrew comedians; knowingness; sex
Myer, Morris, 60, 205, 321, 256n69
Myers, Asher, 246n39

Nager, Arn, 46, 87, 136, 220, 321; adapting songs, 79, 165; London songs, 147, 151, 153, 197, 167–69; places in songs, 80–82, 142–44, 167–68; style, 220–21, 255n48; quoted by Avreml, 205; songsheet, 48
Namerts. *See* Friman, Simon
National Vigilance Association, 138
New York, 10, 33, 41, 57, 96, 155; adapting words, 79–80; cultural overlap, 15, 18, 68–69, 77, 84, 123; moving from London to New York, 35, 45, 97
nonpartisan, 96–98
notitsn, 92, 110, 114–22, 311

Oberman, Zelig, 157, 282n26, 283n2

Pall Mall Gazette, 104, 108, 165
Pavilion theatre, 45, 47, 57, 63, 270n23; people at, 205, 320, 321; in poem, 211; repertoire, 59, 157
pawnbroker, 112, 142, 162, 262n7
Plehve, 59
poetry: complexity, 223; as dialogue, 96–97; English poetic tradition, 33; as history, 3, 10; as performance, 35, 42, 94; as socialist activism, 14, 34, 94; status of Yiddish, 59, 68–69; Yiddish poetic tradition, 31–32, 93, 131, 178
pogroms, 121, 199, 243n95, 263n28; Kishinev, 39, 135, 266n64. *See also* anti-Semitism
Poland, 6, 7, 46, 76
Poor Jews Temporary Shelter, 27
Potter, Beatrice, 26, 280n4, 282n20
Poylisher yidl, 2, 8, 28–29, 92, 121; motto from psalms, 113; poetry, 77, 94; theatre reviews, 41, 43
Prager, Leonard, 8, 74–75, 84, 275n20; Berner Street club, 245n17; dating songs, 229n24, 254n30
Princess' hall, 47, 49, 53, 271n30
Princes Street Club, 43–45, 49, 245n28, 246n39, 319
printers: Mazin, 47; Yozef, 47, 74–75, 79–80, 159, 163, 221
prostitution: advert for missing sister, 167; association with actresses, 50; characters in texts, 82, 104–7, 144, 167–70, 170–71,

328

INDEX

220; child prostitution, 2, 104–5, 170–71; from contemporary debates, 93, 104, 136, 165, 169; in the halls, 57, 138–39; poverty, 161; White Slave Trade, 166–67. *See also* Maiden Tribute of Modern Babylon

Rabbinowitch, Elye, 28
Rakov, Nokhem, 62
reformers: conservative reformers, 32, 47, 55, 138, 240n57; education reformer, 103; social reformers, 26, 108; socialist reformers, 47, 240n57. *See also* Ormiston Chant
Reform Judaism, 101, 216–17
Reingold, Isaac, 79, 277n42
Revolution, revolutionary: abortive revolution (1905), 8, 37, 50; actions on London streets, 38, 126–27; ideas, 30, 91, 191; ideas modified for London workers, 28, 94, 119; internationalists, 13, 122; and religion, 178–79; role of poetry, 33–34, 93, 131, 257n7, 258n9; trade union activists, 23, 119; and Winchevsky, 95, 126, 128–30. *See also* Lieberman, Aaron
rhyming couplets, 2–3, 32, 41, 46, 309; criticism, 93, 130, 258n8; style, 117, 119
Rigoletto, 62, 251n100
Robey, George, 60
Rocker, Rudolf: anarchist leader, 35, 37–38, 321; character in text, 2, 205, 265n59; free love, 274n71; sabotaging the *AF*, 281n13, 284n23, 321; *Zherminal*, 242n79
Rosenfeld, Morris, 46, 240n50
Rosenthal, Max, 46
Rosman, Moshe, 15–16

Rothschild, Nathan Mayer, 7, 80, 85, 127; appearing in song, 2, 52, 127, 147, 217
Russia, 6, 7, 12, 52, 71, 160; abortive revolution (1905), 6, 37; appears in Yiddish texts, 15, 67, 161–62, 170, 184, 221; Bund, 8, 59; language, 31, 35, 46, 70–71, 92; Russian literature, 52, 78–79, 223; Russian politics, 15, 37, 55, 59; Russian socialists as trade unionists, 30; Yiddish theatre, 40–41, 43
Russian Jewish Operatic Company, 43
Russo-Japanese war, 59
Russo-Jewish Committee, 7, 73, 192–93, 276n30

Sabbath, 99, 101, 141, 192, 204; Christian Sabbath, 36; keeping the Sabbath, 46o, 210; liturgy, 70, 183, 204; Sabbath breaking, 7, 44–45, 63, 105, 177, 187; in texts, 94, 187, 193–95
satire, 1, 3, 94; *Bloffer, Der*, 60, 63; *Fonograf, Der*, 59; as local, 3, 14, 67, 84; *Meshugener filozof*, 92; Miatlev, 78; *Poylisher yidl* theatre review, 43; satirising religion, 98–99, 159, 179, 188–89; *shtetl*, 82–83; Winchevsky's style, 94. See also *Bloffer, Der*; Margolin, Avrom (Avreml); Winchevsky, Morris
Schloss, David, 27, 282n20
Schooling, 213–15; Adler's music school, 44; Board schools, 13, 213; schools in the texts, 117, 212, 214. *See also* Jews' Free School; *khadorim* and *talmetoyres*
seasonal work, 25, 26, 39, 237n9, 237n11; Winchevsky on the "slack", 114

329

INDEX

Sephardi, 5, 149
Sex: extramarital sex, 139, 155–60; sex before marriage, 143, 149–52; sexual abuse and harassment, 145, 165; sexual language, 144–45. *See also* lodgers; marriage; prostitution
Shelley, Percy, 111
Sherman, Joseph, 2, 75, 76, 136, 254n24, 321
Shilling, Sam, 62
Shtettin, Dinah, 246n32
Shteynvolf, 205
Shtoyb, Ferdinand, 205, 321
Shund, 41–42, 57–58, 62–63, 244n7, 310; in text and art, 40, 173, 211
Siege of Sidney Street, 38
Singer, Simeon, 99
Smith, Dovid, 44, 45
Social Democratic Federation (SDF), 31, 95, 123, 239n42, 257n5; survey, 108; Winchevsky's criticism, 126
Socialist League, 31, 95, 123, 126, 257n5
socialists: conflict with anarchists, 97, 101; dignity of labour, 113–14, 183; English socialists, 30–33, 35, 114, 123, 125–26, 187; Jewish socialism, 28–30, 34, 91–93; and religion, 176–79, 190–91, 207; and *shund*, 44, 139; socialist aesthetic, 23, 33, 93, 114. *See also* anthems; choirs; Morris, William; strikes; trade unions; Winchevsky, Morris
Socialist Workers' Union, 98
Song: earlier Yiddish popular song, 31–32; power of, 122–24, 259n36; socialist song, 31–33; sol-fa, 32; song lyrics as history, 3, 10; songs in plays, 41; Winchevsky's attitude to, 124–25. *See also* choirs
Standard theatre, 47, 59

Stokes, Martin, 169
Stone, Isaac, 30
strikes: General Council, 98; Shoe and Boot makers strike (1912), 27, 38, 128, 222; Socialists as unionists, 30, 95; in songs, 15, 33, 34, 127–30, 170; Tailor's strike (1889), 27, 38, 127–28. *See also* anthems
suffrage, 148, 158, 208–9, 284n29
Sussman, Moyshe (Morris), 60
sweating system, 23–28, 34; campaigning and publicising, 28, 35; government reports, 36, 181; in poetry, 85, 110–14, 129, 158, 184–87; sweatshop poets, 32, 91, 96–97. *See also* seasonal work; Synagogue Parade
Synagogue Parade, 181, 264n35

Tailor's strike (1889). *See* strikes
talmetoyre. See *khadorim* and *talmetoyres*
Talmud, 140, 176, 178, 207, 262n15, 270n20; Talmudic references in poems, 85, 120, 188–89, 197, 203
Telegraph, 121
Tiszaeszlár blood libel, 121
Torah. *See* Bible
Tottenham Outrage, 37–38
trade unions: and anarchists, 35, 38–39, 95; and Anglo-Jewry, 265n57; English unions, 25–26, 119, 122; Jewish trade unions, 27, 94, 98, 127; religious and unions, 28–29, 81; reluctance to join unions, 26; socialists as union leaders, 23–24, 30; Trade Union Congress, 36; union songs, 122–23, 125–30, 255n37; union success, 131. *See also* anthems; *Arbayter fraynd, Der*; Berner Street Club

INDEX

trafficking, 104, 166, 170, 278n50, 279n64. *See also* Jewish Association for the Protection of Girls and Women (JAPGW)
Transnationalism, 14–18, 67–69, 144, 219, 222–23; carriers of culture, 204; *landsmanshaftn*, 252n9; networks, 252n3; in poetry, 74, 76, 77, 79, 80, 83, 84–85, 87; religion, 187; Winchevsky, 129
Troyke, Karsten, 106–7
Tsayt, Di, 9, 50, 60, 201, 211, 224. *See also* Myer, Morris
Tselniker, Meier and Anna, 277n35
Tsukunft, Di, 8, 28, 106

United Synagogue, 6, 175–76, 216, 280n7; formality, 198; in poem, 179, 182
upward mobility, 2, 5–6, 26–27, 112–13, 160, 185, 275n23

Veker, Der, 8, 92, 98, 128
Victoria, Vesta, 156
Victoria Park, 80–83, 142, 144–45, 168, 170–71, 271n33
Vine Court, 45

Weisenfreund, Salli and Philip, 14, 47, 54, 321; gang violence, 269n14; songs, 75, 254n24
Wess, William, 27, 127, 238n22
White, Arnold, 11, 36, 120–21
Whitechapel Road, 45, 47, 53, 63, 141, 270n23
White Slave Trade, 104, 166, 170, 171, 279n64
Winchevsky, Morris: Awakener (*veker*), 33, 92–93; biography, 91–92; criticism of, 32, 94, 130–32; editor, 28, 92; explaining socialism, 110–14; *notitsn*, 114–22; poems, 77–79, 98–102; poet, 31; poetic adaptations, 33, 34; religion, 179–84, 189–90; *siluetn*, 102–8; socialist anthems, 122–29; on William Morris, 33, 35; writing in English, 257n5. *See also* Edelshtadt, Dovid; *Meshugener filozof*; nonpartisan
women: equality, 129; female performers, 50, 148, 158–59, 247n52; feminism, 275n64; Primrose women, 118, 262n21; and sex, 120, 155–56; sex roles, 136, 141; and strikes, 15, 27; subverting gender roles, 148, 154, 168–69; and work, 25–26, 141, 272n41, 277n43. *See also* courtship; cross-dressing; deserted wives; domestic violence; marriage; prostitution; sex: sexual abuse; suffrage; trafficking
Wonderland, 47, 53, 205
Workman's Times, 33

Yanovsky, Saul, 35
Yiddish Dramatic Club, 245n27
Yidisher faust, Der, 70, 76
York Minster music hall, 47, 51–52, 54, 269n14, 321
Yozef, M. *See* printers

Zalkind, Yankev-Meyer, 205, 284n23
Zangwill, Israel, 11–12, 144
Zionists, 15, 39, 71–75, 87, 205, 284n23
Zunzer, Elyakum, 31–32, 93, 94, 240n49